Raising Your Spirited Child

A GUIDE FOR PARENTS WHOSE CHILD IS MORE INTENSE, SENSITIVE, PERCEPTIVE, PERSISTENT, AND ENERGETIC

THIRD EDITION

Mary Sheedy Kurcinka, Ed.D.

WILLIAM MORROW
An Imprint of HarperCollinsPublishers

HarperCollins books may be purchased for educational, business, or sales promotional use. For information please e-mail the Special Markets Department at SPsales@harpercollins.com.

First Harper Perennial edition published 1992; reissued 1998.
First Harper paperback published 2006.
First William Morrow paperback published 2015.

Designed by Diahann Sturge
Part opener illustration © by Lorelyn Medina/Shutterstock, Inc.

Library of Congress Cataloging-in-Publication Data has been applied for.

ISBN 978-0-06-240306-3

18 19   ov/LSC   10 9 8

Dedicated to:
My husband, Joseph Michael Kurcinka—
without your insight, wit,
and organizational eye I couldn't have done it.

My children, Joshua Thomas and Kristina Leah Sheedy Kurcinka—
without you I wouldn't have known.

My parents, Richard and Beatrice Sheedy—
without you I wouldn't be . . .

Praise for
Raising Your Spirited Child

"All of my pediatric training could not prepare me for the wonderful, crazy, exhausting adventure of raising spirited twin boys. Mary's book gave me the tools not only to help my family survive but also to thrive! *Raising Your Spirited Child* should be essential reading for every pediatrician."

—Jill Simons, M.D., F.A.A.P. Diplomate,
American Board of Pediatrics member

"If you have a child who is 'more'—more intense, more persistent, more sensitive—you probably already know who Mary Sheedy Kurcinka is. She wrote the book on spirited children, literally: *Raising Your Spirited Child*. The newly revised third edition is just as reassuring and eye-opening as the first edition. But it's completely rewritten and updated, with more step-by-step advice, concrete examples, and practical tips. Just the new chapter on helping spirited kids get to sleep will be worth the price of the book for exhausted parents. Kurcinka's great asset is that she helps even the most frustrated parents appreciate their spirited children's strengths. In this book she takes her commitment to positive parenting a step further, giving parents the hands-on tools they need to ease the challenges of life with a spirited child, without resorting to punishment. This book is wonderful."

—Laura Markham, Ph.D., author of *Peaceful Parent, Happy Kids*

"A well-written, comprehensive, and, above all, loving and positive approach to understanding that oh-so-challenging child."
—Evonne Weinhaus and Karen Friedman, coauthors of *Stop Struggling with Your Child* and *Stop Struggling with Your Teen*

"This is a marvelous, inspiring, usable gem of a guide for parents of these challenging and rewarding children. With its positive message of 'progress, not perfection,' *Raising Your Spirited Child* is just what parents need."
—Marjorie Hogan, M.D., pediatrician, Hennepin County Medical Center

"Mary Sheedy Kurcinka packs these pages with wisdom, and has gentle, homey suggestions for keeping peace with children who are unusually intense, sensitive, perceptive, persistent, and energetic."
—*Dallas Morning News*

"Our society values individuality yet organizes its institutions in such a way as to try to homogenize children. Mary Kurcinka's focus is a good antidote. *Raising Your Spirited Child* is an impressive and entertaining book that shows the stamp of Mary Kurcinka's experience as a mother and as a teacher."
—Stella Chess, M.D., professor of child psychiatry, New York Medical Center, and coauthor of *Know Your Child*

"Ten years ago, I would have paid $1,000 for a copy of *Raising Your Spirited Child* if I had known how much trouble it would have saved me."
—*St. Paul Pioneer Press*

"*Raising Your Spirited Child* is loaded with how-tos—not how to change the child, but how to interact positively and minimize difficulties."
—*Bloomington Pantagraph*

Raising
Your
Spirited
Child

Also by Mary Sheedy Kurcinka, Ed.D.

Sleepless in America
Kids, Parents, and Power Struggles
Raising Your Spirited Child Workbook

Contents

Acknowledgments

This revised edition would not have come to fruition without the contributions of many. To them I am deeply grateful and must say thank you.

All of the parents, teachers, and children who shared their stories with me—you asked me not to share your names and I won't, but I have learned so much from you. Without you, this book would not be possible.

Lynn Jessen, friend, colleague, director of Paidea Child Development Center, emotion coach extraordinaire—I have learned so much from you!

Kim Cardwell, my friend and colleague, who was with me through every word, moan, groan, and moment of elation when I was writing the first edition.

Heide Lange, my agent, who continues to believe in me and my work.

Janet Goldstein, editor of the first edition of *Raising Your Spirited Child*, who once again guided me in finding the support I needed to complete this edition.

Nancy Peske, whose editing skills and content knowledge were critical in the completion of this project.

Lyssa Keusch, editor, and Rebecca Lucash, editorial assistant, who smoothly ushered this project through the publication process.

The late JoAnne Ellison, who always believed in me.

The entire ECFE staff, especially Marietta Rice, Jenna Ruble, Janey Whitt, LeeAnn McCarthy, Barbara Dopp, Shannon Dufresne, Beth Hersman, Leta Fox, and Joan Kane, who each in their own way supported me from the very beginning.

Vicki Cronin, friend, colleague, and mother of the other original spirited children—your insights and stories remain invaluable.

Susan Perry, writer and teacher, who has continued to guide me in my writing.

Kelsey K. Sather, my Montana writing teacher—you were inspirational.

Joanne Burke, friend and seeker of knowledge—you ask the best questions!

The late Dr. Stella Chess, originator of the longitudinal temperament research, who graciously answered my questions and always championed my work.

Joseph and Mary Kurcinka, my in-laws, who patiently supported my efforts.

Barbara Majerus, Kathy Kurz, Helen Kennedy, and Sue Nelson, my sisters, who have always been my super cheering team.

The staff of Paidea Child Development Center—I have learned so much watching your sensitive and kind interactions with the children in your care.

Norm Wallace, my high school English teacher, who told me I could write . . .

Thank you!

Greetings!

*You promised me she would be
an awesome adult and she is!*
—Lydia, mother of two

Welcome to *Raising Your Spirited Child*. I'm Mary, your guide, licensed teacher of parents and children, fellow parent of spirited children, now all grown up. I am delighted to inform you that the information and strategies presented in *Raising Your Spirited Child* have soundly stood the test of time.

Sometimes as the parent of a spirited child you can feel like you are the only one. You are not. Thousands have gone before you. There is information that can make it better. Every day testimonials of parents' successes utilizing this information are posted on the Raising Your Spirited Child Facebook Group page and drop into my e-mail box. It was Lydia who wrote, "You taught me to listen to my child. Now because she was listened to and respected she has tremendous confidence and understands herself so well. She recently graduated from college with a triple major. She has been faced with tremendous difficulties and dealt with all of them. I wish I had been parented as I parented her."

In this third edition of *Raising Your Spirited Child*, new information and the latest research has been tucked into each chapter.

Fresh tips are included for focusing on strengths, keeping your cool, diffusing the meltdowns, establishing clear limits, becoming a problem-solving family, reducing the frequency of conflicts with peers and siblings, and guidelines for selecting a school that "fits" your child.

"Bedtime and Night Waking" has also taken on an entirely new look. Years of working individually with families has helped me fine-tune the most helpful information to ensure that your family gets the sleep you need and deserve.

When I first sat down to write the original version of *Raising Your Spirited Child*, I was a mother of little ones, teaching classes for parents through the Minnesota Early Childhood Family Education Program. At the time, I was frustrated by the existing curriculums and secretly needed to talk with other parents who understood what it was like to live with a child who could scream for forty-five minutes because his toast had been cut in triangles when he was expecting rectangles. The kind of kid who would rather die than take no for an answer and could feel the seams in socks. The kind of kid the existing parenting books either failed to address or addressed in terribly negative terms—terms I wasn't willing to accept.

I brought into those first spirited-child classes the latest research reports and studies of child development, communication, personality, temperament, and type. We hashed them over, tore them apart, and figured out ways to use them to help us get resistant little bodies dressed, fed, into bed, or through the grocery store with a little less hassle. By sharing our stories we allowed each other to peek into our homes, schools, and neighborhoods. We discovered similarities in the things we worried and sometimes yelled about. We shared the rules that prevailed in our families, the discipline techniques that worked and those that didn't. We learned what each of us was doing to build a healthy relationship with our spirited child.

In this edition of *Raising Your Spirited Child*, the stories have expanded to include those from parents who have participated in my workshops, sought my advice in private consultations, or written to me to share their experiences. Like their predecessors, these parents were willing to share with you their questions, fears, favorite strategies, and horror stories. All the anecdotes are true, the ages accurate, but all the names, places, and descriptive details are those of a storyteller. People, I have found, don't mind us looking in their windows as long as we don't share their addresses.

But there's one thing I didn't change—the opening pages. All too often, you have told me, "As I read through the first few pages, I found myself crying. Although I logically expected other parents were raising children like my daughter, I had never run across any of them and was beginning to wonder if she was the only one. . . ." And so the beginning remains the same, an invitation for you to join fellow parents of spirited children in the wild, sometimes exasperating, joyous journey of raising a child who is normal but "more."

I have to admit that those fellow parents constitute a much larger group than I ever expected. Never in my wildest dreams did I ever imagine that *Raising Your Spirited Child* would reach around the world. But that is what has happened. It's been a friend to tote along and lay on the bedside table, or to download when there is a question to be answered, a strategy to be learned, and an optimistic vision needed.

I am awed every time I am asked how I could possibly know your children so well, when I've never met them, or if I have somehow managed to hide a video camera in your home. The reality is that I have simply listened to the stories and recognized the commonalities. It appears that while our cultures and countries are different, we are not alone, no matter where we live.

In fact, you have found one another. Twenty-four hours a day, members of the Raising Your Spirited Child Facebook Group are chatting with one another, sharing stories and offering one another support and helpful suggestions. You are visiting my website at http://www.parentchildhelp.com/ to let me know you are grateful for the book that "delivered the goods" or to schedule private consultations. You are stopping one another in stores, schools, and parks to say, "I've been there too and today she is amazing." *Spirited* is not merely a term. It is a vision that draws us together to focus on our children's strengths.

And finally you need to know that our motto for *Raising Your Spirited Child* remains the same:

Progress, Not Perfection

Being a parent, building a healthy relationship with a child is a never-ending process. There are good days and there are lousy days. With progress as our goal we don't have to wait for an obscure finale. We can count every second of understanding gleaned, every power struggle fizzled, every hug held tight as a success. We can be kind to ourselves, rejoicing in moments of peace and hours of "parenting greatness," even if the entire day is not perfection. We can forgive ourselves the times we huff in frustration or flare in anger, recognizing that although we cannot be abusive, we are human. Progress takes time. Changing attitudes, strengthening old skills and learning new ones doesn't happen quickly. That's why we need to count each tiny success. Fortunately those teeny, tiny successes are like wet, sticky snowflakes: they can snowball. Rolled together they build a happy, healthy relationship. And, we hope, one day, like so many others who have gone before you, you'll be able to say, "I've come to believe that spirit is a wonderful gift." Perhaps you will even recognize that you too are spirited!

So grab a cup of coffee, tea, or whatever you prefer and begin to discover the "secrets" of raising a child with "spirit." Take what fits for you. Leave the rest. Only you can truly know what you and your child need. Just remember: progress, not perfection, is our goal.

PART ONE
Understanding Spirit

1

Who Is the Spirited Child?

An opportunity to fall in love, fodder for frustration,
source of anxiety, and an unending puzzle—
this is my spirited child.
—Abby, mother of two

The word that distinguishes spirited children from other children is *more*. They are normal children who are *more* intense, persistent, sensitive, perceptive, and uncomfortable with change than other children. All children possess these characteristics, but spirited kids possess them with a depth and range not available to other children. Spirited kids are the Super Ball in a room full of rubber balls. Other kids bounce three feet off the ground. Every bounce for a spirited child hits the ceiling.

It's difficult to describe what it is like to be the parent of a spirited child. The answer keeps changing; it depends on the day, even the moment. How does one describe the experience of sliding from joy to exasperation in seconds, ten times a day? How does one explain the "sense" at eight in the morning that this will be a good day or a dreadful one?

The good ones couldn't be better. A warm snuggle and sloppy

kiss awaken you. He captures you with his funny antics as he stands in front of the dog, a glob of peanut butter clinging to a butter knife hidden in the palm of his hand, and asks, "Is Grace a rotten sister?" The dog listens attentively. The hand moves just slightly up and down like a magical wand. The dog's nose follows the scent appearing to nod in agreement. You can't help laughing.

Profound statements roll from his mouth, much too mature and intellectual for a child his age. He remembers experiences you've long since forgotten and drags you to the window to watch the raindrops falling like diamonds from the sky. On the good days, being the parent of a spirited child is astounding, dumbfounding, wonderful, funny, interesting, and interspersed with moments of brilliance.

The dreadful days are another story. On those days, you're not sure you can face another twenty-four hours with him. It's hard to feel good as a parent when you can't even get his socks on, when every word you've said to him has been a reprimand, when the innocent act of serving chicken instead of the expected tacos incites a riot, when you realize you've left more public places in a huff with your child in five years than most parents do in a lifetime.

You feel weary, drained, and much too old for this, even if you were only in your twenties when your child was born. It's hard to love a child who keeps you up at night and embarrasses you in shopping centers.

On the bad days, being the parent of a spirited child is confusing, frustrating, taxing, challenging, and guilt-inducing. You may wonder if you are the only parent with a child like this, scared of what is to come in the teen years if you don't figure out what to do now in the early years.

THE DISCOVERY OF SPIRIT

You might have known since pregnancy that this child was different from other kids, normal but different. She might have kicked so hard during pregnancy that you couldn't sleep from six months on. Or it might not have been until birth, when the nurses in the nursery shook their heads in dismay and wished you luck. It could have been years later. At first you may have thought all kids were like this. Your "awakening" might have come with the birth of a second child—one who slept through the family gatherings instead of screaming and let you dress her in a frilly dress instead of ripping at the lace. Or it could have been the birth of your sister in-law's child, the one who could be laid down anywhere and would promptly go to sleep. Your sister-in-law proudly beamed as though she had done something right, while your child continued to fume and fuss, causing all the eyes in the room to turn to you, silently accusing. "What's wrong with yours?" Your intuition has fought the stares and the indictments brought against you, knowing, believing that this child was tougher to parent, but not quite sure if you were right, and if you were, you didn't know why.

WHY "SPIRITED"?

You probably haven't heard the term *spirited children* before. That's because it's mine. When my son, Joshua, was born, there weren't any spirited-child classes or books. In fact, the only information I could find that described a child like him used words such as *difficult, strong-willed, stubborn, mother killer,* or *Dennis the Menace.* Yet I realized that Joshua was much like his father,

nsitive, passionate, and prudent adult whom I
so it was the "good" days that made me search
to describe Josh. On those days I realized that
this child who could drive me crazy possessed personality traits
that were actually strengths when they were understood and well
guided.

My *Webster's* dictionary defines *spirited* as lively, creative, keen,
eager, full of energy and courage, and having a strong assertive
personality. Spirited—it feels good, sounds good, communicates
the exciting potential of these children, and yet honestly captures
the challenge faced by their parents. When we choose to see our
children as spirited, we give them and ourselves hope. It pulls our
focus to their strengths rather than their weaknesses, not as another label but as a tool for understanding.

The Characteristics

Each spirited child is unique, yet there exist distinct characteristics in which *more* is very apparent. Not every spirited child will
possess all of the following five characteristics, but each will ex-
hibit enough of them to make her stand out in the crowd.

1. INTENSITY: The loud, dramatic spirited children are the
easiest to spot. They don't cry; they shriek. They're noisy when
they play, when they laugh, and even when they take a shower,
singing at the top of their lungs while the hot-water tank empties.

But quiet, intently observant children may also be spirited.
They assess each situation before entering it as though developing
a strategy for every move; their intensity is focused inward rather
than outward.

No matter where their intensity is focused, the reactions of spirited children are always powerful. There is rarely a middle of the road. They never whimper; they wail. They can skip into a room, smiling and laughing, only to depart thirty seconds later inflamed. Their tantrums are raw and enduring.

2. PERSISTENCE: If an idea or an activity is important to them, spirited children can "lock" right in. They are committed to their task, goal-oriented, and are unwilling to give up. Getting them to change their minds is a major undertaking. They love to debate and are not afraid to assert themselves.

3. SENSITIVITY: Keenly aware, spirited kids quickly respond to the slightest noises, smells, lights, textures, or changes in mood. They are easily overwhelmed in crowds by the barrage of sensations. Getting them through a shopping center, long religious service, carnival, or family gathering without losing them to a fit of tears is a major achievement. Dressing can be a torture. A wayward string or a scratchy texture can render clothes intolerable.

Every sensation and emotion is absorbed by them, including your feelings. They'll tell you that you are having a rotten day before you realize it yourself, and they'll even scream and sulk for you.

4. PERCEPTIVENESS: Send them to their room to get dressed and they'll never make it. Something along the way—perhaps a flash of light at the window—will catch their attention as they walk by, and they'll forget about getting dressed. It can take ten minutes to get them from the house to the car. They notice everything—

the latest oil spill, the white feather in the bird's nest, and the dew in the spiderweb. They are often accused of not listening.

5. ADAPTABILITY: Spirited children are uncomfortable with change. They hate surprises and do not shift easily from one activity or idea to another. If they're expecting hamburgers on the grill for dinner, heaven forbid if you come home and suggest going out to a restaurant. Even if it is their favorite restaurant, they'll say, "No, I want hamburgers on the grill."

Adapting to change, any change, is tough: ending a game in order to come to lunch, changing clothes for different seasons, sleeping at Grandma's house instead of at home, getting into the car, and getting out of the car. All of these activities signal a struggle for slow-to-adapt spirited children.

WHILE EACH SPIRITED CHILD IS UNIQUE, most are more intense, persistent, sensitive, perceptive, and uncomfortable with change. Many, but not all, possess four additional "bonus" characteristics: aspects of their personality that can make being their parent even more challenging.

6. REGULARITY: Figuring out when they will sleep or eat is a daily puzzle for parents of spirited children who are irregular. It seems impossible to get them onto any kind of schedule. An eight-hour night of undisturbed sleep is a mere memory lingering in your mind from the days before their birth.

7. ENERGY: The tales of spirited kids I hear from parents are truly amazing, like that of the two-week-old baby who "crawled" the entire length of a queen-size bed and was about to land on the

floor when his father found him. Or the toddler who opened the oven door and used it to crawl onto the counter and from there to the top of the refrigerator.

Not all spirited kids are climbers and leapers. But they do tend to be busy—fidgeting, taking things apart, exploring, and creating projects—from the time they wake up until they finally fall asleep. Although sometimes viewed as "wild," their energy is usually focused and has a purpose.

It may surprise you that not all spirited children have a high energy level because for those who do, it is often the energy that first catches a parent's attention, and that is why I have included it in the subtitle of this book. However, if you look more closely, it is usually the intensity of the motion or the persistence of it rather than the energy itself that is at issue.

8. FIRST REACTION: A quick withdrawal from anything new is typical of many spirited kids. Any unfamiliar idea, thing, place, or person may be met with a vehement "NO!" or a quick disappearance behind your leg or to another room. They need time to warm up before they're ready to participate.

9. MOOD: The world is a serious place for some spirited kids. They're analytical, meticulously reviewing experiences, finding the flaws, and making suggestions for change. Even if they scored three goals in a soccer game, they'll focus on the one they missed. If they are excited about an event or pleased with a gift, you may not be aware of it, as their smiles are a rare treat.

THE BONUS CHARACTERISTICS ARE NOT COMMON to all spirited kids, but if your child possesses any of them, you will need to be even more enterprising. Not only are you living with a child who is *more*, but you're also faced with the exhaustion of life with a child who is energetic, rarely falls easily into a predictable sleeping and eating schedule, expresses a strong resistance to new situations and things, and shares fewer rewarding smiles. Don't despair. These too have their potential.

YOU'RE NOT ALONE

Being the parent of a spirited child can be lonely. Because they are *more*, much of the advice that works for raising other children is ineffective with spirited kids. To ignore your child's tantrums is ridiculous. He can rage for an hour because you opened the door when he was expecting to do it himself. Send him to his room for a time-out and he is liable to tear it apart. There is no distracting him from something that he wants. Even if an item is off limits, he'll climb over, under, or around the barriers to return to it. As a result you can feel crazy, wondering what you are doing wrong, chastising yourself for not "getting control," and thinking that you are the only parent in the world with a child who acts this way.

Abby felt like that before she met other parents who understood what it was like to have a child who is *more*. Abby is one of the thousands of parents I have worked with in my family education classes. She smiled to herself as she told me about the first time she had seen the words *spirited children*. They had been written in big blue letters on the whiteboard at the entry to the family center where I was teaching. The one with a lobby filled by a big wooden jungle gym that begged to be climbed, a bouncy blue trampoline, and oversize red pillows.

On that first day she had rushed through the door with her three-year-old son, Owen, in tow. They were late for their class. She told me later that on that particular day they had been waylaid by a string in Owen's sock that had turned the simple task of pulling on socks into a fifteen-minute ordeal, wherein she carefully removed all the loose strings and twisted the sock until it felt just right. That was followed by tears and screams because the tags in the collar of his sweater scratched his neck and the wristbands were too tight.

Now, two months later, her speculation has been confirmed—it does take more to parent the spirited child. But today she can appreciate Owen's sensitivity, predict his "triggers," and avoid the blowups. She has learned that managing spirit well takes understanding, skill, and patience, but it is possible. In fact, it can even be enjoyable.

Like Abby, I have found myself learning from other parents. Laughing with them and worrying with them too. I have appreciated their understanding of life with spirit and valued their support. Over the years I've saved my notes and journal entries, and now I have set for myself the task of capturing the information and techniques that can make living with spirit more rewarding and fun.

As we go along together, there are a few things I'd like you to remember. I've written them in the form of a credo. To me they are the essentials of living with and building a healthy, warm relationship with spirited children. I suggest you hang the credo on your refrigerator for the lousy days—the days when you feel like you are alone—and share it with a friend on the good ones.

A Credo for Parents of Spirited Children

1. You're not alone. According to personality research, 15 to 20 percent of all children fit the description of the spirited child. That means that there are millions of parents who empathize with you and understand the challenges you face. Your child is not an oddity or a freak. You are not the world's worst parent. You are not the only one. You are among friends.

2. You did not make your child spirited. There is a genetic factor to being spirited, but how one's genes are expressed is significantly influenced by life events. You are but one of the many influences in your child's life. Other parents, relatives, siblings, teachers, neighbors, friends, life experiences, and the world at large all play a part. You make a big difference, but not the only difference.

3. You are not powerless. There is information in this book to help you understand your spirited child. You can read it and use it. You can strengthen skills you already have and learn new ones. You can reduce the hassles and live peacefully with your spirited child—most days. Progress, not perfection, is our goal.

4. You have permission to take care of yourself. Your own need for sleep, quiet, uninterrupted adult conversation, lovemaking, a leisurely bath, a walk around the block, and time to complete your own projects is real and legitimate. It is not a sign of failure to ask a friend for help, to hire a sitter, or to allow relatives the opportunity to build a relationship with your child while you take a break. When you address your needs, you calm yourself, making it easier to calm your child.

5. You may celebrate and enjoy the delights of your spirited child. You can concentrate on strengths, appreciate her tender heart, and tickle your fancy with her wild stories and crazy creations. It is appropriate and right to tell her when she is good, instead of when she is bad, to teach her the right way to behave rather than to punish her for innocent errors. Your spirited child possesses personality traits that we value in adults. It is never too early to begin proclaiming her virtues.

WHEN SPIRITED CHILDREN GROW UP

As I have learned to focus on the strengths of spirited children, I have realized that I am surrounded by spirited children grown up. Adults I admire and enjoy: intense, dramatic people.

There are figures from history who I strongly suspect were spirited too. National Public Radio paid tribute to Thomas Edison. I remember chuckling to myself as I heard the announcer say, "Thomas Edison invented the phonograph, the electric lightbulb, the telegraph, and the motion picture camera and projector. He was a man who didn't know when it was time to quit."

I thought of his mother. I wondered how many meals had gone cold when he forgot to come home for dinner or how many times his dad had yelled at him to stop taking apart everything in the house. Today we enjoy his inventions when we relax in front of a movie or read a good book any time of the day. We celebrate his persistence, single-mindedness, perceptiveness, and drive.

Then there are the regular people, not those that we see in movies or hear about, but those we live with each day, like my husband who notices the little things in life and makes me laugh. Or my friend who has the energy to help me out even after taking care of all of her own responsibilities. And my niece who won't give up on the Monopoly game, beating all of us, when the rest of us would have filed for bankruptcy three rounds back.

These are individuals who have learned to understand themselves, to manage their strengths, and to minimize their weaknesses. They are normal. They are more than normal. They are spirited.

SPIRITED OR A MEDICAL ISSUE

It can be frightening to have a child who is so strong and determined, and you may wonder if something else is going on. That's why I am often asked the question, How do you know if your child is spirited or has a medical issue, such as attention deficit with or without hyperactivity, sensory integration issues, oppositional defiant disorder, pervasive developmental disorder, or other conditions?

What I have learned over the decades I have been working with spirited children and their families is that spirited behavior truly falls within the range of typical human behavior—more but normal.

By understanding spirit and using the information you will find in this book, you can teach your child the skills he needs to manage and use his spirit well. As a result, he will be able to focus on the task at hand and be successful at school. Approaching a group on the playground and playing with his peers will go smoothly. And when you ask him to wait his turn, get into the car, or dress himself, he will be able to comply without losing it—at least most of the time. Just like the other children you know, your spirited child, with your guidance, will ultimately be successful negotiating the activities and responsibilities of a regular day. Often, he will excel.

But a spirited child may *also* have a medical condition. For example, he may be spirited *and* have a processing disorder or developmental delay. *Or*, his behavior may reflect a medical condition rather than temperament. Temperament falls along a continuum. Move along that continuum and you begin to shift from "typical" spirited behavior into more extreme variations of those same traits that may reflect a developmental or neurological disorder.

So if you are teaching your child the skills to manage his spirit and giving him opportunities to practice them, yet he continues to struggle with focusing in school, entering a group of peers, or is losing it every time you make a simple request—trust your intuition. That leaden sense in your gut is telling you that the frequency, intensity, or duration of his behavior is different from that of other children you know—even the spirited ones.

Take the time to note and video the behaviors that concern you and then consult your pediatrician, local early childhood screening organization, or other professionals working with children. Their experience and perspective can help you to recognize if your child is spirited *and* has a medical condition, *or* if your child's behavior reflects more than typical temperament issues and your child is indeed experiencing a medical problem.

Then *seek* the medical intervention that your child requires. Early diagnosis and treatment are critical, but even if your child is diagnosed with a medical condition, do not stop reading this book. In addition to therapeutic aids, it is equally important that you continue to teach your child the strategies he needs to express his feelings and needs respectfully, including the words and actions to manage his intensity and sensitivity, to cope with new situations, and to work with others. By doing so you provide him with both the treatment that he requires *and* the necessary information and training he needs to flourish in a positive way. So come along, let me bring you hope and tools for creating a family where spirit thrives.

2

A Different Point of View

Building on the Strengths

*When I was a little boy, they called me a liar, but now that
I am grown up, they call me a writer.*
—Isaac Bashevis Singer

I like to collect labels. Any kind of labels: the kind that stick to cans and the kind that stick to people. Today, I studied the label on a can of soup. It is brilliant red against a sharp white. Bright and cheery, it makes me feel happy. There are splashes of yellow that announce to me that this is "Chicken ALPHABET with vegetables SOUP." It is interesting how they hide the vegetables, and highlight the alphabet. On the back side the label tells me the ingredients, and a stamp verifies that the U.S. government has inspected this soup.

The label tells me a lot. Even before I open it, I know what's inside and that the government approves. Companies spend thousands, even millions, of dollars designing these labels to ensure that we find them enticing and desirable.

LOOKING AT OUR LABELS

The labels that stick to people are not always as captivating. They come in many shapes and forms, nicknames like "Grumpy" and "Whiner," titles like "Lord Know It All" and "the Boss," and tags like *pokey* and *dreamer*. Some are bright and colorful and make me feel good when I hear them, like *scooter* and *love*. Some, like *nitpicky* and *crabby*, are drab and dreary and taste sour when they cross my lips. Each highlights a distinctive quality, an identifiable characteristic. They tell me what's inside of the person even if I've never met him. Unfortunately, these names are not presented in any particular order, so I never know when I hear *crabby* if it means the person is a little crabby or a lot crabby. There isn't a government regulation either, so some names are true and some are not.

Spirited kids seem to beg for labels, and not very positive ones. All kids get called a few names, but spirited kids manage to garner an overabundance of awful, miserable, and poorly designed labels that seem to stick like a mosquito on the back of your neck, leaving welts on tender, smooth skin. It can happen in any family, just as it happened in Caroline's.

"My husband says we should have named her Helen because she's 'hell' on wheels!" Caroline laughed, as we listened to her three-year-old daughter, Hazel, "organize" her buddies in the sandbox. "But seriously, I never realized how easy it is to label her, and I'm beginning to see the impact it has on her. She's the youngest, the surprise baby in our family. She is so different from the other two that we have always referred to her as 'Wild Woman.' Yesterday, my mother reprimanded her for jumping on the couch. Hazel excused herself by saying, 'Grandma, it's okay. I'm supposed to be the wild one.'"

Once a label is set, even if it isn't accurate, we tend to act in ways that are consistent with that label. This seemingly magical leap from label into reality is called the Pygmalion Effect and has been well documented by researchers. The reality is that children learn who they are from others in their lives. Think about the spirited children you know. What words do you use to describe them? Do they sound like the million-dollar words created by advertising companies, words that can make you wish you could have even more children who are spirited? Are they the kind of descriptors that would make others envy you the opportunity of raising a spirited child? Labels that make you puff with pride, smile in appreciation, and chuckle with enjoyment? Positive words that focus on what's right instead of what's wrong?

Let's be honest. It's unlikely.

Most of us find ourselves facing an array of labels spoken and unspoken that affect how we think, feel, and act toward our spirited children. If we are going to build a healthy relationship with them, we must lay the labels out on the table, dissect them, and then redesign those that make us and our kids feel lousy—the ones that cloud our vision and hide the potential within.

THE TOPIC IS LABELS

The labels are different for each family. You'll need to dissect and redesign your own, but let me allow you to join one of the spirited-child classes and hear a few of the labels other parents have composed. Believe me, you're not the only parent ever to harbor a few dismal impressions of a spirited child.

The start of a spirited-child class is a rowdy event with four-teen parents and eighteen kids all arriving at the same time. It's the commotion that strikes you first—a collage of sound. Happy sounds: squeals of excitement, laughter, and calls to moms and dads to "watch this" as agile little bodies leap from the top of the slide and bounce on the trampoline. Sounds of fear: cries of protests and declarations of "I won't do it" as kids wrap their arms around their parents' legs forcing the adults into a stiff-legged walk across the room.

The families spend the first minutes together and then separate. The children continue in their program while the parents move to a discussion group.

"Today the topic is labels," I announce, giving each parent three index cards. I ask them to write on each one a word that describes their child on the "bad days." A few immediately ask for more cards, insisting that three is not nearly enough. Everyone laughs. It feels good to know that other people might also entertain a few unpleasant thoughts.

Several parents instantly complete the cards. Others shift in their chairs, hesitating, their pens hovering. The thought of publicly admitting these horrible thoughts is almost unbearable. I assure them the cards will be passed to the front, shuffled, and redistributed. No one will have to "own" the label they write. They can be completely honest.

Once the cards are shuffled, I pass them back around the table, and each person takes one. Mike, a low-key and observant father of two—one spirited, one not—breaks the silence. "*Argumentative,*" he reads. "Oh yeah, my son Jayden will argue about anything. Yesterday he tried to convince me the sun wasn't shining. I'm not blind; the sun was shining. 'Look out the window,' I told him. 'The sun is shining.' Do you know what Jayden's answer was? 'Well it isn't in China.'"

The others laugh, remembering their own dead-end debates. As the laughter dies down, Jennifer flips a card over. *"Never stops,"* she announces.

Abby jumps in this time. "I've got four kids, and Bea keeps me on duty twenty-four hours a day. I'm on call from the minute she wakes up until she falls asleep. I'm beat. I need a break."

"Me too," Amanda agrees. "Elizabeth is two years old and I'm still waiting for her to sleep through the night. I never know when she'll fall asleep and when she'll be awake." Then, sheepishly glancing around the group, she adds, "Sex. What's that? I think I remember making love. I must have at least once."

The others howl in delight.

"I can't believe someone else wrote this, because I did too," Sarah admits, flipping her card over. *Aggressive* was written in big bold letters.

"If it helps any," Jacob offers, "I wrote *explosive*. The daily blast-offs are almost more than I can endure. I'm beginning to feel like a career astronaut."

"Well, maybe my kid isn't as bad as I thought," chuckles Laura. "I get frustrated because she's so *picky*. The pancakes have to be the same shade of brown on both sides. Her clothes have to *feel right*."

The list grows.

demanding	argumentative
monster madman	stubborn
destructive	picky
defiant	noisy
unpredictable	rude
totally exhausting	whiny
dictator	inflexible
explosive	single-minded

It's a shocking list, one that catches us all by surprise. Silence hangs in the room, the dreadfulness of the list stinging. Each is a label and describes something "inside." When we hear these words, we are not enticed and definitely not filled with desire. Unconsciously we pull away, as though punched.

"Imagine," I begin, keeping my voice low, "a child attempting to develop a healthy sense of self with words such as *stubborn*, *explosive*, and *argumentative* describing him. But it's not only the children who are affected. It's us, too. Let me show you what I mean."

I direct each parent to say, "My child is . . ." and then read the list aloud to a partner. Glancing around the table, I notice Jennifer's neck and face flushing ruby red. Swiping at the tears welling in her eyes, she turns to me shaking her head, and pleads, "I can't do this."

"It's okay to pass," I assure her. Suddenly a cacophony of voices explodes in the room around her, as the other parents read aloud each label. Then another voice catches. The room quiets. Shoulders droop as bodies slide down in the chairs. "What is happening inside of your body?" I ask.

"I feel nauseous," Megan replies, holding her stomach.

Hand on her heart, Abby shudders. "My heart is racing."

Lyssa fans her face, "I'm having a hot flash."

Jennifer wipes another tear.

What the Labels Do to Us

The labels we use may seem like simple words, but they have the power to trigger our fight-or-flight response system. It is an unconscious physiological reaction in which our heart and pulse rates escalate, our breathing quickens, and blood rushes to our extremities—all in preparation to fight or flee. I call this state the "red zone."

In the red zone, we experience tunnel vision. Totally attuned to the potential threat, we lose our ability to think, to solve problems, to hear the voices of others, or to look them in the eye. These reactions make it impossible to empathize with our children. When in this state, we even perceive neutral faces as angry and rejecting. We deem innocent acts intentional and spiteful. Instead of drawing us toward our children to offer comfort and care, the negative labels program our brains to be ready for "battle."

Like a swirling hurricane, negativity is devastating to relationships. It is so powerful that psychologist John Gottman found when listening to couples' conversations that if there was a ratio of 2.9 negative statements for every positive statement, he could predict that they were on the road to divorce. On the other hand, couples with healthy relationships had a ratio of only one negative comment for every five positive statements.

Starting today, you can choose to stop using words that project a negative image of your child. It really is not that far a leap from *picky* to *selective* or even from *obnoxious* to *dramatic*. By changing your vocabulary, you can alter how you and others perceive your child. You can create a new image that feels good, looks good, and meets socially approved standards. Doing so will benefit your child and you as well. It will literally change the physiological responses of your body and brain because negative labels can trigger a flight-or-fight response of fear in the nervous system (which is why the parents who read aloud the labels for their children had strong physical reactions). Using the new language will calm your system and help you feel confident and competent, even on the bad days.

Redesigning the Labels

Grab a piece of paper and on the left side of your sheet, write down all the words that you can think of that describe the crazy, obnoxious things your spirited child does. Be certain to include the worst ones—the ones you believe to have the least possibility of possessing any redeeming qualities. Include on your list words that you've heard relatives, friends, and teachers use to describe your child that made you flare up in anger or shrink in embarrassment. Squeeze them all out.

Now take a deep breath, relax your shoulders, wiggle your toes, and take a look at some of your favorite photographs of your spirited child. Glance at the ones on your computer or phone, the ones in frames—or pull from your memory your favorite images. Focus on those that include the snappy eyes, infectious grin, agile body, or crazy "personal style" outfit. Hold on to that image in your mind as you look at the list of lousy labels. It will help you to discover the hidden potential in each of the words.

If you look closely at the list, you'll see that the lousy labels often reflect strengths that are being overused. Find that strength and name it. For example, with a little direction and skill training, *stubbornness* can be transformed into *persistence*—the number one predictor of future success. *Hyper*, when focused, may be *energetic*. The possibilities are endless.

Your list may look like the one we created in our group.

Old Negative Labels	New Exciting Labels
demanding	holds high standards
monster madman	creative
destructive	passionately curious
defiant	principled

unpredictable	flexible
whiny	expressive
rude	honest
explosive	passionate
argumentative	future attorney
stubborn	committed to goals
picky	selective
dictator	strong
single-minded	focused
inflexible	traditional
totally exhausting	energetic
loud	zestful

"My child is . . ." I invite the group to read aloud with me the new exciting label list. Voices join in. Smiles spread. A sigh of relief punctuates the last word. "How do you feel now?" I inquire.

"Hope," Mike declares. "It's exciting to see the potential."

Abby releases a long, deep breath. "Calm."

Jennifer smiles. "Much better."

When we hold a positive vision, it changes our response. Heart rate and pulse rate slow, allowing us to listen to the voices of others, think, solve problems, and even maintain a sense of humor. The brain tells the body, *We are safe. This is someone we love and who loves us.* The result is that we smile more. We offer more information. Our patience grows and we even give our kids a break. Neutral faces and acts are perceived as just that—neutral. They are no longer misconstrued as a potential threat or intentional goad.

In fact, developmental psychologist J. J. Goodnow found in her research that parents whose children were very socially competent did not see their children's occasional social "tussles" as signs of aggressiveness. Instead, the missteps were attributed to something more temporary, for example, a high-energy child having played for too long. As a result, rather than getting angry with their children, they simply made a mental note to help them avoid getting into trouble in the future by pointing out when to call it quits. That optimistic perspective kept parent and child working together.

You can teach yourself to use your new labels when you talk about your kids and when you discipline them. To the five-year-old who is refusing to wear the new outfit Grandma sent, you can say, "You do have a strong sense of style." And to the eight-year-old who refuses to go to bed until she has finished the last chapter in her book, "You are persistent and committed to your goals."

I realize you might be thinking, *Isn't this child just "getting her way"?* Let me emphasize that this is the beginning of the conversation—not the ending. Ultimately, you will teach your child the skills to be flexible and to be a creative problem solver. But for those lessons to be heard and processed, your child has to be calm. That won't be the case if you are upset, thinking she is being stubborn or difficult.

The feelings and images the new labels create are totally different from those created by the lousy labels. It feels good to be the parent of a child who is assertive, committed, selective, dramatic, analytical, enthusiastic, and charismatic. These words may even describe the child you dreamed of having.

Discipline begins by "drawing your child to you." Visualizing her strengths moves you calmly and empathetically toward her. When you can see before you your passionate, smart, curious child who is struggling right now, it's easier to remind yourself that she can learn skills to make it better. Sensing in your approach someone who loves her, and with whom she is safe, she will turn to you, opening to your guidance and calm enough to hear it.

Getting Past the Barriers

Abby sighs deeply, sinking lower into her chair as she confesses, "I really try. Honestly, I don't wake up planning to call him a 'little jerk.' But some days it's so tough."

It's easy to fall into the trap of labeling kids. Even if you tend to be an incredibly positive person, you might have gotten yourself caught in a whirlpool of negative labeling when it comes to dealing with your child. You may not even be certain how it happened. When you are the parent of a spirited child, emotions can be raw and real, feelings like:

FEAR: "Some days I can't help thinking, 'He's just like my brother.' My brother is *not* doing well in life."

EXHAUSTION: "Every day I think, 'How long before he drives me nuts?' I tell myself I can hold on for another thirty minutes until my husband gets home, but then he calls and tells me he is going to be late!"

INCOMPETENCE: "On the days when I am absolutely overwhelmed, my wife says, 'Call your mother. She raised six kids. Ask Jenna how she did it.' All I can say is, I don't know how Jenna did it, but she cried a lot."

SHAME: "I wonder if I'm doing something wrong. I see a lot of me in him—my bad points. I'm impatient and stubborn and so is he. My parents let me know in no uncertain terms that 'good kids' were not impatient and stubborn. It sets me off when he acts that way."

Like an elephant sitting on your chest, these emotions can crush your best intentions. It does not have to be that way. It really is possible to eject the "beast" from the room. Fears can be quieted once you realize spirited children can excel beyond their peers. Energy replaces exhaustion when self-care is recognized as an essential and noble cause. Efficiency and confidence eradicate incompetence if you have a tool kit of effective strategies in hand. Celebration eclipses shame as you gaze into the mirror recognizing you too are spirited. You are normal. You are more.

Keep reading. I'll provide you with the inside info to show the beast the door.

Good Labels Are Contagious

The exciting thing about changing the vocabulary we use to describe our spirited children is that it is contagious. That's what Erica discovered.

"It was amazing!" she exclaimed. "When I used positive words to describe Silas, so did my relatives and his teacher. If someone complained, 'Silas is awfully loud,' I would respond, 'He is dramatic, isn't he? Let's get him outside where we can appreciate that more.' They'd be taken aback, but after a few minutes they would agree he really can be spectacular. After I'd done it a few times, I overheard my mother say, 'Silas, your dramatic side is coming out again. Let's turn on some music and dance together.' Even at school when his teacher told me he was stubborn, I nodded in agreement but said, 'We find him to be very tenacious at home too.' 'I never thought of it in that light,' the teacher responded. 'I guess it isn't all that bad, is it?' It really changed the way she saw him. It's contagious!"

Jason nodded in agreement. "The labels really made a difference for me too. They gave me more patience. Leo always wants to climb into his car seat by himself. If I try to assist him, he throws a fit. I thought he was being stubborn and uncooperative. But when I saw him as independent and goal oriented, I realized those were good qualities. That thought made it easier to stop and give him a few minutes. Leo noticed the difference. He's not so quick to lose it if I end up helping a bit. I didn't really think a few words could make that much difference. But they did."

Don't let others intimidate you with hurtful labels. Teach them to use words that reflect your child's potential by using them yourself. You don't even have to argue with them. Merely deflect their thoughts in more positive terms.

Like the companies who spend millions of dollars crafting the labels they place on their products, we too must be intentional. When you drop the negative images and introduce to yourself and others the new labels that focus on strengths and potential instead of weaknesses, you are wrapping your child in a protective covering. Those positive labels change not your only your vocabulary, but your perceptions and, as a result, your actions as well.

The first step to building a healthy lifelong relationship with your spirited child begins with the words you use to describe what's inside. It's as simple as that.

3

What Makes Kids Spirited?

Why They Do What They Do

This was a person who had come into my life.
A real person, not a robot to be programmed or a blank
slate to write on, but a person who in his own way talked
to me and told me what he liked and what he hated—
usually in a very loud and demanding voice.
—Sue, mother of three

The windows that wrap around the room on two sides let in the autumn sunset, giving the entire room a rosy hue. Before the families arrive for class, I like to write our agenda for the night on the whiteboard, but today all I write is one question.

What Makes Kids Spirited?

The parents meander into the discussion room, chatting with one another, grabbing a cup of coffee, and finding a chair. Moans, groans, and nervous laughter erupt as they read the words written on the board.

"I've been trying to answer that question for three years,"

Heather exclaimed, not even waiting for everyone to sit down. "I've lain awake more nights than I care to remember, reviewing my pregnancy. What did I eat? What did I do? I've chastised myself for going water skiing when I was two months pregnant. So what if I didn't even know I was pregnant. I never should have gone."

Jason added, "I keep thinking about Seth's birth. How long and difficult it was. Maybe we should have asked for a cesarean."

"I thought it was the cesarean," Kristin piped in.

"I've been thinking it might be because Jayden was premature," Mike remarked thoughtfully. "He arrived six weeks early and was quite ill the first few days."

Abby grimaced. "I can't help feeling I am somehow failing her."

I raised my hand to grab their attention. "Wait a minute!" I almost shouted above the clamor. "You didn't do it." All heads turned to me. An audible sigh of relief escaped in the room.

WHAT IS TEMPERAMENT?

Your actions have not made your child spirited. Current personality research demonstrates that genes influence personality. Being spirited has nothing to do with a difficult pregnancy or birth, or whether you nursed or bottle-fed your child. It appears that children are born with a tendency to act and react to people and events in their lives in specific ways that can be identified and predicted. These behavioral and emotional patterns have biological and neurochemical underpinnings. *This pattern—a child's first and most natural way of reacting to the world around him—is called his temperament.*

Temperament influences a range of characteristics, including how quickly a child gets upset as well as how long he stays upset and how long he takes to recover. Spirited children are wired to "fire" faster, capable of accelerating from 0 to 60 miles per hour in seconds. That's why your child can shift in seconds from being magically awesome to hitting his brother and slamming doors.

Temperament also governs how sensitive we are to sights, sounds, smells, tastes, and the emotions of others. During a trip to the amusement park you can see these differences. One child begs to stay until closing. Another refuses every ride, gags at the smell of hot dogs, and demands to go home after twenty minutes. If you ignore his appeal to depart, he bolts, propelling you into a sprint to catch him before he reaches the exit.

Energy levels vary according to temperament, too. A child who is temperamentally active not only likes to move but *needs* to move. Telling this child to sit still for extended periods of time—and that he could do it if he really wanted to—is like telling you to ignore a full bladder. The pressure builds. Your child's temperament signals a need to act in a particular way—a need that is inside and real.

Children are born with their own temperament just as they are born with black hair or with blond. This is not to imply that temperament is rigid and unchanging. Like hair, which can be styled, trimmed, or colored, but remains hair, temperament may change in appearance according to how it is "managed," while remaining fundamentally the same. The temperamentally active child will always be an energetic individual. How that looks, however, will change over time. The toddler who opened the oven door, used it to boost herself to the counter, and stood on top of the refrigerator to reach the toy you took from her, will have learned by age thirty to refrain from standing on refrigerators. But it's very likely that she is the one who runs four miles during her lunch break, and on weekends, climbs mountains for "fun." She expresses her energy differently, but she is still active.

THE RESEARCH

Temperament is not synonymous with personality. Personality is the combination of temperament, cultural influences, and life experiences. Viewed as a key building block of personality, temperament has intrigued scholars for centuries. Today, temperament research is expanding exponentially. It is of interest to psychologists, cultural anthropologists, behavioral geneticists, neurobiologists, and many others. Unfortunately, they have not reached a consensus on one definition of temperament, nor do they agree completely on the traits. They do concur, however, that temperament reflects individual differences and has genetic, biological, and neurochemical underpinnings. Temperament is also apparent in the early years of life and relatively stable over time, but it may be altered by maturation, experience, and parenting.

There are several different theories of temperament being explored by contemporary researchers. Mary Rothbart, professor emerita of psychology at the University of Oregon, and her colleagues define temperament as individual differences in reactivity and self-regulation. It is a concept I have integrated into my work because it makes me think of temperament as the "engine inside of us." Engines vary in size, power, and responsiveness. Your spirited child's "engine" is like that of a sports car.

I have found the work of Stella Chess and Alexander Thomas foundational for understanding spirited children. In the 1950s, Chess and Thomas, professors of psychiatry at New York University Medical Center, were among the first to question the prevailing theories of the time that all children arrive in this world as "blank slates," their personalities determined by the parenting they receive. According to the blank-slate theory, nurture, not nature, made the difference. Today, remnants of this philosophy can still be heard in comments such as "He wouldn't be that way if you didn't coddle him," or "Give him to me for a week and I'll fix him." This view of temperament ignores or minimizes the biological basis of individual differences.

In their clinical practice and as parents of four very different children, Chess and Thomas saw too many cases in which the one-sided nurture approach did not adequately explain the child's responses. Something was missing.

It was this gap in understanding that led them to conduct the now-famous New York Longitudinal Study. Chess and Thomas, along with their colleague H. G. Birch, observed 133 children eat, dress, and play with friends and also interviewed parents and teachers. From the results of this study, Chess, Thomas, and Birch identified nine distinct differences in how children respond to the world, one of which is intensity of response—similar to Rothbart's identified trait of reactivity. While every researcher may not agree with Chess, Thomas, and Birch's nine dimensions of temperament, from my perspective they got it just right when it comes to understanding spirited children. Once you learn about these, the road of parenting your spirited child will be much smoother, as you'll see. But first, I want you to realize how much power you have to influence your child's expression of his spirited temperament.

YOU DO MAKE A DIFFERENCE

You might be feeling a bit dismayed at this point, thinking that if temperament is biologically and genetically based, there is nothing you can do to influence how it is expressed. Yes, your spirited child is wired to be spirited, but biology is not destiny. We now know that nature and nurture matter. How your child's temperament ultimately manifests depends on his age, his experiences, and how he has been parented. David Reiss, M.D., of George Washington University has said, "Whether and how strongly genes that underlie behaviors are turned on or expressed depends on the interaction and relationships a child has with the important people in his life."

You don't get to choose your child's temperament, nor does your child. Mother Nature does that for us. But you do make a big difference. It is you who will help your child recognize when his engine is running too hot. It is you who will give him the words to describe what he is experiencing. It is you who will teach him the strategies to shift lanes smoothly and brake without spinning out of control. Daily practice with him, researchers tell us, creates new pathways within the brain, making these more efficient skills easily accessible and natural to him.

Initially, in this relationship you are the "driver." Understanding temperament allows you to lift the hood to see what's going on inside your child's engine. Once you understand his responses and the reasons behind them, you can learn to work with them, downshifting through life's curves when needed, recognizing the points at which you need to make adjustments, and running at a pace that allows his engine to purr.

Just as one would never attempt to turn a sports car into a utility truck, it is also critical to avoid the mistake of telling a child who is temperamentally intense, energetic, and sensitive not to be any of those things. By understanding her temperament and working with it, you assist your child in channeling her energy.

Recognizing her persistence, you teach her creative problem solving and flexibility. Appreciating her sensitivity, you help her know when to take a break. You teach her the skills to use the gifts she has been given, allowing her to be all she can be.

Eventually, you will shift your role from driver to leader of the pit crew of support, relinquishing the driver's seat to your spirited child. By then, she will understand how her engine works and be proficient at accelerating smoothly, shifting efficiently, and braking without swerving. Wise, tenacious, and excited about her ability to handle the challenges of the track, she is likely to flash past her peers.

Helping your child gain the skills to drive smoothly on life's course takes time and practice. Until Jason, the father of two, discovered temperament, it was as if there was an undeclared war raging in his home. The lines had been drawn and the battles were being fought every single day.

"To tell the truth," he told me, "the 'war' frightened me. Usually, I'm a low-key, quiet kind of guy. Little things don't rile me. But within five minutes of trying to get my six-year-old into bed, I was a snarling bear.

"Then I learned about temperament. All of a sudden I realized he wasn't doing this just to get me. He had a reason; he needed a forewarning to finish things up. When I recognized that, I could work with it. Little things as simple as giving him a ten-minute heads-up, or taking a few minutes to find out what he wanted to finish before getting ready for bed, really seemed to help. Now I know not to surprise him by announcing, 'Bedtime, now!' It's like we are on the same team.

"I can't believe how much more I enjoy my son when I'm not fighting with him all the time. You know, he's a pretty neat kid."

GETTING A PICTURE
OF YOUR CHILD'S TEMPERAMENT

As I explained, researchers Chess, Thomas, and Birch have shown that there are nine different temperamental traits. Each of these can be placed on a continuum from a mild reaction to a strong reaction, or from high to low. Everyone has her own temperament, her own unique style. Spirited children tend to fall on the strong end of the continuum, but others may fall on that end in one or more traits as well. It's the overall picture that helps us understand the spirited child.

Remember, there isn't a perfect temperament. There are positive and negative aspects of all the temperamental traits. Parents make the difference by helping a child to shape her particular qualities in the most advantageous way.

As you review the traits, think about your child's typical, most natural reactions. What responses have you come to predict?

1. Intensity

How strong are your child's emotional reactions? Does he laugh and cry loudly and energetically or softly and mildly?

1	2	3	4	5
MILD REACTION				INTENSE REACTION
"Squeaks" when cries				Never just cries—wails or explodes
It's almost a surprise when he gets upset				A living staircase of emotion, up one minute and down the next
Reactions are low-key, mild				Every reaction is deep and powerful

Smiles when happy   Shouts with glee

Usually works   Easily frustrated
through a problem
without becoming
frustrated

Daniel Goleman, Ph.D., author of *Emotional Intelligence,* once wrote in the *New York Times:* "Some people, psychologists are observing, find themselves in emotional tumult even in reaction to mundane events, while others remain unperturbed under the most trying of circumstances. These levels of feeling characterize a person's entire emotional life: those with the deepest lows also have the loftiest highs, the research shows. And differences between people seem to emerge early in childhood, if not from birth, and remain a major mark of character throughout life."

Even in the hospital nursery, the differences in emotional intensity are apparent. Some babies "squeak" when they're hungry. Others wail, their cries echoing down the corridor. Spirited kids are born intense, their engines revving. Inevitably, for the parent of a spirited child, one of those squeakers belongs to a relative. At family gatherings, the squeaker whimpers while the spirited one screams!

But there's nothing wrong with the spirited screamer. He is temperamentally more intense. That isn't all bad. It means he is also more enthusiastic, exuberant, and zestful.

Spirited children experience every emotion and sensation deeply and powerfully. There is a physical reaction that occurs more strongly in their bodies than in less intense individuals. Their hearts pound, the adrenaline flows through their bodies, and their pulses race. They are not loud because they know it irritates people; they are loud because they really feel that much excitement, pain, or whatever the emotion or sensation might be. Their intensity is real. It is their first and most natural reaction. If you have circled a 4 or 5, you can predict that your child will be easily excited, frustrated, and emotional. When you know your child is intense, you can expect a strong reaction and develop a plan to help your child express it appropriately or diffuse it.

2. Persistence

If your child is involved in an activity and you tell her to stop, does she stop easily or fight to continue?

1	2	3	4	5
EASILY STOPS				"LOCKS IN"
Can be redirected to participate in another activity quite easily				Sticks to her guns, doesn't easily let go of an idea or activity
Will cry for a few minutes and then stop				Locks in, can cry for hours
Accepts no for an answer				Never takes no for an answer

In their studies, Chess and Thomas observed that some children can easily stop an activity, whereas others continue despite major obstacles. Spirited kids "lock in." If they want to do something, they want to do it now and can't easily give up on it. I remember visiting friends in Colorado. We had gone out for dinner and found ourselves returning to the house in the dark. It was a cold November night, with the wind blowing in gusts, whipping our scarves in our faces and pushing us down the driveway. Without thinking, I picked up their two-year-old daughter and carried her into the house and out of the cold wind. Once inside, she turned around and slugged me! I had spoiled her plans. She had every intention of walking up the steps herself. I tried to cajole her out of her coat, but she wouldn't give it up. A less persistent child might have, but not Claire. She stood screaming at the door, pounding on it with her bare fists. It was obvious that nothing other than opening that door and letting her go out was going to be acceptable to her. I stood back and let her go, reminding her as I did that next time she could say, "I'd like to open the door myself, please." The wind nearly knocked her off the landing, but she marched down those steps and then determinedly back up them. Only after shutting the door herself was she ready to take off her coat. She wasn't about to be distracted from her goal!

The advice to stop a persistent child's cry by ignoring it is worthless, a frustrating joke. Although other children may fall asleep within minutes of being laid in their beds, this child can scream for hours unless Mom or Dad finds a way to soothe her and help her stop. Ignoring doesn't work. Persistent kids only cry louder and longer.

Cleaning up may be another situation where persistence comes into play. This determined child wants to use every block in the bucket before she can stop playing and come to dinner.

Persistent kids are committed to their tasks. If they want a cookie, they'll keep coming back until they get one. They are goal oriented, unwilling to give up easily.

Many parents of spirited children are baffled by the fact that spirited children can be both persistent and perceptive. They wonder how spirited kids can forget two directions from their parents, yet remember their favorite restaurant ten miles back and insist on going there. The answer is simple. Spirited kids are persistent when they are motivated and personally interested in the idea or activity. If it's their idea, they won't let go of it. If it's yours, they are much more interested in what else is going on in the world around them.

The world needs people who are persistent, but as their parent you can expect to expend more energy and skill to win cooperation. However, combine that persistence with the skills to think flexibly and solve problems creatively, and it's awesome what they can accomplish.

3. Sensitivity

How aware is your child of slight noises, emotions, and differences in temperature, taste, and texture? Does he react easily to certain foods, tags in clothing, irritating noises, or your stress level?

1	2	3	4	5
USUALLY NOT SENSITIVE				VERY SENSITIVE
Sleeps through noisy routines				Has to have quiet to sleep
Isn't affected by scratchy textiles				Has to have a sock seam lined up just so
Isn't bothered by funny smells				Complains about lights, noise, and smells, especially in crowds
Eats anything				A "selective" eater
Unaware of your stress				Acts out your stress
Not overly concerned with how things feel				Strong reactions to how things feel, whether pleasant or unpleasant

Researchers have observed a significant difference in how children react to the sights, sounds, and smells around them. Some children seem unperturbed by scratchy clothes, loud noises, or funny smells, whereas others are extremely sensitive.

Spirited children are born with a super set of sensors. Although many other kids can fall asleep in a room full of people, the spirited child stays wide awake, taking in every sound and sight. Sleeping in a hotel or at Grandma's house may be a difficult task. The sheets smell weird and the pillow doesn't feel right. Sensitive kids also respond to emotions, serving as the family's stress gauge. When you feel the worst, they'll act the worst.

To the sensitive child, every experience is a sensual bombardment. He sees, hears, and smells things that others—including his parents and siblings—might miss. In class one day, Mike illustrated this phenomenon with the following story of an outing with his daughter.

The local theater was showing classics. It was to be a great father-daughter experience—just Ellie, *Sleeping Beauty*, and me. I let her skip supper and bought her popcorn and candy. What more could she need? The minute the lights went out she started to scream. "Daddy," she gasped. "It's too dark. I can't see. It makes my skin crawl!"

She leaped into my lap just as the film began.

"It's too loud," she complained, pressing the palms of her hands against her ears. "It's hurting my ears."

I could see she was going to lose it. I've seen it hit before, so I took her out into the lobby. "Ellie, it's all right. We can go home. I don't need to see *Sleeping Beauty*. We can watch it on the Internet," I told her.

"No! No!" she protested. "I can handle it. I want to stay."

We slid back into our seats, crawling over the family sitting next to us, the kind of family where everyone has a barrel chest. She pulled her sweatshirt up over her mouth and ears to help deaden the sound. All seemed to be going well until the family next to us started munching and crunching their popcorn and salted peanuts.

"Daddy, they're chewing too loudly," she complained. "Tell them to close their mouths."

I shot a glance at the guy. One look and I knew he was at least two hundred fifty pounds and counting. I'm one fifty-five on a stretch. There was no way I was going to tell him to shut his mouth. I decided I couldn't hear anything and refused to intervene.

For once she accepted my refusal and buried her head deeper into her sweatshirt. Suddenly she grabbed her stomach.

"Yuck, Daddy, I can smell popcorn and peanuts and some-body's got bad breath. It's making me sick, Daddy."

I grabbed the popcorn container and stuck it in front of her face, but she found her own solution, pulling the sweat-shirt right up over her nose. Now only her eyes showed above the pink collar. I turned to the film, thinking maybe I'd get to watch it now.

Ellie sat hunched in her seat, head buried in the sweatshirt, hands still clamped over her ears. She sighed, and I wondered what was coming next.

Through the sweatshirt she demanded, "What's going to happen next? Where did the witch go? When the nurse pricks my finger, will I fall asleep for a long time?"

She kept a running dialogue going through the entire film. The big guy next to us sent searing glares our way. I slunk further down into my seat. "Shhh," I reprimanded. She lowered her voice, but the questions continued.

"Did the needle prick hurt her? Would you be sad if I fell asleep for a long time?" (I was beginning to think it might be nice.)

The family next to us moved away, the entire row of seats reverberating as they struggled out. I was surprised she didn't complain about that. It seemed like hours, maybe even days before the credits finally appeared. I was exhausted. She skipped out the door, arms flying.

"Let's do that again!" she exclaimed.

Never, I thought. Never!

Ellie was not trying to ruin their special day out. Ellie is temperamentally sensitive. She notices and absorbs all of the sounds, smells, bright lights, and textures around her and reacts to them. As Mike shared, "The level of stimulation necessary to get a response from her is almost indiscernible." Add intensity and she reacts very strongly.

If your child is temperamentally sensitive, hearing, smelling, and feeling things that you may not even discern, you can expect that food, clothing, crowds, noisy celebrations, and other sensory-loaded activities will easily trigger him. Now when it happens, instead of worrying that he is being naughty on purpose, you can recognize it for what it is: his first and most natural reaction, a reaction you can help him learn to manage.

Reading about sensitivity, you may wonder how to discern a temperamentally sensitive child from one who is experiencing sensory processing disorder. It is a matter of degree. But what you will find with a child who is temperamentally sensitive is that, like Ellie, she will keenly notice sensations in her environment, be annoyed or irritated by them, but with your help, be able to find ways to cope. As a result, she may be selective about her clothing, food, or favorite events, and although she may initially be upset, she will not be completely overwhelmed by the sensations or unable to participate.

A child experiencing sensory processing disorder may adamantly retreat from certain sensations or throw his entire body into getting a particular type of stimulation. The reaction is stronger, more intense, and pervasive—as though the child is frightened, ready to "fight or flee." This "drive" can be so strong that it interferes with his daily tasks, making it impossible for him to participate in specific activities.

Unlike children who are temperamentally sensitive, for children experiencing sensory processing disorder, alterations in the environment are not enough to help them cope. In order to be successful, they will need additional therapy with an occupational therapist.

4. Perceptiveness

Does your child notice people, colors, noises, and objects around her? Does she frequently forget to do what you asked because something else has caught her attention?

1	2	3	4	5

HARDLY EVER NOTICES	VERY PERCEPTIVE
Stays on task, isn't watching birds outside the window	Notices things most people miss
Walks past the rainbow that is reflected in the new oil spill	Spends five minutes watching the light in the new oil spill
Can remember and complete multiple directions easily	Forgets multiple directions

Researchers have found stark differences in how aware individuals are of the world around them. Spirited kids are not only more sensitive, they are also more perceptive. They notice everything. Drive down the freeway with them, and they'll point out the hawk sitting forty feet up in the air on top of the light post. Take them for a walk, and they'll notice the shiny coin hidden in the grass.

Their perceptiveness can get them into trouble because it sometimes might appear as though they aren't listening. Ask a spirited child to get dressed and she'll disappear. Thirty minutes later you can find her still in her pajamas staring out the window at the cloud formations or playing with the ball she tripped over on the way to her room. The ten-second journey from your neighbor's yard to yours may take the perceptive child twenty minutes. On her way, she'll notice the dew in the grass, the new bird's nest in the apple tree, and the delicate spiderweb woven in the flowers; she'll stop to enjoy the rainbow reflected in the fresh oil spill on the garage floor.

The keen observations of perceptive kids feed a rich imagination. They'll point out the king's crown left in the carpet by the strokes of the vacuum and the letter B formed by the spaghetti sauce on their plates. They'll act out stories and design crazy costumes.

It may be impossible to nurse the perceptive baby in a room full of people. There's a standing joke among nursing mothers in my spirited child groups—you may become known for your elongated breasts if you attempt to nurse your baby during the discussion because every time someone speaks or walks past, the baby will turn to look or listen, taking the nipple with her. It's a painful stretch.

And for the highly perceptive child, making decisions can also be challenging. Detecting all the options may be overwhelming, which frequently makes even a simple choice excruciating. Leah, a highly perceptive adult, explained to me what happens.

I pulled into my favorite coffee shop thinking, "This will take me five minutes maximum. I will just order my usual, Grande Americano with cream. Simple!" But this morning there were three—not one but three—huge signs promoting the "pumpkin spice collection." This wasn't just any morning at the coffee shop. It was an *autumn* morning.

My heart rate kicked into a discernible roar as the pumpkin battle exploded in my brain. "Should I trade in my Americano for a pumpkin spice latte? No, don't do that. It's too sweet. You're allergic to dairy. It will make you sick. Maybe soy? No, I hate soy." The melee in my brain continued as the line, which initially seemed an insurmountable wall between me and caffeine bliss, morphed into a rushing river.

Much too quickly, the cashier inquired, "May I help you?" I stood frozen, a deer in headlights. My face scrunching and twisting in a last-minute wrestling match with my tongue. I have no doubt that if I were three years old instead of thirty, I would have thrown myself on the ground, kicking and screaming: "MOM, I WANT COFFEE, AND PUMPKIN SPICE!" Two minutes later I departed, drained as though I had completed a four-mile run rather than a six-minute stop at the coffee shop.

"But," she continued, a smile sliding across her face as she remembered, "In my right hand, I held a tall Americano (I had the sense to size it down), and in my left a pumpkin spice latte."

It is this trait, perceptiveness, that is most often confused with children experiencing Attention Deficit Disorder (ADD). Unmanaged perceptiveness may be perceived as distractibility. The difference between a perceptive spirited child and a child experiencing ADD is that a spirited child will notice everything going on around her, but will be able to process that information and ultimately be able to select the most important information to heed. As a result, she will be able to focus on and complete a task, or make a decision. A child experiencing ADD, despite her best efforts, will be unable to figure out what is the most important information to pay attention to and will not be able to focus on or complete a task, even if she wants to.

If you have marked a 4 or a 5 for your child's perceptiveness, you know that your child is engaging more of the world around her than the average person. She will need your help learning how to tune in to the most important messages. Including visual cues such as photos, objects, colors, drawings, or arrows in directions will make it easier for her to "hear" you. Allowing time to process will result in efficient decision making.

5. Adaptability

How quickly does your child adapt to changes in his schedule or routine? How does he cope with surprises?

1	2	3	4	5
ADAPTS QUICKLY				ADAPTS SLOWLY
Easily stops one activity and starts another				Cries or fusses when one activity ends and another begins
Is flexible with changes in the routine				Becomes upset with changes in the routine
Is not upset by surprises				Is upset by surprises
Shifts quickly from awake to sleep or sleep to awake				Requires time to shift from sleep to awake and awake to sleep
Leaves the park, a friend's house, or event with little to no fuss				Becomes upset leaving the park, a friend's house, or event

There are major differences in how individuals adapt to changes and transitions. Some children take little notice of them. For others, transitions or changes of any kind are stressful. Spirited children usually adapt to change very slowly. They hate surprises and need time and forewarning in order to shift from one activity to another. Switching from awake to sleep, or sleep to awake, may also result in lengthy bedtime or morning routines. Rushing sets them off.

The concept of adaptability may be new to you. Perhaps you have not really noticed how your child reacts. Yet adaptability may be one of the major reasons why you and your child are finding yourselves in daily hassles. It's the slow-to-adapt child who loses it because you cut his toast in triangles when he wanted rectangles or you stopped at Burger King when he was expecting Chipotle. Naptime, lunchtime, bedtime, drop-off-at-child-care time, and pick-up-from-school time are all daily transitions that are challenging for this child. If there's a substitute bus driver, teacher, or child-care provider, you can bet the spirited child will have a tough day. Adjusting to daylight savings time may take three weeks. A new season, and the inevitable change in clothing, may prove to be a major source of contention. Stopping a game in order to eat dinner can be a significant intrusion. Even having another child unexpectedly attempt to join a slow-to-adapt child and his friends can lead to tears. Spirited kids honestly do shift this slowly. They often don't realize they are making life challenging for you. They just need time to adjust.

Sasha realized it was Nora's slow adaptability to adjust that turned the task of running errands into a struggle.

I couldn't understand why Nora would start screaming every time I put her in the car and took her out to enter the store. My older child loved to run errands with me. It was a special time, just one child and me. I wanted to share that special time with Nora. But Nora hated it. She couldn't stand going in and out of places. It was a fight to get her in the door and then a bigger battle to get her out again. Now I realize she gets upset because there are too many transitions, too close together. She just can't adapt that quickly. Running errands is *not* a special time with Nora!

Understanding how your child reacts to transitions and changes is a key to winning cooperation. If your child is slow to adapt, you need to teach yourself and him to notice when transitions happen so you can both prepare. Establishing predictable routines allows him to predict what will happen and when, drastically reducing the daily meltdowns. Eliminating unnecessary transitions, like going back upstairs to dress after breakfast instead of getting dressed *before* coming down, is even better.

6. Regularity

Is your child quite regular about eating times, sleeping times, amount of sleep needed, and other bodily functions?

1	2	3	4	5
REGULAR				IRREGULAR
Falls asleep at the same time almost every day				Never falls asleep at the same time
Is hungry at regular intervals				Is hungry at different times each day or "forgets" to eat
Eliminates on a regular schedule				Eliminates on an irregular schedule

In their studies, researchers observed that some children fell easily into regular sleeping and eating schedules, whereas others required much more help from the adults in their lives in order to get into routines. Some days these children napped for three hours; the next they would not nap at all. They were hungry at different times of the day. Irregularity can also affect how children handle mealtime, bedtime, and toilet learning, and when they get up in the morning.

Spirited children who are irregular by nature have bodies that are not easily scheduled into a predictable pattern or rhythm. Frequently, they have a "window for sleep" that's a mere fifteen minutes long. Miss it, and it's another forty-five minutes before you can get them down.

A consistent routine is critical. Allow irregular children to stay up on the weekend and it will take a week, or longer, to get them back on schedule. It may appear that a schedule just does not fit them. However, these children, more than others, need assistance from their parents and cues from their environment to set their biological clock if they are going to get the sleep they need.

Serving six mini-meals evenly distributed throughout the day also helps children who "forget" to eat manage blood sugar and energy levels throughout the day. It also eliminates the frustration of having a child who isn't hungry at dinner, but is the moment you put away the dishes. Understanding her temperament allows you to work together.

If you have marked a 4 or a 5 for regularity, you can expect that establishing regular routines in your household will be challenging but extremely important.

7. Energy

Is your child always on the move and busy or quiet and quiescent? Does he need to run, jump, and use his whole body in order to feel good?

1	2	3	4	5
QUIET				VERY ACTIVE
Stays in one place when sleeping				When forced to stay in one place, seems ready to burst
Sits and plays quietly for extended periods of time				Always on the move, is fidgeting even when sitting
Seems fine on days with no exercise or outside time				Wild and irritable on days of no exercise or outside time

Individual differences in energy levels have also been found. Some children have been observed to sit quietly for long periods of time. Other children are always on the move.

Many spirited children are energetic; however, not all of them are climbers and leapers. Some merely seem to possess incredible energy. They don't walk; they run. They can't pass through a doorframe without jumping up to touch the header. They fall out of their chairs at school and at the dinner table. It isn't that they aren't paying attention or trying to follow rules; they simply have a need to move. A long trip in the car can be a nightmare unless frequent stops are taken to let this child release the energy pumping through his veins.

Energy levels are also a major factor in Attention Deficit Disorder. It is not the amount of activity or energy that is the concern, however, but the focus of that action. For example, the six-year-old who wiggles and jumps in and out of his chair while he completes his work is a child with an active temperament. The child who pings around the room and never completes his work may be experiencing ADD.

It isn't possible for even seasoned professionals to make a diagnosis of ADD simply by observing a child. If you are concerned that your child may be experiencing ADD, it is important that you have the child undergo a full physical and psychological review.

If your child is temperamentally energetic, you can expect that he will need to move. You can predict it and use this information to plan for his success.

8. First Reaction

What is your child's first reaction when she is asked to meet people, try a new activity or idea, or go someplace new?

1	2	3	4	5
JUMPS RIGHT IN				REJECTS AT FIRST OR WATCHES BEFORE JOINING IN
Doesn't hesitate in new situations				Holds back before participating
Seems to learn by doing				Learns by watching
Open to new activities				Is distressed by new activities or things
Usually complies with a new request with little fuss				Immediately says no when you ask her to do something new

Researchers found lifelong differences in how people initially respond to new situations. Some individuals do not hesitate and move right in. They seem to learn by doing. Others hold back and appear to learn by watching. They prefer to check out a new situation before joining in.

A group of spirited children will usually split right down the middle on this trait. Half of the children will jump into new situations, which poses the problem of children literally jumping into trouble. They leap before they look. The other half hang back, often refusing to participate; they may cry and throw themselves on the floor, kicking and screaming the first time they are introduced to anything new. It is this half that poses the greatest challenges for most parents because our culture tends to be more supportive of go-getters.

How a child responds to new situations can be spotted very easily and early. Laura remembers Hazel's hysterical reaction to her first bath.

"If you saw the video of her first bath, you would think there was an error in the color because her skin looks purple. There was no error; she really was screaming that hard."

Whether it's the first bath, the first day of school, a new food, a new car seat, or the first try at swimming lessons, many spirited kids don't want to attempt it and insist that they don't like it. It is important to recognize this as a first reaction—not a final decision. Often, with time and support, as you break new experiences into small, manageable steps, the child will change her mind and really enjoy participating.

Lyssa realized that it was Milo's first reaction that turned a family outing into a major disagreement.

I had planned a day to visit Santa Claus. It was going to be a very special outing to see him downtown. I was so excited because I just knew it was going to be a thrilling day, seeing all of the decorations, talking with Santa, getting the traditional gingerbread cookie afterward, just like the one that I had always gotten when I was a kid. I hadn't told Milo, and when I did, he started crying. He refused to put on his coat and tore his mittens off as fast as I could put them on. I had to carry him kicking and screaming into the car. I kept saying, "You're going to have a great time. We are going to go see Santa and you are going to love it!" I was furious. He was wrecking my special outing! He cried and pouted all the way, thirty minutes in the car. I just turned up the music and let him scream. But I guess that time was what he needed to get used to the idea. When we got there, he walked through the display, and then sat on Santa's lap and told him everything he wanted, so sweet and adorable. I later realized I was lucky because there were other kids there who wouldn't even climb up on Santa's lap. Afterward we both took a two-hour nap. I was exhausted and swore I wouldn't do it again.

This year he said to me, "Mom, when are we going to see Santa? That was so much fun." I almost strangled him on the spot.

How does your child normally react to new situations and people? If you have circled a 4 or 5, you can expect that your child will balk at new situations. You can anticipate what will happen and avoid feeling disappointed, knowing that if you work with her, she may change her mind.

9. Mood

How much of the time does your child feel happy and content compared with serious, analytical, or solemn?

1	2	3	4	5
USUALLY POSITIVE				MORE SERIOUS AND ANALYTICAL
Usually in a good mood				Usually serious
Positive				Sees the flaws, what needs to be fixed

Finally, the ninth temperamental trait describes differences in mood. Many of the children observed by Chess and Thomas were generally happy, positive, and smiley. In contrast, other kids tended to be more serious and analytical and to see the flaws in situations and people.

In my spirited-child classes, approximately half of the children will possess a generally positive, happy mood. The other half is definitely the most challenging for parents. They tend to be much more serious, to cry more, and to appear more negative because they are always offering suggestions for improving an activity. We're used to adults telling us how to make things better, but it's a little tough to take advice from a child who tells you it's time to go home because you've spent enough money, or to add a little more balsamic vinegar to the salad dressing.

When asked a general question such as "How was school today?" the more serious kids will respond with comments like "boring," "dumb," or "fine." They'll tell you they didn't do anything interesting, despite the fact that they took a field trip to

their favorite nature center. They really don't mean to appear un-
appreciative or uninterested. They simply see the world from a
more analytical perspective.

If your child is temperamentally analytical, you can predict that
you will get evaluative responses—or no response from him. This
child will not be the one to rave about an outing or a gift, but he
will provide information on how it could be improved. When you
recognize that he is responding because of a first and most natural
reaction rather than intentionally being contrary or ungrateful,
you can teach him to be more diplomatic and respectful of others'
feelings.

A sudden shift in a child's ongoing mood does not demonstrate
a change in temperament. Rather, it may be cause for concern,
indicating the child is suffering from depression. If you are concerned about your child, a complete medical checkup should be
conducted.

Now go back through each of the temperamental traits and
total your responses. Mark your total on the scale below.

Score

9–18	19–28	29–45
LOW-KEY COOL CHILD	SPUNKY CHILD	SPIRITED CHILD

Of course this is not a scientific analysis; it is merely a sketch,
the initial strokes in the total picture of your child's personality,
a peek under his hood. You can use it as a guide, helping you to
understand who your child is and what gifts and challenges your
child brings to you. It's like a Google map, identifying your starting

point, helping you to plan the best route to take, and predicting where the trouble spots may lie. If your child is temperamentally intense, now you know it. You can expect strong reactions from her and teach her how to diffuse that intensity or to direct it appropriately. If your child doesn't like new situations, you can predict her reaction and teach her the social skills she needs to express herself respectfully and the techniques that will help her feel more comfortable.

Temperament is real: it is inside. It is not the terrible twos, sixes, or thirteens. It doesn't go away. Your child doesn't get to choose his temperament and neither do you, but an understanding of temperament allows you to predict your child's first and most natural reactions and plan for success.

4

Matches and Mismatches

Parents and Kids Fitting Together

Each of us shines in a different way,
but this doesn't make our light less bright.
—Albert Einstein

Gretchen was always the last parent to talk in the group. Her dark eyes drank in the words and gestures of others, but her comments were rare and far apart. Her daughter Asher was the kind of kid you "felt" before you heard and heard before you saw bursting into a room. The temperamental portrait Gretchen saw was not the dream child she had hoped for.

"I never imagined having a baby like Asher," she said. "I thought I would spend hours cuddling her, talking and singing with her. But Asher was born kicking. She never liked to be cuddled unless she chose it. As a baby, she wanted to be carried looking out at the world. I remember when she was fourteen months old, I was holding her on my lap and sobbing, thinking, 'Why can't you be like the other kids? Why can't I do the right things to make you like the child I expected you to be?'

"I tried talking to my wife about it, but she got angry when I told her. It just wasn't an issue for her, but it was for me. I had this phantom child in my mind. I knew how she was supposed to look and act and what our relationship would be like. But our reality was so opposite."

LETTING GO OF THE DREAM CHILD

The temperamental portrait your child presents to you may not be one you expected or wanted to see. For you, like Gretchen, letting go of your "dream child" may be one of the most difficult tasks you face as a parent. You might find yourself grieving, mourning the loss of the child that never materialized. The realization hits—there isn't a quick fix, ten easy steps to success, or a perfect punishment that will make your spirited child into that dream kid.

Your grief can blind you. It can prevent you from seeing the unique qualities of your child. It can force you to expend your time and energy desperately trying to change your child, to make her fit your expectations of the "perfect" child, the child that doesn't really exist.

Julius Segal once wrote, "To reject kids' distinctive natures is to deny one of the central facts of human development: the extraordinary range of individual differences that characterize children from the moment of their birth."

FOCUSING ON RELATIONSHIPS

A spirited child comes to us with not only distinct physical characteristics but a built-in predisposition to be spirited as well. We do not have control over our child's basic temperament, but we can choose to alter our response to him. We can stop thinking of our child as "the problem" and instead focus our energies on discovering more effective ways to relate, to work together, and to enjoy each other's company.

In a conversation with me, Jerome Kagan, a researcher from Harvard University, said, "We try to change our loved ones, and when we can't, we get friction and conflict. People are not really all that changeable. One of the greatest tragedies in human interaction is that we believe 'will' can change everything—it can't."

It is all right to shed your tears, to lament the fantasies that never materialized, but your child needs you to move on, to let go of that image of a dream child so that it does not interfere with your relationship with your spirited child. Now is the time to begin focusing on your child and discovering how to work with her particular temperamental style on an everyday basis; to find the beauty in her "portrait."

WORKING TOGETHER: THE TIES BETWEEN TEMPERAMENT AND DISCIPLINE

Tall, with a barrel chest, a dark thick beard, and a baseball cap pulled low over his eyes, Kevin shoved back from the table, glowering. "I don't get it. What does any of this have to do with discipline?"

I leaped to my feet, grabbed a dry-erase marker and drew flames. Fortunately, despite my severe artistic challenge, they were identifiable.

"How do you put out a fire?" I asked.

"Water!" Kevin snapped.

"What if it's a grease fire?" I continued.

He rolled his eyes at me before replying, "Turn off the burner? Smother it with baking soda?"

"What if it's a forest fire?"

Exasperated, Kevin flung his arms in the air.

The others jumped in, shouting out answers until we had a detailed list.

- Do a back burn
- Make a clear cut
- Use fire retardant

As the room quieted down, I asked, "What happens if you throw water on a grease fire?"

"It will spread like crazy," Jason, our resident firefighter, stated authoritatively.

"And if it's a campfire, are we going to do a back burn?" I continued.

"No!" The group retorted in unison.

"Right!" I declared, pumping my hand in the air. "In order to select the most effective strategy to put out the fire, you have to know what's burning. Temperament helps you identify the fuel source—the feelings and needs behind the flames of your child's challenging behaviors."

When you are the parent of a spirited child, every day can feel like a crapshoot. Time after time, your child melts down and you have no idea what just happened or why. It makes you feel so powerless and inept that you want to raise your hands in surrender, questioning, "Why me? Why did I get this child?"

Recognizing that there are patterns to his behavior that allow you to predict the potential combustion points suddenly shifts the odds in your favor. It's possible to identify the "fuel source," cut it off (at least sometimes), take appropriate precautions, and, when necessary, select the most effective approach to prevent the flames of misbehavior from spreading.

Research demonstrates that if you think a child is spoiled or just crying, you tend to respond harshly. You don't believe his signals or needs. Understanding temperament allows you to identify what the need is and respond compassionately. You can appreciate the challenges your child is facing, instead of thinking he's trying to embarrass you.

Discipline and punishment are not synonymous. Discipline means guiding. Knowledge of temperament allows you to be a skilled guide.

In the chapters that follow, I will help you to see the connections between everyday hassles and your child's temperament. Once you have identified the connections, you can develop strategies that will work with each particular temperamental issue.

For example, in the past you may have thought your child was being disobedient when she didn't come to lunch when you called. By understanding her temperament, you will discover that her reluctant response is actually the result of her slow adaptability, or persistence. She is not deliberately being uncooperative.

A child who is slow to adapt needs time to transition from one activity to another. By learning techniques that respect her temperament, you can work with it and win her cooperation. You can forewarn her that lunch will be served in ten minutes and allow her the time she needs for transition. Or you can develop a consistent routine that includes doing a specific activity such as picking up toys or reading a book and then eating lunch immediately afterward. These techniques allow her the time and consistency she needs to shift from one activity to another smoothly and easily even though she is slow to adapt.

As you work together, you'll also be able to teach her words that you would like her to use, such as: "Sometimes, it's hard for me to stop." Or, "I wish I could have one more minute." Or, "I'll be right there." Or, "Let's talk about the plan for today." The result will be a stronger and healthier relationship because you are working with her temperament rather than trying to change it. You will also be teaching her the skills she needs to be successful.

RECOGNIZING THE TWO-WAY STREET

As I talk about your spirited child's temperament, I'll also talk about yours. Building a healthy relationship with your spirited child is a two-way street. You have to understand your own reactions as well as your child's. Sometimes it isn't the strength of a spirited child's reactions that makes living with him challenging as much as how those reactions match or mismatch yours. Understanding your own temperament can help you work with your child's.

In chapter 3 you reviewed the temperamental traits in order to create a picture of your child's temperament. Now I want you to complete a self-portrait. Using the chart that follows, place yourself on the continuum for each trait. It is more difficult to distinguish temperamental traits in adults because they get mixed up with motivation and learned skills, but try your best to get to your typical response in each of the following situations. Remember there isn't an ideal.

When you have a picture of your own temperament, you can compare yours with that of your child. How are you alike? How are you different? Where do you fit together easily and where do the sparks fly? It is from this information that you will begin to build a more effective relationship with your spirited child.

Taking a Look at Your Own Temperament

1. Intensity

How strong are your emotional reactions? Do you find yourself becoming upset very quickly, or are your reactions more low-key?

1	2	3	4	5
Mild reaction				Intense reaction

2. Persistence

If you are involved in an activity and you are asked to stop, can you do so easily? When a task is frustrating, do you find yourself easily letting it go, or do you push to continue?

1	2	3	4	5
Easily let go				"Lock in," don't let go

3. Sensitivity

How aware are you of slight noises, emotions, differences in temperature, taste, and textures? Do you react easily to certain foods, tags in clothing, or irritating noises?

1	2	3	4	5
Usually not sensitive				Very sensitive

4. Perceptiveness

Are you keenly aware of people, colors, noises, and objects around you? Do you frequently forget to do what you were going to do because something else has caught your attention?

1	2	3	4	5
Hardly ever notice				Very perceptive

5. Adaptability

How quickly do you adapt to changes in your schedule or routine? How do you cope with surprises?

1	2	3	4	5
Adapt quickly				Slow to adapt

6. Regularity

Are you quite regular about eating times, sleeping times, amount of sleep needed, and other bodily functions?

1	2	3	4	5
Regular				Irregular

7. Energy

Are you always on the move and busy, or are you quiet? Do you need to exercise in order to feel good?

1	2	3	4	5
Quiet				Active

8. First Reaction

How do you (usually) react to a new idea, activity, place, or person?

1	2	3	4	5
Jump right in				Reject at first

9. Mood

How much of the time do you feel happy and content compared with serious and analytical?

1	2	3	4	5
Usually positive				More serious and analytical

Score

9–18	19–28	29–45
COOL PARENT	SPUNKY PARENT	SPIRITED PARENT

Now you have it! Your own temperamental portrait.

Compare your portrait with that of your child. What does it tell you?

"I can see that Jayden is very sensitive, but I'm not," Mike commented after completing this exercise in class. "No wonder I'm not very understanding when clothing drives him crazy. I just can't imagine what he must be feeling."

"It looks like we are both sensitive," Abby responded. "We really are tuned to one another, but that also means that the noises that drive her nuts also get under my skin. She needs me to help her stay cool, but I don't have any energy to spare. I need all I've got to keep myself under control."

"Asher and I are both very intense," Gretchen added. "We both lose it over the same things."

"Maybe it's temperament that is getting us into fights at the dinner table," Sarah remarked. "In my family, sitting down to eat dinner together is a special part of the day. I really value it. But Kevin," she said, jabbing an elbow toward him as he sat in the chair next to her, "and our son are constantly eating their meals strolling around the kitchen. Neither of them can tolerate sitting on the dining-room chairs. I've been thinking that they did it to irritate me, but looking at this chart, they both score five on energy and I score one. We don't match. Maybe that's the problem."

Kevin nodded his head. "After working all day," he said, "I just can't sit there. I have to move. It's been hard for Sarah to under-stand that."

Whether you are a spirited parent or a cool parent doesn't really matter. There are benefits and drawbacks to both. What is important is recognizing how you and your child or other family members are alike or different. What triggers set you off? When is it challenging for you to understand each other's reactions? This understanding allows you to respond in a more effective manner.

A week later, Sarah and Kevin arrived at class, beaming. "Guess what we did?" Sarah laughed.

I shrugged. "I haven't the faintest idea."

"We bought new dining-room chairs," she exclaimed. "They rock, roll, and swivel! Now Kevin and our son move to their hearts' content, but they're still at the table and in their chairs. They're happy and so am I."

Understanding their temperamental differences allowed Sarah and Kevin to respect each other's needs and to respond in a way that felt good to both of them. What could have been a contest of wills became a creative problem-solving episode—a more effective way of relating.

You too can build a stronger relationship with your spirited child. You too can learn techniques that will allow you to relate better. As you do, you will be able to let go of the "phantom child" to better enjoy the one who actually lives with you.

By the way, if you checked a 4 or a 5 on first reaction, you can expect it to take more effort for you to make changes in your rela-tionship with your child. That's your style. You approach new ideas and new situations cautiously. Just remember to allow yourself time to reflect. Your first reaction may not be your final decision. Think about it, and then decide.

PART TWO
Working with Spirit

5

Extrovert or Introvert
Finding the Energy to Cope

What really opened my eyes was realizing that,
when I'm at home alone taking care of the kids,
just one phone call, one opportunity to talk with
another adult, can give me hours more of patience.
—Katie, mother of three

The school bus growled through the neighborhood, belching at each corner as it disgorged the children. I walked to the door and unlocked it in anticipation of my spirited son and spunky daughter bursting through. Josh—bigger, older, and faster—hit the door first. Flinging it open, he threw down his book bag in the hallway, ignoring the hooks in the closet (as always), and shouted, "I learned about genetics today," as he disappeared into the family room and his favorite television show.

Kristina was inches behind him until she hit the front steps. She paused long enough to pull her papers out of her bag and then thrust them in my face as she came through the door. "I got to go up on the roof today," she announced, following me into the kitchen.

"It was discovery day," Kristina continued. "I was supposed to go to Creative Dramatics, but I changed my mind, so three of us got to go with Doug, the engineer. We went up on the roof and saw the *thing* in the boiler room that has to be checked every day. Saturday and Sunday, too, even when he's sick, or the whole school could blow up—KABOOM!"

Without taking a breath, she pushed the papers closer to my nose. "I have math sheets to do and I have to read my book to you. Listen, Mom. I want to read my book to you, right now. Oh, Mom, can I play with Kellen? I told Kellen I'd come down to his house. Can I go to Kellen's? Mom, what's for snack?"

She didn't even wait for my answer before she started her next question. Fifteen minutes after she arrived home, I knew everything that had happened that day, including her teacher's mood, how she was feeling, and what her plans were for tomorrow.

I broke away to check on Josh. "What did you learn about genetics?" I asked. "Not much," he mumbled, glued to the show.

"Am I going to hear about it, or do I have to wait?"

"You'll have to wait, Mom," he responded, allowing me to kiss his check for "my" needs, and returned to viewing his show. Silence. Nothing about his day. Two kids, two distinctive styles of recharging at the end of a busy day.

Kristina is an extrovert. She isn't just chattering. She is drawing her energy from me. She prefers to engage the world around her "outside" of her body by talking with people, sharing ideas and experiences. If I don't take the time to talk with her, she gets cranky and even more demanding because she is out of steam. If I allow her to recharge her batteries off mine, she's fine.

Joshua is an introvert. He isn't stubborn or antisocial. He prefers to interact with the world on the "inside" by reflecting on his thoughts and ideas before he shares them with others on the "outside." He refreshes himself by spending time alone. If he gets his downtime, he plays well with the other kids and cooperates with me. If he doesn't get it, he gets surly.

HOW WE GET OUR ENERGY

Extroversion and introversion describe how we get our energy, an important dimension of personality development. We do not get to choose our preferred style. As with the other temperament traits, Mother Nature gives us the preference, encoding it in our genes.

A spirited child may be either an introvert or an extrovert. It doesn't matter which. There isn't a right or wrong preference. Both extroverts and introverts have their strengths and weaknesses. But it does matter that you discover your child's preference, because how introverts and extroverts reenergize is starkly different.

Extroverts seek action to feel good. The more places they have to go, or the more people they can see, the better they feel. If there is a problem, they want to talk about it. However, this bustle of activity and interaction, which recharges extroverts, overloads introverts.

The engines of introverts purr when they have time alone, quiet, and space to themselves to think. An opportunity to ponder a problem before discussing it allows them to clarify their thoughts.

Identifying your child's preference helps you to understand where she gets her energy to cope and allows you to teach her to resupply before she becomes overwhelmed. It takes a great deal of effort to express intensity as assertiveness rather than aggressiveness. It is an exertion to adapt to new situations and to make transitions smoothly. It's hard work to stay cool and calm in a noisy, crowded room. When their energy levels are low, spirited kids fall apart. They just don't have the strength to refine their behavior. When energy levels are high, they have power to demonstrate their strengths. The more your spirited child is allowed to tap into her preferred energy source, the calmer and happier she will be that day.

During a class I was leading, Kelsey explained, "I never could understand why Leah would disappear into her room whenever people spent the day with us, until I learned about introverts and extroverts. Now I know she is an introvert—she needs time alone to recharge. Yesterday I was taking care of a little girl, the same age as Leah. Leah had just gotten up and was not ready to talk or play. Normally I would have told her, 'We have a guest. It isn't good manners not to talk with her and play with her.' But this time I respected Leah. I told the friend that Leah had just woken up and would be ready to play in a little bit. Until then she could have breakfast with me. After thirty minutes Leah was ready, and they played beautifully together."

Introverts

Introverts are the babies who become overwhelmed at the family reunions; the toddlers who play with their grandparents for a while, and then hit to push them away; or the school-age children who suddenly "disappear" when a friend is visiting. After a day at school they are worn out by all of the activity and stimulation. They need a break, a chance to energize by having space and quiet. Siblings can feel left out by the introvert who is perfectly comfortable playing alone.

While introverts may be very sociable, interaction with people, especially those who are not close friends, depletes their energy supplies. They just want to go home, or withdraw to a television show or video game, having recognized that when they do, others will usually leave them alone. (Unfortunately, in the long run, these electronic outlets are not always effective for recharging, but we'll discuss that later.)

It will probably be bedtime before introverts are ready to tell you the highlights of the day. You have to ask questions in order to follow up on events from yesterday and to find out the ending of a few old stories. They share their worries and concerns with you in bits and pieces. You have to listen well, or you will miss them. If you only have to wait until bedtime to find out what's been happening in their lives, you're doing well. Sometimes it takes days or even weeks. And then again, another person (usually the more extroverted friend) might tell you about an event long before your introverted child ever does.

Introverts are outnumbered three-to-one in our society. It is frequently the introvert who is misunderstood and pressured to shape up. This is tough on the introverted spirited child.

Extroverts

Extroverts tend to be the babies who insist on being held up so that they can look around and "talk" to those around them. They are the toddlers who jabber endlessly even if the words don't make sense. They are the school-age kids who jump off the bus and immediately tell you about their day. They need to share their ideas with you while they are fresh in their minds. They follow you around the house, demanding your ear, pulling energy from you. You may not even be able to go to the bathroom without them following you to continue the one-sided conversation. If you remind them that you'd like a little privacy, they seem surprised and step just outside the door, where you can still hear them as they continue sharing their day with you. They're not even breathless after a twenty-minute monologue. Fortunately for you, they are probably ready to play with a friend. If a friend isn't available, you will find yourself engaged in an activity with them as they continue to build their energy off you.

Spirited extroverts can wipe their parents out. The minute they wake up, they have something to say. Brothers and sisters may feel unloved and left out as the spirited "motormouth" gobbles up Mom's and Dad's attention and time.

THE THEORY

The concepts of introversion and extroversion are drawn from the theory of Psychological Type and were first described more than seventy years ago by Carl Jung, a Swiss psychologist. He suggested that human behavior could be classified into predictable categories or preferences. His framework was developed separately from the temperament work completed by Chess and Thomas and describes different dimensions of personality development. Jung, however, like the other temperament researchers, believed we are born with specific preferences that reflect both genetics and early life experiences.

According to Otto Kroeger and Janet Thuesen in *Type Talk*, "Jung believed that healthy development was based on lifelong nurturing of these preferences, not on working to change them." Spurred by Jung's work, Katherine Briggs and her daughter, Isabel Briggs Myers, spent more than twenty years developing the Myers-Briggs Type Indicator to distinguish the preferences described by Jung. Their hope was to help people understand and appreciate differences in individuals.

Today, in addition to these psychological theories, we have precise scientific tools such as magnetic resonance imaging that help us describe the physiological underpinnings of an introvert or extrovert. And through long-term studies we know that the preference for introversion or extroversion is the most stable trait over time.

EVERY FAMILY PROBABLY HAS A MIX of introverts and extroverts. Identifying our preferences and understanding our differences can help us to orchestrate the social activities the extrovert needs and create the quiet retreats the introvert requires. Misbehavior disappears when energy levels are high and coping skills are working smoothly.

Identifying Your Child's Energy Source

For our purposes a formal study in psychological type is not necessary. Your children will give you the information you need if you watch carefully and listen well. Read through the following lists. Check each of those statements you agree with in each group. Both introversion and extroversion are on a continuum.

Your child may demonstrate both extrovert and introvert tendencies, but you want to know which one she prefers (in other words, the preference you would see most frequently).

If your child is an extrovert, she probably . . .

❑ enjoys being around people. She becomes energized by a group, rather than overwhelmed by it, and is eager for more.

❑ wants to tell you about her experiences and ideas immediately.

❑ thinks by talking. She'll walk around the house saying, "I am looking for my backpack," as she hunts for it.

❑ tends to talk more than listen.

❑ gets into trouble for interrupting.

❑ hates being sent to her room to sit alone.

❑ can't imagine why you would want to be alone in a room and always joins you to "cheer you up."

❑ lets you know what she's thinking and feeling.

❑ needs lots of approval. You may find yourself doubting her confidence as she demands that you tell her what a good job she is doing.

If your child is an introvert, she probably . . .

❑ prefers to watch or listen before joining an activity.

❑ enjoys doing things by herself or with one or two special friends or family members.

❑ becomes grouchy if around people for too long, especially strangers, or after being in larger groups.

❑ declines to discuss the day's events until later, even days or weeks later.

❑ has a strong sense of personal space. Does not like people sitting too close or coming into her room. She may stand slightly apart from a group.

❏ seems to enjoy "time-out" in her room.
❏ initially fails to respond to a question when asked.
❏ finds guests in her home "invasive."
❏ talks a lot with family members but is quieter around
unfamiliar outsiders.

Count how many statements you would agree with in each group.

Total

___ Extrovert Statements
___ Introvert Statements

If you are unsure after reading through the statements, you may need to tune in and watch your child more closely in the next few weeks. Think about her past as well: Has she shown a pattern?

In reviewing each of the statements, you may find that your child is a very strong extrovert or introvert, or she may show only a slight preference. Either is fine. Each of us is capable of both extroversion and introversion, but we prefer one over the other. For example, a friend whose daughter is a spirited introvert shared how she saw her daughter displaying both: "McKenzie asked to have a friend over. We've talked about introverts and extroverts, so she knows the terms. Today she said, 'The extrovert part of me says I want to be with a friend, but the introvert side of me says, only for a while.'"

Like McKenzie, if your child is an introvert, she can learn to enjoy aspects of her extroverted side; however, she will continue to recharge as an introvert. The same is true of extroverts experiencing their introverted side, but still seeking stimulation to recharge.

Traditionally the term *introvert* has described someone who is shy and socially unskilled. It's important to remember that in psychological type, introversion and extroversion do *not* describe social skills. They explain how we get our energy. Both introverts and extroverts can be very savvy interacting with people. Your child can be a skilled social extrovert—or a skilled social introvert. The key is what happens afterward. The introvert will be drained and ready for a quiet, solitary activity, whereas the extrovert will be wound up and ready for more action.

The world needs both extroverts and introverts. Our differences create a healthy balance and can actually be fun. We just need to remember that introverts prefer to use the inside energy bank to conduct their recharging business, whereas the extroverts go for the outside version.

WORDS TO USE

In class we referred to twenty-month-old Derrick as our "future medical technician." He bit, drawing blood samples from any piece of anatomy that came near him. Not yet verbally proficient to explain to others his need for personal breathing room, he chomped whenever they got too close. It was a very effective strategy, but the behavior obviously needed to stop. "I need space," his teachers repeatedly coached him to say every time someone came near.

One day, Derrick's teacher noted he was getting irritable, a frequent precursor to the biting. "What do you need, Derrick?" She asked.

In a tiny but firm voice he announced, "I need space." He grabbed his blanket and favorite truck before trudging down the stairs to enter the "cave" under the loft. Soon Derrick will be able to say he needs space before being asked. The biting to get space will end.

Words to describe how they get their energy and what they need to recharge are essential for spirited children. Building that vocabulary allows them to tap into their energy sources without resorting to hitting, biting, yelling, or arguing with you. Here are some phrases to assist you as you work with your child.

Spirited introverts need to hear:	Spirited extroverts need to hear:
You think before you talk.	You are energized by being with people.
You need quiet and downtime to feel good.	You think by talking about your thoughts and feelings.
You enjoy spending time by yourself.	You like to be busy.
You form deep and lasting friendships.	You talk easily with others.

When spirited children hear these messages repeatedly, they learn to appreciate their preference for extroversion or introversion and understand what they need to keep their energy bank full. These same messages also give them hope that soon, they will be able to use words to get what they need. Words like these:

An introverted spirited child can learn to say:	An extroverted spirited child can learn to say:
I need space and quiet.	I like to be busy.
I like to be alone for a little while.	I like to be with people.
Let me think about that.	I need to talk about this.
I need some time to work on this by myself.	Could we work together?

Knowledge of whether she is an extrovert or introvert can end a child's problem behaviors. Erica, whose six-year-old son Jake was an introvert, found this to be very true.

"How was your day?" Erica would cheerily inquire when Jake climbed into the car after school. Much too frequently his response was to shriek, "Everybody shut up!" Taking away his prized video games and even yelling back at him failed to deter his rudeness. It wasn't until Erica learned about introversion and extroversion that she realized he was an introvert who desperately needed quiet after a long day. She explained to Jake, "I think you are an introvert who likes people but needs a break, especially after school. Let's make a plan. It's important to say hello, and it's important for you to have downtime. So from now on, you can say, 'Hi Mom! I'll be ready to talk later.' Then you can put on your headphones, tune into your favorite music, and chill out."

Today both Erica and Jake look forward to pickup time. Understanding what he needed to recharge, and teaching him the vocabulary to express himself respectfully, has allowed Erica and Jake to work together.

Energy Sources for Introverts

Along with building your child's vocabulary you can help her be more successful by keeping her energy bank full. Marti Olsen Laney, in *The Hidden Gifts of the Introverted Child*, writes, "An introvert needs access to her thoughts, feelings, and perceptions in order to have a sense of vitality and equilibrium. Too much external stimulation—activity, noise, chatter—is depleting to her." Although each individual will recharge differently, here are some common sources of energy for introverted spirited children.

1. TIME ALONE: Participating in a group forces introverts to act outside of themselves; this can be exhausting for them. Their energy is sapped as they socialize. If your child is a quarrelsome curmudgeon after a day in school, it may be that he is an introvert in need of time alone.

"I'm a family day-care provider," Kristin explained in a group one night. "My daughter starts picking on the other kids the minute she walks in the door. It's as though she is begging to be sent to her room."

Introverts need their private time. It is often difficult for introverted children to tactfully pull out and play by themselves because of social pressure to be a part of the group. They don't understand that when they are feeling out of sorts, they *need* time away. All they know is that being around people bugs them and makes them feel grumpy. That's why they pick on the other kids until you send them to their rooms. Or they will suddenly stop playing with friends and snap, "I hate you! Go home!" *An unrecognized need for time alone is one of the major reasons spirited children experience meltdowns, fight with siblings, or get nasty.*

If your child is an introvert, you have to help her understand that she needs time alone in order to recharge. When she be-comes agitated, tell her, "I think your body is telling you that you need some time alone." If she is playing with other children, teach her how to tactfully say, "I had a great time. Could we play again later?" If that's not possible, encourage her to step away from the activity get a drink of water, or use the restroom. She can linger there a few extra minutes to get the break she needs. By teaching her to do this, you help her learn appropriate ways to pull out of the group and get the break she needs.

Prevent your child from morphing into a curmudgeon by cre-ating an after-school ritual for recharging: having a snack, along with time in her room to read, daydream, listen to music, or play, before jumping into other activities. Being alone restores her energy bank, allowing her to build up the reserves for interacting with the group again later.

After Thanksgiving a parent in my class shared the following: "Tara went and played by herself. My mother watched her go, and then said, 'What a good idea—let's all find a place to be alone.'"

Younger introverted children, rather than being "alone," may choose to find a quiet spot away from the crowd to snuggle up with a parent or their other favorite adult. They need a break but like to take their "security person" with them.

Extroverts need to resist the temptation to pressure the in-trovert into staying with the group. A few minutes alone for the introvert can mean the difference between a reasonable, conversa-tional human being and a living Scrooge. Introverts are their own best friends. They can have a great time all by themselves. That's hard for an extrovert to understand.

Just as you would plan for your child's nutritional needs, plan for her energy needs. Next time your neighbors invite you to go to the zoo and then for a picnic, stop and think about your introverted child. How will she be able to dip into her energy bank during this long, social day? Could you drive your own car and give her a break between the zoo and the park? Could you plan to separate at the zoo for a while and retreat with her to a quiet corner to watch the snow monkeys?

If it is impossible to create an opportunity for her to recharge, maybe you need to go to the zoo and forget the picnic this time. It is better to be successful at one activity than to attempt both and end the day with a disaster. Remember, your introvert really does like people. She simply gets her energy by taking time alone. As you plan your activities, avoid depleting her energy bank.

2. PHYSICAL SPACE: Physical space is very important to introverts. I recently had a phone call from the mother of a four-year-old. She said her son was getting into trouble at nursery school for pushing in line. I asked her if he had told her why he was doing it.

She said, "All he'll say is he hit the little boy standing next to him because he shouldn't be standing there."

"Makes sense to me," I responded.

"What are you talking about?" the mother queried.

"Introverts need their space. Sharing space takes lots of energy from introverted spirited children. When they get tired, they don't do it very well. Your son needs to learn that he needs space. He can choose to stand at the end of the line, allowing himself more space. He can learn to say, 'Please move over' or 'I feel more comfortable if I have more room.' Simply realizing that sharing space is exhausting to him can help him recognize when his reserves are low and he needs to refuel."

You'll see the need for space in many ways: the child who has to have his own seat in the car, otherwise he grouses about someone touching his leg, breathing in his face, or talking too much; the two-year-old who throws a fit because you pulled off her hat or took off her sweater, not only because she wanted to do it herself—which is normal for two-year-olds—but also because you invaded her personal space; and the seven-year-old who places a jump rope across the center of the couch to mark her half.

Other signs might be the child who can't stand sharing his room with another or the one who posts a sign on his door that says "No Trespassing" to let you know how important space is to his well-being and energy stores. And then it may be the child who gets into trouble at school for refusing to sit close at group time.

This need for space can be hard for extroverts to understand. Extroverts like to be helpful and they like to be together. Space is not an issue for them. Extroverts need to know that sitting too close, standing too near, touching when touch is unwanted, or walking into a private room unannounced will drive introverts nuts and drain their energy. Introverts are not being selfish or rejecting others by asking for their space. Giving introverts space is giving them energy. You can teach your introverted children to be aware of their need for space and help them learn creative and tactful ways to get it even when they are only toddlers.

When two-year-old Seth first started attending a new child-care center, he would scream as the other children rushed to greet him. They were eager to see him, but Seth was an introvert who needed his space—especially when first entering a group. Fortunately for him, his teachers recognized what was happening and pulled out five hula hoops for the kids. Every child was given the choice of having a hula hoop to "define" his space. No one was singled out. It was Seth who chose to keep one right by his coat hook.

Every morning upon arrival his dad helped him hang up his coat and then find a spot where he could sit inside his hoop. There, with his blanket and pacifier close at hand, Seth would play quietly for a few minutes with a favorite toy. His teachers explained to the other children that Seth needed a little time and space before he was ready to play. The toddlers honored the concrete symbol and waited.

The teachers also told Seth that he could let them know when he was ready to move out into the room. Ten minutes after his arrival, he would allow a teacher to assist him in storing his hoop, and begin playing with the other kids. This arrangement continued for three weeks, after which Seth, knowing his "defined space" was available if he needed it, and feeling more comfortable with his new surroundings, simply walked in the door, paused a moment to observe what was happening, and began to play. An understanding and respect of his need for space allowed him to be successful.

3. TIME FOR REFLECTION: Introverts like to think about problems and then talk about them. According to Marti Olsen Laney, "Introverts use a longer brain pathway that integrates unconscious and complex information. As a result processing information requires more time. But introverts also are able to incorporate more emotional and intellectual content relevant to the new data."

Extroverts like to talk about problems and usually have an immediate response. This can be a source of contention. The extrovert who insists that the introvert *talk* about a problem will be frustrated by the introvert who backs off, trying to get the *thinking* space she needs to work through a problem. An introvert isn't ready to share her thoughts before she has had an opportunity to reflect. The more frustrated the extrovert gets with the introvert's lack of enthusiasm for the discussion, the more energy the introvert burns trying to escape. Once introverts have time to think, they will be willing to talk about the issue.

Giving introverts time to think before responding, however, isn't always easy for extroverts who process while talking and want to talk now!

I had a perfect example of this while writing this chapter. I asked my husband to identify the three most important things he needed as an introvert. I stood waiting for his answer. He burst into laughter. "I'll need time to think about that," he replied, and then added, "I know you want an answer right now." He was correct. (By the way, I'm still waiting, but I know that when he does reply, his response will be insightful and worth the wait.)

Extroverts have to remember that an introvert's pause or delayed response does not mean "no thoughts." Nor is he "pouting," having difficulty hearing, or ignoring the question. Allowing your introverted child time to pause and reflect before expecting an answer gives him energy.

If you find yourself getting frustrated because your child isn't immediately answering your questions, change your approach like Megan did. "When I realized my son is an introvert and needs time to think, I changed my strategy," she told us in class one day. "Now I will ask him a question and add, 'Think about it. I'll check back in a few minutes to find out what you decided.' Then I go off and do something else, and when I come back—he has an answer." Giving your introverted child time to think keeps you working together.

Bedtime is a favorite time for introverts to begin talking. Often it feels as though they are stalling, but the reality is that they have had time to reflect about their day and are now ready to share it with you. Begin the bedtime routine early and allow at least ten to fifteen minutes of "talk time." That way you won't feel rushed, or compelled to stop the conversation because it's getting late.

4. UNINTERRUPTED WORK TIME: If you have ever wondered why your child rarely comes to greet you when you come home, it may be that he is an introvert, guarding his energy supplies. If an introvert is busy, he doesn't like it if you stop to say hello to him and expect him to talk to you. In fact, you won't find him unless you go looking for him to greet him. If you want your introvert to be socially respectful, teach him to say hello and then go back to finishing his task. By doing so, you respect his energy supply.

Helping your introverted spirited child to make deposits in her energy bank is a critical step to good behavior. A child who knows how to refuel has the energy to maximize her strengths. Next time your introverted spirited child starts to misbehave, make a mental check of her energy account. Has she been with lots of people? Has she been forced to share space? Has she been required to give quick answers? Has her work been continually interrupted? If the answer to any of these questions is yes, then allowing her to recharge by taking time alone may be all that's needed to bring out your child's "sunny side." Ultimately she will be able to do it herself.

I ran into Libby four years after she'd been in my spirited-child class. "Mary," she exclaimed, "I've been meaning to call you. Remember how Eric, my little introvert, would play well with other kids for a while but inevitably would get cranky and end up fighting? It was so embarrassing. In class I learned how to help him recognize when he needed a break. He's eight now and yesterday spent the entire day with his brother and cousins. They were playing football and then hide-and-seek and a little soccer. I watched as Eric at different points would separate himself from the group. He'd come in for a drink of water and sit down to work with his tablet. Ten minutes later he'd go out again. Ninety minutes later he'd come in to use the restroom, then he'd stop and play with the dog for a few minutes, and then he'd go out again. He played all day without ever losing it. He really has learned how to recharge."

Energy Sources for Extroverts

Energy sources for your extroverted spirited child are very different from those of the introvert. Extroverts are wearied by the quiet and solitude so needed by their introverted counterparts. As with introverts, extroverts are each unique individuals, but here are some common sources of energy you can help them learn to use.

1. TIME WITH PEOPLE: Extroverts collect their energy on the outside. Not only do they like people, they need them. Spirited children who are extroverts are happiest and best mannered when they can be with others. Forcing them to stay home or expecting them to entertain themselves by playing alone for extended periods of time can be exhausting to them. If you are the parent of a spirited extrovert, it's important for you to utilize all of your resources. There is no way one parent, especially an introverted parent, can keep up with the interaction needs of an extroverted spirited child.

In my Spirited Child Facebook Group, parents offered one another suggestions for assisting their extroverted child in filling her energy bank. "Enrolling her in preschool saved both of us," one reported; while another revealed, "We spend three or four hours a day total at the park, library story hour, the playground at the mall, mommy/daddy-and-me classes offered in the community, the beach, hiking, and going to the museum. When we come home I put him down for a nap and collapse!"

If your child is enrolled in school or a child-care program, his need for interaction may be met there, but odds are he will still crave extracurricular activities to keep him recharged. The challenge with this extroverted dynamo is to avoid overscheduling. Since he seeks activity, he has a wide breadth of interests and boundless energy. He likely excels at many things, so teaching him to establish priorities is essential for maintaining balance. Even extroverts need a little downtime.

Sometimes, parents of extroverts worry that their extroverted children lack independence because of the extrovert's need to be with people. That was true for Becca.

"Olivia is the only extrovert in our family. We could never understand why she always wanted friends over. I was worried about too much peer pressure. I began to wonder if we'd done something wrong, because she seemed to need other people so much. We tried to 'toughen her up' by insisting she spend time by herself, but she would just get grouchy. Now I understand what she is doing and encourage her much more. She has been happier and so much better behaved."

Extroverts have lots of friends, need friends, and can't imagine having a good time without them. Being with friends gives extroverts energy. Be sure to provide opportunities for your extrovert to recharge by being with people.

When you do need your extrovert to play or work independently for a bit, begin by engaging her in a hands-on activity and then step away for short periods of time. Be sure to remain within earshot so that she can check in for that energy boost while she works.

2. FEEDBACK: To keep their energy high, extroverts need feedback, love feedback, and can't get enough feedback. A few words of positive reinforcement and the extrovert is flying high, ready to roll. Introverts may wonder why so much reinforcement is needed.

I am a strong extrovert who needs lots of affirmation from my introverted husband. We had agreed to do something for Valentine's Day rather than exchange gifts. But my husband knows me well. Shortly after he left for work, I found a valentine card on the kitchen counter. It said he loved me. An hour later I found another card on the keyboard of my computer—a second affirmation of his love. Making lunch, I found still another card in the refrigerator. I was thrilled, but best of all was the card I found on our bed. Its cover was one continuous rainbow-colored statement: "I love you I love you I love you I love you . . ." Inside the card read, "There, now are you satisfied? Happy Valentine's Day," signed with Joe's scrawl. Four cards just about fulfilled my requirements!

Your spirited extrovert needs feedback to recharge. She isn't just nagging when she asks for your reassurance or response. It isn't a lack of confidence when she needs your words of encouragement. Feedback refuels her energy bank.

Providing enough feedback for the spirited extrovert can be exhausting. You need to teach your child to ask for attention and responses from her other parent, grandparents, friends, teachers, and neighbors as well as from you. Protect yourself from overdrawing your energy account.

3. PEOPLE TO HELP THEM THINK: Extroverts think by talking. To solve a problem or reduce their stress, they need to talk with someone who will listen to them. Many times they don't even need a response from their listener. The opportunity to express themselves is all they need to work through their issues. Tony Bouza, ex-Minneapolis police chief, was once overheard saying, "My mouth runs about eleven minutes ahead of my brain. I'm always amazed to hear what I have to say."

Be certain to provide opportunities for your spirited extrovert to tell you about her worries and concerns and to share her ideas with you. She isn't just chattering; she is thinking and recharging.

The need to think by talking sometimes gets the spirited extrovert in trouble at school. He talks out of turn. The teacher asks the class a question, expecting the kids to raise their hands before answering. The spirited extrovert, however, simply hears a question and responds immediately. His thoughts spill out in words.

Making your child aware that it is difficult for an extrovert to think without talking can help him learn to hold on to his response. Applaud his good ideas, but explain that in the classroom he has to withhold his ideas until the teacher calls on him. Better yet, find a teacher who frequently divides the children into small groups where everyone can talk. Then, raising a hand isn't an issue. We'll talk about that more in chapter 21.

You'll also want to teach your extroverted child to let others know that he's simply "talking to think" or brainstorming out loud. He has not yet made his final decision. Otherwise he may irritate others when it later appears that he has changed his mind.

Identifying Your Own Energy Source

As you work to understand your spirited child, you also need to understand yourself. Where does your energy come from? What is your preference?

To help you identify your type, I've included the following questions. Read through them. Check the statements you agree with in each group. You may find yourself agreeing with statements in both the introvert and extrovert sections. That's because we are capable of using both preferences. Look closely and think carefully: Which feels the most comfortable to you? Which would be your *first choice*—not what you have been taught to choose, but which actually fits who you are? Many introverts do not realize they prefer introversion over extroversion because they have been told that to be an introvert is to be unsociable. Some have so repressed this preference to please others that they have almost lost touch with it. To keep your energies high as the parent of a spirited child, it's important that you find your *true* energy source.

If you are an extrovert, you probably . . .

❑ want to talk with someone at the end of a busy day.

❑ have an immediate answer for a question.

❑ want to be with friends on Friday night.

❑ find yourself rushing from one activity to another.

❑ need and like to hear that others love you and like your work.

❑ start to invite a few friends for dinner and realize you've invited the entire neighborhood.

❑ find yourself telling your introverted child to get out of her room and call a few friends.

❑ solve a problem by talking through the solution with someone else.

❑ feel comfortable initiating a conversation.

❑ call for the babysitter.

❑ are comfortable revealing personal things about yourself.

❑ frequently leave a party chastising yourself for talking too much and not listening.

❑ enjoy and need to interact with other people and feel exhausted when you have spent too much time alone or only with young children.

❑ immediately share a new idea or experience with someone and find joy and energy in the telling.

If you are an introvert, you probably . . .

❏ sit down with your tablet or zone out in front of the television after a hard day.

❏ will do anything, even clean the toilets, if someone else will agree to call the sitter.

❏ can't imagine wanting to invite a group over on Friday night.

❏ find being in a large group for an extended period of time exhausting.

❏ share personal information only with those who are very close to you.

❏ think before answering a question and often berate yourself for not sharing an answer you knew.

❏ frequently have extroverts ask you the same question twice because they assume your pause to reflect indicates you didn't hear the question.

❏ prefer dinner with the family or one special friend, rather than with the whole neighborhood.

❏ find yourself hiding in the bathroom or taking the dog for a walk at large family gatherings.

❏ solve a problem by thinking it through yourself or researching an answer on the Internet before ever talking about it with anyone else.

❏ get tired of telling extroverts what a wonderful job they're doing and how much you love and appreciate them.

❏ have been known to bribe your kids with candy in exchange for five minutes of quiet time.

❏ stay up late to get "alone time."

❏ go to the gym, drop the kids in child care, and then hide out in the sauna.

Count how many statements you agreed with in each group. If you checked more extrovert statements, your energy comes from outside sources. If you checked more introvert statements, your energy comes from inside sources.

TOTAL

____ Extrovert Statements
____ Introvert Statements

Refilling Your Energy Bank

Understanding your own type helps you understand your reactions to your children and helps get your own needs met.

Recognizing she was an introvert gave Laura permission to ask for her space.

"I couldn't understand why it was so upsetting to me when my daughter would crawl all over me and stick her face right in mine when she was talking to me. Now I realize she is an extrovert. She likes to be close. I am an introvert and I need my space. I used to feel so mean pushing her away. Now I let her know I love her, but I need my space!"

For Steve, working with his type has reduced the guilt. "This is the first time in my life I don't feel antifamily," Steve shared. "I am an introvert and I need time alone. I've always felt guilty taking it because it seemed so antifamily. Now we all have an explanation for why I need some time. My wife doesn't resent it anymore because she understands that I'll come back and be happier and more attentive."

And Megan now understands why she felt so drained at the end of a day with her children, even though she enjoyed being home.

"I am a very strong extrovert. I *need* people. I didn't know that interacting with children wasn't fulfilling my needs as an extroverted adult. I like being home with my children and didn't want to change that. I have started planning a lot more activities with other parents, and I'm using my phone to stay connected with others more. My energy is much higher. My husband has noticed the difference and appreciates it."

Marathon runners know that even if they have trained well, they still must pause frequently to eat and drink if they are going to finish the race. If you are an introvert, plan some time alone every day. Get up early enough to have privacy in the bathroom. Stop the car a block from child care and listen to your favorite song before you pick up the kids. Instead of rushing to the grocery store on Saturday afternoon, settle in for a nap even if you end up with peanut butter sandwiches for dinner again.

If you are an extrovert, make sure you have other adults to talk with. If you are employed, take time at lunch for a walk with a friend. Schedule a regular when-the-kids-go-to-sleep time to talk with your partner or another adult. If you are a stay-at-home parent, plan daily outings, allowing the kids to play and you to interact with other adults.

Each of these activities provides you with a few moments to rest your weary brain and body, to nurture yourself so you can nurture your child. It is a must for parents of spirited children.

WORKING TOGETHER

Once you understand both your child's energy source and your own, you can use that information to identify your similarities and your differences. Doing so allows you to work together to keep everyone's energy levels high. Otherwise, you can run into a mismatch, which is what happened to Lindsey and her son.

It was eight A.M. when the phone rang. "Mary, have you got a minute? I need to talk," the voice on the other end responded to my hello. It was Lindsey, and I could tell by the tone of her voice that this was not a one-minute conversation.

"Sure," I responded, knowing full well our minute would stretch.

"I can't figure out how to give Sawyer my attention," she said.

I found this an interesting comment from a woman I knew to be a very committed mother.

"He always wants it at the wrong time." This I understood. "When he comes home from school, I'm ready to talk. He's not. When he's ready to talk, I'm making dinner. I'm not about to stop what I'm doing and interact with him. I'm hungry and I want to eat! He gets energized after dinner. By bedtime he's in full gear and I'm beat. 'Mom, let me tell you about my idea!' he demands.

"My only response is a dragged-out monotone, 'Go to bed, Sawyer.'

"'You never talk to me,' he complains.

"Then I start screaming, 'Stop stalling! Go to bed!' And so the day ends. I'm exhausted, and he hasn't had a chance to share his stories. Our energies never mesh. Both of us are willing to share but not at the same time. It feels like we're never connecting. I'm not sure what to do."

Lindsey and her son were "missing" each other because they

energized and shared information in different ways. As an extrovert, Lindsey wanted to talk immediately after her son arrived home. Sawyer, the introvert, needed to recharge by taking time alone before he was ready to converse. Lindsey felt that Sawyer was ignoring her, refusing to share his day with her. Sawyer thought his mother was pushing him, and it made him back even farther away. Later, when Sawyer was ready to talk, Lindsey was drained by her anger. She was too tired and hurt to be a good listener.

During our conversation I explained to Lindsey the differences between introverts and extroverts. Once she understood their different energy sources, she was able to work out a new approach. She decided that instead of demanding that Sawyer talk with her when he first arrived home, she would call a friend and chat. Talking would refuel her energy bank. Later, when Sawyer was ready for conversation, her energy level would be high from interacting with her friend. She wouldn't be drained by anger because now she understood Sawyer was recharging, not blocking her out.

If we lived alone, personality type wouldn't matter. It's because of our relationships that we need to understand each other's style, to figure out how to work *together*—sharing ideas, solving problems, and recharging—without draining each other.

When you can recognize the needs of both introverts and extroverts, it's easier to accept and appreciate your style and your child's. You can tap into your energy bank more frequently and comfortably. It isn't a hassle. It isn't an intrusion. Energy levels stay high. The good days start to outnumber the bad.

INTROVERTS
A Summary

Introverts get their energy by being alone or with one or two special people. They prefer to interact with the world on the inside by reflecting on their thoughts and ideas before sharing them with others on the outside. They refresh themselves by having quiet time and space. If they get it, they'll play well with other kids and be more cooperative. If they don't get it, they'll become irritable.

Introverted spirited children need to hear:
You think before you talk.
You enjoy spending time by yourself.
You need time alone and quiet to recharge.
You form deep and lasting relationships.

Teaching tips:
Make sure your introverted child has an opportunity to refuel by taking time alone.
Help your child to understand that she needs space and can ask for it without pushing others away.
Allow your introverted child time to think before you expect a response.
Avoid interrupting her when she is working.

If you are an introvert too:
Recognize your need for time alone in order to refuel.
Let others know you need time to think before you can respond.
Appreciate your observation skills.

EXTROVERTS
A Summary

Extroverts draw their energy from others. They prefer to engage the world around them outside of their bodies by talking with people, sharing ideas and experiences. If they don't have the opportunity to talk, they get cranky and more demanding because they are running out of steam.

Extroverted spirited children need to hear:
You enjoy being with people.
You think by talking about your thoughts and feelings.
You like to be busy.

Teaching tips:
Your extroverted child needs other people to help her recharge.
Provide her with lots of feedback.
Spend time talking with her to help her think through
    problems.
Understand that her need for people and feedback is not a
    reflection of a lack of confidence.

If you too are an extrovert:
Avoid isolating yourself at home with small children.
Include outings with other parents and children in your plans
    each day.
Recognize that you need time with other adults in order to
    refuel.
Take time to talk through problems and issues with others
    before making a decision.
Let others know you need feedback.

6

Intensity

Diffusing Your Child's Strong Emotions Begins with You

I've learned that sometimes all a person needs is a hand to hold and a heart to understand.
—Unknown

Dark haired with vivid blue eyes, nine-month-old Dakota perched on his mother's lap intently listening to the teacher reading a story. Suddenly the teacher began to imitate a character weeping. Dakota's body stiffened, his eyes grew wide, and his lip quivered. Turning to his mother, he searched her face for clues. "Am I in danger?" "Should I cry out in alarm?" The "weeping" was only pretend, the story actually silly. Mom laughed and so did Dakota. Unknown to her, she had just "shown" Dakota how to respond.

As parents, we realize that our children turn to us for comfort, but what we may not realize is that children also look to us, the adults in their lives, for assistance figuring out what they feel and help regulating emotions. We are their role models. If we are upset, they'll get upset too. If we can stay calm, they'll be calm as well.

This ability to calm ourselves, or to self-regulate as the researchers describe it, leads to biological changes in our body. Alterations that allow us to think straight and, as a result, manage situations well. Most of us, however, have not been taught to enjoy the richness that intensity adds to our lives; nor have we been instructed in the safety measures needed to use it appropriately. To help our children understand and manage their intense emotions, we have to commit to developing our own self-regulation skills. When we are proficient handling our own emotions, it is far easier to instill those skills in our intense spirited children.

DEALING WITH YOUR OWN INTENSITY

It's hard not to get frustrated when you are the parent of a spirited child—especially when life keeps slapping you around and robs you of sleep, and has sent you a child who can turn a request to put on her shoes into a twenty-minute free-for-all. It's tempting to throw every punishment in the book at her and deny all privileges from screen time to a ride to her friend's house, even when you know darn well that doing so is not going to work. But somehow it seems that you've gotten caught in a vicious cycle from which you just can't escape. That's when the doubts begin to slither in. Maybe you are not meant to be a parent. Perhaps you are not the right parent for this child. Even harder to bear is the fear that things are out of control.

It does not have to feel this way. You really do have the ability to change your child's response.

Have you ever noticed that the first thing out of your mouth either adds fuel to the fire or puts it out? That when you soften your approach, your child becomes more peaceful too? The reality is that your thoughts, words, and actions have the power to change your child's intense responses. True, it does take a lot of work, a team effort, tremendous patience, and a few tears too. But it is possible to learn the skills to keep your cool—and actually enjoy your child—most days.

THE THEORY

Throughout the day your child's body, and your own, move through different stages of well-being. How easily both of you are able to keep your cool and work together depends on sensing what "zone" you are in. In chapter 2, I introduced you to the red zone of tense energy. In this chapter we will explore this concept a bit further and also take a look at the green zone of calm energy.

Imagine for a moment that you are standing on the edge of a cliff. Step to the right and you will tumble into the abyss of intensity that is out of control—the red zone. A step to the left pulls you back from the edge and into a lovely green meadow—the green zone.

In the red zone your body is in a state of tense arousal. A natural warning system in your body has turned on, elevating stress hormones and keeping all systems on alert, ready for battle. In this state you stop listening to the words of your child, don't even want to look at her, and physically pull away. The biological reaction overwhelms both body and mind. Emotions explode.

"Get in the car," you snap at your daughter through clenched teeth. She ignores you. "Get in the car," you repeat once more. But your daughter has something else she wants to do. Getting in the car is not presently on her agenda. You know that if you insist, she's likely to have a full-fledged fit.

Suddenly you find yourself cringing, hoping she'll get in, furious that she's not listening to you, and mad at yourself for being such a chicken. Why are you letting her get away with this? Adrenaline begins to course through your body as your brain screams to all systems, "You are under threat. Be ready to fight or flee!" And that's exactly what you'd like you do.

You can't bear the thought of one more public scene, one more battle, so you stand there and wait, silently counting to ten. But it's not working, and you find yourself hurtling deeper and deeper into a dark pool of emotion until it's as though there is no way of returning to a calm state. Then without any thought, it happens. You scream, "GET IN THE CAR, NOW!" Her scream matches yours in intensity and timing. You and your child have just plunged over the cliff and into the red zone, gasping for breath as you spiral downward into negative emotions. You feel as if you're drowning.

Psychologist John Gottman calls this "flooding" and explains, "Flooding is deadly to relationships. The extreme nature of the body's response makes rational thought unfeasible."

That surge of chaotic emotions also sets you and your child up as adversaries, ensnarled in a fight to the finish. Who will win? But in this battle there are no winners. Ultimately, the power struggle leaves everyone battered and bruised and your relationship damaged. Instead of developing the skill of cooperation, your child may ironically be learning to get angry in order to get you to back off. Or he may be learning to increase the volume of his protests so that you will hear him. Researchers tell us that when we get caught in an adversarial relationship with our children, we end up with more, not fewer, behavior issues in the long run. More troubling, we fall out of love with our sons and daughters.

We do not want to go there. Fortunately, we don't have to.

Go back to that cliff. This time step to the left and enter the green zone of calm energy. Your body and mind are peaceful. In this zone, both you and your child find your hearts thumping slowly, deep within your chests. Your pulse rate is steady and so is your child's. You are focused on each other, able to listen and enjoy each other's presence. It is in the green zone where emotions are easier to manage.

While in this zone, you ask your daughter to get in the car. She simply does it, or if she resists, you are able to think quickly enough to squat down to her eye level, commiserate with her about how frustrating it is to discontinue her activity, and then help her find a stopping point. The two of you remain calm, listen to one another, and work together. The power struggle never occurs.

This positive, calm response results in fewer behavioral problems because your child feels safe and respected. She listens to you because you have listened to her. The green zone allows us to fall in love and stay in love with our children. Staying in the green zone is our goal, and while that won't always happen, there are strategies that can increase the percentage of time it does.

Perspective Matters

Have you ever wondered whether parents who seem to stay calmer have a secret? They do. It's how they view their child. "I recognized this is who he is," Amanda told me one day. "He's very sensitive. I realize that a lot of the time he's scared about something. He's different from other kids. When I think about it that way, I have much more compassion for him."

Steve, a father of three, explained, "I've come to realize it's more about biology than behavior. Usually something upsets her that has nothing to do with me. She doesn't hate me. She just can't get the brakes on without my help."

And for Lydia it was all about falling in love with her daughter. "I was so mad at my daughter and mad at myself because I couldn't figure out how to parent her, but after learning all this stuff, I changed. I began listening to her and respecting her opinions. I stopped punishing her and instead we would talk and work things out."

What these parents are able to do is called depersonalizing. Rather than thinking their child is gunning for them, they are able to step back and recognize there is a reason for the behavior, one not related to them. It's this awareness that allows them to avoid feeling personally attacked, and as a result they stay calm. Their heart rates do not escalate. They remain engaged, which allows them to feel empathy for their children. With empathy also comes an understanding that flooding is frightening to children. They do not want to go there.

It's this shift in perspective that allows them to say: "There's a reason she's upset." "We can figure this out." "We can work together." "We are a team."

CHECK YOUR SELF-TALK

If you find yourself interpreting your child's intense reactions in a negative way, the odds are you will become angry at yourself and your child. Instead of working with your child's intensity or your own, you'll want to get rid of it as fast as you can so the "bad" behavior stops. But if you do that, you're likely to hear yourself say things that send you smack into the red zone. This was Sasha's experience.

"It seemed that every morning my daughter only wanted me and at night it was the same. I could have sworn she was strategically plotting the perfect method to drive me crazy. I kept thinking, 'She's manipulating me. She's pushing my buttons, and I'm not going to let her take control.' Needless to say, all she had to do was open her mouth, and I was catapulted into the red zone."

THE MESSAGES WE CARRY AROUND INSIDE ourselves are called self-talk. It's very important to take them out, pull them apart, and look at them, especially when it comes to messages about intensity. If you find yourself thinking or muttering under your breath messages such as the ones in the list below, it's time to change the self-talk.

> She's manipulating me.
> He's testing me.
> He's being defiant.
> He doesn't like me.
> She's out of control.
> She's trying to get away with everything.

Toss all messages that imply a winner and loser in a battle. Any thoughts that throw down the gauntlet have to go. You and your child are in this *together*, not pitted *against* one another.

Throw out messages that divide you:	Replace with messages that build your "team":
She's manipulating me.	She's scared.
He's testing me.	He's exploring how the world works.
He's being defiant.	Something must be upsetting him. I am feeling defensive, but I can listen before I talk.
He doesn't like me.	Maybe I moved too fast and spoke too loudly.
She's out of control.	She is stressed. It's a wonderful thing to be sensitive and able to read the emotions of others but she hasn't quite learned the skills to manage it yet.
She's trying to get away with everything.	She's trying to learn what's OK and what's not OK.
He intentionally makes me late for work.	It's hard for him to separate from me.

After completing this exercise in class, Sasha reported, "I have been calmer. One of the things that really helped me was telling myself, 'This is because she's tired. She was up late last night.' Or, 'We've been too busy. There have been way too many transitions.' It's made so much difference for both of us."

You might be thinking at this point that we are just making excuses for our spirited children. We're not. We are going to teach them the skills to handle these emotions more effectively. But the lessons must begin with understanding.

Pause

My friend Lynn likes to say, "When working with children, go slow to go fast." A child "losing it" often tempts us to leap into the fray, but if we do, we just react. Our goal is to respond thoughtfully. That requires a pause. Stop! Breathe! Think! Taking a long deep breath provides your brain with the oxygen it needs to reflect, literally increasing blood flow to the part of the brain that needs to be active for you to reason and to plan what to do next. Now you can remind yourself not to yell, grab a toy from your child and throw it across the room, push or criticize him. All things you know you will feel bad about later.

If you realize you're going over the edge with the kids, give yourself permission to step out of the fire. It's much better to take a breather than to create a power struggle and butt heads.

"I'm as intense as he is," Matt shared in class. "The things that irritate him drive me nuts too. It's like two kids going at it instead of one. The only way we can both survive is if I pull away for a few seconds to calm down."

Let your child know you are too upset to deal with him now, but you will be back in a few minutes. Then walk away and take ten deep, slow breaths to calm yourself down. You'll actually clue your nervous system to shut down the alarm system and the fight-or-flight response and increase the blood flow to the thinking parts of your brain. Remind yourself that your child is losing it because she is intense and not because you are a bad parent. Gradually, with maturity and good instruction from you, the frequency and volume of the outbursts will diminish.

Ask for Help

"My husband, Ben, and I have agreed that we'll work together—no matter what," Molly told the group. "This morning we put it to the test!

"I knew nine-year-old Wyatt was building up the minute he awoke," she told us. "He was tired. He had a loose molar that hung by one corner of the root, making eating impossible and shooting sharp stabs of pain whenever anything touched it. I had listened to him moan and groan through breakfast and then watched as he crawled up the stairs to comb his hair. I knew there would be trouble. His hair had grown to the point where it was too long. We had a haircut appointment scheduled for the next day, but my gut said it was one day too late."

She paused for effect and then continued. "I listened to the brewing storm, waiting for the eruption I knew would come but didn't bother to stop because I wanted to eat my breakfast!" We all nodded in understanding. "Sure enough, three bites in, it hit, 'Moooooom!' he roared. 'My hair won't do anything.'

"I grabbed one more bite," she said, "and headed up the stairs. He was right; it was a mess. It resisted his efforts to plaster it to his head. I glanced over his arsenal of chemicals: water, styling sprays, and foam— 'Have you tried gel?' I asked.

" 'There isn't any,' he complained.

"I searched through the shelves and came up with a half-full bottle. 'Try this,' I directed.

"Together we wiped gel all over his head. I thought it was going to work until little tufts of hair popped up around the crown of his head like little suction cups popping off a wall. He lost it, threw himself down on the bed, and started screaming. I was out of ideas and definitely low on patience."

At this point she slouched in her chair, shrugged, and threw her hands up in dismay. We waited for her to continue.

"I went looking for help," she explained. "I glared at my husband, who was downstairs eating.

"'I can't,' he said. 'I'm ready to scream, just listening to him.'

"That's when I gave him my 'look,'" she said, and proceeded to demonstrate for us by crossing her arms, puffing her cheeks, and squinting her eyes at us. Then she went on.

"He got the message and went upstairs.

"'I can't go to school,' Wyatt wailed.

"My husband glanced at our arsenal. 'My gosh, what do you expect?' he quipped. 'You've created a toxic waste site on your head.'

"I couldn't help it—I burst into laughter and so did my son. My husband had used humor to diffuse the situation. The explosion was over. Just like that. We got the hair plastered down the best we could, and he went to school."

When you're in the middle and stuck, you need to know when to back out and call for help. If that person is someone you live with, set up your signals as Molly and her husband did. Use expressions or words that clearly signify "I need your help now!" It is imperative that parents of spirited children work together. It is not a sign of failure to let others assist you. It is a recognition and acceptance of your own intensity and limits.

Blaming or ridiculing only fuels the intensity levels. Teamwork is essential. You have to talk about how you react when your child is upset. You have to decide how you can help and support each other. By working together, you take the sting out of your child's strong responses. You create a lifeline that keeps you from falling into the abyss of the red zone.

If it seems impossible for you and your partner to work together, seek counseling, and make weekly dates a priority so that you can work together. Researchers at the Gottman Institute have found that children of unhappily married parents are chronically aroused physiologically. As a result they get upset more easily and stay upset longer. Your children need you to work together so that they can stay in the green zone, where they are calm and open to your guidance.

If you are a single parent, you might think that you can't ask someone else for help. Single parents often say: "What if I call and interrupt my friend's meal or family time?" Or, "I don't want to bother anyone." But good friends don't mind being called upon. They appreciate the opportunity to help and the joy of giving. Look for someone you know who likes your child and won't be critical of him or you. You have to be able to trust that they'll support you, and then feel free to call. As the parent of a spirited child, you have to know and use your resources well. Someone who "has your back" is essential.

Make Self-Care a Priority

Be kind to yourself. It does require thought, effort, and skill to work with a spirited child. Once you have successfully gotten the kids down for the night, make your own sleep a priority too. When you are well rested, it's so much easier to stay in the green zone. Sleep allows you to be more focused, energetic, patient, and effective working with your children.

Before you begin an evening task, ask yourself if it really needs to be accomplished. Initially flipping on the television, checking e-mail, or going to social media sites can feel restful, but if doing so delays your bedtime, it may not be worth it. If you need a few minutes before sleep will come to you, consider journaling as a way to get in touch with your emotions, meditating, praying, or doing yoga.

Just remember, you can choose to increase the odds that tomorrow will be a great day by simply turning off the lights, fluffing your pillow, and permitting yourself to get the 8.25 hours of sleep you deserve and need. Adequate sleep stops you from being "part of the problem."

By the way, if you are sleeping with a partner, snuggle up. Touch increases the endorphin levels—those soothing, calming agents we need to feel peaceful. Sweet dreams!

Savor Your Successes

Two weeks after our initial discussion about managing intensity, Laura's smile was radiant. "It's really making a difference! I realize now that when I come home, if I just put down my things for five or ten minutes and pay attention to my daughter, I can slide both of us into the green zone. If I do, she's happy and we can sit down and eat. But if I don't and I'm still buzzing from work and running around, she's like a sponge absorbing it all. The whining starts and the evening deteriorates. What I do really does make a difference."

Laura wasn't the only one experiencing success. Angela was also delighted to report, "I'm making sure we get our sleep, and my husband and I are working together more. I let him know 'I need your help,' so that I can step away and come back, and he's right there working with me. It's changing how I respond to my son. Like last night his sister had been invited to a friend's house. He wanted to go, too, but he wasn't invited. In the past I would have yelled at him to stop it. 'You weren't invited. You can't go over to someone's house if you're not invited.' But this time I took a deep breath and I listened. I said, 'It doesn't seem fair. You really wanted to go. How can I help you to make it better?' He stopped and listened to me. And we came up with playing a game together."

Beginning tonight, write down three things that went well today. Include even the small accomplishments. "His intensity was an 11 and now it's 7.5. It's still exhausting but it's getting better." Soon you will recognize that six months ago there was a blowup every day, now it's only once or twice a week. Pat yourself on the back and say, "I promised myself I wouldn't yell today and I didn't!"

Stopping to savor your successes allows you to focus on the hours your child was awake that went well, instead of ruminating on the one hour that was not so great. Your progress will be documented. On the bad days when you need it the most you can reread your entries. There in black-and-white you will see examples of your growing competence and highlights of your child's developing skills.

Spirited children are more exuberant and passionate because of their genetic makeup. But with you as the guide, they really can learn to reel in and redirect those strong emotions. Maybe not every time, but enough to give you hope. By changing your response, you really can transform theirs.

FEELING GOOD ABOUT INTENSITY

It's easier to work with your own intensity when you can think about the ways intensity adds richness and depth to your life. I always like to take a few minutes in class to brainstorm what's great about intense, passionate emotions.

"My intensity allows me to perform," Eric responded. "I can accomplish feats that others can't." His voice started to warm. "I'm enthusiastic about what I do. I can motivate people. At work they always give me the new recruits because they know I'll get them off the ground and build a team."

He paused, and Jennifer took over. "I see it in my husband. He is passionate and committed. His relationships are deep and meaningful. He is an active volunteer. Last year he headed a campaign that raised ten thousand dollars to buy equipment for our school."

"I am demonstrative," Sharon added exuberantly.

Managed well, intensity adds flavor and excitement to our lives. It's the trait that allows us and our spirited children to be animated, vivacious, and zealous. It is the drive needed to become the karate champ, the tumbling tiger, the enthusiastic creator, the lively entertainer, and the charismatic leader. If we can fill ourselves with positive messages about intensity, we can stand in front of a mirror and proudly tell ourselves: "Intensity adds value to my life." "I am comfortable with intensity." "I can accept my intensity." "I can celebrate my child's intensity." "I can help my child learn to manage her intensity." "I do not fear intensity."

(In case you would like more information about how to keep your cool, check out my book *Kids, Parents, and Power Struggles*.)

INTENSITY
A Summary

To help our children understand and manage their intense emotions, we have to commit to developing our own self-regulation skills. When we are proficient handling our own emotions, it is far easier to instill those skills in our intense spirited children.

You need to tell yourself:
She's scared.
He's exploring how the world works.
Something must be upsetting him.
She is stressed.
It's hard for him to separate from me.

Teaching tips:
Pause and breathe before responding.
Ask for help.
Make self-care a priority.

Savor your successes:
Every night write down three things that went well today.
Include even small accomplishments.
Appreciate how intensity adds richness and depth to your
    life.

7

Intensity

Teaching Your Child Self-Regulation Skills

*I don't know why I go to extremes, too high and too low,
there ain't no in-betweens.*
—Billy Joel

Perky in her mukluk boots, black tassels bobbing, Megan arrived at my hotel with her three-year-old daughter Greta. Greta was wearing a red velvet dress trimmed with white fur and shocking pink tights. She was running up and down the stairs when I arrived in the lobby. They had driven two hours, much of it in metropolitan traffic, to pick me up. "I couldn't find a sitter," Megan explained. "The first two hours were great; I can't say what the return trip will be."

The odds were not in our favor. It was lunchtime and we'd be driving through naptime. Megan wanted to wait until we were out of the city to stop for lunch. The first hour went smoothly, but then Greta began to teeter. From the backseat we heard a plaintive plea, "I need Burger King." Then again, louder this time, "I need Burger King." The request was now taking on a note of despair.

We quickly pulled off the highway and into the parking lot of a restaurant. Unfortunately, the restaurant was not a Burger King. Greta's lips trembled in disappointment. Megan said nothing. She simply stepped out of the van, opened the rear door, took Greta out of her car seat, and gently enveloped her in a hug. Perhaps it was a minute, maybe two. But in that moment, something magical happened. Megan's caress pulled Greta back into balance. She was able to regroup, cope with the disappointment of no Burger King, and make it through lunch at the restaurant. What could have become a forty-five-minute public meltdown fizzled in the parking lot. Megan's warm response eased the way, allowing Greta to manage her intensity.

Intensity is the driving force behind your child's strong reactions. It is the invisible power that makes every response of the spirited child immediate and strong. Managed well, intensity allows spirited children a depth and delight of emotion rarely experienced by others. Its potential to create as well as wreak havoc, however, makes it one of the most challenging temperamental traits to learn to manage.

Spirited kids do not understand their own intensity. They don't know why they shriek so loud that it makes our ears burn. They don't know why they still cry over the dog that died two years ago. They don't know why they lose it over things that seem minor to us. They just do.

But you do not have to fear their intensity. While it may feel as though their reactions are completely unpredictable, the fact is that intensity reflects a physiological reaction in the body. It really is possible to recognize when it's building (at least most of the time), as Megan did, and develop effective strategies for defusing it before the blowup ever occurs. You can help spirited children to understand and appreciate the power of their intensity and teach them to direct it instead of letting it direct them. Begin by picking up the cues.

PICKING UP YOUR CHILD'S CUES

I was standing on the edge of the school playground with my colleague Lynn when she left my side to speak to a girl on the swings. "Is something making you sad?" She asked the child. I was puzzled by this question. From my perspective the girl seemed perfectly content. But in response to Lynn's inquiry, tears sprang to the girl's eyes as she pointed to several children and said, "They won't play with me."

Later, I asked Lynn, "How did you know she was sad?"

"I saw a little line between her brows," Lynn explained.

I have watched Lynn over the years and still struggle to be as observant as she is. Lately I have insisted that she tell me her secrets. "What do you look for? What do you feel? What do you hear that allows you to know?" It seems to be so natural for her. Over time I learned that there are very specific cues she picks up on. She sees shifts in body motion and facial expressions, hears alterations in voice intonations, and feels sensations that I had been missing.

It's an awareness of these cues that can inform you that your child's intensity is building. No two children signal growing intensity levels in the same way. But they are sending out identifiable indicators that they are on their way to the red zone. Learning to pick up the cues allows you to take preventive actions before your child becomes overwhelmed.

In class we explored what those cues look, sound, and feel like. Today our topic was managing intensity. As the parents entered the room, I directed them, "If your child was in the red zone this morning, please move to the left side of the room. And if your child was in the green zone, move right."

"Your house too?" Luke inquired, nodding to his fellow partners in the red zone. It's always nice to know you're not alone.

"What did you see, hear, or feel that led you to select red zone?" I asked. Responses came quickly.

"Leo screamed when I said, 'good morning.'"

"Hazel was whining. I think something woke her early."

"Ethan couldn't decide what he wanted for breakfast. He ended up hardly eating anything."

"Ellie refused to get dressed."

Steve snorted, "Not only did Bea fight getting dressed; she wanted me to pick her up out of bed."

Whether they were yelling, not following directions, or fighting with siblings, the kids had begun their day in the red zone.

I turned to the parents standing in the green zone. "What did you hear, sense, or feel this morning that led you to choose this zone?" I asked.

"Claire was cheery. When I walked into her room, she exclaimed, 'Good morning, Mommy!' and gave me a big hug," Heather offered.

"Megan was up and dressed before I stopped by her room."

"The boys played together before breakfast, no fighting," Greg added.

"Silas listened and did what I asked. He ate a great breakfast, too."

Children starting the day in the green zone were happy, cooperative, and independent.

I created a chart from their responses adding one more option to the mix: the yellow zone—revving up, but not quite over the edge.

Green Zone	Yellow Zone	Red Zone
Happy	A little whiny, or louder	Crying, yelling
Independent	Wants help	Shuts down; not able to dress, walk, complete homework, etc.
Coordinated	Stumbles	Falls, drops things
Cooperative	A little trouble listening; says things like, "Who cares?"	Argumentative, resistant
Decisive	Struggles to make a decision	Nothing is "right"
Looks at you	Glances away	Averts eyes, runs away, hides
Engaged	Pauses in play, flits from one thing to another, or goes off to a quiet spot	Revs up, wild, silly
Comfortable Doesn't need pacifier, lovie, etc.	Hot and itchy Fingers in mouth, wants pacifier, chewing on shirt/pencils, etc.	Hitting, kicking, yelling
Eats and sleeps well	Trouble eating and falling asleep	Not sleeping, not eating

Take a minute to review the chart. Place a check mark next to each cue you notice. Are you catching cues when your child first begins moving out of the green zone and into the yellow zone? Or does he have to get to the red zone before you notice?

Whether it's revving up, getting louder, testing the rules, fussing over a decision, or becoming less coordinated, spirited kids are letting you know when their intensity is rising. Psychologist John Gottman states, "You don't have to wait until they are weeping uncontrollably to detect their sadness or screaming in fury to sense their anger." Emotions are much easier to manage when they are at a lower level of intensity—when they are still in the yellow zone.

Think about your child. What cues does he send you? How do his body movements change? What happens to the tone of his voice? What irritates him that doesn't when he is calm? Take note of these changes. Store them in your brain. Next time your child's behavior begins to shift, recognize it as a signal for you to respond. Practice will fine-tune your observation skills. Soon, like Lynn, you'll even notice that "little line" between your child's brows, and you too will find yourself catching him before he goes over the edge.

NOTE YOUR OWN CUES

Anna sighed as we talked about helping our kids manage their intensity. "I just can't see it," she lamented. "I swear there aren't any 'yellow cues.' Rowan just escalates from fine to fury with no stops in between. It's impossible to catch him, and before I know what's happening, I'm right there with him. I want to scream. Sometimes I sit down and cry."

Initially as you begin to focus more on your child's cues, it may feel as though your child plunges into the red zone without warn-ing. But if you pay close attention, you'll begin to realize that when your child's intensity is rising, you can actually feel it in your own body. That's because the yellow cues your child is giving you are often more irritants than blatant signs.

When you offer a choice between yogurt and pancakes for breakfast and she can't make up her mind, it's frustrating. You are trying to be nice to her, but she's drawing out the process and soon you'll be running late. The muscles in your neck tighten; the tone of your voice becomes sharper and more impatient. Suddenly you can feel your pulse rate escalate, your breaths grow shallower and quicker as your irritation increases. These changes in *your* body are cues that you are both moving into the red zone. This awareness can allow you to pause, think, and take steps to calm everyone.

It's likely, however, that you have ignored your child's cues hoping you were wrong. Maybe you were tired, or rushing, thinking that you did not have time to deal with her distress now. Perhaps you disregarded her cues because you believed that responding to your child reinforces her negative behavior. But reading cues is like smelling smoke. If you follow up quickly, you may be able to smother the fire before it engulfs both of you.

When you neglect attending to your child's yellow cues, your own intensity will rise. You'll increase your demands for coopera-tion or compliance. Suddenly you will find yourself and your child in the red zone wondering how the heck you got there.

So as you think about your child's cues, also consider your own. What happens to the tone of your voice or the force of your ac-tions? Are you being irritated by things that on a good day would roll right off your back? Are you losing patience? Are you craving chocolate or other sweets to boost your energy, if only temporarily?

Are you feeling tired or easily overwhelmed? These are all yellow cues that let you know it's time to stop what you're doing and give yourself permission to do something different.

You can teach yourself to monitor your cues. Throughout the day stop and ask yourself, what am I feeling? What is my intensity level?

When we talked about having done this outside of class, Ashley was discouraged. "Every time I stopped to check myself, I was upset, tired, angry, or frustrated. Maybe I didn't stop to check until I got into that state. I don't know."

Tight muscles and our mood are a barometer of our body states. Robert Thayer writes, "Foot wiggling and finger tapping are such unerring indications of tension that if you find yourself doing those things, you can be sure that you are not calm, even if you think you are." Sometimes it can be very difficult to note the sensations in your own body. If you find yourself frequently rushing or short on sleep, mild tension is second nature to you. But do your best to begin to pay attention. That awareness will help you keep your cool. Your child will stay calmer too, allowing you to teach her how to catch the cues herself.

TEACHING KIDS TO READ THE CUES

One day while observing in a classroom, I heard the teacher, Julie Nelson, say to a child, "Oh my gosh, you had so much stress when you came to school today. I could see it in your shoulders." The girl nodded solemnly and whispered, "Oh, Ms. Nelson, I thought it was going to last forever."

Julie, a skilled educator, knows that by describing what she sees, she is teaching the children to notice and name their own cues.

Ultimately we want the children to catch their growing intensity themselves, to rely on their inner control rather than our control. By giving them the words, we can expect that by the time they are three and a half or four years of age, we will be hearing things like: "Mom, I'm bubbling inside." Or, "Dad, I'm really revved up." Or, "I'm having a very hard morning."

Tiffany, a mom in my class, shook her head in dismay when I suggested that children could learn to identify their own cues. "To put it mildly," she said, "I don't find my nine-year-old really open to discussing her rising level of intensity. I can't believe it works."

Tiffany is right. You can't teach kids new words or to pick up their cues when they are in the red zone. But later, after they have calmed and are back in the green zone, or if you catch them in the yellow zone, you can point out to them what you see by saying something like: "Damon, when I see you prowling the house, I know it's time for you to find a quiet place." Or, "Oscar, when you start stumbling, it means you need to stop and read a book." Or, "When you can't decide, it helps if you take a deep breath." Describing the cues once is not enough. You have to keep talking about them all the time. Your role is to empathize, guide, and then wait as they practice.

Laura turned to Tiffany, laughing. "It only takes about four years," she quipped and then explained. "When Connor was four years old, he was the kid who would hurl hurtful words or punch his brother when he became angry. Now he's eight years old. Just yesterday I watched him. He was playing with his brother and cousins. I knew he was getting frustrated. He saw me watching. Instead of losing it, he left the group, shook his head as he walked past me, and muttered, 'I'm steaming.' He then proceeded to step onto the treadmill and run for a few minutes. It was all he needed to calm himself and get back into the green zone. He ended up playing hide-and-seek with them for another half hour. He's really learning to pick up his own cues."

Like Connor, when children learn to notice their own cues, they can short-circuit the meltdowns themselves.

USING WORDS

Learning to observe cues is the first step toward managing their potent reactions. Spirited children also need the vocabulary to name their emotions. If they can tell us they are angry, they don't have to kick us to get the message across. Words control the impulses; without them, children have no protective devices to slow their reactions. Spirited children cannot manage emotions they cannot name.

Focusing on Strengths

Building their vocabulary begins with the words we use to describe and explain intensity.

Three-year-old Al is a blond, tousled-haired mini-tornado. "I've got gusto," he informed me. "My dad says it's okay to do things with gusto—as long as you don't hurt anybody!"

"I'm full of it," a five-year-old shared, "just like my Grandpa Rick."

"My mom plays whisper games with me to help me practice my soft voice because usually I've very dramatic," six-year-old Libby exclaimed.

"I have powerful reactions," eight-year-old Amy told me.

These children, as young as three (and sometimes even two) understand what intensity is and feel good about it. They haven't been told they were wild, aggressive, or explosive. The words to describe their intensity have focused on the vim, vigor, and energy racing through their body in a positive way. It is those words that help them to feel comfortable with their intensity rather than embarrassed or frightened by it. As a result, they don't have to run wild, scream, hit, or throw things to express themselves. They can talk about it instead.

Language development is like an iceberg. A great deal lies hidden beneath the surface. Two-thirds of language development occurs inside the brain, invisible to us. Months, sometimes years, before children are communicating with their own words, they understand those of others.

Parents of spirited children who are learning to manage their intensity well are talking about intensity and naming the emotions. They soothe the wailing baby by telling him that they understand it's frustrating to wait for the food to warm. They tell the toddler that they understand she is angry. It's hard for her to stop playing outside and come into the house. Soon the children will be able to communicate: "I'm getting frustrated." "I'm irritated." "I am tired." It won't happen overnight, but it will happen.

According to psychologist John Gottman from the Gottman Institute, the research demonstrates that children who receive these types of messages are "emotion coached" and are more effective at soothing themselves and focusing attention. As a result, they do better in school and with peers, experience fewer behavior problems, and demonstrate more positive emotions.

It's never too late. Older kids who haven't heard the words need to hear them now. If you are uncertain how comprehensive your child's emotion vocabulary is, try a simple test. Play a game in which you ask your child to give you examples of people he's seen expressing various emotions. For instance, "Can you think of someone who was happy?" (I find it is easier for a child to talk about the emotions of others first and then transfer that knowledge to an awareness of his own emotions.) Wait to see if he can give you an example of feeling happy. If he has no answer, or does not understand what the word means, allow him to pass. Continue asking the same question, but change the emotion each time. Include words like *irritated, frustrated, jealous, scared,* and *anxious.* For example, "Can you think of someone who was irritated?"

Your child's responses, or lack of them, will give you a good indication of how proficient he is at understanding and expressing his emotions. Frequently when I ask these questions during a private consultation, the children are unable to describe a situation in which someone has experienced jealousy or anxiety. Many have no idea what jealousy or anxiety is, yet they are experiencing these emotions daily.

If we are expecting spirited children to manage strong emotions, we have to be naming them and pointing out examples every single day. Think about it. If children can articulate that their brother is irritating them, or that they are feeling jealous, we have a chance to assist them long before the two of them come to blows.

Talking about emotions may be uncomfortable. Frequently I am asked, "Aren't you just begging for a blowup when you talk about intensity with kids? Aren't you feeding them ideas or creating words for feelings that don't really exist?" My experience, observations, and interviews tell me that spirited children feel intensely whether anyone has talked to them about it or not. Ignoring it does not make it go away. Ask children what is happening inside their bodies, and they will tell you that they can feel their blood buzzing in their veins or hornets zipping through their body. If no one has informed them that other people experience these feelings, or if no one has helped them by giving names to these feelings—like anxiety, frustration, excitement, and elation—they become frightened by them. Some worry that they are sick. Some feel odd, others lost and overwhelmed. Talking verifies the sensations and emotions. It gives them legitimacy and allows children to own them without being frightened. It also helps kids to know what to do with them, how to react, and how to manage their intensity. Most important, naming emotions slows the heart rate and makes it easier to move back into the green zone.

"Talk, talk, talk—that's all we do." TJ told me. "My wife is always giving our daughter a word for a feeling or pointing out the body movement that is a sure sign of trouble. I get so tired of listening to her talking—but it works! Now I'm trying to do it too."

Intense spirited kids need to hear phrases like:
You are enthusiastic.
You are expressive and lively.
That can be frustrating.
You are very upset, but you are a problem solver and will
    figure out what to do.
Being intense does not mean being aggressive.
I'm wondering if you are feeling anxious, angry, sad (or
    whatever the emotion might be).
Your body gets very excited.
When kids hear these messages over and over again, they
    are able to turn them into "I" messages.

An intense spirited child can learn to tell himself:
I am getting upset.
I'm going into the red zone.
I can be angry without hurting someone.

I am really excited.

I like being enthusiastic.

My blood is starting to boil. I need to step out of here.

I'm feeling crabby.

I experience very strong emotions, but I don't have to let
    them overwhelm me.

By giving them the words, we give them the tools to get their
needs met appropriately.

"More than once on our vacation," Matt told the group, "our
six-year-old Shane said, 'I think this day is getting too busy. Can
we go back to the hotel and do this activity on another day?'"

The nice thing about using words is that your child may even
be able to help you out like four-year-old Jasper did for his mom.

"We had been shopping in the mall for several hours," she told
the other parents in the class. "I hate shopping. Jasper could see
that I was getting upset with a very slow clerk. 'It's hard to wait,'
he said to me. I couldn't help smiling. How many times have I said
that to him? He saved me from losing it!"

Take a few minutes and write down the words your child uses
to describe her own intensity. Ask her what it feels like inside her
body when she is angry or upset. Give her positive words to use the
next time she feels this way. Let her know you'll listen carefully
and help her diffuse it before she loses it.

SOOTHING/CALMING ACTIVITIES

Catching cues and talking about intensity are both critical steps
for managing strong emotions, but we also need to take preventive measures. Intense spirited kids can roll us right up in their

intensity. Unknowingly, we can add to the level of their intensity rather than diffusing it because we are captured by their zestfulness. When their energy levels become frenzied, we assume they need more stimulation and play wild music, plan more activities, or encourage them to run up and down the hallway, failing to recognize that at this point rather than more activity, what they actually need is help winding down.

Low-key soothing and calming activities distributed throughout the day will help them stay in the green zone. These activities build up their store of natural calming agents, giving them a reserve to draw upon when needed. If you participate with your child in these activities, you will both have fun. Time spent enjoying one another's company builds strong, healthy relationships. The more warm memories you have to savor, the easier it is to let go of the "not so good" ones.

1. SLEEP AND SIESTA TIME: It was 3:50 on a rainy summer afternoon, when I asked my friend Lynn if I could visit the school-age room at her child development center. "They are going into siesta," she said. I was surprised and raised a quizzical eyebrow. "They all go off to evening activities," she explained. "So from four P.M. to five P.M. we have siesta. One hour of quiet time when they are alone in their own 'bubble of space.'"

When I entered their classroom, the lights were low, soft music was playing, and on the shelves was an assortment of quiet activities. There were books to read, baseball cards to sort and stack, Legos, beads and other stringing materials, Zaks building blocks, puzzles, audio books, paper and markers, doodle books, fuse beads, and even a comfy spot or two for sleeping. No electronics were allowed.

One child quickly claimed the cot and fell sound asleep. Rowan headed for a rocking chair where he sat and read. Ben pulled out a puzzle and began to work. Nora created jewelry with the beads she selected. Brookes, Kai, and Connor selected the baseball cards, each taking several hundred and proceeding to build structures with the cards. Shevan selected markers and paper. There was no bickering, no complaints; the children simply played silently, completely engaged in their selected activity. Without realizing it, they practiced feeling comfortable in low-stimulation situations. They also learned a very important lesson about balance, their bodies, and the importance of rest in order to keep their cool. At five P.M. when their parents picked them up to take them to the baseball or soccer field, they were ready, recharged for the evening's activities.

John Bates at Indiana University has found that all children are affected by sleep deprivation, but spirited children are *really* impacted. That's why it is so essential to ensure that your child gets sleep at night and either a nap or downtime during the day. Make sleep a priority for both you and your spirited child. The better rested both of you are, the calmer you'll be.

2. WATER: "When Silas starts to lose it, it's into the bathtub," Laura explained. "There are days the kid looks like a little raisin because he's been in there three times, but it snaps him right out of it. I've got two other kids. They don't need baths the way Silas does, but if necessary I just put them in the tub with him. He needs it and they enjoy it."

"I started putting Elsa in the bathtub to soothe her when she was just a baby," Maggie said. "Now at thirteen, she'll come home from a hard day at school and head straight for the tub. She'll lie there for over an hour, reading, and singing to herself. It's a new person that emerges."

"Water really works for Luke," Caroline added. "When we're away from home, just placing a cool, wet washcloth on his forehead will soothe him."

"Libby doesn't like to get in the tub," Victoria said, "but if I let her play in the sink while I'm making dinner, it slows her down. She especially likes it if I let her scrub the potatoes and carrots for the meal."

Warm or cool, water can be a very soothing entity to spirited children. By immersing their bodies in a warm comfortable bath, pouring water from one container to another, or merely letting it run through their fingers, they can diffuse their intensity and pull themselves back into the green zone.

The nice thing about water is that it is soothing for anyone no matter what his or her age. My friend Rachel has always used the "fun bath" to soothe her very spirited three-year-old daughter. She didn't realize how important these baths were for Jamie until a recent Mother's Day. Clutching a bottle of bath salts in her hand, Jamie insisted that her mother have a bath. While the tub filled with water and bubbles, Jamie ran to get her favorite books. As Rachel lay in the bath with the bubbles tickling her chin, Jamie "read" to her. Then she jumped up and headed downstairs only to reappear with a plate of peanut butter crackers and a glass of milk. "Happy Mother's Day," Jamie exclaimed, delighted to treat her mother to a soothing/calming activity.

3. IMAGINATION: Most spirited children have a vivid imagination. You can use it to help them moderate their intensity and have fun.

Grandma Leah's Dress-Up is an imaginative game that calms a tense child anywhere and at any time. Let your children pretend that they are going to an elegant ball or a costume party.

Then "dress" them up for it. Have them stand in front of you or sit on your lap. First pretend to wash their hair, massaging their heads, and running your fingers along their scalp lines like water spraying from a nozzle. You can tickle their ears with an imaginary diamond earring or a pirate's ring. If their fantasy includes makeup, run the lightest of fingertips along their cheeks, across their eyebrows, along the bridge of their noses and the outline of their lips. The gentle touch soothes and calms them. For boys, you can pretend to shave them—brush shaving cream on their cheeks; then stroke their faces with your fingertips like a razor.

Slide a finger around their necks for a gold chain or a silk necktie. Run your finger down their backbones for a zipper or around their waist for a magic belt. Don't forget the stockings that slide over each individual toe and up along the ankles and even the calves of their legs.

Rings and bracelets are the finishing touches. Place a ring on each finger, sliding down the finger to its base, adding first a ruby, then a diamond, then the gold pinky ring. Finally, end with a watch or gold bracelet, draped around the wrist. They're ready for the ball or party and they're in a much better mood.

Creative dramatics can work too. I once watched a music teacher working with a group of young children. She was trying to teach them the concepts of *forte* and *piano*. She asked the children to pretend that they were leaves. When she played the song forte, the wind would blow and the "leaves" would dance in the air. As the music softened to piano, the wind would die down and the "leaves" would settle to the ground.

At the end of the lesson, one very spirited child was still dancing in the wind. "I think you have lots of wind blowing inside your body," the teacher said to her. "Take a deep breath and blow that wind out of your body." The child puffed her cheeks out and blew a steady burst of air, her chest visibly shrinking as the air diminished.

"There now," the teacher responded. "Do you feel the leaves all settling down inside you? They're in a pile, falling asleep."

The child nodded and quietly walked to the door. Her rich imagination had helped her to release her excitement and energy in a positive way.

Older children and teens can also be encouraged to use their imagination by involving them in theater or improvisational classes. Their perceptiveness of subtle body language and voice intonations can raise their performances to an outstanding level.

4. SENSORY ACTIVITIES: Spirited kids are very sensuous. They enjoy activities that allow them to touch, smell, taste, hear, or see things. Using their senses can calm them.

Older children can benefit from listening to their favorite music, chewing gum, sucking from a straw, rubbing the silk edge of their favorite blanket or stuffed animal (there is no need to "give them up"—they can just be kept private), or using a favorite lotion or oil, especially lavender. Gardening or baking are also favorite sensory activities for all ages.

In a typical preschool program you will usually see one or two sensory activities. For the spirited child, we like to include as many as five. I encourage the teachers to use plenty of sensory materials because the other kids like them and the spirited kids *need* them. It's important that you have them available at home because they are a great way to diffuse intense feelings.

Play-Doh and Silly Putty are favorite sensory activities. Since there isn't a right way to use them, a two-year-old can pull, roll, and stretch them, whereas an eight-year-old can create a log house, imaginary food, or whatever. Many parents of spirited kids keep Play-Doh in the cupboard, ready to pull out when needed.

Every good preschool has a sensory table. Usually it's just a table frame with the middle cut out of the table so that a large tub can be inserted. The tub is then filled with water, sand, oatmeal, cornmeal, snow, shredded paper, or whatever the classroom teacher chooses. Spirited kids are always drawn to the one in our classroom. You can create your own sensory table. All you need is a plastic dishpan or tub. You don't need the table frame. Just put a vinyl tablecloth underneath the tub to keep spills off your floor. Fill the tub with warm sudsy water, and make sure there are turkey basters and sponges for a fun tranquilizing activity. If the kids get tired of the sponges, let them wash their dishes or favorite toys and dolls. If you don't want to use water, try sand, oatmeal, or cornmeal. Include cups, spoons, funnels, and a variety of other containers for hours of fun.

Finger painting the shower wall with shaving cream is another soothing exercise. Wash it down the drain when they're done.

Back scratches and neck massages feel great at any age. We all need healthy nonsexual touch—even adolescents.

Sometimes it's pressure that your child craves. A tight bear hug may be just what he needs, or you might also find it helpful to have him wear a tight stretchy T-shirt, or use a heavy quilt at night when sleeping. The pressure on his body will soothe him. (The adolescent who piles books and clothing on his bedcover and then crawls underneath to sleep may not be intentionally messy, but instead creating his own weighted blanket.)

An infant too young to benefit from a sensory table or weighted blanket may simply need to be held. Researchers in Canada have discovered that the more an infant is carried in contact with your body, the easier it is to calm him. Your physical presence helps him to regulate his body. So unless you are driving and need your child to be in his car seat for safety, get him out of the container carriers and into your arms or a kangaroo pack strapped to your body. He may also be soothed by a massage, a soft lullaby, or a walk outside. Sometimes dimming the lights in a bright room will work.

Any activities that use the senses are normally very inviting and soothing to spirited children.

5. PHYSICAL EXERCISE AND REPETITIVE MOTION: "I was trying to get four-year-old Derrick to put on his shoes so we could go pick up his sister," Nadeen told me. "He was dragging his feet and mumbling as I was trying to rush him along. I told him we really needed to go so we wouldn't be late, and he said, 'But, MOM, what are we going to do about the bees in my body?'

"Shocked, I responded, 'Are you feeling bees in your body?'

"'Yes!' he exclaimed.

"'Well, let's get rid of them! Should we bounce?' And we proceeded to bounce on the mini-trampoline. Five minutes later he got into the car without a fuss."

Exercise, especially repetitive motion, creates natural soothing agents in the body and makes it much easier for your child to remain in the green zone. Plan it into his day, just as you do his meals. If you can, get up in the morning and go outside. Provide lots of opportunities for running, climbing, bicycling, swinging, swimming, or roller-skating. Encourage him to do "heavy work" like pulling, pushing, or carrying heavy—but not too heavy— loads like the laundry basket.

If it's impossible to go outside, suggest that he sit in a rocking chair while reading, use a Sit 'n Spin, cycle on a stationary bicycle, or jump on a mini-trampoline. And when there is no opportunity for using his big muscles, provide fidget toys like a Slinky or finger puzzles to allow him to move his little muscles. All of this physical activity increases the level of Mother Nature's "tranquilizers."

6. READING: When you get stuck—there isn't any water available, sensory activities and your imagination have failed you, and it's raining outside—try reading. Many parents of spirited children have found the simple act of pulling out a book and inviting their child to sit on their lap or next to them, especially in a rocker or glider, is all that is needed to diffuse an accelerating intensity level. Not only does your child learn the power of reading to manage her strong feelings but she is also exposed to the wonder of books. The research on reading states that the child who associates reading with a warm comfortable lap grows up to be the best and most avid reader. Head to your local library or check out those garage sales for used books. Keep your child's favorite titles handy—no matter how old he is.

7. DEEP BREATHING: Even toddlers can learn to use deep breathing to calm their system. Simply say to them, "Breath in." Then exaggerate your own breathing to demonstrate what you mean. You might find it helpful to have your children put their hand on their tummy to feel it sucking in. Follow up with, "Breath out." Again, exaggerate your own slow release of breath. Holding up your thumb as a "birthday candle" to blow out, may also help to draw out that nice long breath.

8. HUMOR: To fully appreciate this story, you need to know a little bit about my husband. He's five feet nine inches tall—if you stretch it—155 pounds, and very spirited. He loves movies where the little guy wins and is a sucker for every kid who comes to the door selling anything. There's another side to him too. His father was raised on the Lake Superior ore docks and liked to regale us with tales of diving off the freighters. I believed him, although no one was ever able to verify his facts. I'm afraid these macho activities have influenced how his son, my husband, sometimes expresses himself.

One day my son came home from school, threw open the door, and stormed into the kitchen throwing his book bag on the floor and kicking at the refrigerator. "Cut it out," I commanded. "What happened to you?"

"That old witch on the playground accused me of fighting and I didn't do it," he roared.

"That must have been embarrassing," I said.

"It wasn't embarrassing," he corrected me. "I wasn't fighting."

"Well, it must have felt lousy then," I responded.

"Stupid aide," he bellowed. "She must be blind."

Losing patience, I tried moralizing. "Next time you might choose where to stand more carefully." I remarked. My comment only added to his fury.

He continued to rage until his father arrived home.

"What's wrong with him?" he asked, noting the steam rising in the kitchen. I quickly filled him in with the details, hopeful that he would know what to do. As he strode over to Josh, I noticed a slight puff in his chest and I knew he was up to something.

"No problem," he announced. I gasped. Josh looked up in total shock. "What do you mean?" he stammered. Joe continued, "Next time just say to the lady, 'Hey, lady, was there blood on the ground?'" Then he jabbed himself in the chest and declared, "When I fight, there's blood on the ground!"

Josh's eyes bugged out. I almost fainted. Years of nonviolence training down the drain. I could just imagine this kid going back

to school, sharing his father's words of wisdom, and being sus-
pended for the remainder of the year.

"You can't say that!" I gasped.

By now they were both roaring, Josh fully realizing that his
father was teasing. The intensity of the fury was literally diffused
by humor. Laughter decreases our stress hormones and increases
"feel-good" hormones. Later, when everyone was calm, we talked
about more productive ways to handle conflict on the playground.

Humor is a frequent visitor to the homes of spirited children
who are learning to manage their intensity well—not sarcasm or
ridicule but gut-busting, yuk-it-up good laughs and fun. Feel free to
enjoy that sense of humor; use it to reduce the tension and bring
your family together. That's what Todd does.

"Sometimes I do something totally unexpected," he said, laughing. "Last night I heard Ben fighting with his sister. I was in a good
mood, so I snuck around the corner on my hands and knees and
growled at them like a dog. They were so surprised they started to
giggle. They jumped on my back for a horse ride and the fight was
over."

Amanda uses humor to back herself out of power struggles.
"McKenzie had really been helpful getting dinner ready. She had
set the table, torn up the lettuce for the salad, and washed some of
the preparation dishes. After dinner I asked her to take her plate
to the sink. She started to balk. 'Oooops, you've been good too
long,' I remarked. She was stunned into silence for a second.

"'Yeah' she responded, smiling, and took her plate to the
kitchen." Humor—a delightful tool for reducing intensity.

9. TIME-OUT—NOT AS A PUNISHMENT: Taking a break is
one of the most effective calming strategies for adolescents and
adults. Unfortunately, we've turned time-out into a punishment

for kids. Instead of being an opportunity to teach our children to take a break in order to regain control, it has become a dreaded order. "Go to your room and don't come out until I tell you to!" Or, "You sit in that chair and don't move an inch!" No pain, no gain, we think, and feel better if they scream and holler to let us know that they are really miserable. But an opportunity to refresh is lost when we struggle to keep them in their room and they expend their energies kicking doors and throwing objects against the wall.

I like to recommend that parents of spirited kids think of time-out as a basketball coach does: an opportunity to take a break from the action, refresh the body, and pull the game plan back together.

It may appear that there is a flaw in comparing time-outs with time-outs in sports. Most three-year-olds, even eight-year-olds, especially spirited ones, don't usually trot easily to the sideline when a time-out is called; nor do they listen intently while the game plan is revised. Instead, they may lie down, kick, scream, and hold their hands over their ears when you try to talk to them. So what is a parent to do?

You can start by reminding your children of the cues their body sends them: messages that say "I'm tired," or "I'm getting overwhelmed." Help them recognize that tight muscles, a loud voice, or the sensation of blood running through their veins is a signal that they need to call a time-out. If we have taught them that time-out is an opportunity to pull out of the action to rest rather than a punishment to endure, they can feel comfortable taking a break. Taking a break means finding a quiet, comfortable spot. It may be a bedroom; it may be a corner of the room you are in. Time-out does not require isolation. At first you will have to gently help them find their spot, away from the action and stimulation. Speak softly to them, help them hear and feel the quiet, sense the frustration draining from their bodies, their heart rate slowing.

You might find yourself groaning right now, wondering what you are going to do with the baby who is crying to be fed, or the toddler who is hanging on your leg, or the phone that is ringing. Forget the phone, lay the baby in the crib for a few minutes, take the toddler with you, or place him in a safe place while you help your spirited child find a comfortable place to take a break.

One way to make that spot more accessible and inviting is to create a calming basket for every room. Fill each basket with stuffed animals, books, Legos, quiet toys, stickers, markers for drawing, and any other things that calm your child. Your child doesn't have to "go" anywhere—the baskets are right there when you need them the most. Encourage your child to select a favorite soothing activity from the basket to play with until his body is calm. Or if he needs help, pick out a book and begin reading it to him. You are not encouraging poor behavior, you are calming him. The teachable moment will come—after he's calm. If he attempts to leave before he is calm, return him to the basket, once again assisting him in finding something to do until his body is peaceful.

Children have to be taught what a relaxed body looks like. Point out that when they are calm their eyes will look at you. Their arms and legs will be still. They can listen and answer. Their voice is quiet. Time-out is not over until you can both see these things and that sense of peacefulness fills their bodies.

What are you going to do for a consequence if time-out is supposed to be a chance to relax? Remember that if kids learn to take a break before they blow up, there won't be any misbehavior.

Once children have learned to respond to the cues their bodies are sending them and understand time-out as a healthy opportunity to deal with their stress, they can call for one themselves. In fact, you may see your children slide out of the action and into their room or to their calming basket for a quick break all by themselves. Intuitively they are bringing their bodies back into the green zone.

Learning to use time-out as a soothing/calming activity is critical for spirited children as they move toward the teen years. As hormones start to pump through their bodies, the challenge to manage their intensity grows. At this point they are physically too big for you to force them into a time-out. They have to choose to do it themselves. If they are comfortable with time-outs, they will use them and will be successful at managing their strong emotions.

When children understand their intensity and recognize that they can control and channel it into athletic, creative, and other appropriate endeavors, they feel good about themselves. The number of full-blown outbursts diminishes drastically. This is preventive discipline. It teaches kids the "right" way to behave, by staying in the green zone where it's easier to manage strong emotions and stop the battles before they ever start.

The challenge in all of this is that we are providing the steadying hand. That's why it's so important to have a plan for the "pivotal moment."

WORKING TOGETHER

Even when you have been monitoring the cues, teaching words, and filling your child's days with soothing/calming activities, there will come a pivotal moment when the kids are on the "edge." Your own emotions surge. It can happen so quickly there is no time to think. The key is having a plan. Knowing exactly what you are going to say and do. Your response is automatic. No thought is required. Let me show you what I mean.

"That's mine! I had it first!" Fighting words erupted from the family room as I sat at the kitchen table with Kate and Todd. Kate shook her head, "There they go again." She groaned. Since I was in their home for a private consultation, I headed toward the boys. Four-year-old Wyatt clutched the iPad to his chest, twisting away from six-year-old Kyle's clawing grasp. Seeing me approach, Kyle shrank back.

"I will help you." I said, moving closer. Kyle glanced at me, a look of confusion in his eyes, as though deciding whether to run or yell in defense. But I bent low and calmly continued, "I saw your hand hit him. What were you trying to tell him?" In that moment he turned toward me, open to working with me.

Why didn't I reprimand them for fighting? Was I just letting them get away with poor behavior? Before the lessons can be taught, we have to draw our spirited children to us. If we move in like a bulldozer, their response will intensify to match ours. That's when the yelling morphs into kicks. Nimble bodies dart from our grasp, and the words *I hate you* stab us in the heart.

Spirited children have to know that the adult approaching them is someone coming to help. Not an enemy or adversary who is going to yell, threaten, or grab them, but someone who will help them calm down and figure out what to do. Someone who is saying words like:

> I will help you.
> I'm trying to understand.
> What do you need?
> I think you had something important to say. What did you want to tell him?

Think about the words you are comfortable using to draw your child to you. Practice them until they are second nature to you. Then when that pivotal moment strikes, you'll be ready.

Choosing to draw your child to you does not mean you are "giving in." A warm, sensitive response to your child's negative emotions actually opens the gate to the "teachable moment." Researchers confirm that children who experience a supportive response when they are upset develop better coping skills. Your response really does change your child's.

"It works," Rob acknowledged in class the next week. "Leo likes to rinse the dishes, which is great. But if someone has left a dirty dish in the sink, he freaks out. I want him to be flexible. So I've been trying to tell him it's not a big deal or suggest he use the sprayer and the other sink. But he just gets more upset. This morning it happened again, but this time I caught myself and said, 'Yuck, there's a dirty dish in there. I will help you. What do you need?' He calmed right down. Then he said to me, 'Dad, why don't I just use the sprayer.'"

Shaking his head, Rob added, "I guess a little empathy goes a long way."

Drawing your child to you calms her.

Being the parent of an intense spirited child requires a great deal of thought, focus, and attention. The payoff for your effort is a dramatic reduction in the frequency of the meltdowns. But let's be honest, sometimes, despite strengthening everyone's skills to manage intensity, there will still be times when things fall apart. I tell you this because when things blow up I do not want you to quit trying. These strategies do work, just not all of the time. That's why it's important that you also know what to do when, regardless of your best efforts, everyone drops over the edge into the red zone. Read on.

INTENSITY
A Summary

Intensity is the driving force behind the strong reactions of the spirited child. It is the invisible punch that makes every response of the spirited child immediate and strong. Managed well, intensity allows spirited children a depth and delight of emotion rarely experienced by others. Its potential to create as well as wreak havoc, however, makes it one of the most challenging temperamental traits to learn to manage.

Intense spirited kids need to hear:
You do everything with zest and gusto.
You are enthusiastic, expressive, and full of energy.
Your intensity can make you a great athlete, leader, performer, etc.
Things can easily frustrate you.
Being intense does not mean being aggressive.

Teaching tips:
Help your child learn to notice her cues—the changes in her body that signify rising intensity.
Teach her the words to express her strong emotions.
Provide activities that soothe and calm, such as warm baths, reading, and quiet imaginative play.
Use humor to diffuse intense reactions.
Protect her sleep.
Make time for exercise.
Teach your child that time-out is a way to take a break and feel better.

If you are intense too:
Do not fear your child's intensity.
Remember you are on the same team.
Plan what you will say in that pivotal moment to draw your
    child to you.

8

Meltdowns

What to Do When Everything Falls Apart

"I was in the black zone."
"What's the black zone?"
"Way worse than the 'red zone.'"
—Dakota, age five

Y ou've got to help me *now!*" blurted the voice on the other end of my phone. It was a plea for assistance from a friend across the country. Seems her son Jayden had spent the day doing everything he could possibly do to get her goat—swearing, punching his sisters, talking back, and refusing to do anything he was told. Out of desperation she had just sent him to his room to rot for the rest of his life. After tearing the sheets and blankets off his bed, he threw himself onto it in a hysterical heap and was still there when she called.

Sometimes, despite your best efforts to work with your spirited child, the words you needed haven't come. The soothing activities haven't been effective. Too many transitions, too much stimulation, or too much stress—and now your child is on a rampage. The force is penetrating. You feel bruised and maybe even powerless to respond.

All kids experience tantrums or meltdowns, whichever you prefer to call them, but spirited children do it with much more vim, muscle, and frequency. My friend who has raised five children, now all grown, says, "If I put on one chart all the meltdowns of the four younger ones, the total wouldn't even come close to what occurred with the oldest one. Today I can tell you she's an absolutely sparkling adult, but it's a miracle we're both still alive to see it."

SPIRITED CHILDREN EXPERIENCE SPILLOVER MELTDOWNS

Jayden's meltdown looked like a classic tantrum. It sounded like one, too, but it wasn't. As I talked with Jayden's mom, I realized that Jayden's meltdown had nothing to do with power or getting attention. It wasn't even meant as a personal attack on his mother. His meltdown had been building for hours, even days. For the last three weeks his father had been locked in negotiation meetings from six in the morning until well past midnight. Alone at home with three preschoolers, Mom was exhausted and short on patience. Jayden is spirited. Jayden is temperamentally sensitive. He absorbed the stress and strains his family was experiencing until he reached his limit. Then he blew, taking the contents of his room with him. This is a spillover meltdown.

Stella Chess and Alexander Thomas were the first to describe this type of meltdown in their now-classic book, *Know Your Child*. They define a spillover meltdown as "an outpouring of emotion in a disorganized way." The genetic makeup of spirited children that fosters a tendency toward steamy reactions makes them much more vulnerable to spillover meltdowns—a flood of emotions that overwhelms them and pushes them beyond their temperamental ability to cope. *In my experience, most of the tantrums experienced by spirited children are actually spillover meltdowns.* They are not premeditated. They are not intended to manipulate. (In truth I believe that children don't intend to manipulate, though sometimes in addition to spillover meltdowns, they may be testing limits or figuring out the rules—we will address those topics later in this chapter.)

A spillover meltdown can't be stopped by ignoring it because ignoring does not address the real fuel source, which is that in this case your child is dealing with a temperamental issue. That issue has triggered a physical reaction and plunged him deeply into the red zone. Your child needs you to help him discover the source of the emotional flood and stop it. He needs your guidance to help him calm himself and regain self-control. Without that guidance, he can rage for hours because his inner restraints have busted, letting loose a hurricane of wild emotions. It's distressing as a parent to witness. It's frightening as a child to experience. Your spirited child does not want to go there.

Seven-year-old Lindsey exemplified this truth. "Will I ever be able to stop myself?" she wailed after experiencing an especially overpowering meltdown." The answer is yes. But it will require patience, support, and assistance from the adults in her life.

SPILLOVER MELTDOWNS
APPEAR DURING INFANCY

Spillover meltdowns, because they are tied to temperament, are apparent even during infancy.

"Travis was only a week old the first time he flooded," Erica offered during a discussion of meltdowns. "Company was arriving just at his naptime. Strangers were holding him and talking to him. The noise level in the room was very high. His dad and I were trying to entertain, pouring coffee, and getting food for everyone. We weren't focusing on him. Travis had been listening and watching everyone very intently, but because he is sensitive and slow to adapt, he couldn't take it. Abruptly his face flushed red and he started to scream. The sobs came from deep inside him, totally overwhelming him."

Spillover meltdowns during infancy are often one of the first signs of spirit for families. For those like Travis the flood results in sobs that emerge from the soul. Their movements are jerky and their faces beet red. But not all spillover meltdowns look the same, especially as children grow and develop.

Casey, whose son Oscar has the gleam of spirit in his eyes, explained, "Oscar doesn't cry. Instead he goes into a frenzy of activity. Last Sunday we invited friends over for dinner. He was so excited that within minutes of their arrival his intensity was out of control. He was a flying saucer whirling around the room in every direction. It was impossible to stop him."

Courtney's son Jasper doesn't scream or act out. His intensity turns inward. "Last week Jasper couldn't tie his shoe," she told the group. "I could tell he was getting really frustrated, but he didn't holler; instead he fell face-first on the floor, his body sagging like a cardboard box left out in the rain. 'I can't do it,' he moaned, then began to weep."

Seven-year-old Luke bolts. "Whenever I tell him it's time to leave the park, he makes a run for it," Luke's dad confessed. "It makes my blood boil." Then, sighing, he admitted, "If I'm truthful, it scares me to death."

Whether your child screams in distress, whirls in a frenzy of excitement, runs away, or completely shuts down, it is critical to recognize that it is a spirited child swamped by his own emotions, pushed beyond his ability to cope. His brain has been hijacked. He does not know what to do about it, or how to stop it. You have to teach him.

USING WORDS

The problem, of course, is that people talk about meltdowns as though kids go out on an island and stand there and scream. Nobody talks about what it *feels* like to be the parent of the kid who can back up an entire checkout line while she gyrates on the floor and lets loose with bloodcurdling wails. Internet chats never discuss how to make excuses for being late because your child wouldn't get in the car (unless you are in the Raising Your Spirited Child Facebook Group, where these types of conversations are common!). And holiday stories fail to include the reality of watching in horror as your eight-year-old bursts into tears because Grandma didn't cut the cranberry gel into turkey shapes as she had done for the last eight years. Meltdowns—it isn't only the kids that are experiencing a major reaction. It's you, me, and any other parent that has to survive the penetrating intensity of spirited children.

Keeping your cool may seem an insurmountable feat. The harder you try to control your child, the more ineffective you feel. Your methods aren't working, but you don't know what to do differently. At this point it's not easy to calmly stop and ask, "What is this really about?" You might just want to scream right along with your child. But you don't have to and, for both your sake and your child's, you do not want to. Instead you can learn to take a deep breath and tell yourself, "My child is in a spillover meltdown. I don't have to go there too."

That one-second pause can make a huge difference in what happens next.

WHAT TO DO IN THE "HEAT OF THE MOMENT"

Today a simple request to get in the shower sparked the blowup. Yesterday it was homework. Earlier, dressing lit the fuse. Laura felt like she had become a character in an unsolvable mystery never knowing what would set off the shrieking, throwing, kicking, and pinching her daughter was prone to in these moments. Laura found herself getting more and more frustrated until she too was screaming and slamming doors. "We've tried everything," she told me when we talked. "We have yelled at her, taken away privileges, sent her to her room, and held her down."

Intimidation does not stop spillover meltdowns, but listening does.

STOP TO LISTEN: Your first reaction when a pillow has been thrown at your head might be to grab your child and scream, "What were you thinking?" A few threats or consequences could be tossed into the mix as well to ensure that your child clearly understands how upset you are with her. I'm going to advise you to resist. Don't get me wrong. Violent and destructive behaviors are unacceptable. You are going to deal with the behavior—but this is not the teachable moment—that will come later. First you have to help her recover from the physiological blast of hormones coursing through her body. Until her body is calmed, she cannot look at you, hear you, or think.

If your child is doing something that is unsafe, hurtful, or disrespectful to self, others, or the environment, you are going to stop it. (I'll give you more tips on how to do that later.) As you move to stop her, however, remind yourself, "My first job is to connect and calm." Use the statement you have chosen for the *pivotal moment* (discussed in chapter 7), such as "I will help." Then take a very long, deep breath and be empathetic, "I see you really do not want to take a shower." Resist stating the fact—you have to take a shower. Or preaching—you have to be clean. Empathy calms. Facts and preaching do not.

But don't stop yet. When I am conducting private consultations with families, I ask, "What do you think your child was feeling or needing in this situation?" All too frequently there is a long pause before they reply, "I never stopped to ask." In order to stop spillover meltdowns, you have to understand what is fueling them. Ask your child questions like: "What is the reason you do not want to take a shower?" Or, "What about these socks do you not like?" If your child has no answer, ask questions or use statements that demonstrate you are trying to understand. Think about what just happened. "Is it the water getting in your eyes or ears that you do not like?"

Run through a mental checklist of your child's temperament in order to identify the source of the flood. If she is an introvert and someone has moved into her space, ask her, "Was he crowding you?"

If adapting is challenging for your child, and there have been lots of transitions, you might say something like, "Did you need more time to finish your game?"

If your child is high energy and has not had any exercise, you might say, "You've sat quietly for a long time. Do you need time to run and play?"

If you have just said no to a persistent child, you could try, "Did it frustrate you when I said no?"

Whatever the trigger, identifying it allows you to stop it if you can. Naming it helps your child understand what is happening to him. This in itself is soothing because naming an emotion slows the heart rate. It also gives your child words to use the next time he experiences a similar rush of emotions or sensations.

Listening does not mean agreeing. It does not mean you are giving up your authority. Nor does it mean you are going to allow your child to "get away" with poor behavior. You're trying to calm her and understand the fuel source.

By the way, talk to spirited infants as you would an older child. You won't get the same kind of response, but someday, sooner than you might imagine, you will.

When I suggested this strategy to Laura, she groaned, "But it is so hard to stop and listen. I'm the kind of person who has a plan. I just want to get things finished."

Unfortunately, pushing harder when your child is resisting (a red-zone cue) only escalates the situation.

Ultimately, Laura figured out that her daughter Marcella is very sensitive. It was the water getting in her eyes and ears that led to Marcella's reluctance to shower. With that understanding Laura could now work with Marcella to come up with a solution. They could choose to bathe instead of showering. Or, Marcella might hold a wash cloth over her eyes. There are many potential solutions.

If Marcella resists, Laura can give her a few more minutes to calm and then establish a clear limit, "You need to be clean. You can think of a plan, or I will think of one, and mine is that I will hold the shower nozzle so we can direct the water away from your eyes. I'm going to set a timer for five minutes. If you do not have a plan, then we will use my plan."

When Laura used this strategy, Marcella immediately said, "I have a plan. I can take a bath."

I know you may fear that the first time you do this, you will get another meltdown because of the timer, but if you follow through, your child will learn that you do what you said you would do. As a result, she will quickly begin coming up with a plan. (I'll show you how to work together and establish clear expectations in chapters 9 and 10.)

At this point you may be sighing in relief. The meltdown is over. You would like to forget about it, but you must not. In order to prevent future meltdowns, you have to follow up.

WORKING TOGETHER: REDO—GOING BACK FOR THE TEACHABLE MOMENT

When your child has experienced a meltdown, it is critical to go back after she is calm to teach her more appropriate words to use and actions to take in the future. I call this a redo. A redo may occur moments after a meltdown, an hour later, or, with an older child, a day or two later—but it must happen.

There are four steps to a redo.

1. HELP YOUR CHILD UNDERSTAND WHAT SHE WAS FEELING OR NEEDING. Select a time when both you and your child are calm. Use your insights gained from understanding her temperament, your conversation with her, and your reflection on what happened before the meltdown to figure it out. What was she trying to communicate when she hit or yelled? When you talk with your child, make it an invitation to work together. You might say, "What happened today did not feel good to anyone. Let's make a plan so that it does not happen again. There is no need for a reprimand that would immediately put your child on the defensive. Knowing your child's temperament provides a guide to her emotions.

If your child is temperamentally . . .	What you can say:
slow to adapt and fell apart when you were running late and told her you could not stop at the ice cream store as planned.	I think I surprised you.
sensitive and lost it in the mall.	I'm wondering if the noise was bothering you.
persistent and refused to go along with your plan.	I'm wondering if you had a different plan.
irregular, skipped her nap, and fell apart at dinner.	I saw you yawn, and it made me think you were tired.
an extrovert and interrupted a conversation.	You like to be part of the conversation.

You'll notice there is no judgment in these words, as there would be if you said, "You were feeling mean today." They are also open ended, allowing for the possibility that you have guessed incorrectly. You are not *telling* your child what he was feeling, you are exploring what you think he *might* have been feeling. He'll let you know if you are wrong. Then you can converse more until you figure it out together.

2. CLARIFY THE EXPECTATION. Expectations focus on your family's values. You can design your own, but here are several that are important to me. In our family:

> No matter how angry we are, we may not hurt someone/ something.
> It's important to be respectful.
> It's important to work together.
> It's important to do what you said you would do.
> It's important to be clean.

3. TEACH THE WORDS OR ACTIONS YOU WANT YOUR CHILD TO USE NEXT TIME SHE EXPERIENCES THIS EMOTION OR NEED. Be specific.

> *Next time you can say:*
> "May I please take a bath so the water won't get in my eyes?"
> "That was a surprise. That's not what I expected."
> "It's too noisy in here. Could we please leave?"
> "I had a different plan. Mom, please listen to me."
> "I'm tired."
> "I don't like that rule. Could we please talk about it?"
> "It's hard to leave. Can we make a plan for when we'll come back again?"
> "That doesn't seem fair."

4. PRACTICE. It is critical that you and your child actually practice the words and actions you want him to use. If possible, go back to the scene of the meltdown. For example, if your child refused to hold your hand or ran away when you left school, once he is calm, go back inside. Walk out again, this time practicing holding hands in the parking lot.

When it is not possible to return to the real event, set the "stage" and act it out with him. If your child is an introvert who is uncomfortable practicing verbally, allow him to listen while you say it. You can ask him, "Do you want to say it, or would you like me to say it and you listen?" If he chooses to listen, model the actions or words for him, but then remind him, "Next time that's what I expect you to say or do."

Later Laura described to me the conversation that ensued with Marcella. "I waited until the next day," she told me. "We were alone together in her room when I said, 'What happened yesterday was really scary for everyone. Let's make a plan so it doesn't happen again.' Marcella was wary. We had never had a conversation like this before.

"I continued, 'I think yesterday you really had fun with your cousins. But you are an introvert. Do you remember what that means? It means that you like being with people but after a while you need a break. I think what happened is that you got worn out and needed some downtime. But right after they left, I asked you to take your shower. You don't like showers because you are sensitive and the water in your eyes irritates you.'

"It was going better than I expected," Laura admitted. "So I reminded her, 'No matter how angry we are, it's not okay to hurt someone.' Marcella looked downcast. I didn't want to dwell on it because I knew she felt bad. 'Let's make a plan,' I invited her. 'Next time you need more time before your shower, you can say, "Mom, may I have a few minutes first?" Or, "Mom, I'm so tired tonight, could I please have a bath instead?"' Marcella looked relieved.

"I knew we were supposed to practice so I invited her to try. 'Time for your shower,' I told her.

"'Mom, may I please take a bath instead of a shower,' she replied.

"We both started laughing and exchanged a high five. The conversation ended with me reminding her, 'Next time that's what I expect you to say.' Marcella bobbed her head in agreement."

REDO WITH TODDLERS: A redo with toddlers needs to be adjusted for their developmental stage. Everything in a toddler's brain is screaming, "Do it! Try it! Find out what will happen!" They also have short memories. Every time, you have to stop them, show them what to do instead.

When a toddler throws a truck at you, hold the truck and say, "You hand me the truck." Invite her to practice placing it in your hand. (Odds are someone has been teaching her to throw a ball. She hasn't figured out yet, we throw balls—but we hand toy trucks.)

Often, parents of spirited children are reluctant to revisit a meltdown. Fearing that doing so will trigger their child again, the subject is avoided. But it's during a redo that your child will gain an understanding of her emotions and learn the words to use and the actions to take. It's like handing her a safety harness to keep her from falling over the edge into the depths of the red zone.

You'll know your child is calm enough for a redo if he's able to look at you. His voice is normal. Limbs still. Ears open to your voice instead of noises around him. He is able to answer your questions. If this is not the case, set him up with his calming basket, or if he's four or older, have him take a break until he is calm. If your child is a toddler, you'll want to follow up quickly, while she still remembers the incident.

MAKING AMENDS: If there has been a "victim" during the spillover meltdown, the redo will also need to include making amends. Once your child has calmed, bring her back together with the victim. Teach her to ask him what he needs. Does he need ice or a Band-Aid? Does he need a hug? Does he need to know you'll play later? Whatever he needs, the protagonist needs to get it for him.

You'll notice that making amends does not force an apology. That's because an obligatory "sorry" is meaningless. When you focus on the needs of the victim, you teach empathy. The result can be remarkable.

After the shower incident, without any prompting Marcella spent thirty minutes handwriting Laura a card that said, in her six-year-old printing skills, "I soree." It was sincere.

GOING BACK FOR YOUR OWN REDO: If we are honest with ourselves, we'll realize that perhaps we played a role in the meltdown too. Not intentionally, of course, but because we too are learners. After a meltdown, think about what happened. Is there anything you could do differently in the future that would help both you and your child stay out of the red zone?

When I asked Laura this question, she replied, "I'm an introvert too. Looking back, I needed a break after the cousins as much as Marcella did. In the future I'm going to plan breaks between major transitions. A few minutes is all we need, but those minutes are crucial."

Laura also recognized that because she was low on energy, she'd missed Marcella's cues that indicated she was moving into the yellow zone—heading toward red. She vowed to pay closer attention.

WHEN YOUR CHILD IS HITTING, KICKING, AND THROWING THINGS: If you change your approach to stop and listen first, you will drastically reduce the odds that your child will get to the point of hitting, kicking, or destroying things. But if despite your efforts to understand what is happening, he still gets to that point, you'll have to stop him. Again, in a firm but calm voice say to him, "If you cannot stop yourself, I will help you." Or, "I cannot allow you to hurt yourself or others." Take a younger child onto your lap. Sitting on the floor, legs outstretched in front of you, place him facing the same direction as you are. Wrap your legs around his so he cannot kick you. Fold your arms around him so he cannot hit you. Hold firmly so that he cannot head butt or bite you, but do not squeeze. Breathe deeply. Tell yourself the following: "He's flooded." "His brain has been hijacked." "He's not doing this 'to me.'" These thoughts will help you remain calmer. Remember, on an airplane you are directed to put on your oxygen mask first. Calm yourself so you can calm him.

It is likely that your child will scream "Let me go!" Assure him that as soon as his voice is soft and his legs and arms are still, you will. Hold him gently but firmly until he calms. Invite him to breathe with you. When he settles, let him go. If he begins thrashing again, hold him once more telling him, "I can see you are not yet ready." Continue embracing him until he is calm.

WHEN YOUR CHILD YELLS, OR SWEARS AT YOU, OR CALLS YOU NAMES: It's not unusual in the midst of a meltdown for your child to hurl nasty words. This is actually progress—he's using words, not hitting. But of course they are not acceptable.

Don't take the bait. You will deal with this later; right now you are attempting to help him pull out of the dive. In a firm but gentle voice say to him, "I know you are really mad at me right now. Try that again. Say it in a way that makes me want to listen." Then wait. Repeat if necessary. "I will help you. Try that again."

A child who is screaming "I hate you!" or "I'm going to whack you in the head" is often a child who is angry about not being listened to or feeling that something was unfair. Now is your chance to help him understand that strong emotions do not need to be feared, but they do need to be expressed respectfully. Pay attention. Let him know you understand he is angry. You will deal with the offensive words once he's calm. It's then you will teach him to say "I don't think that's fair," instead of "I hate you."

Toddlers frequently scream in frustration when they do not have the words to tell you they want the toy you just put away. Due to their intensity it is tempting to immediately stop the shrieking by giving them what they want. However, doing so innocently reinforces this behavior. This is the testing-of-limits meltdown I referred to at the beginning of the chapter. Intense children who have been "rewarded" for screaming continue to do so long after they have the words to ask more appropriately. That's why it is very important that when your child shrieks, you go to him. Connect and calm by saying, "I'm listening. I will help you." Then request that he say it appropriately: "Toy, please." Wait until he does so. Do NOT give him what he wants until he has quieted. Initially, because you are teaching him to stop and try again, you'll then give him what he wants when he asks in a respectful tone. (Affirm even the slightest change in voice tone in the beginning.) Once he has learned to use a more respectful voice, then you will expect him to work with you to come up with a solution that is acceptable to both of you. (More about that in chapter 9.)

BE PRESENT AND OFFER TOUCH: Not every child's brain goes into "fight" mode when experiencing a spillover meltdown; some shut down like a deer in headlights and simply need time and space to recover. Your presence is essential. I was observing at a child-care center one morning when a mom dropped off her preschooler. The little girl started to scream and kick the minute Mom started out the door. I recognized a slow-to-adapt child who was having trouble with a transition, but the teachers and her mom weren't familiar with temperament and didn't understand what was happening. They sent her to the corner to cry it out on her own while they went on with their business. I moved close to her. She didn't know me, and I sensed that she did not want me to touch her. Keeping my body relaxed, I told her I would not come near her unless she wanted me to. I sat on the floor close by, present and available. Gradually she moved nearer until her head rested on my lap. Only then did she stop crying.

To be left alone with such strong emotions can be very frightening to children. They need your calm physical presence to let them know that you care and that you are available.

If a hug will calm your child, give it to her. Do not worry about creating a bad habit. Even if you believe it's what she wants and fear that doing so will reinforce poor behavior, do it. If she had fallen and skinned a knee, you would offer comfort. During a meltdown she is experiencing emotional pain. She needs your compassion.

John Gottman calls this a sliding-door moment. Your child expresses a need for connection. You have a choice. If you slide the door open and walk through, you let your child know you are there to help her. If you shut it and turn away, you force your child to escalate to draw you back. Responding warmly is not a "bad habit." Touch increases the level of soothing, calming hormones in your child's body, slows her pulse rate, and stops the flood. The great thing about a hug is that it is good for your heart too.

If you find you are getting upset, you may need to walk away for a few minutes. Tell your child you are stepping away to calm yourself, but assure her that you will be back. You are not "breaking off." You are taking a break. That's a good thing.

GIVE YOUR CHILD SPACE: Sometimes, rather than soothing, touch may add to the intensity of spirited children. This is especially true for those who are more introverted. These children need their space. They'll let you know by withdrawing, or pushing your hand away. Or they'll say things like: "Don't look at me!" "Go away." Or, "Get out of my room!" If this is true for your children, and they are preschoolers or older and not hurting themselves or anything else, respect their boundaries and move away slightly. Let them know you'll be checking back. You are available. You care. Recognize that later in a redo you will teach them more appropriate words, such as: "I need some space right now." Or, "I will be ready to talk after I take a break." Or, "I just need a few minutes."

Christina agreed. "The worst thing I can do is try to pick Rowan up. He needs to be near me, but he doesn't want to be held."

If you are an extroverted parent, it's often very difficult for you to not touch your child or talk through the problem. When he's upset, you see his withdrawal or hear his cries as a request for contact. That's because when you are upset, touch and connection are often what you prefer and need. But this is where you have to make the effort to stop your initial, "natural" reaction and instead respect your child's need for space and quiet. He'll be ready to cuddle or talk with you soon; it will just be a little bit later. You can tell him, "I will not touch you, but I will stay near you until your body is calm."

ENCOURAGE YOUR CHILD TO MOVE: When your child slips into a spillover meltdown, blood rushes to his muscles, and adrenaline and cortisol, the stress hormones, are released into his system, telling him to move. This is why your child may "bolt." He needs a release for all of that energy. We just have to teach him how to get it safely and appropriately. If he's little, take him by the hand and walk briskly with him. If he's older, encourage him to get up and pace up and down the hallway, climb some stairs, or move his body in some other way. If he is older and needs to run, help him find a safe place to do so like running around the outside of the house, or go with him to a local track, playground, or park.

I prefer to direct the movement to the legs rather than the hands or arms, which means I don't encourage kids to punch a bag or pillow. I want them to have physical outlets that they can use at school and ultimately in the workplace. It's almost always acceptable to get up and get a drink of water or go to a restroom, but it's rarely acceptable to pound a table.

WHEN YOU ARE IN PUBLIC, TALK OUT LOUD: Maggie listened attentively as we discussed how to cope with the spillover meltdowns and then shook her head. "At home I can give him a hug or move with him, and it works perfectly. I can feel him relax. He starts talking, the tone of his voice changes from whining to conversational. But I've tried the same thing at the grocery store, and it doesn't work."

There's nothing like a child losing it in a restaurant, place of worship, or at a family gathering. The challenge with public situations is that it's harder to slow the heart rate and calm the body because of higher stimulation levels. Often, too, you're not focused on your child, and as a result, the intensity is very high before you ever realize it. Also, there's always the pressure of others' expectations and social rules on you—and your child.

Alice Honig, professor at Syracuse University, says, "Forget about the strangers. You'll never see them again anyway." Take care of yourself and your child. If you're with friends or family, ask for help. If you're not comfortable doing that, focus on what you need to do to calm yourself and then your child. Know that you'll deal with the relatives or the other parents on the playground later.

As you calm your child, raise your voice enough for the others around you to hear your clear, confident tone. It will make you feel better that they know you are handling the situation effectively. It also keeps them from offering unwanted advice.

"We had just finished eating at a restaurant," Hillary explained during a class on tantrums. "Wyatt didn't want to leave. He was coloring the placemat and wanted to finish. I couldn't wait for him because I needed to pick up my daughter at school. 'Time to go,' I told him.

"He started to squirm and protest. I knew I wasn't going to get him out of there easily. Everyone was looking at us. I started talking out loud. 'I know it's hard for you to leave. You haven't had a chance to finish your picture. We have to pick up your sister; you can take it with you and finish it at home.' I don't know if it helped him, but it kept me under control."

Don't second-guess those around you. If they are strangers, who cares what they think? If they are friends, they'll support you, and if they don't, they're probably not really friends anyway. If they're relatives, listen to them and then decide what you want to do with their advice. It may be helpful or it may not fit your child. You can decide.

SPANKING DOESN'T WORK: In fact, it only intensifies the reaction and sends the child over the edge because it adds to the flood of emotions. And let's be honest—if we are hitting, we are experiencing our own spillover meltdown. My advice, my plea, is *DO NOT* spank the spirited child. Behind the tough-cookie demeanor of a spirited child is a very soft center. And because of the penetrating intensity of a spirited child, it is very easy for the spanking to get out of control.

LOOK FOR THE FUEL SOURCE

Spillover meltdowns feel awful to everyone involved. Recognizing common fuel sources helps you prevent the meltdowns from occurring in the first place.

PEAK TIMES

Spillover meltdowns can occur at any time of the day or week, but there appear to be certain peak occasions when you really need to be prepared. I once asked a group of parents when their children experienced the most spillover meltdowns. They told me between four and six P.M. I didn't hear their response correctly and thought they had said, "When their parents wanted to have sex," which could be true too. The time of the day or the situations in which your child loses it may vary with every child, but merely understanding that there are peak periods for spillover meltdowns can help you to tune in to his cues and be more patient.

LATE AFTERNOONS: A high frequency of meltdowns occur during the late afternoon because it's easier to flood when everyone is tired and hungry, when you've had the whole day to collect sensations, or when the transitions have piled up. If this is happening, it's *very* likely that your child is short on sleep. Record how much sleep your child is getting and note the difference in his behavior according to how much sleep he has had. In my private practice I've found that over 90 percent of the children experiencing daily meltdowns are sleep deprived. This is true for all ages, toddlers to teens. If there is one magic cure for meltdowns, it's adequate sleep.

On the days when your child hasn't gotten the sleep he needs, or when he's experienced a time-zone change, think carefully about your plans for late afternoon. Consider dropping one or more activities, especially those that require your child to work with others, stay focused, block out stimulation, or control his body. He just doesn't have the energy to do it at this time of the day. He floods more easily when he's short on sleep. It's also very likely that you will have less energy to help him.

MORNINGS: It's tricky for all children to get up, get dressed, and say good-bye, but when your child is slow to adapt, sensitive, and intense, mornings can be ripe for spillover meltdowns. Not only does the slow-to-adapt child find it challenging to move from one task to another in the morning, but his brain also struggles to shift from being asleep to being awake. If you have to wake your child in the morning, the odds are significantly increased that he'll experience a meltdown.

In order to ease those morning meltdowns, avoid rushing. Allow your child enough time to awaken slowly before he has to act. Get as much as you can of the morning routine set up the night before. Include time to connect and cuddle. A few minutes spent eating together and time to empathize with how hard it is to get going and to say good-bye can help prevent the morning spillover.

WHEN YOUR STRESS IS HIGH: When I was first asked to speak about spirited children, the requests came from local community groups and churches, so I often had supper with my family and then dashed off to conduct the workshop. Inevitably, it seemed that as I sprinted out the door to tell other parents how to work effectively with their spirited children, I was screaming at my own. Frustrated and even more embarrassed, I found myself yelling back one night, "I can't do this! I'm a fraud! How can I tell other people how to work effectively with their spirited child when I'm screaming at mine?"

Fortunately, I figured out that Joshua was picking up my anxiety about the speaking engagements. As the tension built and I withdrew into myself and away from him, I frightened him. Everything in his little brain told him to go after me and get me back—and he did. Unfortunately, I didn't recognize what he was doing, and because he was young and unskilled, his methods left much to be desired. We both ended up even more distressed.

Once I understood what was happening, I chose to spend time with him before leaving and then to depart before my anxiety started to peak. Instead of fighting with him in the kitchen, I sat in the parking lot at the workshop location until it was time to set up. The difference was huge. Instead of screams, we separated with kisses and hugs. Our parting was peaceful, and I didn't feel like a fraud.

Your spirited child picks up your stress like a top-of-the-line vacuum. His spillover meltdowns are a warning sign.

Stop and think about what's been happening. Has one parent been traveling more or working longer hours? Are you worried about job security? Has there been a new addition to the family? Was someone ill? Did you experience a significant disruption in your schedule? Are you experiencing marital conflict? Has there been a natural disaster? Spirited children suck it all up, absorbing it until they burst. No one is immune to life's stressful events, but by monitoring your own stress levels you can protect your child.

"I'd been working in L.A. all week," Andrea told us. "When I walked in the door, I found the kitchen a mess and the grocery list I'd left on the counter as a 'hint' to my husband still sitting there. I was furious. Libby, my spirited one, picked up my stress, immediately demanding my attention. 'Mom, will you drop me off at my friend's house? Mom, you're not listening to me!'

"I could feel my face flushing, but fortunately before I started yelling, I stopped and thought, 'What am I feeling? What do I need?' I realized I was utterly exhausted, and I wanted my husband to read my mind that we needed groceries and he should get them. Reality check: I had never asked him to do it. I'd merely left the list in sight. It wasn't fair to be angry at him. And I had promised Libby that when I got home, she could play with her friend. I sat down. 'Just give me a minute,' I said. 'I need a minute to rest.' After just a few minutes, we were able to work together."

By managing your stress, you provide the steadying hand for your child. When you recognize that you are on the verge of your own spillover meltdown, acknowledge that what you are doing isn't working and choose to do something different.

Consider playing with your child. Select an activity that leaves both of you giggling, reminding you of how much fun this child can be. Sit down in a comfy rocker and read together. The repetitive motion will soothe both of you. Get outside—everything feels more manageable when you're in the open air. If it's nasty or dark outside, pop everyone into the tub.

By recognizing your own emotions and needs, you really can help your child avoid slipping into the depths of a spillover meltdown.

DEVELOPMENTAL SURGES: Kids go through developmental surges. You can mark it on your calendar. Somewhere around their birthday *and* their half birthday, you can expect trouble. You'll also want to note significant developmental changes like learning to walk, shooting up in height, or hitting puberty. Starting school, entering middle school, or other significant developmental points are also tender for meltdowns.

You'll know a developmental surge is striking because your children will get cranky and uncooperative. They might be incapable of doing what they were able to do just a few weeks before. Nothing seems right. They're easily frustrated. Every time you turn around, they're crying about something else. They won't cooperate. They want to be held and then push you away when you hold them. They're angry—angry at you, at the world, and at themselves. They are *more* easily upset by *anything*.

The developmental theorists tell us that this is a time of disintegration, a time when children are moving from one stage of development to another. Their inner systems are restructuring, creating a new, more complex way of understanding the world.

Think of five building blocks. Stack them one on top of the other until you have a tower of five blocks. This is your five-year-old—his inner structure that controls how he sees the world and responds to it. It works well for him, but as he nears his sixth birthday, changes begin to occur. A new block will be added to the structure, but it won't just be added to the top of the stack. Instead, the tower will come crashing down; it will disintegrate and a new structure with six blocks will be formed. This time it may be in the shape of a pyramid, with three blocks on the bottom, two in the middle, and the sixth resting on top. It will be a totally different structure. During this construction, which can take three to six weeks, everything that was working well for your child doesn't seem to be operating anymore. He becomes overwhelmed easily and is more vulnerable to spillover meltdowns.

Slow down the schedule. Be proactive. During growth spurts children regress. The child who could dress himself yesterday is suddenly incapable of putting on his own socks. Expect it and stay a step ahead of him so you don't feel "manipulated." Before he demands your help, ask him, "Is today a day you need help dressing, or can you do it yourself?" If he says he needs help, help him. But gently nudge him forward by saying, "Maybe tomorrow you'll be ready to do it yourself and then we'll have time to read together." One day soon, he will.

Developmental surges happen to all kids, but as is always true for spirited children, their reactions are much stronger. Mark your calendar and be ready for the surges.

EMPTY ENERGY BANKS: Empty energy banks can also lead to spillover meltdowns. If your child is an introvert and hasn't had any time alone to recharge, she'll be on edge. Another child merely "looking at her," much less moving into her space, can send her to the moon. If your child is an extrovert and hasn't had an opportunity to play with other children or interact with you, expect her to lose it. When coping levels are low, there's nothing to stop the flood of emotions.

FEAR: "This is stupid." "I won't!" "You can't make me!" Spill-over meltdowns often occur in new situations or when spirited children are afraid they may make a mistake. Unfortunately, when they do not understand that fear, instead of telling us they are afraid, they become resistant and nasty, often spewing words that push us away when what they actually need is our support.

Recognize that opposition is likely fear and talk about it. Break new skills into small, easily accomplished steps. Success builds on success. Fear eases as your child moves from one step to the next.

This is just a sample of common fuel sources behind spillover meltdowns. Observe closely to discover when your child is most vulnerable.

SAVOR SUCCESSES: We help our spirited children manage their strong feelings best by focusing on what they did right. Learning to put on the brakes takes time. It's important to celebrate along the way. Savor the little successes. Tell your child: "You were very upset, but you remembered not to hit me." Or, "I heard you say you were getting frustrated. You're really growing up." Or, "I saw you walk away instead of pushing your brother. You must be proud of yourself." Focus on what your child did that was appropriate. This is the action you want to see repeated in the future. Look for it. There is always something that she did right. Find it.

TAKE CARE OF YOURSELF: Meltdowns are exhausting for everyone. At the end of a long, emotional day, call a sitter and plan a night out, or hop into a hot bath, or simply allow yourself an early night to bed. Handling meltdowns drains moms and dads. Take care of yourself. Then you can be loyal to your child.

WHEN THE MELTDOWNS DON'T STOP

There are times when, despite your best efforts to understand your child's intensity and teach him effective ways to diffuse and use it, the meltdowns continue. If you find yourself angry, resenting your child, unable to see his potential, or dreading another day with him, it's time to enlist professional help. Potentially you are dealing with a medical issue as well as a spirited temperament. Or a medical issue rather than a temperament one. Follow your gut. There really are people who can help you.

Make that appointment. Take care of your relationship, and get your child the support and services he needs to be successful. Children are not replaceable. Now is the time to build your relationship for a lifetime. It is worth the time, effort, and money.

SPILLOVER MELTDOWNS
A Summary

The steamy reactions of spirited kids make them much more vulnerable to spillover meltdowns—a flood of emotions that overwhelms them and pushes them beyond their ability to cope.

> *Spirited kids experiencing a spillover meltdown*
> *need to hear:*
> This is a flood.
> You are being overwhelmed by your emotions.
> I am here. I will help you.
> It is all right to cry, but you may not kick or bite.
> If we can, we will stop what is flooding you.

Teaching tips:

Stay with or near your child. To be left alone with such strong emotions can be very frightening to your child.

Run through a mental checklist of your child's temperament in order to identify the source of the flood (too many transitions, an overload of stimulation, etc.). Stop it if you can.

Reduce the demands on your child during peak meltdown times, especially late afternoons, during developmental surges, when your stress is high, and when energy banks are low.

Ensure that your child gets the sleep he needs.

Do not spank your child. Spanking can easily get out of hand when everyone is upset.

Go back later when everyone is calm to help your child understand what she was feeling and teach her more appropriate words and actions to use.

Savor successes—even if they are small.

Dealing with your own strong feelings:

Recognize that your child is overwhelmed.

Take care of yourself so you will have the energy to help your child.

If the meltdowns continue despite your best efforts, know when to enlist the help of professionals.

9

Persistence

Choosing Your Battles—
When to Say Yes

The difference between perseverance and obstinacy
is that one comes from a strong will
and the other from a strong won't.
—Henry Ward Beecher

When my daughter went off to college, she selected a university tucked in a valley surrounded by mountains. One fall day she and another young woman decided that they would go hiking. It was a beautiful, warm day in the valley, so they didn't really think about being prepared for the mountains. Imagine their surprise when, after driving several thousand feet higher and going off onto a logging road, they found themselves stuck in two feet of snow. They had no shovel with them. No coats, no one knew where they were, and their cell phone had no reception.

I asked her, "What did you do?"

"Well, Mom," she replied dryly, "I have to admit at first it was a bit scary and my friend was freaking out. But I took a deep breath and told her, 'Sarah, I come from a problem-solving family!' It was enough to make her laugh and calm us both down. Then we got out, started searching in the trunk, and found a coffee can. We used it to dig ourselves out."

When I tell this story in my workshops, the audience inevitably laughs, but *"We're a problem-solving family"* is actually a very powerful statement. It is a phrase that immediately connotes that in this family we listen to one another and work together. Problem solving with others is an essential skill for persistent children.

Living with the "raw gem" of a persistent child is not easy. To tell these kids no, to thwart their efforts, is to risk their wrath. Even as infants they are incredibly determined and strong. They push where other kids don't push. They demand more than other kids demand. And they never give up. It is nearly impossible to ignore them or distract them.

Persistence is the temperamental trait that plays a major role in power struggles. Unrefined it can provoke daily tugs of war that leave both your arms and heart aching. When you have a persistent child, it's crucial to stop tugging on opposite ends of that rope, and instead team up. If your child pulls east (declaring, "I won't"), don't dig in your heels and pull west (retorting, "Yes, you will"). Instead, loosen your grip and step to the north (saying, "Let's work together"). When you do so, your child will relax, and step north too, allowing you to travel forward as a team—at least most of the time. You don't have to fight every day. You can be a problem-solving family where persistence and commitment to one's goals are celebrated, and the ability to work with others is a honed skill. It begins by talking about persistence.

USING WORDS

Persistence is a key predictor of future success. Tenacity can even trump talent. Perseverance, determination, grit, and diligence are all synonyms for persistence. Martin Luther King and the Wright brothers were very persistent individuals. Spirited kids need to hear from us that we value their persistence.

"I used to go crazy," Kim told me during an interview. "Whenever I would tell my daughter to do something, she would insist on doing it her way. It wasn't until I took a look at my own temperament that I realized I was persistent too. It's true that there have been times when my persistence has gotten me into trouble, but for the most part it really has been an asset for me. Now when she says she wants something different, at least I can listen without getting upset. I don't discourage her determination."

Look at your labels—the words you use to describe persistence. Do they help your child understand and feel good about it?

> *Persistent spirited kids need to hear phrases like:*
> You are committed and decisive.
> You know what you want.
> You're assertive.
> Your friends will never talk you into doing something you
>   do not want to do.
> You are independent and capable.
> You have the drive to achieve great things.

When children hear these words, they quickly learn to turn them into messages they can use to work with others:

I have an idea.
Could we talk about this?
Let's make a plan.
Let's work together.
I know I can accomplish this!

When we appreciate our children's persistence and give them the words to express their determination respectfully, they are more open to working with us. They view us as a helpful resource rather than a brick wall hindering their efforts. It is our task to encourage their persistence and at the same time teach them to respect us, other people, and the world around them. For us it is a matter of learning to recognize that "Yes—we can work together" is a very acceptable and healthy answer. It is a mind-set that instills a can-do sense of resiliency in our children that will protect them all through their lives.

GOOD PARENTS DO SAY YES

Choosing to solve problems together is a process in which you and the other side have some interests that are shared and others that are opposed. In order to reach an agreement that both of you can accept, you communicate back and forth. Most of us have had the experience of being told that back-and-forth communication meant talking back to our parents—a taboo behavior on our part. Working together to reach agreement was not an obvious goal. If Dad told us to do something, we were supposed to carry it out whether we agreed or not. Negotiation was not an option. The reason is that in the past we thought there were only two possible outcomes: you win, or I win. Fortunately, there is another way that leads to a win-win solution.

Becoming a problem-solving family doesn't lock us into wrestling matches designed to determine a winner and a loser. It focuses not on what each side says it will or won't do but on finding common interests and solutions. It brings down the intensity, allows creative problem solving, and fosters a sense of teamwork: two individuals working together, respecting each other, and finding solutions that allow both a sense of dignity and personal power. This is the kind of relationship that keeps our spirited kids working with us—and can even make the teen years much easier to manage.

Becoming a problem-solving family involves three steps:

1. **Y**ou seek understanding of what is important to your child.
2. **E**xplain what is important to you.
3. **S**olve the problem together.

Put those steps together and you get YES!

You Seek Understanding

Choosing to seek understanding first does not imply giving up your authority. Winning coaches have a plethora of strategies from which they pull. Depending on the situation, they can opt to seek understanding, hold the line, or let go. It's a choice they control as the leader on life's playing field.

My colleague Lynn recently demonstrated this. Paidea Child Development Center, which Lynn owns and directs, is open from 6:45 A.M. until 6:00 P.M. Within those hours the school day runs from 9:00 A.M. to 4:30 P.M. The rule is that during the nonschool hours children can have a toy from home to share with their friends or play with by themselves. But at 9:00 A.M. all home toys must be tucked away in a child's cubby until the end of the school day.

On this morning Jacob had brought his favorite dinosaur to Paidea. When his teachers told him the school day was about to begin and it was time to put away his dinosaur, Jacob lost it. That's when Lynn walked into the classroom.

"You really want your dinosaur," she offered.

Jacob protested, "It's not a home toy."

"Oh, is that dinosaur for everyone?" Lynn inquired. "If it's only for you, it's a home toy. Paidea toys are for everyone." And then she simply paused, letting it sink in for a moment before continuing, "It's yours, so do you want to put in it my office or in your cubby to keep it safe until you can play with it again?"

Jacob thought for a moment before replying, "Your office," then walked with Lynn to put it there.

Stopping to seek understanding doesn't require convincing a child he is wrong. It does not necessitate that he agree with you. Nor does it imply that you will just do what he wants without consideration for your own interests. It's simply a process of understanding what the child is thinking and feeling. Seeking understanding gives you the information you need to make a decision about what to do next.

The key to seeking understanding is being a good listener.

BECOMING A "GOOD" LISTENER: During class one day I asked the group, "How do you know if someone is listening to you?" Followed by the question, "How do you know if someone is NOT listening to you?" A quick brainstorming provided us with this list:

You know someone is listening to you if she . . .	You know someone is NOT listening if she . . .
looks at you.	doesn't look at you.
is calm.	interrupts you.
focuses on you and what you are saying.	is doing other things.
responds in ways that fit what you are talking about.	responds inappropriately or off topic.
is not doing something else.	rolls her eyes.
nods.	has a glazed look.
lets her arms lie relaxed near her body.	crosses her arms across her chest.
has a look on her face that "fits" what is being said.	frowns, or looks down her nose, as though ready to pounce.

Abby reflected, "I can always tell when I'm on the phone talking to my brother if he's on the computer. I know by his responses that he's not really listening."

Looking at the "not listening" list, Crystal quipped, "That's my house every day."

"Let's see what this feels like," I directed the group. "Find a partner. One of you will be the speaker and one of you the listener. If you are a speaker, share something that is important to you. Listeners, use the good-listener skills."

I quickly lost the group in deep conversations. Laughter resounding and heads nodding, their bodies moved toward one another as they engaged. I had to flicker the lights to catch their attention. "What did that feel like?" I asked.

"Really validating," Maddie replied. "I wanted to share more."

Steve agreed, "Good. I felt respected."

"Switch roles," I directed. "If you were the speaker, you are now the listener, but this time I want listeners to NOT listen." Voices erupted, rapidly gaining volume. Suddenly Abby was shouting and when Heather actually pushed Rob, I stopped the activity. "Whoa, how did that feel?" I asked.

Heather glared. "He kept looking at his phone. He wasn't even listening to me!"

"Really crappy," Abby proclaimed shaking her head.

Shrugging Matt stated, "I just stopped talking."

When we don't *really* listen to our kids, they feel the same way.

Choosing to listen requires a commitment on our part to stop multitasking or thinking about what we want to say instead of focusing on what our child has to say. We have to check our body language to ensure that it's communicating, "I want to understand." When you choose to fully engage you'll discover that listening diffuses your child's defensiveness.

If you find yourself too upset to focus, you may have to go back to the "keeping your cool" techniques, explained in chapter 6, and say to your child, "Wait. I have to have a minute for myself before I can really listen to you." Then step back, take a breath, and cool yourself down. Once you are calm, you can continue seeking understanding.

After completing this exercise, I asked the parents to think back to the last time they argued with their persistent kids. "What did you fight about?" I asked. It was an easy question. Their answers were immediate.

"Yesterday at lunch," Christopher said, "I asked Dylan if he wanted water or milk. His answer was, 'I want soda.'"

"Lunch was our battleground too," Crystal added. "I told my ten-year-old to sit down for lunch. She insisted she wasn't hungry and wanted to go to her friend's house."

When you ask your child if he wants water or milk for lunch and he replies "I want soda," you have each taken a position— water and milk versus soda. Positions express what you want. They can be anything from "I want to" versus "I won't let you" to "I want to go visit a friend" versus "You'll sit here and have lunch."

These are positions that slam us into corners every time. Like two boxers in the ring, we can almost hear a gong ringing in our heads, marking the beginning of the fight. The question hangs in the air: Who will win and who will lose? The challenge is to get out of our corners and find a solution that is acceptable to both of us; to focus on our common interests—*why* we want this—rather than on our positions—*what* we want. Instead of grabbing our gloves, we can teach ourselves to stop and seek clarification of *why* this is important. We begin by asking "What's up?"

WHAT'S UP: Every time you and your child lock into a position, there is a reason: an interest or need you are trying to meet. In order to resolve our differences, we have to clarify those interests. *Why* is this important? When your child's position is different from yours, resist pushing harder or beginning the conversation with criticism or contempt. Instead, remain open to understanding what's important to your child. What is she feeling or needing?

In class I asked Christopher what he thought was important to Dylan about soda.

"Maybe he wanted it because I hid soda in my coffee cup?" He laughed. The group chuckled with him—we'd all tried that a few times.

"What other reason might he have had?" I asked the group, just to be sure we explored all of the possible interests.

"Maybe he's sick of milk and water," Greg suggested.

"My daughter likes ice cubes," Stephanie said. "She wants soda so she can get the ice cubes."

I asked a similar question of Crystal. "Why do you think your daughter wanted to skip lunch and go to a friend's house?"

"She'd been playing alone all morning," Crystal answered. "She's an extrovert, and I'm sure she was ready to recharge."

"What other reasons could there be?" I asked.

"Maybe she wasn't hungry," Crystal offered.

Whatever the feeling or need, it's important to do our best to figure it out. Get down to eye level with your child and start listening—really listening. Invite your child to tell you more. "What about going to your friend's house is so important?" You'll notice I used the word *what* not *why*. Children typically find it very difficult to discern *why* they are feeling or needing something.

If your child is too young to answer you, or offers you no response, you may have to guess by describing what you see, hear, or know about the situation: "I see you don't want to eat lunch today. What's up?" Or, "I hear you saying you do not want to leave. What's up?" "Are you sad because Mom is gone?" "You have been home all morning. Do you need to get out?"

If you stay tuned in, you'll know what has been occurring and recognize that your child wanted a toy or is feeling drained. Feel free to throw in a little humor by saying something silly: "Are you mad because there are no elephants in the yard?"

Even a two-year-old will begin to realize that you are trying to understand what is important to her. Her tension will diminish as you try.

Dig deep. If your child's response is something that sounds ridiculous to you, keep digging. One day while I was visiting Paidea, three-year-old Lily refused to put her coat on to go outside. I watched as Tammy, her teacher said to her, "I see you don't want to put your coat on today. What's up?"

"It's too windy," Lily declared.

It wasn't windy, but rather than disagreeing with her, Tammy clarified, "Oh, you don't want to go outside because it's too windy?"

Lily nodded, this time adding, "And there is a big garbage truck in the parking lot."

"Oh," Tammy replied, checking to be certain she fully understood. "You want to stay inside because there is a big garbage truck out there, not because it's too windy." Lily sighed, her shoulders relaxing as she realized her teacher had helped her figure out what was really going on. Lily was afraid of the big, noisy truck.

Digging deeper may feel uncomfortable to you. In class Casey told us, "I would ask Leo what he was feeling, but he'd reply, 'Nothing.' That would stop me cold. I didn't want to steamroll him. I thought prying would just make it worse. But when I pointed out to him that he was saying nothing was wrong, but I could see a frown on his face, it was as though a lightbulb went off in his head. A channel opened allowing him to express himself."

Don't be afraid to dig deep. But do check your tone of voice and monitor the questions you are asking. If you hear yourself saying things like "Why are you pouting?" or "Why are you angry—again!" your words carry judgment. You sound more like an intimidator interrogating a witness than someone who is seeking understanding. Remember too you are not trying to cheer up your child or talk him out of feeling as he does. If no words come to mind, simply ask, "What's up? Tell me more. I really want to understand," and "Is there anything else you want me to know?" You will recognize that you truly understand what your child is feeling when you see his body relax.

Once you have gained that understanding, it's your turn to explain what's important to you. Knowing that can help you to avoid getting pulled into a power struggle—which happened to me the other day when I was attempting to seek understanding. Dismayed, I called Lynn, "Help me understand what happened. I just lost it!"

She reminded me, "Listening doesn't mean you are going to give up anything that is important to you."

My blood pressure dropped precipitously. (Later I repeated to myself, "It's a never-ending process—progress, not perfection, is our goal.")

Explaining What Is Important to You

It takes two to lock into positions, and it takes two to unlock. Your interest is just as important as your child's. It is during this step that you not only get to communicate to your child what is important to you, but impart your family values as well. It might seem faster and easier to insist that your child comply by declaring, "Because I said so!" But without conversation, your child has no idea why this particular issue is important to you. Taking the time to explain clarifies your values. Your child now has the information she needs to make them her own.

Turning back to Christopher in class I asked, "Why did you want Dylan to have milk or water?"

"Because that was the only thing left in the refrigerator," he responded.

"What other reasons might we have?" I asked the group.

"Good nutrition," Stephanie offered.

"What about you, Crystal?" I asked. "Why did you want your daughter to eat lunch?"

"Because she goes crazy if she doesn't eat," she answered. "And anyway, I didn't want to be making lunch again at two o'clock."

Explaining what's important to you does not include preaching or accusing, as in "I did not like the rude way you talked to me." It is a simple statement you own, like:

> I expect to be treated respectfully.
> I am worried that if you don't eat you'll feel awful.
> I need to know you are eating nutritiously.
> It's important to me that you are safe.
> It's important to me to be on time.

Stating what is important to you helps you to clarify your own feelings and needs. When you begin to look at why you are both in positions, you will realize there is a reason other than determining a winner or a loser. Now that it's clear what is important to *both* you and your child, you are ready to solve the problem together.

Solving the Problem Together

"How could we make this better?" Tammy asked Lily. "You want to stay inside because there is a big garbage truck out there, not because it's too windy. I am worried that there are no teachers inside and it would not be safe for you to stay inside. Can you think of three things we could do to make this better?"

Lily frowned. "But I don't want to go outside."

"Well, what if you put on your coat and I wait with you until the garbage truck leaves? Then we'll go out to the playground together." Lily put on her coat and once the garbage truck roared away, walked out holding Tammy's hand.

Solving the problem together means addressing the interests of *both* parties. There are no losers. Everyone wins. Children feel empowered while at the same time they are learning the importance of considering the interests of others. When you invite your child to solve the problem with you, begin by restating what's important to both of you. "You want to be with your friends. I need to make dinner right now."

Then invite her to solve the problem with you by adding a phrase like:

> How can we make this better?
> Can you think of three things we could do to make this work for both of us?
> What could we do?

If your child suggests, "Take me to my friend's house," there's no need to get upset or immediately say no. Simply state, "That's one idea. Give me three more." Continue exploring potential solutions together until you come up with an idea that satisfies everyone. Brainstorming helps you to find *yes*. The rule for brainstorming is that anything goes. At this point nothing is evaluated, thrown out, or ridiculed. You can come up with any solutions. In fact, tossing in a few humorous ideas often eases the tension and keeps you working together until you find just the right solution.

I divided my class into two small groups, one to help Christopher and Dylan find an acceptable solution and one for Crystal and her daughter.

Christopher's group returned with these suggestions:
Have milk or water for lunch and soda with popcorn for a
    snack.
Put ice cubes in the water.
Christopher can drink milk with his lunch, too, and save
    his soda for later when Dylan is outside.

Crystal's group suggested:
Skip lunch.
Have the daughter pack a bag lunch and take it with her to
    the friend's house.
Invite the friend to lunch.
Make lunch at two o'clock.

After reviewing the lists, I asked Christopher and Crystal to
pick the solution they thought would be most acceptable to their
child and to them. Christopher chose to put ice cubes in the water
because that's what he thought Dylan really wanted. Crystal selected inviting the friend to lunch.

Brainstorming together with your child allows you to see that
there are a multitude of solutions available to you—solutions that
will feel good to both of you. The younger the child, the more
you'll be developing the solutions. The older the child, the more
you'll be stepping back and letting him use his flexible thinking
skills to solve the problem.

As you look for solutions, feel free to be imaginative. Spirited
kids are incredibly creative. One parent told me she had stopped a
preschooler's demands for fruit snacks simply by handing the child
a pretend packet and munching loudly. Another parent mimed
driving in a car when his toddler wanted a car ride. Spirited kids

can learn to use that wonderful imagination to help them be very good problem solvers.

Choosing to say yes and to allow our spirited children to try a new idea or come up with the solution to a problem is a decision we make in order to teach them an essential life skill. In fact, realizing that they are good problem solvers is a major breakthrough for persistent kids. It helps them to stop the struggles before they ever start. Recently, Jessica, a mom from one of my classes, told me:

> Aiden, my five-year-old, came downstairs with his pajamas in his hand. They were inside out. In the past this would have turned into a forty-five-minute fit. Hearing his huffs of irritation, I said to him, "What's up? I will help you." He paused, looked at me, and in a matter-of-fact tone replied, "Mom, just give me a minute. I'm a problem-solving kid!" He took a deep breath, spread the pajamas out on the floor, and put them on. Teaching him to problem solve has been a miracle.

Think back to the fights you've had recently with your spirited child. Decide whether "looking for yes" could have eliminated any of them. Next time you run into a similar situation, be ready to begin your child's lessons in what it means to be a problem-solving family.

WHEN YOUR CHILD DOESN'T TALK YET

Getting to yes requires communication skills that infants and toddlers don't have, but they still have strong ideas of their own.

Parenting the spirited toddler and infant is exhausting. The fewer times you have to get up and go after your avid explorer or stop your determined-to-try kid, the more energy you save and the fewer battles you wage. For this age group, there is another way to say yes.

Say *Yes* with Your Environment

Walk into a good early-childhood classroom and you'll find a planned "*yes* environment." There are chairs kids can get on and off by themselves. There are toddler tables where there are no chairs. The kids just sit on the floor or stand leaning against the table, learning how to use a table before they're expected to use a chair as well. There are shelves and hooks at heights children can reach without assistance. There are little cups that are easy to handle for their water. Paper, crayons, and other supplies are out and available. A trampoline, rocking boat, or jungle gym is ready for the wild leaps and jumps of the energetic child. There are push and ride toys. Shatterproof mirrors hang horizontally an inch off the floor instead of vertically, so even very young babies can raise their heads and watch themselves. Everything in the room says: "Show me what you can do, all by yourself," "Explore," "Learn," and "Feel self-sufficient." This is a *yes* environment. The adults have chosen what materials and furniture to have available for the children, thus freeing up their time to talk with the kids, teaching them rather than reprimanding or fighting with them.

We can't make our homes into early-childhood classrooms and we wouldn't want to, but we can look around our home and plan for a *yes* environment that fosters peace. Is your home a good place for kids to live, or is it a battlefield pitting parents against determined, energetic explorers? Are there cupboards available for little investigators? Or is it a struggle every time your toddler heads for the kitchen? Is there somewhere to jump, other than the couch? Where are the books? Are they easy to grab? Where is the media center? Are you begging to have buttons pushed or wires pulled? Where are the hooks for coats? Can a child get her sweater down without assistance? How big are the drinking glasses and where are they stored? Are they easy for a child to get to and handle without spills? The more places in your home that are child-safe and manageable, the less you'll have to fight with your tenacious child about "getting out and staying out" of things and places.

Yes, a child does need to learn to respect the things that belong to others, but during the early years everything in your child's brain is telling her to find out how her world works. It is an essential stage of development. Add a persistent temperament, and the need to explore is stronger than her ability to stop herself. By saying yes with your environment, you are working with your child's temperament instead of against it. You are appreciating and enjoying her inquisitiveness and her resolve and are avoiding a fight that doesn't need to happen. This isn't giving in. This is *working together.*

WORKING TOGETHER

Looking for *yes* requires effort and takes time, but in the end it can save you time. David, a father of two, was raised in a very strict, authoritarian family. "If Dad said jump, you jumped. I've had my doubts about 'looking for *yes*,'" he said, staring at me sternly. "In fact, part of me gets angry just thinking about it. Last Saturday morning, my wife and I wanted to go downtown together and look for a bookcase. The kids had a fit. They hate shopping. They didn't want to go. I was furious. Why wouldn't they just obey and get in the car without a fight? I was losing it, so my wife took over."

"Dad wants to go and you don't," she said. "What could we do?"

"How about calling the neighbors?" the older one piped up. "You took care of their kids last week. Maybe we can stay with them, and you and Dad can have a date."

"Yeah," the younger one said. "Let's do it."

At first I was reluctant to bother the neighbors, and I'd been thinking that this would be a nice family time together. I relented, however, when I realized we had watched their kids and it obviously was not going to be a "nice" time together. The kids called, the neighbors agreed, and my wife and I took off on our own.

It was peaceful having just the two of us during the drive, yet there was a part of me that was still frustrated. It was my wife who pointed out the fact that most of the time they did come with us and with very little hassle. It was also she who said, "We want to raise adults who can speak up for their own needs, solve problems, and sometimes question authority."

That wasn't how I was raised, of course, but I've been working for years to try to speak up and have the guts to stand up for myself sometimes. It just isn't easy to parent this way when I wasn't raised this way.

I calmed down a little, but then I thought of the twenty minutes it took to come up with this solution. I got mad all over again. It seemed like twenty minutes of wasted time. My weekends are precious to me. I don't want to spend them negotiating with the kids.

I was still steamed when we got home, but the kids were in a great mood when we picked them up. We had to run the oldest to his basketball game and then decided to look at a couple more places for bookcases. They went along, no complaints. In fact, they seemed to enjoy themselves. Even the next day it paid off. I had suggested a family walk.

The oldest jumped in with, "We never get to do what we want!"

"Wait a minute. What about yesterday?" I reminded him.

"Oh, well," he stuttered, and put on his coat.

It was a lovely family walk. That night I figured out that our twenty minutes spent finding *yes* had allowed the morning to pass peacefully. Everyone was happy. Everyone had been listened to and had gotten to do what he or she wanted. The goodwill it created carried into the afternoon with the basketball game and the shopping trip. There had been no hassle. Negotiation wasn't necessary. The next day it stopped a potential power struggle over a family walk. In fact, that twenty minutes spent on Saturday morning had carried over for a good twenty-four hours of harmony—I'd call that a very good investment!

I can't guarantee that every search for *yes* will buy twenty-four hours of harmony, but it is a good investment. Looking for *yes* teaches our persistent children to consider the needs of others, to solve problems amicably, to think flexibly and to make decisions that everyone can live with. It builds the foundation for a healthy relationship—a relationship that can survive adolescence and more.

When You Are Persistent Too

Like David, many of us find looking for *yes* difficult. It may be because of the way we were raised, or it may be because we're persistent too. We lock in as strongly and as adamantly as our kids do.

"Oh yeah, am I persistent!" Kimberly explained during our group discussion:

> Jackson and I are like two bulls with horns locked. My hot button is when he tells me I'm wrong! That one *really* sets me off.
>
> Yesterday afternoon, Jackson was working on a letter. Asher, our eight-year-old, was doing spelling words and needed my help. They were both driving me crazy. Jackson demanded to know how to spell *neighbor*.
>
> "N-e-i," I said.
>
> "No, it's n-a," he insisted.
>
> I said, "It's n-e-i."
>
> "No, it's n-a," he maintained.
>
> It made me angry. He'd asked me a question, and now he was telling me my answer was wrong. I was in no mood for this kind of treatment.
>
> "If you don't want to know the right answer, then don't ask me," I snapped. He was so frustrated that he tore up the letter he'd been working so hard on. It wasn't until

later that I realized that he had already written "n-a" on his sheet before he asked me the question. If the right answer was "n-e-i," he had a mistake on his paper that couldn't be erased. I hadn't bothered to find out why he was disagreeing with me or why he was so frustrated with my answer. I didn't want to take the time. Anyway, I was busy with his sister, who was moaning in my face.

It so happened that we visited friends that night. I overheard the five-year-old tell his sister that a red block was black.

"It's red," she responded.

"It's black," he claimed.

I couldn't help remembering a very similar conversation held just a few hours earlier. This one, however, had a less frustrating ending. The sister sighed, looked at him, and replied, "You certainly have a creative way of looking at things."

I couldn't believe I had heard a seven-year-old respond in this way. She knew it was red and, quite frankly, so did he, but at that point in time he wanted it to be black. Her response said "You're creative," not "You're wrong." Yet she knew that she was not wrong either. They both just walked away from it.

Persistent kids have persistent parents. Sometimes to avoid a power struggle with our kids, we are the ones who have to unlock. We must realize there doesn't have to be a battle. We don't have to be frustrated. There are just two strong, opinionated people with a very different perception of the same situation. The world needs people of conviction.

So next time you realize you are arguing with your child over something quite superfluous, think of that wise seven-year-old and know when to simply let it drop or remind your child that you are problem solvers.

Next time Kimberly and Jackson disagree, Kimberly might say to Jackson, "Tell me more. I'm saying it's n-e-i and you're saying it's n-a. What's up?" Or, in another situation, "I want you to clean your room and you want to play video games. What could we do to work together?" These simple clarifications of what's important to each of you and reminders that you work together can prevent the power struggle.

Getting Past the Roadblocks to Solving Problems Together

Amanda frowned. "I'm trying to solve problems with Bea, but she just ramps up. Even if I attempt to empathize she amps up, and once she's in a storm, she doesn't want to be touched. The other day I said to her, 'I think you're getting tired.'

" 'I'm not tired. You are!' she roared.

"It's really hard to figure out what she's feeling, and when she gets so nasty about it, I don't even want to try."

In order to effectively solve problems with your child, sometimes you have to take a look at her entire temperament profile. If your persistent child is also analytical and serious, she's likely a more factual kid. Exploring emotions makes her feel vulnerable. She does not like to go there. If you can hear her stomach growling and you remark, "I think you may be hungry," she'll likely retort, "I'm not hungry! I'm mad!" Admitting mistakes or revisiting them leads to shouts and slammed doors.

If this is what happens with your child, switch to the concrete facts: "Did someone do something you did not like?" "What did they say?" "How would you like it to be?"

Or, because this child tends to have a very strong sense of justice, you can ask, "Was something unfair?" That will get her talking! Only after this persistent and analytical child has had an opportunity to tell you about her plan, or describe what happened, or what was unfair will she be ready to solve the problem with you.

There is a little test you can try to determine if your child is analytical. Next time she gets upset, offer her a hug. If she pushes you away, you've got a factual child. Stick with the facts. Later, when everyone is calm, go back for a redo, as described in chapter 8, "Meltdowns," to talk about what she may have been feeling. It's tempting to skip the redo because the problem has been solved, but for your factual child to be able to tune in to her emotions, it is essential not to skip it. Ultimately even serious and analytical spirited children can learn to value and articulate their emotions.

Keep in mind that introverts need time to experience and process their emotions. It's the introverted child who may go to her room and not come out, even when you tell her you are willing to work with her. If she's old enough to read, you can help this child be a problem solver by writing notes. Lyssa tried this idea with her nine-year-old son.

The cousins were visiting. We'd had a great morning. Then it was lunchtime and I had them choose a number before picking their jobs. The next thing I knew Luke ran into his room and locked the door. I tried talking to him through the door, but he wouldn't open it. So I grabbed a notepad and on it wrote:

I am not feeling good about today and want to know what happened. Could you please help me understand better by checking the box that explains?

❑ Did you want a different job?
❑ Did you want a different lunch?
❑ Did you think choosing numbers was unfair?
❑ Did you want to drive the car? ("I was trying to be silly, like you told us to be.")
❑ Other—please fill in . . .

Thank you for helping me understand. Now I'll know so next time I can do something different and not do it again. Love, Mom

I slid the note under the door. Ten minutes later it came sliding back out. He'd checked the box next to "Did you want a different job?" And next to the "Other" box, he wrote, "It seems like they are luckier than me." He added a P.S. "Sorry for the way I behaved."

Even if your child initially resists, vary your techniques, and take the time to discover what he is feeling. Being in touch with one's emotions is an essential life skill.

Sometimes your child's resistance to solve problems is due to his sensitivity.

Cason pulled his dripping-wet favorite purple jersey out of the washer. "It's team day today. I wanted to wear it!" he wailed.

"I'm so sorry." His mom replied. "I had no idea. That's so disappointing. But we're problem solvers. What could we do?"

Tears slipped down Cason's cheeks.

"What if we find a different purple shirt?" Mom offered, but Cason just crumpled onto the couch, hiding his face in the pillows. Cason needed to be sad for a while.

Highly sensitive children need time to recover from that stab of deep emotion. Pause, give them time and space. They have to "feel" before they are ready to solve the problem.

If you are running into roadblocks, stop and check:

- ✔ Is everyone calm? If not, take a break and come back to it.
- ✔ Have the introverts and highly sensitive family members been given time to process what they are feeling? The introverts can include you as well as your child.
- ✔ Have the analytical family members been allowed to review the facts and what was unfair?
- ✔ Are you rushing? Problem solving takes time, but in the end you'll save time. The more you practice, the faster and more proficient your child will get.

If you are running into barriers, don't push harder. Instead, stop and analyze what's going on. You can get past those roadblocks. Even persistent spirited children can learn to be flexible thinkers. In fact, with their intelligence and creative minds they can be awesome problem solvers.

FEELING GOOD ABOUT PERSISTENCE

Whether it's buying a pint-size pitcher so your three-year-old can pour her own juice, or spending twenty minutes with your twelve-year-old trying to figure out a mutually agreeable solution, you can win cooperation by looking for ways to say yes.

Kids can amaze you with their ability and ingenuity. Don't be afraid to be flexible. Take time to understand what is important to your child and to explain what is significant to you. Even if it takes longer to have this conversation than simply insisting on his doing what you asked, you have eliminated the fight, shared your values, and fostered an I-can-do attitude.

We never know what life will throw at our persistent kids. But if they come from a problem-solving family, they will probably figure it out—even if they get stuck in the mountains!

PERSISTENCE
A Summary

Persistent, spirited children push where other kids don't push. They demand more than other kids demand. It is nearly impossible to ignore them or distract them. That's why it is so important to teach them to be problem solvers.

Persistent spirited children need to hear:
We are a problem-solving family.
You can be a flexible thinker.
You are committed and decisive.
You know what you want.
You are independent and capable.

Teaching tips:
Focus on working together.
Seek understanding of why this issue is important to your child.

Explain what is important to you.
Invite your child to brainstorm with you potential solutions
   that work for both of you.

If you are persistent too:
Allow yourself time to unlock.
Recognize that good parents do say yes.

10

Persistence

Choosing Your Battles—Saying No

You can't show your underpants in public.
—Sue, mother of three

GOOD PARENTS DO SAY NO

The story is told that years ago, when Lou Holtz became the head football coach at Notre Dame, there was a talented young quarterback on the team. After reviewing the previous season's statistics, however, Holtz noted that the quarterback had thrown many interceptions. He called the young quarterback into his office. "You're a great athlete," he told him. "And you can expect to continue as the starting quarterback. However, you're not going to throw more than seven interceptions next year."

The young quarterback gave Holtz a puzzled look and asked, "How do you know that?"

"Because," Holtz drawled, "after your seventh, you'll be sitting on the bench next to me."

By the end of this discussion the quarterback knew:

- What he was expected to do.
- What would happen if he did not meet that expectation.
- At what point that action would be implemented.
- That he had a choice. He could choose whether to work hard and play, or slack off and get benched.
- The responsibility was his.

Coach Holtz's quarterback never did sit on the bench that year. He threw only six interceptions.

What Coach Holtz did is called transparency in setting limits. Transparency in limits means there are no surprises and no sudden proclamations of mysterious penalties. Expectations and consequences are concrete and presented up front. Everyone is forewarned and knows what to expect. Researchers tell us that this is how competent parents set limits.

While saying yes is essential to living in harmony with our spirited children and teaching them problem-solving skills, just as important as our yes is our very clear no. Spirited kids, more than other children, need confident parents—adults who, when it comes to teaching the basic rules and values in their lives, are willing to be just as persistent and adamant as their children. Parents who understand that establishing and enforcing clear limits rather than being "mean" provides children with a sense of security.

My friend Peni pointed this out to me in a rather roundabout way. Peni owns a cattle ranch in Nebraska. One day we were discussing what we had learned from raising our children. Peni replied, "Oh, raising children is just like raising cattle." I have to admit I was taken aback, since I would not typically compare a child to a cow. It sounded like a bunch of bull to me. (Sorry, I couldn't resist.) I looked at her quizzically. She continued, "You gotta give them a good-size pasture with a sound fence. Provide them lots of room to roam, but within safe boundaries. And just like kids, they need to know that you'll be there for them."

A sound fence encircles us, protecting us from harm. It de-marks a clear boundary, a moat that keeps trouble away. When we establish clear limits, spirited children never say to us, "Thanks, that's exactly what I needed." In fact they may scream "I hate you" or "You are the meanest parent in the world." It isn't easy to stand strong, especially if you're not as temperamentally persistent as your spirited children. But clear limits fortify our children, providing them with a sturdy, dependable foundation. It's worth the effort to establish those boundaries. We begin with the words we use.

Using Words

Two-year-old Emily loved her dad's phone. If he laid it down even for a second, Emily snatched it. "Bring me my phone," her dad requested. Emily glanced in his direction before squealing in delight then dashing away, phone in hand. When her dad attempted to retrieve it, the chase was on, but before he ever caught her, Emily would throw it across the room.

There are two important lessons in this scenario. First, Emily's behavior exemplifies classic toddler behavior. Toddlers are learning: What are the rules around here? What are the results of my actions? What happens if I run away? What if I throw a phone? Is that different from what happens when I throw a ball? Her "testing" is not predictive of a future troublemaker. Her laughter is not an act of defiance; it's a reflection of her amazement at how her actions draw a response from adults. That's why it is critical that the adults in her life get up, move to her, and help her stop. Doing so allows her to clarify: "Oh, that's what happens. That's where the fence is. It's nice and solid."

Secondly, this scenario raises the question, "When do I say no?". Here's the guideline I use:

> *If something is unsafe, hurtful, or disrespectful to self, others, or the environment, it needs to be stopped.*

Spirited children need to hear from us, the adults in their lives, phrases like:

> I will keep you safe.
> You can count on me to do what I said I would do.
> If you cannot stop yourself, I will help you stop.
> I will let you know what to expect. I will not surprise you.
> You can make a choice with your behavior.

Statements like these let children know they can depend on us. They can trust us to keep them secure. We have their backs.

ESTABLISHING TRANSPARENT LIMITS

Coach Holtz did not yell across the football field to his young quarterback, "Hey, you! Stop throwing interceptions or you will be benched!" No harsh threats to frighten him into compliance.

In fact, researchers tell us that a harsh, rigid approach increases behavior problems and leads to more aggression. Holtz held a private face-to-face meeting.

If you need to stop your child, do not yell across the room at him. Go to him and bend down to his level. Look him in the eye. If necessary, put a hand on him to prevent him from bolting. If he attempts to twist away, say to him: "I will help you." "I will keep you safe." "I will help you stop." Pause to let your child calm enough to be able to hear you. Then follow these three steps:

1. Tell your child what you want him to do.
2. Tell him what you will do if he does not do it.
3. Tell him when you will do that.

You'll use a firm voice. A firm voice is not harsh or loud. It is simply a voice of conviction—a voice that states clearly, "The expectation is . . . I will help you meet the expectation." The tone communicates to your spirited child that you are committed and willing to get up and follow through every time. It is this style of calm, confident direction that leads to children who are more flexible and agreeable.

After one too many frustrating chases after Emily, her dad, Luke, contacted me. Together we made a plan. Next time Emily snatched the phone he would move toward her, bend down, put out his hand and say, "Emily you can choose to hand the phone to me and we will look at it together. If you do not choose to hand it to me, I will put the phone away. I am going to count to three and you can choose. If you have not chosen by the time I say three, I will put the phone away. The choice is yours." Still holding his hand out and hanging on to Emily, if needed, he would commence counting in a confident voice. His words did not need to resound as a threat. He knows what actions he is going to take if necessary. He is simply stating the facts.

"One. You can hand it to me and we will look at it together. If you do not choose to hand it to me, I will put the phone away." At this point, he pauses for a few seconds.

"Two." He repeats the expectation. "You can hand it to me and we will look at it together. If you do not choose to hand it to me, I will put the phone away." Again, he pauses.

"Three. You did not choose to hand the phone to me so I will put the phone away."

This is the point at which Emily will throw herself down on the floor screaming "I'll do it." It is critical, however, that Luke follow through by saying to her: "I'm sorry. You made a choice. Next time you can make a different one." Because he did what he said he would do, Emily will learn she can trust her dad. It will only take a few practices before she will figure out it's to her benefit to make a decision to do what is being asked.

Transparent limits are effective because they let your children know what to expect. They are a promise to your children, "I will do what I said I would do and I've let you know what that is. You can predict my response. There are no surprises. You get to choose through your behavior what will happen." It's this knowledge and predictability that allows children to feel safe and secure.

Let me give you a few more examples.

What your child's choice is:	What you will do:	When you will do what you said you would do:
You can choose to sit on the chair.	If you choose not to sit on the chair, I will hold you on my lap.	If I see you get off the chair, I will know you are choosing to sit on my lap.
You can choose to use a quiet voice in the car and go to practice.	If you choose to yell in the car, I will take you home and you will need to tell your coach why you missed practice.	If I hear you raise your voice, I will know you have chosen for me to turn around and take you home.
You can choose to hold my hand and walk in the parking lot.	If you choose not to hold my hand, I will carry you.	Before we get out of the car, I am going to count to three. If you have not decided to hold my hand, then I will know you have decided I will carry you.
You can choose to clean your room and go to the party.	If you choose not to clean, I will choose not to take you to the party.	If your room is not clean by 5:00 P.M., I will know that you have chosen not to go. The choice is yours.
You may choose to use electronics for thirty minutes and then turn them off.	If you choose not to turn off the electronics when the time is up, I will put them away for two days.	If you choose not to turn off the electronics, I will know you are choosing not to use them for the next two days. The choice is yours.

Make Your Expectations Clear and Concrete

Transparent limits require that the choice you give your child is specific and precise. If it is not, you may find yourself debating with your little future attorney like Nicole did.

"The rule in our house has been that electronics use is limited," Nicole told me. "We were constantly fighting about it. I'd tell the kids to turn off the devices, and they'd fuss and fume that they had just started or they hadn't been playing very long. It wasn't until we talked about it in class that I realized that our expectation wasn't clear. What was too much time spent on electronics? How long could they use it? I went home and said, 'We need a clear rule. Let's say one hour of nonhomework electronics a day is the maximum.'

"'But what if we are in the middle of a game?' they complained.

"So I had them open their favorite game and then note how long it took to shut it down. With that information in hand we agreed upon a time limit to play, allowing for the shutdown to occur after that point.

"They moaned, but the electronics did go off. I'm sure it helped, too, that they were included in deciding on the final rule. Now when they are playing, I ask, 'Is this your choice for the time?' If they say yes, they play it; if they say no, they turn it off themselves, recognizing they are using up their limit on junk. The arguments have stopped—even with Kyle, who is incredibly tenacious."

Examine your expectations closely. Are they clear and concrete? What time is bedtime? What toys are shared? Where can your child ride her bike? What chores are to be completed? Ask your kids what they think the expectations are in your house. Look at them together and, if they need it, give them a precision tune-up.

Know too that children do not think like adults do and have

to transition to adult thinking over the course of childhood and adolescence. The world is black-and-white to toddlers. If you want your toddler to hold your hand in a parking lot, that has to be true every time. Toddlers do not understand ambiguity. If you choose to let your toddler run free when a lot is empty, but expect him to hold your hand if it's busy, he gets confused. The line has to be solid for him to see it. If it wavers, he can't figure it out. Expectations are learned and internalized when they remain the same every time no matter what the circumstances. Children older than preschoolers are developmentally ready for more flexibility in what the rules are—they understand time and can accept that an extra thirty minutes of screen time today means thirty minutes less tomorrow. Before about age five, however, you need to be more concrete in your rules and expectations.

"It worked," Luke reported a week later. "The first two times I had to put the phone away and, just as you predicted, she did throw a fit. By the third time, however, she was willing to hand it to me so we could look at it together." Then he paused before adding, "I realized, though, that sometimes I know what I want her to do, but I don't know what I am going to do."

Just as important as knowing what you want your child to do is deciding what you will do if your child chooses not to comply.

Follow Through

It's virtually impossible to "make" a spirited child do something. That knowledge can leave you feeling powerless. But transparent expectations include taking a moment to determine how you will respond. Pause and consider what you can do. If your child is small, can you pick her up and remove her? If something is not cared for, can it be put away? When bedtime is not honored, is it possible to move it fifteen minutes earlier the next night? Can you separate two children who are fighting? Are you willing to turn around and go home when children are acting up in the car? Whatever you decide, make certain it is something you can do, and are willing to do.

Sometimes doing what you said you would do requires waiting until your child is calm. If your preschooler is dragging out the day's clothing selection, you can say, "I am going to set the timer for five minutes. You can choose an outfit. If you have not chosen one by the time the buzzer sounds, I will choose this outfit for you to wear. The choice is yours." When the buzzer sounds and no choice has been made, to avoid a struggle you will have to take a few minutes to calm your child down. But once she is calm, because she did not make a choice, she needs to wear the outfit you selected. Next time she can make a different decision.

Whether it is saving a pile of toys to pick up, or completing a chore, waiting your child out the first time will take patience. She can go to her calming basket or space (see chapter 7). She can still eat if it's a mealtime, sleep if it's bedtime, or go to school. She does not have to be miserable. But before she goes on to another fun activity, or uses any electronics, the task has to be completed, and you have to make sure that happens. It's not a threat. It's a promise.

The first time you implement this strategy, do so on the weekend or another time when you are not worried about being late. You have to be as committed to your goal to follow through as your persistent child is to his. The more you practice doing what you said you would do, the more cooperative your child will become. (If your child is older and resistant, read on for how to go back and solve this problem together.)

Sometimes, doing what you said you would do requires being

willing to do it. Laura grimaced before admitting, "I got caught in a real bind. Eleanor has been kicking the back of my seat when I'm driving on the freeway. She loves story hour at the library. So I told her that we could go to the library for story hour if she could keep her legs still in the car. But if she kicked my seat, I would turn around and take her home. She agreed, but two miles down the road, she kicked my seat. I pulled off at the next exit.

"Realizing I was turning around, she begged me not to go home and promised she would stop kicking. I really did not want to go home. I needed that break. So I relented and headed for the library. We hadn't gone a mile before she kicked the seat again."

Failing to do what you said you would do leads to "amplifying." Your child escalates her behavior to figure out where the line is. So before you tell your child what you will do, stop and ask yourself, "Can I do it?" and "Am I willing to do it?" If not, think of something else you can and will do. Your child needs to know she can trust that you will do what you said you would do.

FINE-TUNE THE TIMING

When Luke and I developed his plan for addressing the phone issue, I advised him to count to three so Emily would know at what point he would act. If Emily had been five or older, I would not have advised Luke to count. Counting escalates older kids. And, sometimes, more anxious kids, too—they hear "one" and freak out that they won't be able to calm down and make the right choice in time. Instead, set an agreed-upon time limit—by 5:00 P.M. the room will be cleaned. Then step away and give your child space and time to complete the task. Avoid hovering or reminding. You may choose to give a twenty-minute warning, "Remember, in twenty minutes if you are choosing to go to the party, your room needs to be cleaned." That's it, no more. He is making the choice.

If the situation is not time sensitive, then establish a specific behavior like Coach Holtz did. Instead of seven interceptions as the concrete boundary, yours might be "If I hear you yell" or "If I see you hit your brother." No need for arguments or debate. It's specific.

When you are very clear about what your expectations are and know what you are going to do if your child does not comply, you will feel much more confident. Confidence gives you strength even when faced with the force of a very strong, persistent spirited child.

WORKING TOGETHER

Ultimately you want your children to stop themselves. Rather than being dependent on you as the external control center, you want them to have self-control. As your children enter the later preschool years and definitely once they are in school, you will put your energy into helping them stop themselves and make good decisions.

"Eight-year-old Steven came home late again last night," Tiffany told the other parents in her group. "Today I sat down with him and said, 'Steven, when you're late, I get worried. What can we do to help you remember to come home on time?'

"He looked at me and then said, 'What if I wear the watch Grandma gave me? It has an alarm on it. If you teach me how to set it, I can use it to remind myself to come home.'

"Can you believe it? He thought of that all by himself!"

When your children are toddlers, you'll be leaning more toward stopping them in order to help them understand where the line is.

But as children grow, you will lean toward saying, "Yes, let's work together to make this better." By involving them in the process, you help them develop the skills for self-control. This is especially true if the problem is occurring repeatedly. If every night there is a fight over homework or siblings squabble after school, there is a reason, a feeling and need that has not been identified. It's time to sit down and be a *problem-solving family*.

FINDING THE BALANCE

Spirited kids don't like it when we say no. The intensity and duration of their reaction can invade us, forcing us to question our own judgment. Finding a balance of control can be difficult. We are forced to be confident when we may not feel confident, to walk a battle line that is not clearly marked. When we say no, we may wonder if we are wounding their spirit or misusing our parental authority. How do we know if we are overcontrolling? Battling more than we should be? How do we know if we're undercontrolling? Letting our spirited child take control? Will we know when we have found balanced control? By checking in with how we feel, we can know whether we are finding balance.

Undercontrol Makes Us Feel Resentful

Ashley wrapped her arms around her body as though to hide from the world. When it came to establishing clear expectations for her son Jackson, she found herself crumbling.

"I don't want to stifle him," she told me. "Maybe this is what boys are like. My mother was ill when I was growing up, and my father traveled all of the time. No one ever set limits for me. I don't know what limits feel like. I can walk right into a brick wall and never know it was there until I hit it. Jackson knows when I'm uncertain, and he keeps pushing. I think he's trying to find the bottom line, but I don't know what the bottom line is. Then I get angry because I feel like he's getting away with murder."

If your spirited child is more persistent than you, there is a very important question to ask yourself before establishing an expectation: Do you believe that this expectation is in the best interest of your child and your family? If you find yourself uncertain, or responding no, do not move forward. Only when you can look in the mirror and with conviction in your voice say "Yes, this is in everyone's best interest" will you be ready to establish an expectation and confidently follow through. Your confidence in what you are doing will come through. Your child will resist much less than you ever expected.

Think about it. Even if you are one of the most sensitive, nonpersistent parents on earth, if your child vehemently resists being buckled into a car seat, you are resolute in getting him safely tucked into it. You never worry about wounding his spirit. Being buckled in is a law designed to ensure his safety. It's in everyone's best interest. You don't cave in on that. The reality is that you *do* know how to enforce clear expectations. Build off that success.

Here is a tip that may help. Social psychologist Amy Cudder has found that body language affects how others see us and also changes how we see ourselves. Even if you do not feel confident, she advises, by standing in a posture of confidence, you change the hormones in your brain and, as a result, increase your chance of success. Starting today, you can choose to stand in front of the mirror with hands on your hips, feet shoulder-width apart, and head up. Firmly and loudly declare, "I am an effective parent. I know what I am doing. There is a reason I was given this task. I can find the tools to successfully accomplish it." Hold that stance for two minutes, and then go about your day. You'll find that by "faking it" you'll become it.

Overcontrol Makes Us Feel Like a Drill Sergeant

Audrey was someone you noticed the minute she walked into a room, your attention caught by her big and commanding gestures. "I know I am controlling," she said. "I hear myself barking out reprimands to my son. 'Stop that! Watch out! Move over here. Get out of the way. Be careful. Don't touch that.' It creates tension that electrifies our home, as though each nerve ending is exposed. To protect himself, he goes 'mother deaf' and ignores everything I say, and if he doesn't ignore me, he fights with me."

Rob nodded as Audrey spoke. "I won't let him do anything," he added. "When I am overcontrolling, I always think I can do it better. I won't take the time to let him zip his own coat. I do it because I can do it faster. The other day I took a paintbrush out of his hand at the easel and said, 'Here, let me show you; I can do it better.' My son's eyes filled with tears, and he said, 'I don't want you to be part of our family anymore.'"

"I know I'm not saying yes enough," Deb admitted, "when I realize I've said no without even really listening to him, or I interrupt him before he can finish his sentence."

If you are feeling like a drill sergeant or are filled with guilt because you are constantly dragged into battles and hassles with your persistent child, it may be a sign that you need to say "Yes, let's work together" more frequently in your relationship. Step back and ask yourself if you are allowing your child to practice making decisions or to complete tasks he is capable of doing. Are you encouraging him to say "I can do it" and "I've got a great idea"? Are you letting him know you respect and value persistence?

Balanced Control Feels Like
You're Making Progress

Our real goal is to achieve a sense of balanced control, one in which both persistent spirited kids and their parents feel as if they are being listened to and respected, where we are a problem-solving family and expectations are clear.

> *What does balanced control feel like? This is what other parents say:*
> It feels like everyone is getting what they need without anyone coming out on the short end.
> Everyone feels respected and is respectful.
> People stop to listen to one another. There are no winners or losers.
> Everyone knows what to expect. There are no surprises.

It's a fine line we walk to balanced control; as your child grows, you will work on it together. A spate of "arm farts" that broke out at Paidea one summer demonstrates well how it can be done. It started in the school-age classroom when some of the boys discovered the thrill of making noise with their armpits. Soon the guttural spurts of sound had been titled "arm farts." Lynn shares my guidelines of what is and is not acceptable behavior. Specifically, if it's unsafe, hurtful, or disrespectful to self, others, or the environment, it needs to stop. But anyone who knows school-age boys, and the glee they can garner from their friends' responses to sounds that remind one of bodily functions, knows that a simple rule will never stop them. So Lynn held a meeting. Mind you this was not a top-down, here-are-the-orders meeting, but rather a conversation about respect and appropriate behavior.

Drawing the children together, she let them know that she was not comfortable with that language. This clarified the limit, but rather than forbidding arm farts and threatening that if they used that term, there would be consequences, she invited the children to come up with a different title. Soon thirty-eight kids were brainstorming alternatives to "arm farts," ultimately creating seven variations. Then they put the list to a vote. "Pits of fire" won the vote by a landslide. But Lynn didn't stop there.

"Okay," she replied, "so we are going to call making music with our armpits 'pits of fire.' Now let's talk about when and where it is acceptable to do this." The children fell silent, thoughtfully pondering this question. Then one declared, "When making music in a band!" Quickly another burst out, "On the playground!" Lynn clarified, her voice rising into a question. "Okay, so it's acceptable to make music with your armpits on the playground and if you're playing in a band?" The children solemnly nodded their heads in agreement. Lynn paused, reflecting, before asking, "When would it not be appropriate to make music with your armpits?" Once more the children exploded into action, exclaiming, "In the classroom," while another cried out, "When the teacher is talking." Still a third, waving his hand confidently, confirmed, "At dinner!"

"There aren't many places where it is appropriate to make music with your armpits," Lynn replied thoughtfully. "So let's see if I have this correct. It would be acceptable on the playground or if you were playing in a band? But it would never be acceptable in the classroom or at dinner?" The children nodded as one. That was it—end of meeting. And so too, the saga of "armpit farts" that somehow lost their luster when altered to "pits of fire" and relegated to the playground.

No consequences, threats, or declaration that this was forbidden behavior had been uttered. Instead there was a conversation, one in which both adults' and children's perspectives were addressed. The children had a voice, and an opportunity to practice limit setting, problem solving, decision making, and negotiation skills with an adult guide. Did it take time? Yes. But by having that conversation the children now appreciate the importance of respect, why limits are important, how to determine where a limit should be, and, most important, enough information to make that value their own. Balanced control allows persistent children to work with us without breaking their spirit. And during the teen years it will be what keeps your spirited adolescent working with you.

PERSISTENCE
A Summary

Spirited kids, more than other children, need confident parents— adults who, when it comes to teaching the basic rules and values in their lives, are willing to be just as persistent and adamant as their children. Parents who understand that establishing and enforcing clear limits rather than being "mean" provides children with a sense of security.

> *Persistent spirited children need to hear:*
> I will keep you safe.
> You can count on me to do what I said I would do.
> If you cannot stop yourself, I will help you stop.
> You can choose by your behavior what will happen.

Teaching tips:
Tell your child what he can do.
Tell your child what you will do if he does not comply.
Tell your child when you will do that.

If you are not persistent:
Ask yourself if you believe that this expectation is in your
　　child's best interest.
Build off past successes.
Recognize that good parents do say *no*.

11

Sensitivity

Understanding How They Feel

How do you deal with a child who can feel the "seams" in her socks and refuses to wear them?
—Kelsey, mother of three

My daughter Claire wasn't getting her work done at school," Kim told the group. Her brown curls bounced, emphasizing each word. "The teacher had told the kids at the beginning of the year that if they didn't finish their work, they would have to stay in the media center instead of going outside for recess. Claire's work kept getting slower and slower. It wasn't long before she was spending every recess period in the media center. Finally, in frustration, I demanded to know why she wasn't finishing her work.

" 'Because the noise on the playground drives me crazy,' she responded. 'The only way I can get some peace and quiet is to not finish my work!' "

Sensitive spirited kids feel emotions, see sights, hear sounds, and smell odors to a degree that most of us mortals will never know. They are not teasing when they tell us their socks are hurting their feet. They're dead serious when they refuse to eat lunch at school because the other kids make slurping sounds. If, on a cold winter day, you catch them standing in their shirtsleeves at the bus stop, it's actually true that they're *hot* rather than defiant. They recognize the difference between brands of applesauce, and if you check, you'll find out it's a fact that the toilet paper at school smells and feels different from the toilet paper at home, just as they told you.

Sensitivity allows the spirited child to form deep attachments and to nurture others. Noted humanitarians are blessed with the gift of sensitivity.

Problems occur for sensitive children when they are overwhelmed by the amount of stimulation and emotional stress around them. It can happen easily because within sensitive children emotions and sensations are collected and concentrated. They are soaked up rather than diffused. When this occurs, a pressure can build that overpowers their control systems.

Sharon Heller writes in *Too Loud, Too Bright, Too Fast, Too Tight*, "If we feel 'touchy,' our whole nervous system is out of whack and affects other sensory systems as well: when you get a mosquito bite, chapped lips or a hangnail, you feel on edge and the world gets louder and brighter."

Managing all of these sensations can be exhausting to our spirited children. It is our job to help them learn to monitor the concentration of stimulation in their bodies and to teach them how to manage their keen sensitivity in a positive way.

CHECK STIMULATION LEVELS

I always tell the parents in my classes that if they ever feel as if they are the only parents in the world with a sensitive spirited child, they should head for the largest, noisiest, most congested store in their area. There they will find spirited kids dropping like little bombs: two down in aisle one; three in aisle four (the candy shelf); and six in aisle seven (the toy department). At first glance it will appear that the explosions are triggered by a refusal to buy a candy bar, a desire to push the cart, or some other insignificant issue. The real trigger, however, is hidden in the fluorescent lights, piped-in music, flashing signs, colorful packages, and crush of people that create more stimulation than a sensitive child can endure, especially if his energy bank is low.

As the parent of a spirited child, you need to focus on the environment around you. You have to become aware of stimulation cues and recognize the breaking point for your child—the level of stimulation that pushes her beyond her ability to cope.

Jessica and Steve had never realized how sensitive their son Kip was until they started the spirited-child classes. As they participated in the discussions, they began to understand that too much stimulation was a major reason for his wild behavior. Behavior they could prevent simply by monitoring the level of stimulation to which he was exposed. In class, Jessica proudly told us how they had stopped one flare-up before it ever started.

"On Saturday, we took the kids to a huge craft fair," she said. "I wasn't two steps in the door before I was struck by the sound of craftspeople hawking their wares. Splashes of red, orange, purple, and green assaulted my eyes. Dangling lights hung from the ceiling and swung in the air forming patterns on the floor. And the people—there wasn't room to turn around. I looked at Kip and realized he would never make it through. The stimulation would drive him crazy. I was so disappointed and frustrated too. I knew we couldn't get our entrance fee back. I took a very long, deep breath, and then I pleaded with Steve, 'Please, give me thirty minutes. Can you help him last thirty minutes? I just need thirty minutes!'"

Before learning about sensitivity, Jessica and Steve had not been aware of stimulation cues, but they were now. Jessica immediately recognized a potential catastrophe in the making. It was likely that Kip would start to fuss and fume not because he was naughty but because the stimulation was so penetrating to him.

Monitoring the stimulation level around your child is critical to helping him learn to manage his sensitivity well. When you are able to read the cues that inform you a sensitive child will feel bombarded in this situation, you will know how to respond and be able to avoid a meltdown. Be especially observant at shopping centers, fairs, parks, beaches, and parties. Anywhere there is a substantial amount of noise, smells, bright lights, and big crowds, your sensitive child is vulnerable.

USING WORDS

Because they had participated in my class, Jessica and Steve knew they needed to help Kip understand the impact on him of the crowd and the commotion. Kip didn't understand that the irritation and discomfort he felt were caused by the people, the bright lights, and noisy hawkers. He needed to know he wasn't sick; he wasn't in danger. He was reacting to the stimulation.

"What did you tell Kip?" I asked them.

Steve responded. "I told him, 'It's pretty crowded in here. There's lots of noise and bright colors. You might start to get that weird feeling inside of you again.' I knew he would remember that because he had lost it at a party last week, and we had talked about the 'weird feeling.' Anyway, I told him that if he started to feel that way again, he should let me know. I would help him find a quiet spot."

By pointing out the lights, colors, and people, Steve was teaching Kip to recognize the cues necessary to read the stimulation level. Someday it won't be Jessica realizing that the craft fair may be over stimulating for Kip. It will be Kip himself.

If your child has been using tears for years to express himself, he doesn't know that words can be more effective. You have to teach him the terms that describe the sensations and emotions he experiences and demonstrate for him the power of these words to communicate.

Check your child's vocabulary. Does he know what *scratchy*, *bumpy*, *sticky*, *tight*, *stinky*, *noisy*, or *screechy* mean? Can he tell you when he is sad, lonesome, scared, hot, irritated, or overwhelmed? Are you honest with him when he asks if you are upset or sad? Sensitive kids need their observations confirmed, and they need to possess in their vocabularies the words that can help them communicate the profound emotions and sensations that they experience.

REDUCE THE STIMULATION

"Jessica took off on her own," Steve continued. "And I strolled through the rows of crafts with Kip. I watched him really carefully, ready to catch the first hint that he was ready to explode. It only took about ten minutes before I noticed he was starting to forget the rules. He was picking up things roughly and jostling people back. I told him, 'I think you're getting the weird feeling,' then I led him over to the snack bar. It was quiet there. He devoured a yogurt parfait and settled down, but I didn't trust him to go back near the booths. I knew we'd pushed it as far as we could, so I took him out to the front of the building and just let him run up and down the ramps.'"

Steve had learned that when the stimulation levels are too high for a child, you need to reduce them if you can. Taking your child to a quiet room; suggesting a walk outside; getting the scratchy, irritating sweater off; using the calming activities described in chapter 7; or anything else you can do to reduce the stimulation your child is receiving will help.

If your child is three or older, let him help you figure out what he needs. Ask him: "Is it the noise that is bothering you? Then let's find a quiet place." "Is it the jacket that is making you hot? Then let's take it off." Teach him how to reduce the stimulation level himself so he feels in control—capable of managing his own sensitivity.

KNOW WHEN TO LEAVE

From experience Jessica knew Kip could handle the commotion of the craft fair for about thirty minutes, but after that they would be pushing their luck.

"It wasn't long," Steve told us, "before Jessica reappeared with a lamp in hand, ready to head home. It hadn't been the outing we had expected, but in its own way, it had been successful. Kip had lasted thirty minutes. There hadn't been any fits—no embarrassing screams. We had worked together and that felt good. I know someday Kip will be able to tell us he has had enough and needs to get out of there."

Mica had sat quietly listening to Jessica and Steve tell their story. As it ended, she acknowledged, "You did a great job, but what do you do if you're at someone's house? You can't just leave."

"I've got a great technique for getting out of situations without hurting other people's feelings," Andrea exclaimed. "Whenever we go to a gathering, I always let the host know we have another appointment and will probably have to leave early. I don't tell them the appointment is my tactful 'escape' for my daughter and me. I keep my eye on her. As long as she's doing well, I let her play, but the minute I hear her start to get cranky or demanding, I know she's about to blow. That's when I say, 'Time for our appointment. We have to run.' I pick her up and get her out fast. She's only sixteen months, so it works. I realize when she's older I'm going to have to fill her in to watch for the blowup herself. But for now it's just nice to have people say she did a great job and invite us back again. Before my 'mysterious appointments,' we weren't always welcomed back."

If you watch closely, you will realize how draining crowded, stimulating situations are for your sensitive child. It can be frustrating especially if you're having a good time and are not ready to leave. But recognizing when it is time to pull out is critical to your child's success and your own confidence as a parent. Departing with a sour, cranky kid feels lousy. It is much better to exit while everyone is still in good spirits. That way your child experiences success rather than failure. Gradually, with practice, he will learn the skills to tolerate the situation longer, but that takes time.

LIMIT ELECTRONICS USE

Craft fairs, shopping malls, and beaches aren't the only places sensitive kids can easily receive too much stimulation. A study that measured recreational (nonschool) use of electronics found that the total amount of media content young people are exposed to each day has increased by more than an hour over the past five years. And not only is there more exposure, but the children are "multitasking"—using several media at the same time.

Many spirited kids seek electronic entertainment. The bright colors and fast pace of electronics can seem to entrance them, making it appear that they are calming them. As a result, it is very tempting to allow spirited kids to use electronics for a few hours because for that period of time they won't be demanding anything from you. Watch closely, however, what happens after the electronics are turned off. Some kids may indeed be calmer, but for most, rather than calming, electronics may overstimulate, resulting in even more challenging behavior after their use.

If there are any electronics in their bedroom, remove them. Avoid using electronics to entertain your children in the car. (Audio books are an exception.)

Balance screen time with time spent in other activities such as playing outdoors, playing with toys, reading, and doing artwork, all of which can be calming for sensitive children. By limiting the amount of time your spirited children spend with electronics, you'll prevent overstimulation and give them more opportunities to practice their interpersonal skills. Your children's behavior might improve dramatically, and so might their reading scores.

CHECK YOUR EMOTIONAL BAROMETER

Spirited kids are the emotional barometer of any group. Not only do lights, noise, and other sensations lead to overstimulation for them, but so does an overabundance of stress. Susan Cain writes in *Quiet*, "It's as if they have thinner boundaries separating them from other people's emotions and from the tragedies and cruelties of the world." Spirited children have keen radar for anyone who is in the red zone. If you are distressed or harried, they will be the first to respond. You might not think they are noticing your fears or anxieties, but they do—even as infants.

Spirited kids know these feelings and sense them in others. If we don't talk about such feelings, the spirited child may be frightened by them. Scared kids balk. They don't cooperate, and some vehemently protest any separation from you. It's as though their brain is telling them, "My family is under threat. I am very little and I don't want to be left alone!" Others tend to shut down.

"Krissa won't talk to me about feelings," Crystal groaned. "She won't tell me why she's sad or mad. She just says she doesn't want to talk about it."

"Isn't Krissa an introvert?" I asked.

"Yes, she is," Crystal replied.

"Remember, introverts only like to share feelings after they've had a chance to think about them," I said. "Let her know you're available when she is ready to talk, but give her time to think through her emotions before you expect her to share them. If you push her, she'll only withdraw. Introverts need their space."

Even introverted spirited kids will open up to you if you let them know you are willing to listen when they are ready to talk. If they need a little help, try using books or puppets as a stimulus for conversation. Sometimes it's easier to talk about how "Mr. Pickles" feels than it is for a child to talk about how she feels.

"My problem isn't that Ethan won't talk," Mya said, "it's that he is so sensitive. He is devastated when he loses a game. He'll cry for hours if a favorite toy gets broken or he loses a mitten. How do you deal with it when he has too much feeling?"

Sensitivity combines with intensity to make spirited kids very tenderhearted. They form deep and lasting relationships. They have a tremendous sense of justice. They are easily hurt. It is critical that they understand both their sensitivity and their intensity, to realize that life may have dumped a bucket of water on their head but they aren't drowning. They will survive.

Talk about their feelings and direct them to soothing, calming activities. Help them to understand that although they cannot control the emotions they experience, they can manage their responses. It is all right to feel sad and to cry. It is all right to take a break. It is perfectly acceptable to go for a run or to read a good book. It can be very comforting to confide in a friend.

CONSIDER OCCUPATIONAL THERAPY

"We have told four-year-old Eleanor over and over that she may not go near the lake without supervision. We've even taken her home when she does it, but no matter what we say or do, it doesn't make any difference. She just keeps going back," Stephanie complained. "It's as though the sensation of the water is a 'siren' call to her."

"Ben can't stand to ride in a wagon or to swing at the playground. He'll scream hysterically if you try to force him. And he hates to be kissed on the cheek. If you do, he'll wipe it off. Are all spirited kids this sensitive?" John needed to know.

Sometimes as we are working with our sensitive spirited kids, we begin to realize that their sensitivity seems even "more" than other spirited children. On the continuum they seem to have moved up a notch, and the level of their sensitivity is seriously disrupting daily life. If, despite all of the actions you take, your child seems to crave sensations so intensely that he'll keep going back into the water, tackle his friends, or continue to put everything into his mouth even though he's four years old, listen to your gut. Or, if he resists and avoids other sensations, especially light touch (like a kiss on his cheek), water on his head, or movement on a swing, be on alert. Combine these behaviors with poor coordination and stiff or rag-doll muscle tone, and as Sharon Heller, author of *Too Loud, Too Bright, Too Fast, Too Tight*, states, "They are a red flag for sensory-processing problems."

Listen to your intuition. Ask your doctor or school district for a referral to an occupational therapist who is trained and experienced in working with children who have sensory processing differences. She can evaluate your child and provide noninvasive strategies such as deep touch, joint compression, listening therapies that use music, and "heavy work" to help him manage everyday situations more easily. She can set up a sensory diet of activities and accommodations to help your child function better.

DAILY TOUGH TIMES

Sensitivity is a major issue when we try to get spirited kids dressed, bathed, fed, and groomed. It is their keen sensitivity that makes them very selective eaters and their cognizance of textures and sensations that make bathing, teeth brushing, and dressing major ventures. These daily events, however, are also challenging because of the spirited child's adaptability, perceptiveness, and persistence. In chapters 17 and 18 I'll describe for you how to successfully negotiate your way through these daily tough times.

WORKING TOGETHER

Helping our children understand and manage their sensitivity means working with our own. "What happens if you're sensitive too?" I asked the group of parents. They laughed. They moaned and they shuddered.

"Let me tell you it ain't easy!" Megan joked. "The same things that drive Silas crazy bug me too. I can't stand noise and commotion either. I feel myself getting irritated and tingly, and his crying only adds to the stimulation. I want to scream."

Dealing with Your Own Sensitivity

If you, too, are sensitive, it is very important that you constantly check the stimulation level around you and take note of the discomfort you are feeling. Be sure to fill your energy bank before going into a stimulating situation or immediately afterward because otherwise, you will feel drained.

Over the years you might have learned to cope with your sensitivity and may not even be aware that you are annoyed by the excitement and sensations around you. But if you listen carefully to your body, you will decipher those warning signs that tell you your own pressure valves are being tested. You are moving toward the red zone. Focus on those cues. Teach yourself to either quit or lower the stimulation level while you still have the stamina to take care of yourself and your child as well.

"I've learned so much about myself from watching Leo," Brent remarked. "I never realized how sensitive I was. I just thought I was hyper and I didn't like it. Learning to pick up the stimulation cues for Leo has helped me. A few weeks ago we went to an ice show. My wife and daughter loved it, but Leo and I were going crazy. I used to force myself to stay, even though it was pure tor-ture. Now, because Leo needs to get out too, I have an excuse to leave. Boy, do I appreciate him. My wife doesn't mind because she understands what's happening and appreciates our sensitivity in other ways."

Look at Your Message Board

Sensitive spirited kids need to enjoy and be comfortable with their heightened responses and tender emotions.

"What words do you use to help your children understand their sensitivity?" I asked the group.

"'You are loving,'" Melissa responded. "Rowan is so warm and affectionate. He really is a neat kid."

"'You're sensitive,'" Laura added. "But Alex is more sensitive to light, textures, tastes, and colors than feelings."

"'You're selective,'" John offered. "Everything has to feel just right for Peyton. You have to cut the tags out of his clothes. The cuffs can't be too tight. The potatoes can't be lumpy. He's going to make a great designer or chef someday."

Michael listened quietly to the group and then asked, "How can I tell my son I'm glad he's sensitive when it makes me flinch inside? I am embarrassed by my sensitivity and my son's too. When I grew up, boys didn't cry, and I cried over everything. I have spent years trying to control my sensitivity."

Appreciating sensitivity in our children, especially our male children, sometimes requires throwing out old messages and re-placing them with new ones that reflect the value of sensitive, caring individuals. We have to revisit the strengths of sensitivity and fill our minds and our vocabularies with the words that cel-ebrate its worth. When that happens, a special bond can develop between parents and their children—a bond that leads to personal growth for parent and child alike.

FEELING GOOD ABOUT SENSITIVITY

Katie waved her hand wildly when I asked the group if anyone had experienced a success the previous week. "I kept my cool!" She exclaimed.

"What helped you stay calm?" I asked her.

"I recognized Jayden is a really sensitive little guy. He's tuned into others and reads their emotions. That thought helps me be so much more compassionate. And I know I can teach him skills to manage it and use that gift well."

Justin nodded in agreement. "They really can learn. Abigail is now seven. She said to me, 'Dad I want to go to the fireworks with my cousins, but the noise hurts my ears. Would you help me find clear earplugs, so no one would notice them?' I did. Once during the evening she stopped, looked at me, and gave me a thumbs up. She knows I get it."

A special bond can exist, a nonverbal communication between parents and children, when you both understand sensitivity.

If you aren't as sensitive as your child, it may be challenging to understand her. To you, her reactions may seem to be *oversensitive* or *super* emotional. Be kind to your sensitive child. Appreciate that she may feel what you do not feel, that she may hear what you do not hear, that she may see what you do not see. Invite her to share her experiences with you and enhance your own sensitivity.

If it weren't for my sensitive son, I would never have noticed that when I am walking around a lake, the wind feels cooler on my cheek facing the water. I would never have fully appreciated the aroma of pumpkin pies baking. I would have missed hundreds of sounds, smells, sights, and feelings that have enriched my life.

SENSITIVITY
A Summary

Sensitive spirited kids feel emotions, see sights, hear sounds, and smell odors to a degree and depth that most of us mortals will never know. They are not teasing when they tell us their socks hurt their feet. They truly know the difference between brands of applesauce and if you check, you'll find out it's a fact that the toilet paper at schools smells and feels different from that in at home, just as they told you.

Problems occur for sensitive children when they are overwhelmed by the amount of stimulation or emotional stress around them.

> *Sensitive spirited kids need to hear:*
> You're tenderhearted.
> Noise bothers you.
> You are loving.
> You are very sensitive to feelings and care about people.
> You can feel other people's stress.
> You are very selective.
> You'll make a wonderful chef, artist, designer, photographer, teacher, etc.

Teaching tips:

Talk with your child about the rich array of sensations and
emotions she experiences. Give her the words to describe
them.

Be sensitive to how much stimulation your child is
receiving. Noise, smells, bright lights, crowds, etc., bother
her; protect her from overstimulation.

Limit the amount of time your child spends using
electronics.

Teach your child to recognize when she is getting
overstimulated and to ask for help stopping or reducing
the stimulation.

If you are sensitive too:

Be aware that stimulation that bothers your child also
irritates you.

Reduce stimulation while you still have the energy to
manage your own sensitivity and to help your child
manage hers.

Refill your energy bank after being in a stimulating
situation.

12

Distractible or Perceptive

Helping Them Hear Our Directions

We are able to process your call. We just don't feel like it.
—Ziggy

I was standing at a checkout in the discount store one day. A child-care provider with three preschoolers in tow was attempting to make a purchase.

"Oscar, over here," she called. Oscar stood in his tracks.

"Oscar, I need you to come over here," she repeated sternly. No movement. Finally she went over to him, touched his shoulder, and growled, "Oscar, I asked you to come over here." He looked up at her with his finger at his lips. "Shhhh, listen to the bell. I hate it," he whispered.

I tensed, straining to hear the bell. At first I couldn't distinguish anything, and then suddenly I realized he was talking about the bell rung by the Salvation Army person soliciting donations outside the store. The child-care provider was also puzzled. She darted a glance around the store, but seeing no bell she started to speak again. It was then that the faint tinkle of the bell reached her. "The Salvation Army bell," she exclaimed, her brow wrinkled in exasperation. "You hate the Salvation Army bell?"

"It reminds me of morning," he soberly replied. "Every morning when the bell rings, I have to get up!"

From outside appearances it looked as if Oscar wasn't listening. In fact, he was. The problem arose because he heard every sound around him and didn't know which was the most important for him to tune in to and respond. He heard the child-care provider, but he did not react because he was attending to the bell outside. He wasn't being willful. He was doing what his brain was telling him to do.

USING WORDS

There's a *Ziggy* cartoon that reads, "We are able to process your call. We just don't feel like it." But it may be that Ziggy, rather than choosing not to process the information, may actually be so distracted by the barrage of sounds bombarding him that he is unable to decipher the message. According to research completed by Dr. Stephen W. Porges of the University of Illinois at Chicago, our nervous system continuously evaluates risk by processing information from the environment through the senses. When a child feels safe, his brain unconsciously directs his facial muscles to make eye contact, vocalize with an appealing inflection and rhythm, and adjust the middle ear muscle to distinguish the human voice from background sounds more efficiently. But if he feels threatened, the brain spontaneously signals these same muscles to let the eyelids droop, reduce voice inflection, and adjust the muscle in the middle ear so that the human voice becomes less acute and the sounds in the environment more pronounced instead.

Spirited kids are highly perceptive. Their senses are keen, drawing in every aspect of the stimulation around them, constantly evaluating risk. They need us to tell them that they hear what others do not. They see what others do not. They feel when others do not. It is this ability to perceive that gives them an understanding and insight beyond their years. It is the basis of a sharp sense of humor and creative thought. To be perceptive is a special gift.

Problems occur for the perceptive child when he is barraged by information from his senses and unable to sort it out. He struggles to decide what the most important message is or where his focus should be. When this occurs, he becomes overwhelmed, confused, unable to concentrate on the task at hand or the instruction he has just been given by his parent or teacher. It appears as though he is not listening. It is our job to help kids like this understand what is happening and to teach them techniques for distinguishing the most important messages in their lives.

HELPING KIDS TO LISTEN

To prompt kids to listen, we can start thinking and acting like the marketing director of a major company. We have to help them feel comfortable and make them believe that among the rush of messages they are receiving, ours is the most important.

Coca-Cola is almost indiscernible from its competitors. Yet their marketing people have to convince people to buy it rather than the other brands. They do this by using what advertisers call "emotion extension." They embed into the ads images of families playing games, dancing, and celebrating together. They aren't simply selling a fizzy, brown, sweet liquid; they're selling optimism and contentment. Coke's message stands out. Buyers like it. They listen and respond.

Advertisers study neurobiology. They know that the strategy of creating a good feeling is effective because it promotes a sense of well-being. When we feel good, our brain communicates to the muscle in the middle ear, "All is well; go ahead and tune in to the human voice." Then we listen to the words.

So just like the advertising directors, we have to develop our own emotional extension with spirited kids. It has to be one that lets them know we love them. We want to communicate that it feels good to be around us and to do the things we ask.

One day I yelled at my kids. I told them I was tired of them not listening or doing what I asked them to do. "But, Mom," my son protested, "you're not listening to us. You're crabby. You're not giving us any choices. We ask for your help and you walk away. You even pick up our toys before we're done playing with them."

I was not pleased. I had not started this lecture as an opportunity to discuss my behavior. But drill sergeants who bark out commands send us into the red zone ready for fight or flight. In a state of fight or flight, we need to take in all sound, so much so that we can't even process what's being said.

"KRISSSSSS, turn off the television and GET YOUR PAJAMAS ON NOW!" brings on a case of "parent deafness." "Kris, sit on my lap and I'll scratch your back before we get your pajamas on" brings her running. Hugs, a thank-you, a compliment, a question about her day, or which book would she like to read tonight, all *draw* your child to you. Your warm messages create a good feeling, the one that *allows* our spirited kids to listen to our message rather than the other sounds around them. Check your messages. Are they creating that good feeling? Are they helping your child's brain heed your messages?

Vary Your Methods to Get Your Message Across

Our brain hungers for novelty and quickly tunes into it. Through extensive market research, companies have learned that if they want their customers to actually respond to their message, they must vary their approach. So they inundate us, utilizing every conceivable shape, form, and matter. They sing it to us; they picture it for us. It's on the truck that just rolled down the street, in YouTube videos, and on the highway billboard, a friend's T-shirt or baseball cap, and the city bus.

Experiment with your child. Does she respond best when you verbally tell her to do something or when you write a note or draw a picture for her? What happens if you sing it to her? One of the most effective classroom techniques is the "clean-up song." The simple little tune that pleasantly reminds us that "it's time to put your work away so we can have a snack today." If you don't sing, try changing the tone of your voice. A robot voice or a whisper easily captures your child's attention. Blink lights, freeze in place, raise a hand, or let the timer ring. Vary the techniques that are most effective for you, or use a couple of them together.

When you vary your techniques, it's also easier to send your message more than once without feeling repetitive or as though you're nagging. Watch a classroom teacher, and you'll see her step over to the light switch and blink the lights. That is a visual signal that says, "Stop. Listen to me." Then she'll sing, "It's time to put your work away," an auditory message. To those who are not responding, she will walk over, touch, and remind—a physical message. Finally she may begin helping some of the children pick up the blocks they are playing with—a demonstration. In four different ways she has sent her message. With this approach she is assured that everyone has heard it and knows this is where their attention should be focused.

Touch seems to be a very important way of signaling a spirited child that this message is important. In our spirited-child classes we make a general announcement of what is to come and then walk around the classroom, gently but firmly (not tickling) touching each child on the arm or shoulder and repeating the message. This touch is critical to helping the children focus on the information we are giving them. Try catching your child's attention with touch.

Once you've learned which techniques are most effective with your child, teach him what you are doing. Let him learn to ask for directions in a written form or to sit close to a teacher so it is easy for her to touch him and cue him in.

Make Eye Contact

To get potential customers to pay attention to their messages, advertisers have learned to catch their eye. Walk through the grocery store. If it's an adult's product, you will find it standing at an adult's eye level. If it's a kid's product, it will be at a child's eye level. If you are online, images will show up next to what you are viewing. Companies actually squabble over space that will give them the most direct eye contact.

You can use the same technique. If you want your children to listen to you, avoid hollering at them from across the room. This strategy lets off steam for you, but for spirited kids it is the least effective way of getting them to pay attention. Instead, walk over to them, bend down, and look them in the eye. If you don't want to bend down, pick them up and set them on a counter or table that brings them up to eye level with you. When you have direct eye contact, it means their brain is working with you and it's much easier for them to process your message. Eye contact is especially important when your children are in a situation where they may feel uncomfortable, like meeting a stranger or visiting a new place. It is also true if they are feeling edgy, experiencing pain or discomfort, and, finally, if your home is filled with relatives, music, activities, and other background noise. By drawing them to you, you catch their attention and help them hear your message.

What if they won't look you in the eye? It does happen, and not because they want to annoy you. It's very likely that it's occurring because they are in the red zone. Making eye contact requires giving up hyper vigilance caused by overstimulation and taking in everything. You have to calm them.

It's important to remember that every time we ask our spirited children to do something or to stop doing something, it's a transition—a change that can easily overwhelm them. We ask them to turn off electronics and come to dinner. Stop hitting their brother and instead use their words. Most spirited kids find any change or transition difficult. To stop doing what they are doing requires a shift in their brains, a processing of what's new and different.

If your child turns away from you, making a deliberate move that seems to say, "If I can't see you, I can't hear you," stay calm. Your child's body is in the red zone and he is trying to bring himself back into balance. Wait a moment. If he'll let you, gently touch his back, but often if he's gotten to this point, he doesn't want to be touched. If that's the case, simply say to him, "I can see you are not ready to talk yet. I will wait."

Emma used these strategies the day she looked out the window just in time to see her four-year-old son and his buddy urinate into a bucket lying near the sandbox. "I waited until he came into the house," she told the class, "and then I said to him, 'I saw you peeing in the bucket.'

"'We were making a pee trap,' he calmly informed me.

"'There are germs in pee,' I told him. 'The rule in our family is that you only go in the toilet, so you need to say, "Mom, I will only put my pee in the toilet."' He didn't like this idea, and I think it embarrassed him. The next thing I knew he had dropped to the floor, rolled under the table, and covered his ears.

"Initially I was really ticked off, but then I remembered what we'd talked about in class. I took a deep breath and said to him. 'I can see you're not ready to talk yet.'

"He uncovered one ear, 'I can hear with one ear,' he informed me.

"'But you're still not completely ready,' I told him. 'I'll wait.'

"It probably took him another two or three minutes, but it worked. He came out from under the table and said, 'Mom, I'm only going to put my pee in the toilet.' That was it, no thirty-minute tantrum and at least for the last three days, no more pee traps."

Whether your child turns away, closes his eyes, hides under the table, or covers his ears, it's important to remember he's not intentionally being disrespectful. He's overwhelmed and needs a little time before he's ready to listen to you. Wait, and then teach him that next time he can say, "I need a minute, Mom," or "I'm too upset to talk right now," instead of turning away.

Keep It Simple

You'll notice that Coke doesn't tell us you're going to feel good because it's really good stuff. "It's got formula XYZ in it, just developed by HW and Co., and we think you're really going to like it." No way. Coca-Cola knows that, given our busy lives, they have only a few seconds to catch our attention and get their message across. They keep it simple. In a recent commercial the feel-good images ended with one last photograph of a Coca-Cola bottle standing next to the words *Open Happiness.*

With spirited kids who are taking in everything around them, we too can expect to catch their attention only for a few seconds. That means our messages need to be succinct and to the point: Snack time. Shoes. Outside. Come. Freeze. The reasons why we want them to stop or why we want them to get into bed are important, but we can save the reasons until we know we have their full attention. Our initial interaction with them is just the headline— the words that grab their attention and pull them away from other distractions. When we know they are listening to our message, we can give them further directions. Sometimes we are running into trouble without even realizing it merely because our initial message is too complex. If you do not like how your child is responding to your direction, check the clarity of your messages.

Say What You Mean

Did you ever notice that companies never say "Please buy Nike," or "Buy Nike, okay?" Nope. Nike says, *Just Do It*. They know that *please* and *okay* can get you into trouble because they change a clear directive into a question. For example, at eight o'clock at night, after a long day, you want the kids to go to bed, right? Right! So you tell them "Time for bed," and you mean it. But without realizing it at all, you may have sabotaged yourself by adding *okay* or *please* to your directive. Instead of clearly saying "It's time for bed," you say "It's time for bed, okay?" or "Go to bed, please." It's easy to do. Spirited kids can muster such a fierce reaction to our directives that we add *please* and *okay* as a bit of a buffer. It is a tool on our part to diffuse the intense reaction we know we're going to get. But when *please* and *okay* are added, our spirited kids hear our directive as a question and immediately answer with a resounding no.

Choosing the right words is critical to winning your child's co-operation. If you want your child to do something and don't wish to debate it, be sure your message is a clear direction: "It's time for bed." "You may play in the yard." "It's time to leave." "Wash your hands before eating." And "The rule is you must wear shoes in school." These are all straightforward directives. They clearly and simply tell the child exactly what he may do. Make sure you are not unintentionally blurring your direction by adding the words *please* or *okay* or even raising your voice at the end of your statement as though asking a question, when there really isn't any choice.

Tell Them What They Can Do

Notice that Disneyland doesn't tell us not to go to Six Flags. That's because people don't like to be told what they can't do. They want to hear what they *can* do. This is especially true for intense, persistent spirited kids. To get the response you want, focus your instructions on the things they can do.

I was visiting a preschool when one of the children, a new arrival to the class, dashed across the room. It was the kind of action that often solicits a firm warning like "WATCH OUT" or "STOP" or even a time-out for inappropriate behavior. But instead of reprimanding him, his teacher redirected him to what she wanted him to do. Catching him midstride, she whispered in his ear, "Damon, in this classroom, we walk slowly." Then in an animated voice, she declared, "Let's practice!" Standing tall, puffing out her chest, and lifting each leg in an exaggerated step, she began walking toward the table. Holding her hand, he matched her stride for stride. When they reached their destination, both were laughing as she offered him a high five in congratulations. Pointing to a red chair across the room, she challenged him, "Try again, this time on your own!" Slowly, methodically he moved forward, each step a concentrated effort of controlling his body. Reaching the chair, he turned to her with a huge grin on his face. "You are really learning!" she exclaimed. "That's how we walk in our classroom." He smiled, confident in his new skill.

Yet not two minutes later, excited by the sight of a new toy, he raced from the table to the loft. As she went after him, she bent down and whispered to him once more, "Remember how we walk slowly?" He nodded gravely and calmly took her hand as she moved him back to the table with her. "Try again," she invited him, "I know you can do it." And then she stood back to validate his efforts. Once more he deliberately took one step and then another, each time looking back over his shoulder for her nod of approval. When he reached his destination, she moved toward him, beaming. "I knew you could do it!" Now standing in the loft, he flashed a smile, then leaned down and gave her a big, tight hug! "Thanks!" he declared.

Watching the two of them, I had to smile to myself. By telling him what he could do, she had won his cooperation—and his heart.

This teacher recognized that this persistent, active child worked hard to slow his body. She appreciated his energy and yet realized she needed to teach him how to move safely through the classroom. To ensure that she was heard, she gave her directions both verbally and physically. She not only said "Walk slowly" but also demonstrated her words with her entire body, taking big, deliberate steps. She emphasized her points. And she did it in a way that let this child know it was safe and even fun to work with her. As a result, the teacher received the response she wanted.

Listen to your directions. Are they telling your child what she can do? Do they say "Sit on your chair" rather than "Get off the table"? "Drink your water" rather than "Stop playing with it"? Is your tone inviting? When your message informs your spirited child of what she can do, it's much more likely that you'll get the response you had hoped for.

WORKING TOGETHER

Perceptive kids tend to have perceptive parents. Like your child, you may be working very hard to decide which information is the most important to you. It isn't easy to do, especially if you are distractible yourself.

Marni called me at home one day, troubled about her three-year-old son. It was a typical question: "How do I get him dressed, fed, and out of the house in the morning without a fight?"

I asked her what she had been doing. She explained that she had set up a routine that they followed every morning. They would get up at seven; cuddle for a few minutes; dress, eat, brush teeth and hair; and have a few minutes to play before it was time to put on coats and leave. "Sounds good," I responded. She told me it was working pretty well. They were fighting less, but she still felt rushed going out the door.

"We always seem to run out of time, no matter how early we get up," she lamented.

As she talked more about her morning routine, we both began to realize that like her son, Marni was very perceptive and easily distracted. When she helped him get dressed, he would run to the window to watch a bird. She would go with him and watch it too. When she asked him to come and eat, he would say, "Just a minute." She would give him the minute and start on a differ- ent task. Suddenly the minute had stretched to five. The cycle continued until the clock struck eight and they found themselves frustrated and rushed to get out the door.

Becoming aware of our own distractibility helps us to commu- nicate more clearly with our spirited children. It's important that we teach ourselves to recognize interruptions and not let them pull us off in another direction unless we choose to do so. This is easier said than done when you're living in a house full of kids. Next time you are working with your spirited child and are inter- rupted by another child, a call, or text message, consciously ask yourself, "Do I wish to change my focus, deal with the call, the other child, or text message, or do I need to say I will check in later and continue with my spirited child?"

You can choose how to deal with distractions, recognize them, and alter your communication accordingly.

Share with your child the techniques you use to keep your focus. When you feel pulled to do something else, tell your child, "My phone is ringing. Part of me wants to talk to the caller, but I know I need to finish what I'm doing and call back later." He will learn from watching you what he can do to stay focused.

Establish Quiet Settings for Tasks

When you and your children need to concentrate on a task, create a quiet, safe place to work. Think about what each of you needs to be successful. Check background noise levels. Loud noise can trigger the red zone. However, the *right* white noise or music can improve focus if it masks other disruptive sounds. What the sounds are will depend on you and your child.

Reduce options. Perceptive spirited children use more eye

movements than others to compare choices before making a decision. They process extra deeply and spend more time considering alternatives. An overabundance of choices can overwhelm them. When selecting a shirt, pull two out of the closet and place them in the bathroom so he can make his choice there. Avoid opening the closet door and letting him view all the possibilities.

Break large tasks into small steps. Otherwise, finding a starting point can become an insurmountable task. If he has ten spelling words, begin working on three. Set the others aside until these are mastered. If there are fifteen pages to read, break the reading into three segments of five pages each.

Understanding how and where you and your perceptive child work most effectively allows you to stay focused. Tasks efficiently completed reduce the frequency of those harried, last-minute dashes to the finish line.

Avoid Interrupting

When you are distractible, it is very tempting to share with your spirited child the thoughts that come to your mind. You see her building with blocks and say, "Good job." The compliment is appreciated, but your words interrupt her work, breaking her concentration. You tell her to get dressed, and then think to tell her to make her bed while she's in her room. She stops dressing and starts working on the bed. Five minutes later you're frustrated because she isn't dressed.

Better to save your compliments or your next instruction until she has finished her task. Otherwise her concentration will be broken, and she may fail to complete the job at hand.

Identify Your Attention-Getters

I talked earlier about getting your child's attention with multiple mediums: eye contact, touch, and short, simple phrases. If you are distractible, it may also be difficult for your child to get your attention. Think about the last twenty-four hours. What did your child have to do to get your attention, to get you to listen to him?

> *Your list may look like the one from a recent
> spirited-child class:*
> He hits or yells at me.
> She stands right in front of me and puts her face in
>   my face.
> He bites the baby.
> She whines.
> She hangs on me.

Or your story might sound like Matt's. "It was late and I was tired. As usual, my night stalker couldn't sleep. I soon felt his presence next to me on the couch. I tried to ignore it. I'd already sat with him, tucked him in, and read him a story. Enough is enough, I thought. Suddenly my ear was assaulted by inorganic flatulent noises. Not the real thing, mind you—this one created by the flapping of one's lips and the rolling of a tongue. It was grotesque. There isn't another word for it.

" 'What are you doing?' I demanded in my best authoritarian voice.

" 'Getting your attention,' he quipped, a big smile wiping his cheeks. 'You look at me when I make that noise.'

"You bet I look at you, I thought. The better to eat you alive!"

If you don't want to be hit, bitten, whined at, hung on, or disgusted, you have to teach your children how to get your attention. Decide how you would like them to approach you and then show them. Do you want words? What words? "I want attention," "I need a hug," or "Please listen to me." Do you want actions? A tap on the shoulder or the shaking of your hand? Do you need eye contact? Do you want them to stand in front of you? Do you want them to pull you down to their level and talk to you?

There isn't one right way, but just as you have to learn how to get your child's attention, your child has to learn how to get yours. Next time he whines, say, "Stop. I'm listening. I think you are telling me you want attention. Say it with words." Or if she hits you, say, "Stop. Hitting hurts. If you want my attention, take my hand." Then you have to be willing to garner your forces and give your attention to her.

Remaining focused takes a great deal of energy on your part if you are distractible. High-stimulation situations like airports, family gatherings, shopping malls, and restaurants are the most challenging because, like your perceptive child, you too may be flooded. Teach yourself to stop, take a deep breath, and think before entering one of those situations with your children. Do you have the energy to clearly direct them and help them to be successful, or are you exhausted, needing all of your remaining energy for yourself?

Don't forget to give yourself and your child a break after you've been working hard to keep your focus.

FEELING GOOD ABOUT BEING PERCEPTIVE

In *Essays*, author E. B. White draws our attention to the white feathers in the swallow's nest that allow the bird to fly directly to its nest after swooping into a darkened barn from the bright sunlight outside. He describes the smells of the farm and the light playing on the pond. He is a perceptive individual who has used his talents to enrich our lives.

The world needs perceptive individuals. It is very possible to enjoy our children's keen awareness and still teach them to listen to our messages. It does take more energy, especially when you first begin. Spirited children do listen. They listen well. With your help, they will also learn to identify the most important messages in their lives.

PERCEPTIVENESS
A Summary

Spirited kids are perceptive. Their senses are keen, drawing in every aspect of the stimulation around them. They see and hear what others do not.

Problems occur when they are barraged by information from their senses and are unable to sort it out. They often struggle to decide what the most important message is or where their focus should be. When this occurs, they become distracted, confused, and unable to concentrate on the task at hand or the instruction that has just been given.

Perceptive spirited kids need to hear:
You notice everything that is going on around you.
Sometimes it is hard for you to hear instructions when you
    are feeling uncomfortable.
You are very creative because you notice things other
    people miss.
You are perceptive.
You have a wonderful sense of humor.

Teaching tips:
Motivate your child to listen with words of support and love
    that let him know he is safe with you.
Send your message in many different ways, including
    talking, writing, drawing, and demonstrating.
Touch your child to help him attend to your instructions.
Make sure you have his attention by making eye contact.
Keep your message simple.
Avoid asking a question if there really isn't a choice.
Tell him what he *can* do.

If you are perceptive too:
Be aware of your own distractibility.
Don't let it stop you from following through with your
    spirited child.
Provide quiet places to work, rest, eat, and play.
Refill your energy bank after working hard to stay focused.

13

Adaptability

Making Transitions Easier

*Transitions are like a virus. They are the little things that
disrupt our days.*
—Becca, mother of two

Anna's shoulders slumped as she ushered her two youngest into the family center. Tears welled in her eyes when I greeted her. "What's up?" I asked, offering her a hug.

"I just put Hazel on the bus screaming and crying because the outfit she was wearing did not have pockets," she replied. "I've worked so hard to set up a routine and not rush in the morning. We were right on schedule just a few minutes before getting on the bus when she realized she didn't have pockets. I didn't have enough time to change her pants at that point. I stayed calm and tried to problem solve with her, but she couldn't think of a solution. Time was running out and nothing I suggested was acceptable to her. And now, I feel terrible. I want to help her control these emotions and come up with solutions, but it's so hard when the bus is waiting and the neighborhood is watching."

Transitions are one of those little things that can make or break a day. A transition is a change in routine, a shift from one place, activity, or state of being to another, or a need to adjust to an unexpected event like pants with no pockets. Transitions can be as simple as stopping play to come to eat, as common as switching from asleep to awake, or as significant as moving from one house to another. Spirited children adapt slowly to any transition. Each shift requires regulating their arousal system for the new activity without dropping over the edge into the red zone. When the intensity goes up, adaptability goes down. Switching gears requires a wrenching, grinding effort on their part. If you can't even get the kids out the door, in the car, to the table, from school, or cleaned up without a major hassle, the good parts of the day can lose their sparkle. Listening to their shrieks of protest can make you feel that a major overhaul is needed to correct the problem. Fortunately, a mere tune-up will do the job.

Smooth transitions are one of the most significant aspects of a good day. All kids benefit from planned transitions. Spirited kids *need* them. Temperamentally, most spirited kids are like Hazel. They are not trying to frustrate their parents or make them look bad in public. They simply find dealing with change and surprises extremely challenging. This is most apparent when they actually *want* lunch or *like* going to school and yet find themselves in a tizzy, failing to cooperate and fighting every step of the way. Change is so difficult for them that they'll get upset that the neighbors painted their house a different color, the bank replaced its sign, or you took a different route to school. Transitions will never be easy for slow-to-adapt individuals, but spirited kids can learn to manage them well.

USING WORDS

The beginning or ending of anything—a visit, a video, school, a meal—is treacherous ground for the slow-to-adapt child. To help spirited kids cope, we have to help them recognize and understand transitions, then give them the words they need to express their feelings about them. By identifying transitions and naming them, we can prepare for them and handle the discomfort they create.

It's easiest to focus on the transitions that we can predict. We can begin by looking closely at our day and asking, "Where are the beginnings and the endings of activities and events?" and "How will today be different from our normal routine?" Think about the most difficult times in your day. Odds are they are transitions like getting up and out in the morning, returning home at the end of the day, bedtime, entering or leaving places and activities, going to or returning from the other parent when custody is shared, and changes in routines due to vacations and holidays. (Check out the *Raising Your Spirited Child Workbook* for an entire list of daily transitions.) Once we recognize them, we can plan for success. As a result, your child will experience fewer meltdowns tied to daily transitions and free up extra energy to manage those that cannot be predicted.

> *Spirited children—even infants—need to hear words that help them feel good about their adaptability:*
> You like to know what is going to happen.
> You like routines.
> You like to have a plan.
> You can be flexible.

Spirited children need to hear words that help them recognize transitions:
That was a surprise.
That was different from what you expected.
You feel uncomfortable the first day your stepsister
     comes to stay with us because it changes our routine.
It's hard to leave when you are having a good time.

Spirited children need to hear words that help them manage transitions:
Change is difficult for you, but you can change and
     you do all of the time. Remember last week when
     you . . .
The shift from school to home is very tough for you,
     but together we can come up with a plan to make it
     better.
You like to know what to expect. Let's talk about the
     plan for the day.
What do you need to finish in order to be ready to go?
Where would you like to save that?
What would you like to take with you?

As you point out the transitions in her life and use words such as *routine, plan, time,* and *shift,* your child will begin to look for them herself. Mike discovered that even four-year-olds can do it. After recognizing that the nightly transition to bath time was triggering his daughter's meltdowns, Mike talked with her about the bath-time routine. Together they decided to set the alarm on his watch to give her a five-minute warning. Now when the alarm beeps, she says, "Dad, it's time for my bath." The battles have disappeared. Her confidence and ability to cope is increasing.

Your slow-to-adapt child needs to know she is not alone in her need for unrushed and planned transitions. Introduce her to other people you know who are thoughtful and cautious during transitions. Let her know she isn't odd. She isn't different. There are many people who share her same feelings, people who make us aware of our traditions and history.

ESTABLISH A ROUTINE

Routines are the lifelines of spirited kids who are slow to adapt. Routines provide a sense of predictability and safety. It is calming to know what to expect when awakening in the morning, who will be picking them up after school, or when they are expected to do their homework. When spirited kids know what to expect, they can begin making the change themselves. Routine reduces their discomfort and allows them to have the energy to manage transitions smoothly.

Look at your day. Does your child know what time she gets up in the morning? When she will eat? When she's supposed to get dressed? When you go on outings? When she can invite a friend to your home, or when she may use electronics? A spirited child needs to know these things—if she doesn't, you can expect a fight. A handy tool to help even toddlers and preschoolers learn the routine is a visual plan.

CREATE VISUAL PLANS

"Every morning was a tug-of-war at our house," Sarah explained during class one day. "Alex absolutely would not cooperate about going to child care even though once he got there, he loved it. I tried leaving quickly. I tried staying longer, but nothing seemed to work. He'd just lie on the floor whining or cling to me and cry. We were both a wreck."

"It was tough on his teacher, too," she continued, "because Alex's crying would upset the other kids. She suggested that we develop a chart with pictures on it so that Alex would know what to expect."

"At that point," Sarah said, "I was willing to try anything. I told him, 'Alex, let's work together to make going to school easier. What would make it better?' He told me that he was worried about leaving home and that he didn't know when I was coming back. I'd never thought about that."

She continued, "I crafted a six-frame blank cartoon form for our plan. I explained it to Alex and asked him, 'What's the first thing we do when we get to school?'

"'Put away my coat!' he replied.

"I drew a picture of his coat in the first frame. 'What happens next?' I asked. He shrugged, and I said, 'Well, what if we said you will find something to play while I watch?' He agreed and drew a picture of the blocks in the second frame of our plan. We continued with illustrations of waving good-bye and smiling, lunchtime, and a book for story time."

Sarah wasn't finished yet. "I pick him up right after

story time," she added. "So I said to Alex, 'Let's draw a clock. We'll make it say five P.M.—that's the time I'll pick you up.'"

Then Sarah and Alex read the plan together, putting words to the pictures: "We'll take off your coat, find something to play with, wave good-bye, have lunch, read stories, and when the clock says five, Mom will come to pick you up."

Sarah then folded up the plan and helped Alex slide it into his pocket, telling him he could check it any time he liked.

"The response was immediate," Sarah declared. "Instead of starting our day in tears, he put away his coat, found something to play with, and then waved to me. We used the chart for two months. After that we had the routine down and didn't really have problems anymore. I can't tell you how grateful I am to that teacher."

Adaptability isn't an issue when your child knows what to expect. By creating a visual plan with your child you give him a sense of comfort. You or your child can draw it, or use photos, or clip art. It does not need to include more than about four to six drawings illustrating the concrete steps of his routine. You can also create different plans for morning, evening, or drop-off, etc.

Clear and consistent routines win the cooperation of the child who is uncomfortable with change. That doesn't mean that you will never have a spontaneous moment again, but now you'll have a plan to refer to when there is a change. Not only will it allow you to point out exactly where the alteration will be, but it will also provide you with a checkpoint: are you making modifications daily? If so, the changes are too frequent. Your child needs predict-ability in his daily routine. If you are constantly altering what is going to happen, you may be unintentionally pushing him off the edge into the red zone. Routines provide a sturdy foundation that helps your spirited child stay in the green zone. If you find it dif-ficult to create and maintain routines, one way to make it easier is to limit the number of transitions.

ELIMINATE UNNECESSARY TRANSITIONS

When five-year-old Derrick gets up in the morning, he goes down-stairs to watch television. Getting him dressed requires turning off the television and going back upstairs to his bedroom. Some days he is asked to get dressed shortly after awakening. Other days he stays in his pajamas until noon. The one constant is a battle every time he is faced with a transition.

Every transition opens you and your child up to a potential meltdown. Turning on electronics then switching them off is a transition. Going downstairs to eat breakfast and then back up-stairs to dress is another. Dressing some days at 8:00 A.M. and other times at noon turns a request to dress into a surprise every time. When you are the parent of a slow-to-adapt spirited child, life is much easier if you eliminate those unnecessary transitions.

After consulting with me, Derrick's parents created a predict-able routine that they follow seven days a week. Now when Der-rick awakens he has a picture plan that reminds him to dress, use the toilet, and brush his hair and teeth before going downstairs. The use of morning electronics is banned. I know—that last sug-gestion made his parents shudder too. But think about it: How many fights occur over turning off electronics? Instead of playing a video game or watching videos, Derrick assists his parents in preparing breakfast, and as a result, they get to spend more time together before separating for the day. It also means that Derrick is already in the kitchen prepared to eat. They don't have to drag him from another activity to get him to the table.

Check your routines. Are there transitions like turning on and off electronics or inconsistencies in the routine that simply do not need to be there?

Unnecessary transitions can also slip into daily outings. If you are planning on going out, count the number of times you'll be in and out of the car. Know that for your child to be successful, you will have to *limit* the number of transitions. When taking the kids to an after-school event, instead of stopping to get something to eat, bring a snack with you. You will eliminate three major transitions and potential meltdown triggers: getting out of the car, taking off jackets, and getting back in the car. If you head straight to your destination instead, you will have extra time to relax together and enjoy your snack.

Sometimes unnecessary transitions seem necessary, like getting your child to one more activity. But if your child is balking when it's time to go, stop and ask if the real issue might be overscheduling. That was the case for ten-year-old Nora. "I know when she gets home from school she's tired," her mom told me. "But there is homework to be completed, piano to practice, and gymnastic lessons. When I ask her why she is fighting me, she says, 'I want to be free.'"

Spirited kids can take only so many transitions each day, especially if the transitions are major ones. Overdo it and you will lose them. Look carefully at the number of transitions you have included in your plans. Consider skipping a class or canceling an activity, especially if it is one that disrupts sleep or mealtimes.

Listen carefully: your child may be telling you she needs to slow down. Don't force her to yell, or have a meltdown, to be heard.

Knowing when to let go of an activity can bring harmony to your family. Look for a way to readjust your schedule or accomplish what you need to in a different way, rather than pushing and shoving until someone goes over the edge. There is always a solution, a way to respect your child's needs and your own. Look for it. The gift of a slow-to-adapt child is often that he is the first to let us know: "We're doing too much and it's time for our family to slow down and take a break."

ALLOW TIME

"If I rush Charlie, we're sunk," Kim said during an interview. "I can never throw him into a situation. The more time that I can give us, the happier we both are. But it means I have to be one step ahead all of the time."

Time—spirited kids need plenty of it to make transitions. You might not feel that you have that much time, especially if you have other kids. Anna, a mother of four, felt overwhelmed by the needs of her spirited daughter.

"I don't have *more* time," she snapped during our class discussion. "Getting Libby out the door is a full-time job as it is, and I've got three other kids. Our routine is clear, and she still doesn't cooperate."

Transitions are tough on our spirited kids. In order for them to go smoothly, we have to consciously allow ourselves enough time to assist them when needed. I convinced Anna to set her alarm fifteen minutes early by saying, "You won't be rushed. What do you have to lose?"

The following week she arrived at class *early*. "I've got good news," she reported as she breezed into the center. "You know how I resisted the idea of allowing more time? Well, after I thought about it, I decided to try it. I guess I'm slow to adapt too. Anyway, I set my alarm fifteen minutes earlier. Libby was already awake, but I let her lie in bed while I took a quick shower. When I was dressed, I got Libby out of bed. I didn't feel frantic because I was already showered and dressed. When she needed help with a blouse, I helped her instead of telling her I didn't have time (which I usually don't). When I was calmer, she was calmer, which allowed me more time for the other kids. I can't believe what a difference fifteen minutes made. You were right."

Then, just to make sure I didn't get a big head, she added, "But I'm *really* tired!"

"We'll work on that," I quipped.

Over the years I have learned that every five minutes spent in prevention saves you fifteen minutes of turmoil. If you would like more time in your day, allow yourself and your child extra time for transitions. Slow-to-adapt kids are not wasting time. They are working into the change and often need assistance.

Other people can sabotage your efforts to allow your child time to warm up. Sometimes you have to be assertive. At your physician's office you may have to ask the doctor to talk with your child and show him the stethoscope before she tries to touch your child. If you are going to an event with a group, you may decide to drive your own car so you can arrive early and allow your child the time he needs to acclimate. Even at athletic events you might have to discourage the coach from judging your child's performance by her first game, knowing that after she has warmed up, her performance will be much stronger.

It almost seems un-American, at times, to have kids who are

slow to warm up. Other people tell us to push them—to force them to jump in—and they reprimand us for babying them. When your child adapts slowly, remind yourself that you will appreciate it when he is an adolescent. While all the other kids are running off on some ridiculous impulsive venture, yours will be thinking, moving slowly and cautiously. There are strengths to every temperamental characteristic.

FOREWARNING IS CRITICAL

Forewarning is the process of giving a picture of the future. Slow-to-adapt kids need to know what the future holds. Whether you will be eating lunch, going to the doctor, having company, going to an event, trying a new toothbrush, or washing a favorite T-shirt, spirited kids need to be apprised of what will happen. Make sure they know what they will be doing, how long it will take you to get there, what you will be taking along, when you will be leaving home, who will be there, and anything else you know might happen.

The timing of forewarnings is important. Some kids need to be told hours, days, even weeks in advance what they will be doing. This gives them time to ask their questions and mentally prepare. Others will mull it over and get wired if you tell them too far in advance. You'll have to decide what works best for your child. Here are a few forewarnings used by teachers and other parents:

> You have ten minutes. What else do you need to do in order to be ready to go?
> In five minutes your time is up. Let's find a stopping point.

After this show we will . . .

Today when I pick you up, we won't be going home; we will
    go to . . .

When the timer goes off, it's time to go . . .

Three more jumps and then it is Mica's turn.

"We have to prepare Leo for everything that will happen," Melissa told the group. "Like today," she said, "my friend came over to visit. I had to tell Leo who she was, why she was coming, and how long I expected her to be here. He needs to know the 'little' things. I can't take anything for granted with him. He does fine as long as he knows what to expect."

"Learning to prepare for transitions really made my husband feel better," Heather explained. "Our two-year-old son, Braden, would scream whenever his dad arrived home. He would refuse to let him touch him and pushed him away. Thirty minutes later, however, he wanted to sit on Dad's lap.

"My husband started to take the 'greetings' personally and was really feeling bad. From our discussion in class I realized this was a transition. I started letting Braden know it was almost time for Dad to come home. When I heard the car, I would pick him up and hold him as my husband came in the door and tell him he could let Dad know when he was ready for a hug. He started reaching out right away. I think it was the forewarning that helped."

It isn't uncommon to give a toddler a "one more time" warning only to have him start crying because you've given the warning. You can empathize with him by saying, "You wish we didn't have to leave." Even though the shift may still be challenging, keep giving forewarnings. Gradually it will get easier for both of you.

Remember that the younger the child, the less he understands about time. Tell a two-year-old that in five minutes he'll need to stop, and you may still be picking up a screaming child five minutes later. Kids this age don't understand the concept of time unless you make it concrete. Directions such as "You can throw the ball five more times," "When the music stops," and "When the alarm sounds" all make time something real and easy to understand. You can also purchase a color timer or app which allows a child to "see" time pass. When you set the timer for a designated amount of time, the dial shows red. Gradually, as time passes, the color disappears. The child can *see* when the time is almost up.

If it seems like extra work to clue your child in on what will be happening and when, take note of how many times you check the time and think "in ten minutes" or review your schedule and make your plans. Or, imagine if your friend unexpectedly showed up at your door and asked you to "jump in" her car and refused to tell you the destination. Instead she simply said, "Trust me."

Just like you, your children need that information, but little kids can't get it themselves. You have to provide it. All you have to do is share your thoughts and actions with them. As kids get older, you can put more responsibility on them. For example, you might say to an older child, "What's your plan for getting your chores and homework done today before bedtime?" Eventually they'll prepare themselves for transitions.

ALLOW TIME FOR CLOSURE

Spirited kids like to finish what they're doing. Before they move to a new activity, we have to help them put closure on the existing one. You can acknowledge their feelings by saying something like, "It's hard to stop doing this." Or, "You can go back to it later."

Once you have forewarned them, give them the space and time they need to finish what they are doing. If it's hard for you to wait, don't watch them; instead, start putting things in the car or make a last-minute phone call. That's what Maggie did. "It was time to get ready for school," she told us, "but Jake, my four-year-old, was deeply engrossed in his Legos. He didn't want to get ready. Usually I would have screamed, *Stop right now!* And the argument would have begun. But this time, I asked him, 'How many more minutes do you need?'

"'Ten,' he responded. We didn't have ten minutes.

"'How about five?' I countered.

"'Ten,' he replied once more.

"'All right,' I said, 'I'm going to set the timer for five minutes and you see how far you get. And while you are working, I'm going to get other things ready.' I walked away.

"Soon I heard, 'I'm finished and the timer hasn't even gone off yet!'"

If you're short on time, you may need to help your children bring closure by closing the paints they aren't using, putting away toys, or storing all of the markers except for the one in their hand. Invite them to put their project in a safe place so they can return to it later; ask them, "Where would you like to save this?" Sometimes to bring closure and move spirited kids to the next activity, you will need to allow them a "transitional" object. Let them take a toy with them in the car or bring the ball to the table, asking them to lay it next to their chair.

At the same time that you are helping your child bring closure to her present activity, remember that you'll need to remind her of the good things to come by saying things like "We'll be having your favorite apple crisp for dessert," or "You'll get to see your friend." Knowing what's next eases the transition.

USE IMAGINATION

Spirited kids have a wonderful imagination. You can use it to move them from one activity to another.

I've watched parents get their kids to wash their hands by pretending they were a dump truck opening and shutting their hands under the faucet "dumping" water. I've seen toddlers so engrossed in walking backward or four-year-olds so excited about galloping like a pony that they didn't even realize they were in transition. All of these little imaginative journeys win cooperation.

This isn't playing games. It's being smart.

HELP THEM DEAL WITH DISAPPOINTMENT

Disappointment hits spirited kids hard. That's because disappointment is actually a transition—a change in plans, an unexpected surprise. Spirited kids need to understand that disappointment is very difficult for them. They experience a rush of emotions that easily overwhelms them. If they don't understand this, they may turn on you with retorts of "I won't" or "You can't make me." Or, like Hazel, who was saddened to discover she had no pockets, they may melt into tears.

Spirited kids are deep feelers. They can learn to handle their disappointment without letting it drown them, but it still is real and requires an outlet. In that critical moment they need words to use. You can teach them that they can say:

That's not what I expected. I need a minute to recover.
I'm having a tough time with this change.

Can we talk about this?

May I please have one more minute?

That was a surprise, but I'm a problem solver. I can figure
this out.

Words calm when they clarify what just happened and create a
mind-set of empowerment.

You can also help take the sting out of disappointments by
playing *what if* with your children. Before an event occurs, talk
through the things that could possibly happen. For example, if you
are going to a movie, ask your child: "What if we got there and all
of the tickets were sold out? How would you feel? What would we
do?" Or, "What if you went to a birthday party and they served
fruit salad instead of birthday cake? How would you feel? What
would you do?" Or, "What if you went to swimming lessons and
they called everyone's name but yours?"

What if teaches kids to be good problem solvers and sets them
up for success. If the *what if* actually happens, they're already prepared. They can name their emotions, and *know* what to do. Even
if you haven't predicted a surprise, practicing *what if* strengthens
problem-solving skills, making it easier to cope when something
unexpected pops up.

"Doesn't this raise anxieties?" parents ask me. The emphasis of
what if is not on what terrible disappointment or calamity could
happen. The emphasis is on our confidence in their ability to
solve the problem. What they *can* do. This is a supportive, comforting message. Kids don't become overwhelmed when they feel
in control.

I remember a New Year's Eve celebration in which we had
planned to go out to dinner with neighbors and then to see a

movie. We finished dinner earlier than we had expected and found ourselves at the theater forty-five minutes before show time. My neighbor glanced at the advertisements for other movies. "What if we go to this one instead?" he suggested. The other kids cheered. I darted a quick glance at my son, wondering if he would survive this "surprise." I saw his face flush and pulled him aside.

"Can you handle this?" I asked. "I know you didn't expect it."

"You promised we'd go to my movie," he stammered.

"I know," I said, "but you have also talked about this one. Think about it for a minute and then we can decide."

Amazingly my son survived the switch in movies. At five he wouldn't have, but at eight he did. I was pleased, but afterward I could tell he was still upset. The neighbors had invited us to their house for treats after the movie. I was pretty certain he wouldn't make this transition without some kind of "refueling."

"I need to check on our puppy," I said, excusing myself. "Josh, would you like to help me?" I didn't really need to check on the puppy, but I knew I needed to give my son a chance to let it out. He did, too—walked in the house and let loose.

"You said we could see my movie. You promised. That movie was *awful* [he was right]. Why did we have to change?"

I let him blow, and then said, "That's it, buddy, time's up. Change is always hard for you, but that's enough for now. You did a great job at the theater. Maybe later this week we can see your movie. We've got to go back to the neighbors' now." Together, we walked out the door. He had survived and so had I. Disappointment doesn't simply seep away. You and your spirited child need to find a respectful release.

WORKING TOGETHER

You might be thinking, "I don't have time for this; I can't be late for work," or "What if others are watching?" If you are in public, pull your child away from prying eyes. Acknowledge that this is a surprise, a change from what was expected. Give him a moment to calm. Then you can decide what to do. True, the clock may be ticking, but taking a few minutes to work with your child makes the entire day better for both of you. If the problem occurs repeatedly, take time to look for the *real* fuel source so you are not continually late. That's what Matt did.

Three mornings a week it was Matt's job to get his daughters fed, dressed, and out the door to drop the older one at preschool. The girls would dress, eat, and play together with no problems until it was time to leave. Then Amy, the two-year-old, would fall apart; dropping to the floor kicking away her shoes and twisting from her coat. "The routine is always the same," Matt said. "I set the alarm on my watch. They always get a forewarning, but it still isn't working."

It was time to dig deeper. What was Amy's resistance really about? "What do you think Amy is feeling or needing at that moment?" I asked Matt. He pondered for a moment before replying, "She really likes playing with her sister," he replied. Then suddenly it hit him, "Going out the door to preschool means Amy loses her playmate."

Recognizing Amy's disappointment, Matt now makes it a point to let her know all of the fun things they will do after dropping Elsa at school. Putting on Amy's coat is no longer a tussle.

The investment of time it takes to plan effective transitions is well worth the results. When the daily routine provides a foundation of predictability, spirited children have more energy to cope with surprises. There are fewer hassles and more successes. The good days start to outnumber the bad ones.

FEELING GOOD ABOUT ADAPTABILITY

As the frequency of successes increases, let your children know how proud you are that they have made the transition well. Appreciate how they stopped riding their bicycle and came in for lunch. Cheer when they get in the car without a fight—not sarcastically but triumphantly because they are growing and learning to adapt. Remark about the preparations they themselves have made to get ready for school or to go to a friend's house. Thank them for their flexibility. Let them know how pleased you are when, instead of screaming at you, they *tell* you that you've surprised them. In these little ways you reinforce their cooperation. Celebrate their successes, always remembering that one success leads to another.

If you are slow to adapt, too, you are working harder to cope during transitions. Establish a predictable plan for those transitions you can predict. Allow yourself a few minutes to center yourself before beginning transitions. Pause and breathe deeply when you are surprised. Appreciate your own limits. Sometimes staying home, dropping an activity, or even allowing yourself to occasionally be late may be exactly what everyone needs.

ADAPTABILITY
A Summary

Spirited children adapt slowly to transitions—any transition. To shift gears, to pass from one activity, place, or topic to another requires effort on their part. Smooth transitions are one of the most significant aspects for a good day.

Slow-to-adapt spirited kids need to hear:
Change is difficult for you.
You like to be organized.
You need to know what to expect.
You can be flexible.

Teaching tips:
Establish a routine and explain the plans for the day to your
    slow-to-adapt child.
Allow time for the transition from one activity to another.
Forewarn your child of what is to come.
Allow time for closure.
Eliminate unnecessary transitions.
Recognize when your child has been surprised or
    disappointed.

If you are slow to adapt too:
Allow yourself time to transition.
Plan to dip into your energy bank when your day has been
    filled with transitions—especially unexpected ones.

14

Regularity, Energy, First Reaction, and Mood

Understanding the "Bonus" Traits

He's got them all. No wonder I'm tired!
—Martha, mother of three

"Wait a minute!" Cody exclaimed, as he scanned the class outline. "There isn't a discussion scheduled for energy. Isn't high energy an issue for spirited kids?"

"It isn't for mine," Zoe answered.

"What about first reaction? No matter what we suggest, she says no," Katie grumbled.

"I wish it was just a first reaction," Rob added. "McKenzie wakes up in a bad mood. Don't we get to talk about mood? We used to refer to this kid as 'grump baby.' Of course," he added quickly, a twinkle in his eye, "that was before we learned about labels."

The conversation scattered around the room, with small groups spinning off. Our cohesive group was experiencing dissension among the ranks. They looked to me to explain it because one of the best things about the group was finding other people who understood what it was like to have a spirited child. "You're talking about the bonus traits," I remarked. "They include regularity, energy, first reaction, and mood. As you can tell, some kids score high on the temperament scale in these categories and some don't. That's why I call them the bonus traits. Unlike the first five temperamental traits (intensity, persistence, perceptiveness, sensitivity, and slow adaptability), which are common to almost all spirited kids, the bonus traits run about a fifty-fifty chance of appearing in the 'five column' for your child. Because they aren't common to every spirited child, I thought we'd cover them when we discussed bedtime, eating, dressing, holidays, and other typically tough times." I paused, waiting for a reaction to my suggestion. One glance around the room told me it had not gone over well! We needed to talk more about the bonus traits *now*!

REGULARITY

"I can hang in there all day, knowing I just have to make it until eight o'clock," Zoe stated. "I put him to bed at eight, and he sleeps until eight the next morning."

Erin turned to her in dismay. "Twelve hours." She practically choked. "I can't even remember the last time I got eight hours of uninterrupted sleep. Sawyer is sixteen months old, and I'm still waiting for him to sleep through the night."

Some spirited kids are quite regular and their parents can count on a good night's sleep after a hectic day. It is their saving grace. Others, however, are unpredictable. Their bodies do not seem to fall into natural rhythms. They're never hungry at the same time, can go days without having a bowel movement, and it's anyone's guess as to when they will be tired.

It is important to remember that if your child is irregular, he has a body rhythm that moves to its own drummer. He doesn't know why he lies awake at night, unable to fall asleep. It is a mystery to him why he isn't hungry when everyone else is, and all this fuss about regular bowel movements is rather confusing. You aren't doing anything wrong. He simply has a body that works differently. He needs you to help him adapt to social schedules and learn the skills he needs to survive as an irregular person in a very scheduled world.

Using Words

Irregular kids are often the odd man out. Because their body rhythms frequently don't match with those of others, they (and you) may think there is something wrong with them, but there isn't. It's important that they hear words from you that help them understand their irregularity and feel good about it.

"What can you say to your irregular child?" I asked the group. Blank stares met me.

"'You drive me crazy,' probably doesn't count, right?" Cody joked.

I laughed, noting that a sense of humor is essential to the survival of a parent with an irregular child, but I encouraged him to try again.

"You really are very flexible," Zoe offered, and the others followed.

"I don't have to worry about having dinner ready right at six o'clock. If you're not hungry, we can eat later."

"You are full of surprises."

"You can be a police officer like your dad and work the swing shift."

Our brainstorming ended as Rob quipped, "You're going to

love college life." Then dropping his voice, he whispered, "I'm not going to tell him that I am going to send him very far away so I can get some rest!"

Sometimes when your brain is fogged from lack of sleep, it is difficult to think of positive messages to give your irregular child, but he needs to know that you understand his style and that other people—even adults—experience irregular body rhythms too.

Creating Cues

Lack of sleep, the disruption of routines, digression from "social schedules," and the inability to plan are major issues facing the parent of an irregular child. In order for you to survive and avoid chaos in your family, you have to help your irregular child adapt enough to be able to function within a school and family schedule. It isn't easy, but it is important to do. Their natural body cues may be so erratic that you don't know where to start. In fact, mealtime and bedtime are such frequent issues for spirited kids that I have included a chapter on each. In chapters 16 and 17 you will find information that will help you to develop a routine that includes external cues—predictable signals—that help your irregular child set his body clock and function within your family's schedule.

As you face the challenge of moving an irregular child toward a more workable schedule, remember that it will take time. You will be gently nudging him. You are dealing with Mother Nature—the child's innate temperament. It can easily take three to six weeks to reap the rewards of your labors. In the meantime, remind yourself that your neighbors are not better parents because their child slips promptly into sleep at eight o'clock every evening. Their child simply experiences regular body rhythms. Your child is irregular. He arrived that way, but he can eventually become more regular if you support him in developing routines. You will still get to enjoy his flexibility, but once he's become more regular, you'll be able to savor mealtimes and get the sleep your family needs.

Working Together

"I hate routines myself," Zoe noted. "They are *booooring*. Ellie's irregularity isn't an issue for me. If she wants to stay up, I stay up. If she wants to sleep, I sleep. When I was working, I never drove home the same way twice. I can't imagine anything more mundane."

If you are irregular, too, your child's irregularity may not pose a problem for you. Be aware, however, that researchers have found that an erratic schedule is more detrimental to well-being than sleep deprivation alone. That's because an erratic schedule puts you and your child in a constant state of jet lag. Your brain has no idea when to be awake and when to be asleep. As a result your child may need more consistency than is natural for you to provide. Although it's unlikely that you will ever develop (or want to, for that matter) the kind of routine a temperamentally regular parent may, you do need to be sure that there is enough predictability in your home for your child to get the rest and meals she needs. One day she will also have to function on a school schedule, and her peak performance will be tied to adequate sleep. Fortunately, once you begin establishing more of a routine, you may discover that while you and your child don't seem to "need" or even like a routine, you excel and feel better when one is in place.

If you are a temperamentally regular parent, understand that your irregular child's body just doesn't work like yours. Within you lies an inner clock that tells you it's noon, time to eat. Or it's ten o'clock at night, time for bed. Your child's clock does not have these inner alarms, but you can help him set them. Gradually he will be able to accept a schedule and can thrive when it is in place. His body rhythms, however, will naturally want to *fall out of sync* any time the schedule is not maintained. The most effective routines for this child are maintained, as much as possible, seven days a week.

Feeling Good About Regularity

Take heart as you work with your irregular children. We need them. They grow up to be the nurses and doctors in the emergency room at two A.M. and the firefighters, police officers, pilots, chefs, and other professionals who work crazy hours while the rest of us sleep. It isn't easy to live with an irregular two-year-old, but sooner than we might think, they'll move away and let us sleep and eat in peace!

ENERGY

"So what about energy?" Cody demanded. "The kid sleeps, but he never stops moving all day long. I'm worn out from chasing him. Is there anything I can do?"

Immediately banter erupted. "Coffee? That's what keeps me sane—lots of it," Katie joked.

"The good stuff," Brooklyn insisted. "Lattes and cappuccinos."

Laura was adamant, "No, chocolate—it has to be chocolate!"

Cody rolled his eyes.

Laughing, I agreed with the daily dose of chocolate. Then more thoughtfully, I replied, "Imagine for a moment that you are trapped in this room. It will be at least five hours until you are released. Take note—there is no restroom. A quick mental check on your bladder should let you know how comfortable the next five hours will be for you. You might be in big trouble. Inside your abdominal cavity, you sense a growing pressure. Your bladder is announcing to you a grave need for release. Your brain is telling you to tough it out, ignore the mounting tension within you, but if Mother Nature provided you with a small-capacity bladder, no matter how tough your brain might tell you to be, this may not be a case of mind over matter. If you don't get out of here, you're going to be embarrassed. The sense of urgency increases. You feel strained, stretched to capacity. Your body practically screams for release."

Out of the corner of my eye, I noted that Cody was squirming in his chair and a few others had crossed their legs. I stopped. I didn't want to lose the whole group to the restroom! But it's important to remember that sense of pressure because just as your bladder signals a need for you and creates a pressure when that need goes unanswered, a child who is temperamentally active has a body that not only likes to move but *needs* to move. Your high-energy child isn't leaping off the furniture in order to scare you to death or trying to wear you out with his constant motion. He's on the move because he was born with a high energy level, and he needs you to help him direct it in positive and fun ways.

Using Words

High-energy kids need to hear from us that we appreciate and value their energy. Look at the messages you give to your child about her energy. Do they help her to understand and feel good about it? If they do, they might sound like these:

Your body is full of energy.

I wish I had your energy.

You need to wiggle and be on the move.

You'll make a great athlete and parent.

You are an energetic worker.

You like to learn by using your body.

These messages and others like them help a high-energy child to understand the urge to move that lies within her body. They let her know that her energy is a valuable trait.

Plan Positive Energy Outlets

It isn't your imagination that your high-energy kid is on the move more than other children. Recently I observed two eighteen-month-old children in our early childhood classroom. During the fifteen minutes that I watched, one child sat quietly at a table and played with a button game for ten of the fifteen minutes. His parents had rated him a 2 for energy level on the temperament chart. During that same fifteen minutes the other toddler climbed into the rocking boat, climbed out of the rocking boat, climbed into the boat again, leaped out of it, grabbed a phone off the shelf, ran to show it to his teacher, and threw the phone into the rocking boat before climbing in after it. In the time that I watched, his body never stopped moving for more than a few moments. Even when he sat down to "read" a book, he alternated between standing and sitting. His parents had ranked him 5-plus for energy.

All toddlers are on the move, pushing, shoving, dumping, climbing, and taking things apart. Toddlers learn with their bodies; however, the high-energy toddler is the epitome of energy—an energy that follows her into adulthood.

If your child is a high-energy kid, expect it; don't fight it. Plan for it. "After we completed the temperament chart," Katie said, "I realized that Imogen has a high energy level. Before, when she was continuously getting out of her chair, I thought I was doing something wrong. I just couldn't figure out how to get her to sit. I felt as though I wasn't in control of my child and it felt awful. When I realized that she has a high energy level, I started planning active play time every morning right after breakfast. If we take care of her need to move, everything else seems to go more smoothly."

"What kinds of things can you do?" I asked the group.

"We've learned Ellie needs to use her big muscles—jumping, pushing, pulling, swinging, pumping, digging, and pedaling," Kristin offered. "If the weather is nasty, we go outside anyway to dig in the snow or splash in puddles." She paused, as though wondering whether to continue or not. Then she shrugged and added, "If it's really nasty, I have her help me move the furniture, or we push the walls." She glanced around the room, nodding. "That's right—we push the walls, lift mattresses, and wrap up in a blanket like a mummy. It's magical."

"We enrolled McKenzie in swimming lessons," Rob said. "She loves them and is so much calmer."

"We only go to quick-serve restaurants," Cody remarked. "If we have to wait for a table, I know he'll be in the fish tank. He's only two, so I'm hoping someday soon we'll be able to go to other places."

"We let her be the errand runner at dinner," Katie added. "We send her for another carton of milk, the napkins, or whatever. That way it isn't as noticeable when she's constantly getting in and out of her chair."

Matt leaned forward, anxious to offer his advice. "I went to school and looked for the most active third-grade teacher. The guy was on the floor with the kids, he even had exercise balls and bikes in the room. No worksheets in sight. The kids were building and experimenting. I said, 'Put my daughter in that classroom,' and they did. She's doing really well."

I nodded in agreement, recognizing a teacher who knew the latest research: movement, included in and interspersed between lessons, enhances focus and attention. Test scores soar when bodies move.

No matter what the situation, it's essential to plan for your child's high energy. Expect it. Don't set him up for failure. Dance, take walks, sing songs with motions, and play ball daily. Select athletic activities where lines are short and the action is fast, such as soccer, basketball, and karate, rather than baseball, where there may be a great deal of downtime. Tour your home from an active child's point of view. Recognize that high-energy kids need more space and opportunities to move. A mini-trampoline or exercise bicycle may be more useful than another chair in a room. When you plan a trip, include stops for energy releases. By recognizing your child's innate need to move and preparing for it, you help him to direct his energy in a positive way.

Recognize How Energy Is Tied to Other Traits

When your kitchen sink overflows, water running across the floor may be the first indication that you have a problem. But unless you find the faucet and turn off the water—the real source of the problem—mopping the floor won't do you any good.

The same is true when your high-energy child "revs up." While it may be a leap off the steps that catches your attention, the real issue may not be "wild" behavior but an underlying emotion that he is expressing—an emotion tied to one of the other temperamental traits. Stopping him or slowing him down may not solve the problem unless you discover what he is really trying to say and teach him more appropriate ways to express himself.

Think about the last time your child got revved up and out of control. Was there another temperamental trait involved?

"Company was arriving," Mark offered when I asked the group this question. "The first person knocked at the door, and Nora took off racing around the room. It's embarrassing trying to greet people while your child is pinging around the room. I thought she was just misbehaving, but when you think about it, it was a transition. She really is slow to adapt. Maybe she was uncomfortable."

"Last holiday I thought someone had put drugs in my son's food," Laura added. "He was in overdrive. I wasn't prepared for that. I guess it could have been from too much stimulation. He really is sensitive." Then she asked, "Would it be sensitivity that makes him tackle other kids, or squeeze them?"

"Yes," I answered. "Sometimes with sensitivity it's an issue of too much stimulation, but other times it's getting the right sensation to calm. Pressure calms. That's why high-energy kids who are also sensitive love to wrestle and get into trouble for pushing or tackling. They are trying to calm themselves!"

"Perhaps for Justin it's about regularity," Mari offered. "He needs to be in bed by eight. If it's 8:15 he's overtired and becomes a wild man."

"I think the issue for Braden is intensity," Cody added. "He's intense about everything. When he's playing, he doesn't just grab one ball—he grabs four and then throws them all at the same time."

"Persistence is the problem for Ryan. I took him to play at the gym. They let the kids play on all of the equipment and then have parents and kids sit in a circle to sing songs. The other kids run to find a spot on the circle, but he won't get off the trampoline. He absolutely locks in."

High-energy kids express themselves with their whole bodies. If something distresses or excites them, they pop right into the red zone. Blood rushes to their muscles, immediately preparing them for action. That means if a child is energetic and intense, he may bodycheck his friend because he is excited to see him. If he is energetic and slow to adapt, he may run wildly around the room when grandparents arrive. If he is energetic and sensitive, his activity may turn into frenzy when he is overwhelmed by stimulation. And if he's missed his bedtime and is overtired, he becomes the "feral man" running up and down the hallway.

If you have a high-energy child, watch carefully for rev-up. When you start to sense that the activity is getting out of control, move in and check closely. Is your child just being active or is he acting out another temperamental trait? If it is another temperamental trait, you will have to help him deal with that particular need. For example, if he is intense and excited about seeing his friend, talk with him about the appropriate way to greet the friend and how to diffuse his energy and intensity by inviting the friend to play ball. If a transition is the issue, you may need to talk him through it. If the real issue is overstimulation, you may need to direct him to a soothing, calming activity or remove him from the situation. If he revs up when he misses his bedtime, protect his sleep.

If your child is expressing another temperamental trait rather than just being energetic, more climbing or jumping will not slow him down. High-energy kids don't wear out. In order to channel his energy well and to teach him to express his needs appropriately, find the real reason for his frenzy. Don't let the movement mask the true issue—another temperamental need. Use that awareness to help him calm his body; only then can he engage and listen to you.

Expect to Direct Him with Gentle Touch

High-energy kids are usually very kinesthetic learners. They solve problems by using their bodies. That's why they are always taking things apart or climbing across the table to get a toy rather than asking for it. They think with their whole body. As a result, it is very difficult if not impossible to direct the high-energy child with words alone. When the temperamental traits of high energy and perceptiveness are linked together, one way to let this child know that your message is important is to touch him.

Be aware, however, that grabbing him will only result in a struggle. Observe closely. When you see a slight slowing of his body, gently touch his arm or shoulder. In this situation your touch can be calming. Once he can look at you, you know he's ready to work with you.

If his activity is frenzied and you have to stop him immediately from hurting himself or others, wrap your arms around him and say to him, "I'll help you stop. I'll keep you snug as a bug in a rug." These lighthearted words help you stay calm and, as a result, help your child stay calm as well. Stay with him until his body calms, then he can hear you. If he's older, point out to him that he's revving up and help him find a safe release. Once he has slowed his body, he'll be ready to listen.

Working Together

High-energy kids demand a great deal of attention from their parents. Safety is a constant issue. Do not leave the high-energy infant sitting in a seat on the table or counter. She can flip right out. In a parking lot, insist that your young child hold your hand until he demonstrates that he will respond immediately when you ask him to stop. You can help him learn to stop his body by playing games like Simon Says. Simon says *run fast in place;* your child runs in place until Simon says *stop!* Simon says *jump;* your child jumps until Simon says *stop!* You can also practice slowing his body by giving him landmarks: "You can run to the tree." Or, "You can run to the steps, but then you need to stop." Only when he consistently demonstrates that he will stop when you ask him to can you trust him to walk next to you rather than holding your hand or being strapped into a stroller or child carrier backpack.

Monitoring the whereabouts and activities of high-energy kids and getting up to direct them requires stamina. If they are extroverted, their energy may come out of their mouths as a continual chatter from morning to night. Each word from them demands your full attention, and every toy they pick up may be brought to you for your appraisal. If you are a high-energy person yourself, you may be doing well keeping up with your energetic child. If, however, your energy level is lower than your child's, by the end of the day you may feel as if a Mack truck has hit you.

Of course, the obvious answer is to get a sitter to allow yourself a break, but as Cody reminded me in class one night, this may be easier said than done.

"Who," he asked, "are you supposed to leave him with? He wears out an older person, and a younger sitter may not be able to keep him safe."

True, this is a problem, especially with a young toddler, but you need to get a break. Talk with teachers at your local high school, or check with youth leaders to find a responsible teen you can educate to watch your child. Then invite her to your home to get to know your child and play with him until you feel comfortable leaving them alone together. If you still don't feel comfortable, wait until your child falls asleep and then go out, leaving the sitter to watch him. If you take this tack, be sure your child is familiar with the sitter and knows she's coming; otherwise, he may be very upset if he awakens while you're gone.

If you are a high-energy person, realize that when you have to sit still for long periods of time at a desk, or are confined in the house with small children, the pressure to move builds up within you too. You can't cope as well when you're trying to manage your own surging need to move. Exercise is a very important outlet for you. Plan it into your day.

As high-activity kids grow and learn to channel their energy in appropriate ways, the drain on you will be reduced. In fact, if you are also a high-energy person, you may enjoy biking, playing ball, and exercising together. If you're not, the opportunity to sit on the bench and watch while your child runs around a soccer field may be a wonderful break.

Feeling Good About Energy

Although not all high-energy people become professional athletes, in our fast-paced society adults with a high energy level are generally esteemed. They can keep up with a household of kids, the demands of the workplace, and still find the energy to volunteer in the community. Being energetic is an asset.

FIRST REACTION

"'No!' That's Asher's first response to anything new," Jared told me. "It's always been that way." He continued, "The latest issue is toileting. She's using the toilet at home, but refuses to use the one at school, because it's scary—at least that's what she is telling us.

They've been great, letting her just look at it, reading books in the bathroom, and even allowing her to choose which teacher would assist her, but she is still refusing to go."

"How did you get her to use the toilet at home?" I asked, wanting to build off successes.

Jared turned to his wife, Sara. Sara sighed. "It wasn't easy. We tried reminding her, pushing and pressing her, which did not work. We tried reward charts. She wasn't interested. We talked about other kids she admires who use the toilet at school. That had no effect. I've been firm." She paused, "I even forced her, like other people told me to do, but she just got hysterical and wet herself.

"What finally turned the situation around was when we were no longer pressuring her, or urging her to go to the potty. We let her go back to using diapers for a while. Then I suggested—not pushed her—to use the potty, which worked. I would ask her, 'Is today a day you would like to try using the potty?' When she said no, I didn't insist. But I kept asking each time. One day when I asked her, she said yes."

Asher is one of those children born with a tendency to become upset in new and unfamiliar situations. Their blood pressure rises, pupils dilate, pulse rate escalates, and vocal cords tense. They may complain of stomachaches and even gag or vomit. It is not a "learned" response.

When your child experiences a cautious first reaction, withdrawing from something new, it may be hard to imagine why he's doing so. It's bewildering when he suddenly refuses go into the water, when he asked to be signed up for swimming lessons. It can be extremely frustrating when you take your child shopping, and she rejects everything in the store; or when you prepare a new dish, and she pushes it away. It is draining when your child is upset all day because you sold the old couch and bought a new one. According to psychologist Jerome Kagan, "These kids inherit a neurochemistry that makes them very excitable." Anything new can send them into the red zone.

For these children their first and most natural reaction to every new food, stranger, place, and even smell is to push it away. If they are also intense, that reaction may include ear-splitting screams. But the research demonstrates that while we need to respect their caution, it is very important to help them work through it. Avoid using force or pressure, which, as Asher's parents discovered, does not work. However, don't avoid new situations, since avoidance actually increases their anxiety.

Cautious children need to feel that we believe they are capable of mastering new skills, a gentle, firm insistence that they move forward, and strategies that help them to feel competent in unfamiliar situations. By working them through their initial negative reaction, we foster the creation of new pathways in their brain, which literally changes the physical reaction in their body. I call this approach the *gentle nudge*. It begins with the words we use to help them understand what they are experiencing.

Using Words

Cautious kids need to hear from us that we appreciate and value their slow-to-warm approach. Look at the messages you give to your child. Do they help her to understand and feel good about it? If they do, they might sound like these:

> You like to watch before jumping into things.
> You think before doing.
> You are capable.
> You can break this down into steps so it will be easier.

You have bubbles in your tummy right now, but you are
  not ill.
Practice makes better.

It's words like these that help your cautious child understand
what she is experiencing. They let her know that her reserve is
an asset. She is thoughtful, not impulsive. And while her first response may initially be to resist, that does not have to be her final
decision. She can choose.

Lessons in the Gentle Nudge

"What's the difference between nudging and pushing?" I asked
the group. "Nudging makes me feel confident," Alicia replied.
"Pushing makes me feel out of control." Understanding the difference between pushing and nudging is critical when your child's
first reaction to new situations, people, or things is to reject them.
Spirited kids who experience a negative first reaction need our
nudge—not our push.

I first thought about the *gentle nudge* one day when I was waiting for my kids to finish swimming lessons. On that particular
day there was a four-year-old sobbing at poolside. His eyes red and
swollen, he shook his head in dismay, refusing to respond to the
instructor's words. She jumped out of the pool to bring him closer,
but his spindly wrist slipped through her grasp as he backed away
from the edge. He stood shivering, wanting to run yet hating to
give up. He looked imploringly at his mother, who was sitting next
to me. I wondered what she would do, and as I watched, she clearly
taught me a lesson in the steps to the *gentle nudge*.

Without any hesitation she walked confidently toward her son
and warmly gave him a hug. She didn't let his reluctance or tears

embarrass or frighten her. She recognized that he was afraid. Her actions said, "I am here for you. I understand. I am not angry. I am confident that you can do it. I will help you." *The first lesson in the gentle nudge: I will support you. I believe you can do it.*

I heard her ask him what he was feeling inside. Did his stomach feel pinched? Could he feel his heart pounding? He nodded. "That's fear," she explained. "You haven't had swimming lessons before, and your body is telling you to be careful. It is all right to be afraid. I feel fear sometimes too." *Lesson number two: The gentle nudge helps us name our feelings and know that others have felt that way too.*

The mother continued talking. "What helps me when I am afraid," she said, "is to sit back and watch for a while. I like to see how the other people get the water out of their eyes, how they kick their feet, and move their arms. Then I plan what I will do." *Lesson number three: The gentle nudge allows us time to think and an opportunity to observe so that we feel in control.*

Together, mother and son moved back to the bench along the wall and sat there watching the other swimmers. She reminded him how he used to hate having his hair washed when he was a toddler, and now he never cried and could almost wash it all by himself. "Maybe," she said with a smile, "you know more about swimming than you think." *Lesson number four: The gentle nudge builds bridges from our past successes to the present situations.*

The mom and son sat silently for a while, his body resting against her arm. His breathing slowed visibly as he relaxed, realizing he wasn't alone in this venture. The teacher came back to poolside and invited him to dangle his feet in the water. She promised not to pull him in. He looked at his mom. She nodded. "You can do it. Remember, it's just like the bathtub."

He sat down gingerly, first dangling a toe in the water, and then letting his feet sink in to his ankles. Soon he was kicking with both feet, and a shy smile crept up his cheeks as the water splashed on his legs and then on his face. The teacher clapped. "Great kicks," she exclaimed. "Maybe tomorrow you'll be ready to hang on to the edge and slide into the pool." *Lesson number five: The gentle nudge helps us to see the parts of a task so we don't feel overwhelmed and allows us to choose when we are ready.*

I saw the boy and his mother leave. His head held high, a smile on his face. He hadn't entered the pool on his own, but I could tell he was feeling confident. He didn't feel like a failure. He didn't feel pushed. He felt encouraged, capable, and hopeful for success. Who knows? Maybe tomorrow he'll be ready to say, "I can do it." *Lesson number six: The gentle nudge takes time.*

You cannot convince a cautious child with facts that she shouldn't be uncomfortable. The fact is, she is uncomfortable. Her heart is pounding, her mouth is dry, and her blood pressure is rising. She needs time to be successful. In order to respectfully voice her need for time, you can teach her to say things like: "I'd like to watch first." Or, "I'll be right there; I just need a minute." These words offer her an alternative to screaming *no!*

You can also help her recognize that it's helpful to bring along a friend, arrive early to watch the class before her own, view a video, or create a picture planner depicting the steps of what will happen. These strategies allow her to watch, listen, think, and calm herself before she is expected to participate.

Katie had been listening intently to my story, and as I finished, she nodded in agreement. "Keelin is so active. We wanted her to play basketball, but she absolutely refused. She wasn't going to try it. I knew that she would love it if only I could get her on the court. I told her, 'Keelin, I know you haven't done this before and you're feeling that you won't like it, but I think it will be fun—think about it.'

"Our neighbor Claire was playing on the eighth-grade team. We went to a game. Keelin observed intently. She asked a lot of questions, but I couldn't tell if she liked it or not. I kept my mouth shut. The next morning she handed me the registration form and said. 'Fill this out, will you? I want to play like Claire.'"

It's important not to let a negative first reaction trap your child in a corner. By giving her a chance to think, to observe, to gather information, Katie allowed Keelin the opportunity to let go of her first reaction and participate. It's important to give spirited kids this second chance—to let them know it is all right to change their minds. This isn't coddling. It's recognizing their temperament and working with it.

Our encouragement is very important for children who experience a strong first reaction; without it they may miss out on many opportunities, not realizing that with time, thought, and practice they'll truly enjoy themselves.

Recognize How a Cautious First Reaction Is Tied to Other Traits

Psychologist Elaine Aron explains in *The Highly Sensitive Child* that sometimes a cautious first reaction occurs when a highly sensitive person is overwhelmed by a barrage of stimulation. If this is the case for your child, you can teach him that it's easier to manage new social situations if he arrives early before the crowd and finds a comfortable place to sit. Research demonstrates that sitting in a new environment is more comfortable than standing.

If he abhors automatic flush toilets, he can carry sticky notes to cover the sensor before sitting down so there will be no surprise flushes. Wearing sunglasses at outside events reduces the discomfort caused by glaring light. If sensitivity is the real fuel source for your child's negative response in new situations, go back to chapter 11 for more suggestions of how to manage high stimulation levels.

Working Together

When kids demonstrate an immediate resistance, it tends to bring out a similar reaction in us, especially if our first reaction is rejection too.

"I know exactly how my son is feeling," Nicole told the group. "That's why I tend to just stay home with him to avoid the situations."

While you do not want to overwhelm this child with too many new experiences, the research strongly advocates teaching her that you will support her in figuring out how she can do something when she wants to say "I can't." She needs your gentle insistence that she is capable, and your steadfast belief that learning to manage new situations is an essential life skill. Avoidance is not the answer. Ultimately she may choose not to participate, but it must be a choice, not because she feels incapable.

Encouraging your child to try new things may also nudge you out of your comfort zone. Allow yourself to recharge as needed. Celebrate successes for both of you while also appreciating your thoughtful observations and decisions.

Feeling Good About First Reaction

Helping your child work through her first reaction takes time. It is, however, a trait that most parents come to appreciate as they begin to realize that their child thinks before she acts. During adolescence the value of this trait will be even greater. Your child will be the prudent one who moves through life thoughtfully.

If you experience a strong first reaction, reread this book! You may find helpful information that you passed by in your first reading.

MOOD

Kristin was laughing when she walked into class. It was evident she had a story. "This morning my eleven-year-old son Kyle was on his way to basketball camp," she began. "'Have a good day,' I called as he opened the door to leave.

"He stopped dead in his tracks. 'Have a good day,' he exclaimed incredulously. 'How can I have a good day? There's fighting in the Middle East, and the stock market fell ninety-three points. How can I possibly have a good day?'

"'Do the best that you can, honey,' I remarked and gave him a quick kiss on the cheek."

Kyle is a temperamentally serious and analytical child. Studies show that the secret to a child's disposition may lie in a specific pattern of brain activity. Some individuals are more upset by distressing events and less cheered by amusing things than individuals with a less serious disposition.

"It's true," Brandon remarked. "I never see the positive first. I always think about what's not working, and because I'm an extrovert, my emotions flow right out. Everyone knows when I don't like something."

For children who are serious and analytical, their mood is directly linked to their brain patterns. They need your help understanding their disposition and learning to be positive and tactful as well as cognizant of the things that need to be fixed.

Using Words

Serious and analytical kids see the world from a very serious perspective. They need us to give them the words to express those serious thoughts without offending others or creating a sense of hopelessness. There's a classic children's book called *Puppy Too Small* by Cyndy Szekeres, which provides a delightful lesson for analytical kids. In the book Little Puppy wails, "I'm too small! I can't reach the doorknob," and focuses on all the things he cannot do, like pull a toy. Others, however, gently remind him what he can do, like reach the cookies.

Analytical kids go through life like Little Puppy. They need our help recognizing what's working, as well as what's not. We can say to them, "Tell me what you enjoyed today, and then tell me what you didn't like." Or ask them, "If you can't do that, what can you do?" Let them know that you appreciate their analytical point of view by saying things like: "You're a good analyst." "You notice the things that need to be fixed." Or, "You think deeply. You will make a great judge or market analyst." Teach them to break things into parts so that they can clearly see the pieces they enjoyed as well as those that need to be reviewed or revised.

When you watch the world news, point out to your analytical child the anchor's serious presentation of the information. If there are other people in your family who share this perspective, let your child know that others see the world from an analytical point of view too.

Teach Good Manners

Small children are egocentric. If they feel it, they say it, believing that everyone must feel as they do. Help your serious and analytical child stay on good terms with relatives and neighbors by teaching her good manners. This is especially true when it comes to receiving gifts or enjoying a holiday meal. I'll talk about this more in chapter 20.

Working Together

If you are a serious and analytical parent, it is easy to overlook what went well and instead focus on what you want to be better. Remind yourself to pat yourself on the back for your accomplishments and celebrate each success, no matter how small it might be. Don't let one problem rob you of the joy of the good moments.

Remember, too, that your first inclination is to see the flaws. Allow yourself to look for strengths as well as weaknesses in your spirited child, in the people you work and live with, and in the situations you face daily. Hold a vision that maximizes their potential.

If you are not an analytical individual, understand that your serious child is seeing the world from his own perspective. When he points out to you the things he doesn't like or those that didn't come out quite right, he isn't necessarily unhappy—to him it is just a fact. Listen to his concerns, address those that are significant, and let go of those that are simply an expression of his view.

Feeling Good About Your Child's Mood

Serious and analytical kids can come in handy, especially when you are making a major purchase. In class, Ryan told us his twelve-year-old son Travis helped them make a very important decision.

"We were looking at a new house," he said. "My wife and I really liked it, and we were just bringing the kids through to get their reaction. Travis is a real estate agent's nightmare. As we went through the house, he kept pointing to different things saying, 'Our furniture would never fit in this room. Why would you want this? Look at this carpeting—what a dreadful color! The garage is too small. Look at the hill in the yard. You don't expect me to mow that, do you?' His critical eye took in everything. My wife and I really hadn't noticed those things. He was right."

The world needs people with a critical eye. They grow up to be evaluators making sure our programs are well run. They aren't afraid to make the tough decisions—and they can save you money . . . just ask Ryan.

REGULARITY
A Summary

Unpredictable describes many but not all spirited kids. Their bodies do not seem to fall into natural rhythms. They're rarely hungry at the same time, and it's a good guess as to when they will be tired. It is important for you to create routines that help them function within your family and the world at large.

> *Irregular spirited kids need to hear:*
> You are really flexible.
> You are full of surprises.
> You'll make a great emergency room doctor, pilot, or other professional who works irregular hours.
> You're going to love college life.

Teaching tips:

Provide a routine and a schedule that is consistent so your child can gradually adapt to it.

Expect your irregular child to take longer to adapt to a routine, but with patience and consistency he can.

If you are irregular too:

Be aware that you may be inconsistent with mealtimes and bedtimes because you are irregular. Your child may need more consistency than you are providing.

ENERGY
A Summary

Many but not all spirited kids are energetic. The need for them to move is real and inside. The challenge for their parents is to keep them safe and to teach them to use their energy in positive and fun ways.

Energetic spirited kids need to hear:

Your body is full of energy.

I wish I had your energy.

You need to wiggle and move.

You like to learn by using your body.

You are an energetic worker.

Teaching tips:

Plan for your child's energy. Provide many opportunities to run, jump, and climb, but monitor stimulation levels closely to prevent rev-up.

Avoid activities that require sitting for a long period of time.
After your child has been confined to a small space, expect
that you'll need to allow him time and space to move.
Recognize that wild activity is often related to the other
temperamental traits such as overstimulation, too many
transitions, or fatigue.

If you are energetic too:
Plan exercise in your day.
Know that it is difficult for you to cope when you have not
had exercise.
Enjoy athletic activities with your child.

FIRST REACTION
A Summary

Studies conducted by Dr. Jerome Kagan at Harvard University
have demonstrated that about 15 percent of all children are born
with a tendency to become upset in new and unfamiliar situations.
Spirited kids who experience a strong first reaction need our encouragement and a gentle nudge—not our push.

*Spirited kids who experience a strong first reaction need
to hear:*
I will support you.
It is all right to watch before participating.
You like to check things out before you jump right in.
You can think about it and then decide.
New things and situations are difficult for you, but
remember last time . . . when you were successful.

Teaching tips:

Encourage your child. Don't push him.

Forewarn your child about new things that will be
    happening. Talk about what to expect.

Allow your child time to observe.

Break new skills into small, easily managed steps.

Remind your child of similar situations that she rejected at
    first but now enjoys.

Allow your child a second chance.

If your first reaction is negative too:

Reread this book! There may be information you rejected
    the first time you read it, but with a second reading you
    may find it useful.

Recognize that your first reaction may not be your final one.

Do not avoid new situations. Remember, practice makes
    better.

MOOD
A Summary

Studies show that the secret to a child's disposition may lie in a
specific pattern of brain activity. She needs your help understanding her disposition and learning to be positive and tactful as well
as analytical.

Serious and analytical kids need to hear:

I appreciate your suggestions.

You are a good evaluator.

You think deeply. You will make a great judge, analyst, etc.

You are a serious person. That doesn't mean you are
   unhappy.
Tell me what you enjoyed. Then tell me what you would
   like to see done differently.

Teaching tips:
Help your child see the positives. If she can't do something,
   help her to see what she can do.
Teach your child good manners.
Ask specific questions that require her to think about the
   segments of an issue or situation rather than making one
   general analytical statement about the entire thing.

If you are serious and analytical too:
Practice looking for the positive aspects of people and
   situations as you analyze them.
Celebrate the little successes. Don't let one problem rob you
   of the joy of the good moments.

PART THREE
Living with Spirit

15

Planning for Success
*Predicting and Preventing
the Trouble Spots*

*I never thought about planning for success.
I just worried about surviving.*
—Kate, mother of one

When my kids were little, grocery shopping was a family outing—with two grocery carts. One for my husband and the children to meander around the store and one for me to actually get the food we needed. You might see this as a luxury. In our case it was a basic survival technique and cheaper than divorce court. (Neither one of us was willing to pack two weeks' worth of groceries alone.) It had to be early Saturday morning before the crowds hit or a Saturday-night family date. Not what I imagined for excitement when I was sixteen, but what the heck.

The kids *always* chose to go with their dad. There were times I felt a few pangs of guilt. Fortunately my insanity was short-lived, and if I was honest, I would have chosen to go with Dad too. Instead of struggling with them to stay in the cart, he loaded them up firefighter's style. The one who got the seat was the driver;

the one hanging on the outside was the tillerman. It didn't really matter because everybody got in and out of the cart a dozen times anyway.

They started at the dairy case. That was where everyone first jumped off the cart and started perusing the yogurt shelves, checking out the little containers and the big containers, deciding what looked best. The next step was determined by how they *felt*. Sometimes they went back to the front of the store for the bakery. It just *felt* like they should have a treat so they got one. Then it was down the aisles in random order, ten then five then two then six. In the end they hit all of them, but the cart rolled with the whim of the moment.

Forty-five minutes later I met them at the checkout counter. I had a basket bulging with fruit, vegetables, meat, and canned goods. The dog food was hanging off the bottom shelf, and the bread was teetering on the top. They had five half-gallons of milk, two flavors of ice cream, three boxes of cereal, an empty doughnut sack, three empty milk containers, and big smiles.

It hadn't always been this way. With a spirited son *and* husband, one spunky daughter, and a very persistent and focused mom, grocery shopping was ripe for turmoil in our household—until we figured out how to *plan for success*.

What we learned is that grocery shopping is repetitive, just like 75 percent of the activities in life. When something is repetitive, you can *predict* how you and your child will respond because it has happened before. If you can predict everyone's typical reaction, you can plan for success. You don't have to wait for the blowups. You can prevent them from ever occurring.

Think about it. In the last twenty-four hours, what have you and your child been butting heads about? If you're like the parents in my classes, it's very likely that you've spent thirty minutes with either you or your child in tears over her getting dressed. Someone left the table in disgust, and either the kitchen is still a mess or you have picked it up yourself. Homework was a bust again, and there was at least one hassle over going somewhere.

You *know* these things will happen because they happen all the time. As the parent of a spirited child, you can use that awareness *to plan for your child's success!* You can put into use your knowledge of temperament, the words that you have learned to use, and the techniques that work for managing spirit to prevent daily hassles. I've designed four simple steps that you can follow. They are:

1. Predict the reactions
2. Organize the setting
3. Work together
4. Enjoy the Rewards

Just remember POWER. (Yes, I cheated to make the acronym, but I'm close!)

PREDICT

Predicting the reactions means beginning each day thinking about how you can help your spirited child be successful. An interesting thought, isn't it? Not focusing on how to make him behave or how to survive, but how to be successful.

In the morning mentally run through the day. What will your child be doing? What typical tough times will you both encounter? Will his routine be normal or disrupted for some reason? Who will your child be talking with or meeting for the first time? Where will he be going? Will he be exposed to any new experiences? Will he have to wear clothing that is unfamiliar to him or less comfortable? Will he have to be quieter than usual? Will there be lots of stimulation?

If you answered yes to any of these questions, think about what type of reaction you could expect from your child in these situations. If you always fight about getting dressed, expect to fight today. If you are going to start gymnastics lessons and your child hates new things, expect a reaction.

In class, I asked the parents to predict some typical tough times. Their list looked like this:

- getting dressed
- coming home from school or child care
- taking medication
- leaving dance class
- going to bed
- trying new things

"Now," I said to the group, "review the temperamental traits— all of them, including the bonus points. Which ones might explain your child's reaction?"

Rob looked at his list and answered, "Dressing is a hassle because McKenzie is persistent. She always wants to do it herself. She is sensitive, so the textures bother her, and she is slow to adapt, so changing clothes is difficult."

"You've got it!" I exclaimed.

We quickly ran through the others. The reaction to coming home after school is an issue of adaptability. Taking medication is difficult because of persistence, sensitivity, and intensity. Leaving dance class is challenging because of adaptability and sensitivity—there has been a lot of stimulation. Going to bed is a major effort because of persistence, adaptability, sensitivity, intensity, and if you throw in the bonus traits of regularity and energy for good measure, it can be really tough! And trying new things involves managing intensity and moving through a cautious first reaction.

By using the temperament charts, you can predict your child's reactions to typical situations. Remember, your child can't change her temperament, but she can learn how to express it in an acceptable and positive manner. As your child grows older, include her in predicting her reactions. Help her to identify situations that may be stressful for her. The older she is, the more you can expect her to take over this responsibility herself. Eight-year-old Amy can do it.

"I wanted to run to the grocery store before supper last Friday night," Amy's mother explained.

Amy was watching television. She seemed pretty wiped out, but I didn't want to wait until Saturday when the crowds are like a nervous hive. I forewarned her, "Amy, at the next commercial, we're going to the grocery store; you have to come with me."

She groaned. I braced myself. "Mom, I just can't do it. I can't take all of the people and noise and the lights in the store today. Can't you wait until Dad comes home? Then you can go all by yourself and I can stay home."

I didn't know what to do. Part of me said that I should make her go because not going would be giving in. Part of me said that I should listen to her. She's not trying to control me. She's telling me she can't be successful in the store today. It wouldn't kill me to wait thirty minutes. But I'm persistent, and this was tough on me.

I called my husband to find out what time he would be coming home and to talk through my decision with him. I am an extrovert, and I need to hear myself think. He's a good sounding board and helps me unlock. His perspective is helpful because he is a lot more like Amy and understands her better than I do.

"I can empathize," he said. "It's been a hard week. We were out on both Tuesday and Thursday nights. I'm exhausted too. I couldn't face going to the grocery store tonight."

I folded another load of laundry and waited until he got home to go to the store. I wasn't sure whether to be happy she had used words and hadn't thrown a fit or to be angry that I had to wait. I still wasn't certain if this was giving in. But I did it. I have to say it was a lot easier to shop without her, and when I came home, they had supper ready. That was nice. I guess in the end we both got what we wanted.

Amy had predicted her reaction and a potential trouble spot. Her mother had respected her prediction. Together they avoided a blowup in the store. Respecting temperament means thinking about it and trying to set up situations so that everyone wins.

For infants and toddlers you will have to do all of the predicting, but make a habit of telling them what you are thinking. They will learn from listening to you, and they will begin doing it themselves when they are ready.

Preschoolers can begin making some predictions for themselves. You can help them by asking questions such as: "We're going to the store today. What do you need to be comfortable?" Or, "Tomorrow is a school day. What do you need to be ready in the morning?"

School-age children can begin taking over much of the planning themselves. You can say to them: "It's always hard for you to leave your dad's on Sunday night; transitions are tough for you. What will make it better?" Or, "Noise wears you out. After being in school all day, it's hard for you to get in the car with your talkative sister. Would it help if you had a headphone so you could control the sound?"

Be careful not to fall into a rut. Your predictions will change as your child grows and develops and becomes more competent in managing her temperament. Although a spirited two-year-old may not be successful at a birthday party for twelve kids, a spirited six-year-old may be. The reactions and skill levels change and so must our predictions.

After thinking through your day, expand to your week and even your month. You can predict that the shift to daylight savings time will cause problems at bedtime and morning time for your slow-to-adapt child, so be ready for it. Changing seasons means switching from shorts to jeans; expect a problem for the sensitive kid. Your mother schedules Thanksgiving dinner for 2:30 P.M.—smack in the middle of your two-year-old's naptime—and she expects him at the table. A slow-to-adjust child will not be happy.

As you make your predictions, think about your own reactions as well. Is the switch to daylight savings time difficult for you too? Does the stimulation level in a store give you a headache? By predicting both your reaction and your child's, you can create a plan for success.

ORGANIZE THE SETTING

In theater production there is a stage designer—the person who takes the script and creates the environment in which the action can happen. Along with a lighting director, he also creates the cues for the changing of scenes or the passing of time.

Once the stage is set and the cues are established, a stage manager makes sure the actors always have the objects they need to go forward—the clothes in the closet, the chair to sit on, or the water to drink. And it is the stage manager who ensures that the cues for the transitions from one setting to another occur smoothly and consistently at every performance.

As the parent of a spirited child, you have to think like a stage designer and act like a stage manager. Knowing that your child is spirited, you have to create the environment that will help her behave appropriately. You have to decide what cues she will need to help her perform. And you have to consistently provide her with the props she will need to be successful. Ultimately she'll take over these tasks herself.

We actually have many choices for altering our environment in a way that promotes our child's success. The more we can organize the setting to fit with our child's temperament, the happier everyone will be. Daniel found this to be very true.

"Whenever we get together with my family, they insist on going out to eat," Daniel told the group.

It's a two-hour drive to their house. My son, Milo, is very active. The last thing he needs is to sit in a chair again for another hour. I know it won't work, but my father is insistent. I don't want to get in a fight with Dad, so I force Milo to go and I try to make him sit. Of course he won't, and I get snarled at for not controlling him. I can't win. If I take him, he's a brat, and if I refuse to go because he can't handle it, they say I'm spoiling him.

Last weekend I finally realized that *both* my dad and Milo are spirited. So I decided to try planning for success. Knowing that Milo wouldn't be successful in a restaurant but that my dad, who is incredibly regular, would want to eat, I planned a picnic for noon—just when Dad likes to eat. I called ahead and had him meet us at the park—just like old times, I said. He bought it. It was the best visit we've had in years. My dad was actually boasting about Milo, pointing out to other people that his grandson was only four years old and could hang by one knee on the monkey bars!

Daniel had predicted that high-energy Milo could not be successful in a restaurant after traveling two hours in a car. He also understood that his very regular father would need to eat. So Daniel planned a picnic. He selected a location where he knew Milo could be successful and provided the food his dad's body required. Daniel organized the setting for success.

Sometimes, without thinking, we put our kids in situations where it is impossible for them to be successful, such as taking the spirited toddler to a formal wedding reception or planning a gourmet dinner for twelve and expecting our six-year-old to just hang around quietly. But carefully creating and selecting a setting can help your spirited child be more successful. (Considering the temperament of the relatives or other adults involved can help too!)

Think about stimulation levels, amount of space for movement, and/or touchable versus breakable items as you make your selection. Don't be afraid to remove tempting nontouchable objects.

Avoid toys that promote aggressive play, like make-believe guns or action video games. Choose a familiar site over an unfamiliar one if your child will also be changing his schedule or meeting new people. Create a setting that helps your child be successful.

Plan Appropriate Activities

The set manager knows that if he wants the actors to eat, there has to be food. If he wants them to put on a hat, there has to be a hat. The right props have to be available for the proper behavior to occur.

As the parent of a spirited child, you have to make sure that the right props are available for your child—the objects that encourage the kind of behavior you want. If you know your child will have to sit quietly, make sure she has books to read and paper and markers to use. Before handing over an electronic device, observe closely whether electronics provide a helpful distraction or in the long run end up overstimulating your child.

Remember, intense kids need soothing, calming activities. Sensitive kids like things they can touch, taste, and smell. Energetic kids like to move. By bringing along or including activities and objects that your spirited child will enjoy, you prevent him from getting into trouble. If he doesn't have the appropriate things to do, you will find him touching things that shouldn't be touched or jumping on things that shouldn't be jumped on.

"I always take along our survival kit," Christie offered. "It includes Handi Wipes, water, crackers, a notepad, crayons, a Nerf ball, and a blanket. I've told Olivia, who is only three, what I'm doing and have had her help. Lately she has started packing her own backpack. She brings it everywhere. But if I don't want her to take it in, she is willing to leave it in the car."

Activities, objects, and props allow the actors to do what they are supposed to do. The same holds true for kids.

Create a Space for Introverts

To recharge, introverts need a quiet out-of-the-way space. Many settings, however, even classrooms especially designed for kids, don't include a hideaway for introverts to refuel. As you organize the setting, be sure that you have created a space for your introverted child. He'll need it to keep his energy level high.

WORK TOGETHER

We can't plan for success all by ourselves. We also have to get cooperation from our spirited kids. Working together is *not* playing games. It is respecting temperament.

In theater it is the director who creates the vision of what should occur. In planning for success, you are the director, and it is you who hold the vision of your child's success. Like a director, it is you who adapt the expectations to fit the situation and your particular child. It is you who help your child to understand what is expected of her and to perform to the very best of her ability. In the previous chapters you have learned many techniques that allow you to work together with your child to bring out her best. Use this new awareness as you plan for success.

CONSIDER ENERGY LEVELS: To ensure your child's maximum performance, consider energy levels when you schedule appointments, classes, parties, or outings. Energy levels are usually highest at the beginning of the day and lowest in the late afternoon or evening. By carefully selecting the best time of day for your child, you are helping her to be successful.

"I used to schedule Ellie's gymnastic classes in the evenings because I liked to keep my weekends free," Zoe said. "But it was always a fight getting her there and getting her out again, even though she loved gymnastics. Once we missed a sign-up date and were forced to take a Saturday-morning class. What a difference. Her energy level is so much higher. She's up and ready to go. Even getting her out is less of a hassle, and I find myself more patient too. We may never take an evening class again."

The more you can schedule activities and events during your spirited child's peak energy times, the better her performance. Look for the schedules and times that will fit your child best. Resolutely protect her sleep times. You will be expending energy in a positive and preventive way, rather than in a struggle.

Of course, not everything can be scheduled around your child's peak performance times, but if the majority of events fit, those that don't will be easier to handle. If you know you can't change the schedule, then do your best to help your child refill her energy bank before the activity begins.

SHARE YOUR VISION OF SUCCESS: What is success? If you don't tell your child, she won't know. Make sure your child knows what *being successful* means as you work together.

    a. *If your child is intense.* Remind him of his cues and let him know what soothing/calming activities are available if he needs them.

    b. *If your child is persistent.* Look for *yes* with him. "I take away the mystique," Cassidy told the group. "I let him do something to participate. If I say no, it's too hard or too dangerous, he'll be right there in the way. But if I give him a job to do, like pick up the log and carry it to the garage, he'll work and work. You have to expect it will slow you down and it won't be a perfect job, but he sure feels good about himself."

And remember to clarify the expectations with your persistent child. "Abigail is five. We sit down together and talk about what the expectations will be. It's easier for her to follow them when we review them before we go or if she helps make them up."

c. *If your child is sensitive.* Talk about feelings and remind him of his cues for overstimulation.

d. *If your child is perceptive.* Talk about how you will get his attention. Write down directions or schedules or make a picture planner together.

e. *If your child is slow to adapt.* Let him know the agenda.

Jake wins his son Maverick's cooperation by making sure he knows the specific details. Jake explained, "I'll say things like, 'We're going in the car. We will drive down Cedar, past City Hall and the gas station, until we get to Chipotle. We will have dinner there. You can order a taco or a burrito. Think about which one you would like.'"

Letting Maverick know the agenda gives him the time he needs to make a decision and to make a transition easily.

KNOW WHEN TO QUIT: A good director also knows that selecting the appropriate length for a performance is a key to its success. Plan your family activities with the kids in mind. Often that means making them shorter than the adults would like them to be, but overall, everyone has a better time if the kids are still smiling at the end of the trip. For spirited kids who are sensitive, intense, and sometimes energetic, this may be a shorter period of time than for other children their age. That's because spirited children must work much harder to cope than children who are not quite as spirited.

ENJOY THE REWARDS

At the end of a great performance the actors are rewarded with applause and cheers from the audience. When you and your child have been successful, you too deserve recognition for a job well done. Capture those moments of success and celebrate them.

RECOGNIZE YOUR CHILD'S ACHIEVEMENTS: It is very easy with a spirited child to focus on what she has done wrong instead of what she has done right. Let your child know how proud you are of her good behavior. Say it with smiles, hugs, and words. If you have not been taught to celebrate strengths, you may find this difficult to do.

John was afraid of creating an egomaniac. "I never told Peyton how proud I was of him when he behaved well. I thought he should just do it. I was worried that if I praised him, he would get conceited or would expect it all the time. My wife pointed out to me how good I felt when my boss told me I had done a great job on a project. 'Don't you think Peyton would like to hear he did well too?' she said.

"I couldn't disagree. Peyton really seems to be responding. The other day he said to me, 'Dad, you did a good job keeping your cool with that mean clerk.'

"How's that? My kid giving me pats on the back!"

"I thank him," Erica, the mother of seven-year-old Jasper, said. "I make sure he knows exactly what I am thanking him for, like,

'Thanks for sitting so quietly in the restaurant. We'll have to do that again because you did such a good job.' "

You don't have to restrict your good words just to your child. Hearing you tell other people how well she picked up her room or how competently she handled swimming lessons can be a great incentive to spirited kids to repeat that super behavior.

APPRECIATE YOURSELF: As the parent of a spirited child, you have to remember to pat yourself on the back for the little successes, to celebrate your moments of greatness. When you have predicted a difficult situation and prevented it, tell a friend, write it down in your journal, or stand in front of the mirror and tell yourself, "I'm good!" Treasure the moments of success. Don't let them slip away without the recognition they deserve. Remember, directors and stage designers win awards too.

PLANNING FOR SUCCESS CAN BE USED ANY TIME

Planning for success—learning to Predict your child's reactions, Organize the setting for success, Work together, and Enjoy the Rewards—gives you POWER to face those typical tough times head-on.

My friend Jenna and I were having lunch one day. She works with three-year-olds and finds it fascinating to figure out how they think. One little guy named Jake was known among the staff for his loud protests and determined nos. "It's been very difficult, trying to help him be successful," she told me. Just that day she'd introduced a handprint turkey activity to the kids. Making the turkey print required painting each child's hand. Jake's response to this activity was a resounding *"No!"* Now, making a turkey print is really not going to make or break a child's chances for success in school. Jenna knew that, but she also knew that such strong protests were likely to get Jake into trouble in other classrooms and that learning to try new things and work together were essential life skills. She also foresaw his disappointment when all the other children had the turkey-print table decoration to hand to their parents and he didn't.

I told her about planning for success. Her eyes lit up. "I think it would work." She decided to implement her plan the very next day. "Initially," she told me later, "I couldn't figure out why he reacted so strongly. But then I began to recognize that he gets upset every time there is something new or a 'surprise.' He is also incredibly sensitive, noticing the fuzz inside of his mitten, insisting he needs a new shirt when his sleeve gets wet, and refusing to try the finger paints. I checked the temperament chart. Intensity certainly fit, but that wasn't the trigger. Then I saw sensitivity, adaptability, and first reaction. Aha—I realized he's highly sensitive to touch, and his first reaction is definitely cautious. Even thinking about starting something different sends him into a spin. I could work with that!"

Jake was having a good day, so Jenna decided to grab the teachable moment and work with him. Like the stage director, she created a vision of what was to come. "Remember," she reminded Jake, "how I told you that there are times in school when we don't have choices and sometimes we do?" He nodded, recalling their earlier conversation. "Well," she said, "this is one of the times we don't have a choice. It's important to make a turkey print to take home for your mom, and it's important to practice trying different things."

"I won't!" He protested loudly, his intensity flashing. Jenna didn't perceive his protest as a threat to her but simply as a message of how strongly he felt about this activity. She kept her voice low and calm. "I know it's hard," she whispered. "We can wait until you're ready." ..

He glared at her. "You can't make me!"

"No, I won't make you," she responded. "We'll just wait until you're ready."

Thoughts tumbled through her mind. What might he be feeling? How could she organize the setting so that he would feel safe enough to try the activity? "Do you know that the paint will come off?" she asked him, guessing that perhaps he feared his hand would be rainbow-colored for the rest of his life."

He twisted, refusing to look at her, and then bolted. "Remember, you can play when we're finished," she reminded him as she gently brought him back.

Then she guessed, "Do you wonder if it would tickle?" Demonstrating on her own hand, she lightly caressed her palm with the bristles of the brush, to show him what she would do. He watched silently. "We could just run the brush across your hand without paint, if you'd like to see how it would feel." He held his hand out, and she lightly caressed his palm with the bristles. "We could put brown paint on your thumb for the head. What color would you like on your pinky?"

He listened, sinking his hands deep into his pockets before mumbling, "Red."

"Okay, we'll put red on your pinky, and what about your pointer? What color would you like on that finger?" she asked, holding up her own.

"Yellow," he announced more quickly this time.

"All right."

He snorted. "I'm not taking my hands out of my pockets and you can't make me."

"I know, you're not ready yet."

He sighed as though reconciling himself to the inevitable.

Jenna noticed and paused, thinking perhaps just a few more questions would help him move through his strong negative reaction. "What about your ring finger? We haven't decided about that one yet."

His brows furrowed in thought. "Green."

"Okay, now we have red, yellow, and green, and for the middle finger?"

"Blue," he announced, his shoulders noticeably beginning to relax.

Jenna held up her own finger, touching it lightly with the brush. "If you'd like to see how it feels, we can put just a dab on the point of your finger like this."

He slid his hand out of his pocket. Carefully, she placed a minute speck of paint on his fingertip.

"That doesn't tickle," he exclaimed in surprise.

"Shall we try the next finger? I'll run the paint down the entire finger this time. And if you want me to stop, you can say 'Stop!' and I will." Once again she demonstrated on her own finger.

He nodded seriously, sighing deeply when she finished. "That's not too bad," he reported.

They continued working slowly through the activity until he had in front of him his own turkey handprint ready to take home. His entire face was glowing in a rapturous smile. "They're going to love this!" he shouted, leaping up from his chair and holding the turkey handprint high in the air. "That wasn't too bad. That wasn't too bad at all! Wait until they see this!"

Jenna laughed with him. "You did it! You made a turkey hand-print. It wasn't easy, because you are very sensitive and you like to think about things before you try them, but you did it! And next time it will be even easier!"

Planning for success allows you to see your child's negative response not as a threat to your authority but simply as a strong communication of his feelings. Predicting those feelings allows you to work with them.

It's not easy to know what a child may be feeling, but by thinking about his temperament and making an effort to see a situation from his point of view, you clearly communicate that you are trying to understand. Your child will sense it, feel safe, and as a result his intensity will come down.

Jenna also worked together with Jake, not forcing him but gently nudging him through the activity. When he resisted, she didn't jerk him back, yet she didn't let him go. She simply said, "We'll wait." No push, no shove, just a gentle nudge and clear expectation—we're going to practice. Practice will make it better. You can do it.

The researchers call this scaffolding: letting a child *know* what we are going to do together, *showing* him what we're going to do, and then actually helping him *do* it. It's like learning to climb a mountain. You don't start on your own. Someone else initially helps you, pointing out the hand and footholds to make it easier for you to climb. It's that same person who actually controls your safety rope—your belayer—who gradually releases the rope as you move up the mountain and yet, like a supportive hand on your back, keeps it taut to catch you, just in case.

I was so proud of my friend Jenna and Jake that when I told my class about them, I plunged through the story, hardly pausing for a breath. By planning for success you can:

- avoid daily battles,
- prevent meltdowns, and
- help your child handle frustration, anger, and other intense feelings.

Nods of agreement from several parents in the group kept me rolling:

- plan birthday parties and family gatherings that are fun for everyone,
- travel comfortably with your spirited child, and
- reduce the fighting between brothers and sisters.

I was breathless as I finished my list and glanced at the faces of the people sitting in front of me. Several sat quietly in their chairs, averting their eyes.

I reined in my excitement and asked them, "What are you feeling right now?"

"Overwhelmed," Sasha confessed. "I feel distraught. It seems like there are sixty things to remember. I don't think I can do it because I don't have that kind of time."

The others listened intently. Cory remarked, "I feel angry. Why should I have to plan for success for Brandon? I don't have to do it for the other kids. Why should I have to do it for him?"

Katie sagged in her chair. "I don't know if I have the confidence to pull it off," she groaned.

Feeling like Katie, Sasha, or Cory is not unusual. Planning for success does take effort, especially in the beginning. Changing parenting styles isn't easy, but with practice, planning for success becomes almost automatic. You don't even have to think about it anymore. You just do it and soon your child will take it over herself.

It's true your other children may not need your help planning for success, but they will benefit from it too. They will appreciate the peace and extra time you have for them because planning for success can save so much time. When you aren't engaged in quarrels or seething with frustration, you have energy and time for other endeavors. There will always be something that surprises us, but by planning for success we can go back to the many things that are working right. Each year our planning gets better, the surprises fewer, and the successes more frequent. The result is a sense of confidence for both parents and kids.

It isn't possible for me to address all the daily tough times with spirited kids. But planning for success with the POWER approach is your key to addressing most of the problems you may encounter. In the chapters that follow I'll show you how the process works with some of the most common daily tough times.

PLANNING FOR SUCCESS
The POWER Approach—A Summary

As the parent of a spirited child, you can plan for your child's success. You can put into use your knowledge of temperament, the words that you have learned to use, and the techniques that work for managing spirit to prevent daily hassles.

Predict:
How might your child feel in this situation?
List the temperamental traits that may affect how your
    child reacts to this situation.

Organize the setting:
Can your child be successful in this setting or location?
What activities or objects can you bring along that will
    help your child be successful?
Have you created a hideaway for introverts?

Work together:
How will you help your child manage her intensity?
Is there a way to say *yes* to your child?
How will you get his attention?
Are the agenda and expectations clear?
Does the length of the activity promote success?

Enjoy the Rewards:
What has your child done well?
What have you done well?

16

Bedtime and Night Waking

I now protect sleep like a fire-eating dragon.
—Zoe, mother of three

Kristin had hit the breaking point. As she gazed into her bathroom mirror, she saw that the energetic thirty-three-year-old she had been just two years before had vanished. Reflected back to her was a stranger with dark under-eye circles, hair that was limp and desperately in need of a cut, and jowls sagging beneath what had once been a dimple. There is torture in sleep deprivation, and a spirited child can cause a parent to struggle to get enough sleep.

You'd think that after expending so much energy during the day, sleep would come easily to spirited children, but alas, that is rarely the case. Indeed there are a few spirited children who appear to be naturals, slipping easily into sleep and sleeping soundly until the next morning. They are a minority, and if you have one, celebrate your good fortune.

The majority of spirited kids, however, tend to keep us up at night and awaken early, leaving everyone in the family exhausted.

It's as though their brain is stuck on *go*, resulting too frequently in epic bedtime battles and middle-of-the-night brawls. Falling asleep and staying asleep can be so challenging for spirited children that people often believe they require less sleep. Parents will tell me, "My spirited child has never slept well. He just doesn't seem to need as much sleep as other kids." Or, "I try to put him to bed, but he won't fall asleep."

Sometimes spirited children have been sleep deprived for so long that parents mistakenly assume their crabby demeanor is simply their personality. They never realize how exhausted the children are. Over the years, however, I have come to realize that those frequent awakenings, bedtime tussles, and early awakenings are not because spirited children do not need or want sleep. Rather, they may be a reflection of what's happened during the day that has left them too wired to sleep. It's not that they *won't* sleep but that they *can't* sleep.

Yet it is critical that spirited children get the sleep they need. In class one day, Zoe said it well. "When she is tired—you'd better watch out!"

It's true you cannot *make* children sleep, but it is possible to make it better—much better. We can examine and change the things that may be innocently disrupting their ability to fall asleep and stay asleep. By considering their temperament, we can create a routine that sets their body clock and cue them for sleep. Selecting the techniques that "fit" allows everyone to get the sleep they need and deserve.

Unfortunately, in our culture, people still brag about getting by on only a few hours of sleep—a major coffee company uses the slogan, "Life is short. Stay awake for it"—and demands on our time promote everything but sleep. It's not easy to make sleep a priority. Being aware of the latest research can help you dig in your heels and, as Zoe once told me, start protecting sleep like a fire-eating dragon.

PREDICT

If I told you there was one thing that could bring more joy and harmony to your home; keep your spirited children healthy; reduce their risk of developing cavities, obesity, depression, heart disease, and type 2 diabetes; improve their mathematical reasoning skills; raise their reading scores; foster impulse control and quicker reactions; improve focus and attention; and reduce conflicts and accidents, would you be interested?

That one thing is sleep.

The field of sleep research has burgeoned. The data are clear: adequate sleep is critical for our well-being. Protecting your child's sleep is just as, if not more important than, buckling him into a car seat. You wouldn't drive down the freeway with him unbuckled as a *treat*. It's time to recognize that staying up late or skipping a nap must not be a treat either.

Predicting how to help your family get the sleep you need begins by establishing a goal. That requires knowing how much you really need. Listed below are the average sleep requirements according to a National Sleep Foundation Survey.

Average total sleep needs in a 24-hour period (and notes on how much sleep is typical):		
Infants (birth to 17 months)	14–18 hours	May include three or more naps each day
Toddlers (18–36 months)	13–14 hours	May include one or two naps each day
Preschoolers (3–5 years)	11–12 hours	Currently averaging 8 hours and 40 minutes at night and 9.5 hours with a nap
School Age (6–12 years)	10–11 hours	Many 6-year-olds still need 12 hours
Adolescents (onset of puberty)	9.25 hours	Currently averaging 6 hours and 50 minutes
Adults	8.25 hours	Currently averaging 6 hours and 54 minutes

When I shared this graph in class, Cory nearly choked on his laughter. "That's ludicrous." He retorted. "No way am I going to get eight hours of sleep. It's just not possible." Snorting in disbelief, he paused before asking, "Is this a bad joke or is someone just that out of touch?"

It's not a joke. While eight hours a night sleep for yourself may seem like an unrealistic dream at this moment, it's critical to have a goal in mind. If you don't have a goal, sleep deprivation can unknowingly snowball. Sleep deprivation is cumulative. If your child is short on sleep one hour each night of the week, by the end of the week it's as though he's missed nearly an entire night's sleep. Even if he sleeps longer on the weekend, he can't recoup the learning that was never imbedded in his long-term memory or the restorative repair work his body would have completed if he'd gotten the sleep he needed. It's important to have a goal to aim toward, even if you can't get the recommended amount of sleep right now.

Let me stress that these figures are averages; half of people will require more sleep and half will need less. We are biologically programmed to tend to want additional sleep during the late fall and winter when nights are long and less in spring and summer when nights are short. It's as though during the winter our brains are saying, "It's cold out there. We should sleep."

Since the figures in the chart are only averages, you'll have to determine how much sleep your children need. Watch and they'll show you. *If you have to awaken your children in the morning, they are not getting enough sleep.* Children should be awakening on their own. However, that said, some individuals are genetically wired to be morning larks. These children wake early no matter what time they are put to bed. Thus they may awaken on their own, but still be sleep deprived. In that case, you can tell by their behavior.

You will know your children are getting enough sleep when they are generally happy, flexible, creative, and more tolerant of stimulation and siblings—even during the late-afternoon *poison hours*. This is true even for spirited children. They will still be busy, but their energy will not be frenzied. And while adequate sleep does not totally eliminate meltdowns, it does dramatically decrease the frequency of them and fosters quicker recovery when meltdowns do occur. Well-rested children are also more patient, cooperative, and focused. Perhaps best of all, they fall asleep more easily and stay asleep. By protecting sleep, you can say good-bye to daily bedtime struggles and frequent middle-of-the-night awakenings. It won't be perfect but it will be a whole lot better.

When protecting your family's sleep becomes a priority in your home, your children's demeanor will change for the better and so will yours. You will have the energy to stay tuned-in, allowing you to catch cues earlier before anyone has moved into the red zone. When brains are not fogged by fatigue, creative problem solving becomes much easier. Patience grows with every minute of sleep you get. Promise yourself today to make protecting your family's sleep a goal. You can do it by establishing a routine that makes sleep a priority instead of something you do in your spare time.

ORGANIZE THE SETTING

Awake and asleep are opposite states. The most vulnerable point in your child's ability to sleep is when the brain must switch from one state to the other. Like the stage designer who creates the environment in which the action can happen, you will need to establish an environment that cues your child's brain for sleep. The brain's ability to switch to sleep is not something that just miraculously occurs at bedtime. The cues for a good night's sleep begin in the morning.

Inside our brain is a body clock that tells us when to be asleep and when to be awake. It runs on a twenty-five-hour cycle, which means that if we don't "set it," we gradually shift to later and later bedtimes. To help your spirited child sleep well, it's essential that you take the steps to "set" his body clock so that you have Mother Nature helping you to ease him into sound restorative sleep.

Begin by establishing a regular wake time. This is your cornerstone. It's upon this foundation that everything else will revolve. In order to determine your child's wake time, check your calendar. During the week, what's the earliest time your child has to awaken? Establish that time as his wake time seven days a week.

Before you stop reading in disgust, let me explain. A regular wake time clearly indicates to the brain it is morning and time to be awake! If, however, your child has to be awakened one day at 6:00 A.M., but then sleeps until 8:00 A.M. the next, it's as though one day he awoke in Minneapolis and the next in San Francisco: his brain is jet-lagged, not knowing when it's supposed to *go* and when it's supposed to sleep.

I know you may crave those mornings when you can sleep in, but two things will happen if you establish a regular wake and bedtime: First, you won't need to sleep in because you and your child will be getting adequate sleep. Second, it's not as though you will never sleep in at all; you will, just limit it to a thirty- or maybe sixty-minute window. (How much variance you can allow will depend on your child. For some it may need to be as little as fifteen minutes. Even if that's the case for your child now, it will not be true forever.)

Now establish regular mealtimes. Meals help to set the body clock. If your child is attending school or a child-care center, match your meals with those served at school so that you are working together to provide a consistent schedule.

I follow the recommendations of nutritionist Ellyn Satter. She recommends six mini-meals a day, each containing a little protein, carbohydrate, fruit/vegetables, and fat. Meals are about two and a half to three hours apart. So if your child eats breakfast at 7:00 A.M., midmorning snack will be at 9:30 A.M. with lunch at noon.

Plan exercise time. It's best if your child can awaken and get outside to soak up the rays of the morning sun. But also include time in the late afternoon for active play. Avoid exercising late in the day, especially under artificial light, which can interfere with the production of melatonin, the hormone that tells us it's time to fall asleep.

Don't stop yet. If your child is five years old or younger, establish a naptime. Spirited infants may be ready for their first nap of the day a mere forty-five minutes after awakening. Toddlers up to about nineteen months often need two naps a day, with the first one beginning about two and a half to three hours after they awaken. If they are only taking one nap, that often begins about four hours after awakening for the day. Naptime for preschoolers typically begins about five hours after awakening in the morning. After lunch there is a natural dip in energy, which makes this a great naptime for everyone, including us. It seems to work best if naps are completed by 3:00–4:00 P.M. (except for young infants, who need a short thirty-minute catnap at about 5:00 P.M.).

When it comes to naptime, don't forget your own. A power nap lasting twenty to thirty minutes maximum is documented to not only improve your focus and attention for the remainder of the day, but also protect you from heart disease.

Now select night-sleep time. If, for example, your preschooler arises at 7:00 A.M. every morning and takes a ninety-minute nap, sleep time will be around 8:30 P.M. for a total of twelve hours of sleep in a twenty-four hour period. If he's school age and arises at 7:00 A.M., he'll need to be asleep between 8:00 and 9:00 P.M. This is *not* bedtime, this is sleep time—the moment you want your child to actually be sound asleep.

Before you finish, establish the time to begin your bedtime routine. This will be about thirty to forty-five minutes before you want your child to fall asleep.

Here is a graph depicting potential schedules depending on your child's age and wake time.

Sample schedules:						
Age	Tiny Toddler (12–18 months)	Toddler (19–36 months)	Preschooler (3–5 years)	School Age (6–12 years)	Adolescent (13–19 years)	Adult
Avg. sleep needs (hours)	14–15	13–14	11–12	10–11	9.25	8.25
Wake time	6:30	6:30	6:30	6:30	6:30***	6:00
Breakfast	7:00	7:00	7:00	7:00	7:00	7:00
Activities	7:30–9:00	7:30–10:30	7:30–11:30	7:30–12:00	7:30–12:00	7:30–12:00
Midmorning snack	9:00	9:00	9:00	9:00	9:00	9:00
Nap	9:30–11:00					
Lunch	11:30	11:00	12:00	12:00	12:00	12:00
Nap	2:00–3:30	11:30–2:30	12:30–2:00	Power nap*	Power nap*	Power nap*
Midafternoon snack	3:30	3:00	3:00	3:00	3:00	3:00
Activities	3:30–5:00	2:30–5:00	2:00–5:00	12:30–5:00	12:30–5:00	12:30–5:00
Dinner	5:30	5:30	5:30	5:30	6:00	6:00
Activities	6:00–7:15	6:00–7:15	6:00–7:45	6:00–8:00	6:30–8:30	6:30–9:00
Bedtime routine starts (with snack)	7:00	7:15	6:00 if no nap; 7:15–7:30 with nap	8:00	8:45	9:15
Asleep	7:30	8:00	6:30 if no nap; 8:00 with nap	8:30	9:15	9:45
Total sleep (hours)	14	13.5	12	10**	9.25	8.25

*Power nap is twenty to thirty minutes in length.

**Younger school-age children will need closer to eleven hours of sleep—
adjust sleep time to 8:00 P.M.

***Puberty shifts the melatonin cycle, which tells us when to go to sleep, later
into the evening. If possible, choose a school with a start time of 8:30 A.M. or
later so your adolescent is not struggling to fall asleep before his body and
brain are physiologically ready. Turn off all electronic devices and dim lights
before bedtime to cue melatonin production.

This schedule is merely an example. You will have to create one that works for your family and adjust it as needed. If you have moved your child's bedtime earlier but still need to wake her, move bedtime fifteen minutes earlier for five to seven days. Repeat if needed, until she is waking on her own. If it's taking your son forty-five minutes or longer to fall asleep, move his bedtime later. The average time to fall asleep when we hit the *sleep window* is twenty-seven to thirty-five minutes. Maintaining a sleep log over several weeks can help you see what's working best for your child and family.

Audrey found doing so extremely helpful. Following up after a private consultation she wrote, "You asked me to record times (wake, nap, play/exercise, eat, bedtime, etc.) and then use that information to create a schedule that worked for our family. That schedule is priceless. It took nearly three months to slowly adjust everything, but it worked! It really helped me to have that schedule to refer to when we struggled. I have stuck to it religiously, modifying it slightly over several months to accommodate our needs. I learned I could not just change his schedule on a whim."

Sound sleep requires a consistent schedule that sets the body clock.

Creating a schedule also allows you to see the best times to schedule doctor and dentist appointments or activities so they don't disrupt nap or bedtime. When a friend asks you to meet at the park at 2:00, it's easy to say, "Let's make that 3:30—after naps."

Working with families over the years I have found that the most effective schedules allow parents to arise before the kids so they can have a few minutes for themselves before meeting the needs of children. Mealtimes that are consistent for everyone eliminate the feeling that you are a short-order cook. Some families prefer a common evening snack time so it can be their family meal if a parent arrives home later from work. After the bedtime routine is completed, some families prefer to stagger bedtimes so they can put each child down separately. Others find both a common snack and bedtime for the little ones most workable so that they all can go down at once. If you have a spirited adolescent and a school choice, select the one with a start time of 8:30 A.M. or later. Puberty shifts the melatonin cycle later, making it very difficult for an adolescent to fall asleep before 10:00 P.M.

Setting the body clock takes time. Expect at least three to six weeks to pass before you see significant progress. Somewhere about seven to ten days into the process things will suddenly be worse than ever. I do not know why this occurs, but it is very predictable. Perhaps the old system has to crash before the new one fits into place. During this upheaval do NOT throw out the routine. You are not doing something wrong. Keep going.

By creating a predictable routine that you are comfortable implementing seven days a week, you put Mother Nature on your side. Your child's brain is now *set* for sleep. The result is a child who "switches" from *go* to *asleep* without the wrestling match—at least most of the time. Now, because things normally go smoothly, if there is a tussle, it's blatantly apparent that something is *up*.

Your child is getting sick, stressed, going through a growth spurt, or something else that is disrupting his sleep.

WORKING TOGETHER

One of the most frustrating issues parents of spirited children face is the fact that what works for other kids is frequently ineffective for ours. What *everyone* tells us is the *right* way to respond may be *wrong* for our kids. This is especially true when it comes to sleep. Helping spirited children shut off the *go* button and switch to sleep requires finding the strategies that fit their temperaments. Sometimes those strategies are NOT what most people recommend.

1. If Your Child Is Intense

"How do you know your child is ready for sleep?" I asked the group. Puzzled, Amy raised her eyebrow, offering more a question than a statement, "When we are finished with dinner and homework?" Cody cocked his head, not certain he should admit, "When the movie ends?"

Leaving bedtime to happenchance does not work for spirited children. We have to be tuned in to the cues that tell us their body and brain are ready for sleep.

PICK UP THE CUES: Finding your child's window for sleep is critical. This is the point where melatonin levels have risen, telling the brain it's time for sleep. If you miss that window, your intense child's engine revs. A shot of adrenaline zooms through his body, making it impossible for him to fall asleep until forty-five to ninety minutes later when it has finally dissipated. To avoid your intense child getting a second wind, watch, listen, and pay attention to what you feel. If you do, you'll catch the magical sleep window when it's easy for even an intense child to slip into sleep. Frequently it's much earlier than you might have been expecting.

There are three levels of sleep cues:

Level One	Level Two	Level Three
Red under the eyes	Yawning	Burst of energy/silly/wild
Staring off	Rubbing eyes	Screaming
Slowing of play/motion	Stumbling/loss of coordination	Resistant
Glazed look	Laying head down	Unable to settle
Change in skin color/pallor	Seeking contact/clingy	Falling apart
Looking away	A little difficulty listening but not too bad	Not listening
Slight sagging of cheeks	Change in voice tone	Whining, irritable
Slight drooping of eyelids	Some difficulty complying, starts to lose focus	Arching, thrashing
Tired eyes	Going for a comfort object	Not complying

Level-one cues are the point at which we want to put spirited babies down. By level two or three their engines are flooding. Level-one cues for toddlers and older children signal, "I'm getting tired." Check the clock when you see them. These cues tell you that it's either time to begin the sleep routine, or it soon will be—depending on your child.

Level-two cues signal it's time for sleep. Do not wait for the second yawn, eye rub, or stumble. Move immediately to get your child down for sleep. Check the clock so you know what time you typically see these cues. Set an alarm on your phone to ensure that each night at that time you will be fully engaged, ready to help your child prepare to sleep.

Level-three cues signal an overtired child. You have missed the window. It will now take another forty-five to ninety minutes to get your child down while that second wind blows through his system. Expect that he will need extra help calming down. Note the time. Reset your phone alarm to be certain that in the future, you will begin watching and listening for cues earlier. Move bedtime accordingly until you find that spot where sleep comes easily.

The ability to read your child's subtle cues is challenging. It requires a focus that is sometimes tough to garner. Kelsey was laughing when she told me this story. "We were all lying on my bed. The kids were playing, and I was on my laptop, not really paying any attention to them. Just as I was concluding a long e-mail, Marcus stepped over to my computer and turned it off. 'Oh, Marcus,' I said. 'Mommy was working on something and now it's gone!'

" 'Now it's gone,' he repeated as he stepped away."

Catch the moment—it's worth the effort.

EXPECT TO CALM YOUR CHILD: You probably realized when your spirited child was born that if you held her, she slept. If you laid her down, she woke up. Years later you may still find yourself rocking, scratching a back, snuggling or sitting with your spirited child, wondering if you are doing something wrong. That's why I was not surprised when Shelly divulged to the group, "I'm embarrassed to admit this. My twenty-one-month-old son has been having lots of trouble falling asleep. We recently moved and shortly afterward he started crawling out of his crib. So we purchased a 'big boy' bed for him, but he keeps falling out of it and fussing and crying when I put him in it. He can really get himself worked up.

"In the past, I've always rocked him for a few minutes before he went to sleep. My friends have told me not to do it, but it relaxes him and he seems to need it, so I've done it. I suspect they think that I'm just 'giving in.' But all I have ever had to do is rock him for about five minutes until he is drowsy. Then I lay him in his crib, give him a few pats, and he falls asleep. Most nights he has been sleeping ten uninterrupted hours.

"With the new room and bed, even rocking isn't working. When I lay him down and walk out, he becomes frantic. The only way I can get him to sleep is to lie down with him. Everyone is telling me I should just let him scream or I'll be starting a bad habit. I honestly don't mind, yet I do worry. I don't want to be doing this forever."

Shelly had sensed her son's discomfort and intuitively had realized that he needed her close in order to calm his body enough for sleep. She was comfortable with that decision until others told her she *should* be responding in a different way.

To slip into sleep easily and to sleep well, your child's body must be calm. Touch calms.

Researchers have found that intense spirited children have

more "alerting" transmitters in their system, while those transmitters that tell them it's all right to sleep remain lower. This is why they need more *outside* help from us to feel serene.

Unfortunately, many of the books that address sleep problems will encourage you to let your child cry it out. However, even these authors are beginning to recognize that there is a flaw in this advice. Supposedly the child stops crying after a few minutes. Spirited kids don't. Left to their own devices, intense, spirited children become physiologically flooded. They are unable to stop crying without assistance.

Spirited children may react so strongly that they will vomit. Some experts raise a warning that to respond sympathetically is to be controlled by your child. "If they vomit," they advise, "clean it up and put them back to bed." But children don't vomit to control their parents; they vomit because they are highly stressed. They also rarely vomit in a neat little pile. There is nothing worse than walking into a room with vomit sprayed on the walls, the carpet, stuffed animals, and each individual bar of the crib. If your child is prone to vomiting, go to him, help him to take deep breaths and calm down so that he won't regurgitate. Your support at this point will save you both a great deal of frustration and discomfort when you are much too tired to deal with it.

Unlike other children who are not as intense, the spirited child needs much more help soothing and calming his body. Your presence and your smell calm your intense child. I am very comfortable recommending that if rocking your child, or massaging and scratching his back, help him to relax and fall asleep soundly, feel free to do so as part of your bedtime routine. Later in this chapter we will talk about how to gradually reduce the physical contact if that is your wish.

As we discussed staying with our kids at bedtime in class one night, Katie groaned. "I don't *want* to sit with her. I've got other things to do and I need a break!"

We can all empathize with Katie. At the end of a long day we're tired too. I have a friend who had adolescents when my kids were little. "Part of being a parent," she told me, "is waiting. When they're little, it's waiting for them to fall asleep. When they're older, it's waiting for them to finish a dance lesson or to come home from a date, but you'll always be waiting."

Intense spirited kids need our help settling down. You can expect it. Try to think of it as a treat for yourself rather than one more demand to meet, a time when you don't talk to them anymore; you just sit and daydream or read. Make it an enjoyable part of your day rather than a hassle—you know you'll be dealing with them anyway if they are too agitated to sleep. If you try to do something else, you'll just be chasing them back into their beds and yelling at them, raising everyone's intensity. Rather than frustrating yourself, expect it and plan it into your day. Sooner than you might ever think, they won't be as interested in cuddling with you anymore.

You may not mind staying with your child as she unwinds and learns to stay in bed, but you may be wondering what to do about the other kids. That's where creativity comes in. Not every child needs this much help unwinding. Some kids hit the bed and are out. That child requires your time and attention at another time of the day. Give it to her when she needs it, after naptime or after school. You don't have to feel guilty if you sit with one child and not another at bedtime. You meet the needs of both of them but in different ways.

If more than one needs your help unwinding, you may have to sit on the floor between their rooms or take turns—Monday night one room, Tuesday night another. Develop a routine that includes "calm time" with you and also alone. Read to one child while the other reads to himself, and then switch places, leaving the first child to fall asleep or to look at books himself, and go to the child who was reading independently. Once both children know they will get their "calm time" with you, you'll find that they are much more open to practicing a little on their own.

DECIDE WHERE EVERYONE WILL SLEEP: A very important question for the intense child is—your bed or mine? With a child who does not fall asleep easily and wakes up frequently, you will soon be faced with the question of the family bed. In most cultures of the world the family bed is not a question. It is an expectation. In our society, however, it is a question that needs to be answered or it can become a major source of contention.

Intense infants seem to quickly realize that they need the adults in their lives to help them calm their bodies. (Some researchers also suggest to regulate their body temperature.) As a result, they seek your company and don't want to sleep alone. Frequently this is the child who will sleep only on you or next to you. So what are you to do?

The American Academy of Pediatrics recommends that infants be placed in a bed separate from their parents but in the same room. Breast-feeding groups, such as the National La Leche League believe that the academy's recommendation to avoid co-sleeping reflects a lack of basic understanding about breast-feeding management. To support the benefits of co-sleeping, they utilize the research of James McKenna, director of the Mother-Baby Behavior Sleep Laboratory at the University of Notre Dame.

The concern for both groups is safety. The key is to find safe strategies for soothing and calming your intense child. If you do find that co-sleeping works best for your family, follow safe sleeping procedures. Select a sleeping surface that does not have any crevices or creases that can trap an infant. Keep the bedding simple: no feather beds, heavy quilts, or thick pillows. Choose a mattress that is large enough so there is no worry of rolling over on your baby. And consider taking your mattress off the frame and putting it on the floor to avoid falls. If your hair is long, pull it back so that the baby cannot become entangled.

Do *not* co-sleep on recliners, couches, or chairs. Do *not* co-sleep if you smoke, have consumed alcoholic beverages or mind-altering drugs, are taking medications, or are retaining significant weight. Do not let babysitters or other children co-sleep with a baby. These are all factors that can reduce the sensitivity to where the baby is in the bed.

There isn't a right or wrong answer to how your family sleeps as long as it's safe for your child and everyone can sleep. Take time to do your own research. Talk about your choices with your partner. Select the strategies that you both agree upon.

Some families put a crib or bassinet right next to their bed. Others help their older child to sleep in his own room so that parents can have time alone at bedtime, but they allow their child to join them in the middle of the night. Or they put a sleeping bag on the floor next to them for the middle of the night "connection." The goal is to find a way to calm the spirited child easily, quickly, and with as little stress as possible so all of you can sleep more peacefully.

As you make your decision about the family bed, realize that it's a decision you can change after a few months or after a number of years. The choice will be yours. While it may take practice and time, whenever you and your child are both ready to do so, it is possible to gradually help him feel comfortable sleeping in his own bed.

PROTECT NAPS: Intense spirited children work much harder to manage their strong emotions. That's why it is so essential to protect their naps. Often they seem to resist napping because they so easily get wired, but this is the child more than any other who needs you to take the time to help him calm his body so that he can rest in the middle of the day.

2. If Your Child Is Persistent

MAKE BEDTIME ROUTINES SIMPLE: Bedtime is a favorite time for persistent kids to push the limits. "I am willing to spend time putting Emma to bed," Brandon said, "but I get tired of her demands. She always wants one more drink of water or one more book."

Successful bedtime routines are simple and nonalerting. Spirited children are often highly intelligent children with vivid imaginations. They love to read and who doesn't want to encourage reading? But I'm going to suggest that reading become a routine for early evening, not bedtime, for the very reason that they do not want to stop. One book turns into five with a persistent child. Suddenly the sleep window has been missed. You can prevent that from happening by keeping things simple.

Begin your bedtime routine with a snack. Few spirited children can resist this. Sitting down with the child for a snack slows everyone down and helps you focus on the goal at hand. Afterward, it's to the bedroom area for toileting/diaper changing and teeth brushing. Then it's into the bedroom for pajamas, a cuddle, talk time, song/prayer, and good night. That's it.

You'll notice bath is absent from this routine. That's because for spirited children, getting into and out of the bath is often alerting.

They resist getting in and squabble about getting out. Bathing can also raise the body temperature, whereas sleep requires a drop in body temperature. Like reading, the bath is frequently best moved to morning, late afternoon, or right after dinner. (If a bath calms your child, however, continue to include it in your routine. Adding a bit of Epsom salts can be helpful.)

A routine such as the one above, which takes about thirty minutes, will make it much easier to catch your child's window for sleep and avoid accidently pushing past it. If on a particular night you recognize that your child is experiencing more difficulty settling, simply extend the cuddle time until you sense her body relaxing, and hear her breathing slow. At this point she's ready for sleep.

CREATE A PICTURE PLANNER: When persistent kids know what to expect, it is easier for them to comply. Once you have established the steps of your simple bedtime routine, work with your child to create a picture planner depicting each step.

Rob and Sara used this method to stop the bedtime fights at their house.

"McKenzie is our first child. We had never heard of a bedtime routine. We didn't even know what it meant. When we learned about it, we decided to try it. We took photos of her going through each step, printed them out, and made a book that we read while she ate her snack. If she resisted using the toilet, we'd point to that photo and say, 'What does the book say?' She'd do it. We used the book for about three weeks. Now she just knows the steps and often completes many of them on her own."

Picture planners let your persistent child know the plan. When the plan is the same every night, power struggles disappear.

SWITCH TO SLEEP: The final step is the switch to sleep. You may choose to continue to sit near your child or lie down with him (your arm across him provides calming pressure), but the interaction stops. If a few pats are needed, that's fine, but gradually, as you hear his breathing change, lift your hand from his body. Your goal is for him to fall asleep in such a way that the conditions will be the same when he rouses in the middle of the night. If you'll be next to him, it's fine to be there as he switches to sleep, but if you're planning on going to a different bed, then let him snuggle up to the silky blanket or stuffed animal that will stay with him during the night. You may still be near, but the sensation next to his body needs to be what will continue to be there all night long. If your child is an infant, you'll be laying him on his back and you won't be leaving a stuffed animal with him.

3. If Your Child Is Sensitive

CREATE A NEST: "I'm scared!" "I'm thirsty." "I can't sleep!" It can be a real struggle to get your sensitive child down for the night, but without sleep his ability to manage sensations and cope is drastically reduced. The trouble is that because he is so aware of every emotion and sensation in his environment, it's often challenging for him to "shut down" and go to sleep. This is the child who requires a "nest," a quiet, low-stimulation place where his brain can clearly note that it's safe to sleep. He has to be able to block out noises, lights, and even smells to be able to sleep.

If you can, give him the quietest bedroom in the house. Usually that means the bedroom farthest away from the street, but it can also mean the one the greatest distance from the furnace or air conditioner. In order to help him sleep past sunrise, consider the room on the north or west side of your home. Blackout shades, pillows to "nest him in," lavender spray, a fan or other soothing white noise can all be used to block sensations that may disrupt his sleep. If your child insists on a night-light, use an outlet behind a dresser to avoid overstimulation. Keep the wattage as low as possible.

Being close may be more important than quiet and dark for some sensitive children. For them, select the bedroom closest to you, or have them share a room with a sibling.

Highly sensitive children also need their nests to include pleasant sensations. Don't overlook the bedding. Take note of how your child sleeps best. Is it snuggled under a heavy quilt? Or does he prefer to sleep with no covers at all? What colors, textures, and smells seem to soothe him? Often he's most comfortable with his bed pushed into the corner of the room rather than "floating" in the middle.

Eliminate clutter from your child's room, including all electronics, toys, mobiles hanging from the ceiling, and even visually interesting murals. Temperature is also important to him. If he tends to be hot, be sure the room is cool enough. And if his hands and feet are frequently cold, encourage him to wear socks to bed.

FIGHTING OVER PAJAMAS IS NOT WORTH IT: Forget about the cute pajamas with feet in them, elastic cuffs, and lacy collars. Sensitive kids can't stand pajamas that are scratchy, that irritate them in any way, or that are too hot. Consider letting your child sleep in sweats, an oversize T-shirt, baggy cotton shorts, a loose nightgown, or in the buff. Or, if she is the child who prefers pressure on her body, try a stretchy tight shirt.

TALK ABOUT FEELINGS: Because they often worry, spirited kids also need an opportunity to debrief before sleep. An opportunity to talk with you, write in a journal, or simply spend time reflecting on the concerns of their day may be enough to allow them to slip easily into sleep.

Some sensitive children become anxious worrying that they won't fall asleep. I didn't realize this until one day a ten-year-old told me she gets sick at bedtime. "What happens?" I asked her.

"I have the sleeping sickness," she said. "I can never go to sleep like other people. There must be something wrong with me."

Spirited kids have vivid imaginations. If we don't give them factual reasons as to why they need time to unwind, they'll come up with their own. They need to hear:

> You're very sensitive to noises, smells, sights, and
>   feelings. You can create a comfortable nest to help
>   you sleep.
> Dad is out of town and that's always stressful to all of us.
> It is all right to lie here quietly. Take deep breaths. Relax
>   your muscles. You will fall asleep soon. If you would
>   like me to stay near you, let me know.
> You are a deep thinker and feeler, sometimes it helps to
>   write down your thoughts in a journal so that you can
>   close the book and leave them behind you while you
>   sleep.
> Let's go upstairs and put things away in your room
>   together so you have time to talk and wind down.
> Let's do a meditation.

4. If Your Child Is Perceptive

HELP HIM HEAR YOUR MESSAGES: At bedtime our children have to follow many directions. Remember to make eye contact. Don't try to direct your child to get ready for bed from across the room, or while you're doing something else. Focus on your child. Avoid distractions that pull you away from the task at hand.

5. If Your Child Is Slow to Adapt

ALLOW ENOUGH TIME: It takes time to get slow-to-adapt kids to bed. Trying to rush or skip part of the routine only extends the process as they go into overload from too many transitions too close together. That's why it is important to keep your bedtime routine simple. While the steps are minimal, you may have to allow time for your child to make the physiological switch from being active to sleep.

Once pajamas are on, some children benefit by taking time to unwind by playing quietly in their room before moving through the remaining steps of the routine. If this is true for your child, go through the initial steps of snack, toileting, teeth, and pajamas with all the kids and then let this one chill out while you put another child down. Given that time, he'll be ready for cuddling and closure for the night.

BEGIN WITH CLOSURE: It sounds crazy, doesn't it? Start with closure? But one of the major reasons we can't get spirited kids into bed is that they don't want to stop their activities. A bedtime routine needs to start with closure on the existing activity. Before you begin your transition activity, bring closure to what your child is doing by an announcement such as:

It will be time to start getting ready for bed in ten minutes.
Where would you like to save that?
What do you need to complete so you'll be ready to stop
   and go to bed?

It may be helpful to set a timer. Timers are a wonderful way to
allow slow-to-adapt kids time to transition, especially those that
show color gradually disappearing, so that your child can see time
pass. Some families use a music box that plays for ten minutes and
then gradually winds down. The sound is more pleasant for noise-
sensitive kids. Dimming or turning off lights also gently signal
that the day is about to end. Finally, moving into snack time is
much easier than moving directly into brushing teeth or toileting,
both of which are often triggers for conflict.

6. If Your Child Is Irregular—A Bonus Trait

To prevent your hard work from being sabotaged, mark the change
to daylight savings time on your calendar. It can take spirited kids
three weeks to adjust to this time change. Start the process of
change at least two weeks in advance of everybody else. Otherwise
the week of change will very likely be a disaster. Gradually move
your child's bedtime and wake time fifteen minutes every day or
two until you get him to the new time. Adjust your schedule too.
Mark the first Monday and Tuesday of the daylight savings time
switch on your calendar. If possible, schedule no appointments
before 10:30 A.M. That way, if things are rough at home, you can
deal with them without feeling rushed. Otherwise get yourself up
early enough so you have the time you need to help your child.
(Tuesday is usually the worst because by then they are really out
of whack.)

You can't *make* an irregular child fall asleep, but you can insist on a definite bedtime. Gradually, with a consistent routine that is carried out *even on weekends,* your child will begin to adapt relatively smoothly. The payoff in good behavior will be well worth your efforts.

7. If Your Child Is Energetic

CATCH HIS WINDOW: Many kids get *wild* at bedtime. They dash around the house, leaping, jumping, and wrestling. It is easy to get pulled into their energy and start roughhousing with them, but that frenzy of energy is actually a signal that you've missed your child's window for sleep.

High-energy children tend to have a window that's a mere fifteen minutes long. If you miss it, you have a "wild child" who can't fall asleep. When this happens, gradually wind him down. Rock him vigorously; then slow your movements. Let him move out of your arms. Then pick him up and rock again, this time more slowly. If he's older, encourage him to take deep breaths and slowly let them out. Teach him to tense each muscle in his body and then relax it. You might also find that if you tuck him tightly under his covers, or give him a deep pressure massage, it will help him to slow his body down.

On a preventive basis, make certain this child has exercise and roughhousing time daily, just not at bedtime.

8. If Your Child Has a Cautious First Reaction

Two weeks after our initial conversation in class, Shelly reported the results of changes to her son's bedtime routine. "During our conversation," she said, "I heard you say that to help my son I must truly listen to what he is telling me and trust that message. I can also trust myself to advocate for him.

"After we talked, it was pretty clear to me that he wasn't feeling safe in his new room after our move. He needed a little extra support. I still rocked him like I've always done and then lay down with him. But after a couple of nights, I slowly began cutting back, moving from his bed to the floor, and then to sitting in the chair.

"He'd lie in his bed and listen to his music, but he wasn't upset. He'd look up at me to see if I was still there. When he flipped over and I could hear his breathing change, I knew he was settling in but not quite asleep, so I would go out. Last night I was in his room at most five minutes after I put him in his bed. It took three weeks, but we got there—without screaming."

If your child has a cautious first reaction, listen and trust the messages that he sends you. Meet his needs, even if that means bringing him into your bed so everyone can sleep. Once you begin to sense he is feeling comfortable, begin using the gentle nudge to gradually back off your support.

Like Shelley, if your child needs you near to fall asleep, lie with him, or pull a chair into his room. Simply daydream or fold the laundry until he falls asleep. Gradually, over time, begin to move farther away, then step out of the room, initially for a mere fifteen to thirty seconds, assuring him as you do that you will be right back. Continue to practice, each night stretching the time a little longer until he's comfortable falling asleep independently. He will get there.

To prevent those nighttime hassles with spirited kids, we've got to be creative, willing to recognize their individuality, and strong enough sometimes to buck the crowd. The payoff is children who are more willing to work with us—and children who can sleep soundly—most of the time.

GET YOUR OWN NEEDS MET: Once your child is off to dreamland, make your sleep a priority too. Remind yourself that you're aiming for 8.25 hours of sleep. When you consciously choose to protect your own sleep, you will be amazed how much your child's behavior improves. Her challenging behaviors will not be fueled by your own lack of sleep.

WHEN YOUR CHILD CONTINUES TO STRUGGLE WITH SLEEP: If you implement all of the suggestions in this chapter, and your child is still not sleeping, it's time to dig deeper. There may be a medical factor playing havoc with her sleep. I suggest that you:

- Ask your doctor to check iron levels, specifically the ferritin count. Low iron can disrupt sleep.
- Ask your doctor to check adenoids and tonsils. If either is enlarged, they can be blocking your child's breathing, causing frequent wake-ups.
- Interview family members to discover if anyone has been diagnosed with restless leg syndrome or sleep apnea. There tends to be a genetic link.
- Check for allergies and food intolerances.
- Schedule a sleep study at a pediatric sleep center.
- Honestly review your own stress. Research has documented that when there are marital issues, children's sleep is disrupted.

On a temporary basis, sound sleep may be disrupted if you have recently moved, your child's friend has moved, there's been a natural disaster or major life stressors such as the birth of a new sibling or death of a family member, or your child is experiencing a growth spurt, just to name a few.

ENJOY THE REWARDS AND CELEBRATE SUCCESSES: It is true that helping spirited children become sound sleepers does take time, patience, and significant effort. But Hillary discovered it can be done.

When Hillary contacted me, her two-and-a-half-year-old daughter was waking as frequently as six times a night. Both she and her husband were exhausted and desperate for some help. They hadn't had a full night's sleep since their daughter's birth, and now they were expecting another child.

After working together, she sent me an update. "Our daughter is sleeping almost all night long now. She awoke only once last night. And not only are the nights better, but she is brushing her teeth, sitting down for meals, getting off the teacher's lap at school, and opening up to family members she never approached before. They have noticed and commented how sweet she is these days.

"I'm just completely shocked that we could have this level of change. I know it's tied to her getting more sleep. Now, she even allows her dad to put her to bed. While he's doing it, I'm sitting downstairs thinking, 'Is this how other people live?' We feel like a miracle has happened to our family."

Bedtime tussles and middle-of-the-night awakenings do not have to be nightly events. It can be better—much better.

Sleep is so important for the spirited child that I've written an entire book about it. If you'd like more information about how to help your family get the sleep you need and deserve, look for *Sleepless in America: Is Your Child Misbehaving or Missing Sleep?*

BEDTIME AND NIGHT WAKING
A Summary
———————————

Bedtime and night waking are two of the most frequent and frustrating issues for parents of spirited kids. It is possible, however, to help them get the sleep they need.

Predict:

Predicting how to help your family get the sleep you need begins by establishing a goal. That requires knowing how much sleep you and your child need.

Organize the setting:

Create a routine that cues your child that it is time to sleep.

Work together:

Pay attention to your child's sleep cues so that you catch his window for sleep.

Keep the bedtime routine simple.

Help your child create a *nest* for sleep.

Allow enough time to prepare your child for bed. Rushing or skipping part of the routine only extends the process.

Use the gentle nudge to help your child adjust.

Enjoy the Rewards:

Protect your own sleep.

Believe it can be better—much better.

17

Mealtime

Heaven forbid if you take the cereal box down for him.
If you do, you have to put it back up on the shelf and
let him take it down or he won't eat.
—Maggie, mother of four

The topic was mealtime. The week before, I'd asked the parents to bring a sack lunch for the noon-hour class. Today when they sat down, I instructed them to take out their lunch, unwrap their food, and place it in front of them. Once this task was completed, I had them stand up and move one chair to the right, leaving their lunches at their original spot. I explained that today they'd be trading lunches and would get the one that was now in front of them. The looks I got nearly dropped me in my tracks. Zoe gasped, near panic. She had food allergies and had no idea what was in the salad in front of her. Ryan was famished and not happy. Lyssa, whose spot he now filled, had forgotten to bring a lunch. Lyssa had been remiss because she rarely ate lunch or only a light one, if she ate at all. Now she shuddered, looking at the sandwich, chips, Clementine, and banana that sat in front of her.

Pausing just a moment for effect, I continued, "I want you to eat any fruit or vegetables before you eat anything else. You have ten minutes to finish because we've got another exercise to do after this one. And just for your information, you'll need to stay here until you have eaten every last bite." Then I sat back in my chair, casually folded my arms, and smiled. Quick glances shot around the table as they wondered if I could really be this socially inept.

Suddenly Jason growled low in his throat. "I'm not touching this yogurt. I hate the texture of yogurt. If I was on a desert island starving to death, I wouldn't eat yogurt."

Christina, whose yogurt he was berating, raised her hands in the air and shrugged, "I didn't know I was making lunch for you."

"No offense," Jason quickly offered.

From the corner of my eye, I caught a slow grin spreading across Melissa's face as she perused a slice of chocolate cake topped with caramel sauce and pecans, a bright red apple, and a hoagie sandwich stacked high with turkey, ham, and cheese. Sam, who had prepared that lunch for himself, appeared ashen as he bleakly took in the squished peanut butter and jelly sandwich sitting in front of him.

Fortunately for the parents in my group, I really am not this socially naive. This was merely an exercise in empathy, and they were quickly allowed to reclaim their own lunches before any bites were taken. But for many spirited children, this emotional mix of surprise, apprehension, excitement, disappointment, dismay, disgust, and joy may be their experience every time they sit down to eat unless we work with them as a team.

Spirited children have a keen sense of taste, texture, and smell. They can discriminate between name brands, and the texture of meat may make them sick. They have defined rules about what foods may touch each other or be mixed together. The mere thought of beans touching the mashed potatoes may be *absolutely* repulsive to them.

Getting spirited kids to the table, keeping them there, and ensuring that they eat some semblance of a nutritional diet is a major source of consternation for parents of spirited kids. By working with your child's temperament, it is possible to make mealtime not only more tranquil, but a joyful opportunity to unwind together.

PREDICT

What makes mealtime tricky for your child? For many spirited children their sensitivity fosters strong opinions about what they will and will not eat. Intensity makes their reactions forceful. Persistence results in little tigers who want to do it themselves! Perceptiveness leads to "grazing"—eating, playing, browsing, talking, eating—but never quite finishing anything. And slow adaptability makes it tough to get them to the table in the first place. The bonus traits may also affect mealtime. Irregularity leads to erratic hunger pangs. High energy promotes a desire to eat on the run, and a negative first reaction leads to frequent refusals.

Believe it or not, your spirited child isn't really all that different from other young children. The developmental books will tell you that all young children are prone to food jags (insisting on eating one particular food) or food strikes (not eating at all). Other kids also dawdle, spit out foods, wiggle in their chairs, spill their milk, react negatively to new foods, and eat erratically. This is the picture of the *average* child. Add to that the greater temperamental strength of the spirited child and you have the potential for a very interesting situation.

Problems often arise during the toddler years when a normal reduction in appetite occurs. Think about it. An average infant triples her weight by one year. If she continued to gain weight that quickly, you would have a sixty-pound toddler! Instead, during the next year and a half growth slows down. A toddler gains only six to eight pounds in eighteen months. It stands to reason that her appetite should become smaller too.

Many parents are not aware of this normal change in appetite. A sudden refusal by their toddler to eat sparks the beginning of the feeding wars—concerned parents pitted against toddlers with a declining appetite. Mealtime does not need to be a point of dissension. By predicting your child's typical temperamental reactions and understanding the natural and necessary reduction in appetite, you can respond in a positive manner.

ORGANIZE THE SETTING

Nutritionist Ellyn Satter offers a guiding principle for maintaining a positive feeding relationship: "You are responsible for the what, when, and where of feeding. Your child is responsible for the how much, and whether, of eating."

"This principle," she continues, "both charges you with what is your responsibility to do and lets you off the hook when you have done it. It is up to you to get healthy food into the house. It is you that makes sure the meals and snacks are nutritious and served on a predictable schedule. But once you have done that, you simply have to let go of it, turn the rest over to your child, and trust her to do her part."

Many years ago Dr. Clara Davis conducted an experiment in which she demonstrated that young children, if given the chance, will choose to eat a healthful diet. She found that when babies between eight and ten months were offered foods and given the power to choose what to eat, and how much, they didn't eat balanced meals every time—but nutritional balance was achieved over the course of several days.

CONTROL THE PROPS: As Ellyn Satter states, you are responsible for providing nutritious food. If you do, you can trust even very small children to use good judgment. Your child can't fill up on cookies if they aren't in the cupboard. He can't drink soda if it isn't in the refrigerator. You get to control what food is available. If you want your child to eat fruit, keep it handy for snacks, or serve it with your child's favorite macaroni and cheese. If you want your child to drink milk, make sure it's served at the temperature he enjoys. Better yet, let him see you drinking it too. This is creating the setting—providing the props that allow the appropriate action to occur.

MAKE SNACKS A PREDICTABLE PART OF THE SCHEDULE: Snacks are actually an important part of meeting the nutritional needs of children but can be a source of trouble with the child who wants to eat all the time or sporadically. You don't need to worry about your child's snacking if you offer a nutritious snack every two or three hours between meals. The key is to offer it on a *predictable* basis, when your child is hungry but before he is starved.

Ellyn Satter recommends that a snack be a "mini-meal" that keeps your child from being hungry for a while. In order for this to occur, it needs to contain a protein, a carbohydrate, a fruit or vegetable, and a little fat. This combination will be satisfying and stay with your child, yet let her be comfortably hungry for her next meal. An example might be whole-grain crackers and cheese and an apple slice with water; peanut butter on a banana;

or oatmeal–peanut butter cookies with milk. By occasionally offering cookies as part of a snack, they don't become the "forbidden fruit."

When you are predictably offering your child a pleasurable and nutritious snack, there's less likely to be "begging" for another treat thirty minutes later. And if by chance he does beg for another, you can feel more comfortable suggesting another inviting activity instead of more to eat. In this way he learns to eat when he's hungry, to stop when he's full, and to search out an activity or person rather than food when he's bored or in need of an emotional boost. If he is growing fast and really is hungry, you can always serve fresh vegetables and fruits.

EAT MEALS TOGETHER: Schedules are busy and it's easy to "eat on the run." But Leslie Lytle, Ph.D., of the University of Minnesota states, "Family meals are incredibly important." Studies clearly indicate that children who regularly eat family meals have better overall nutrient intake than children who do not regularly eat family meals. If sitting down together seems impossible in your family, start by selecting one meal a week to which you will all commit. No excuses allowed, not even working late, going to a friend's house, or soccer practice. It may be a Sunday-noon meal, a Wednesday-night dinner, or a Saturday breakfast. Turn off the electronics and converse. If this is new to your family, give it time to take root. You'll be amazed at how quickly the entire family will come to look forward to this ritual.

If you don't know how to cook or don't like cooking, subscribe to Ellyn Satter's newsletter at http://www.ellynsatterinstitute.org. But even if you are serving a take-out pizza, remove it from the box, serve it with fresh fruit or a salad, set the table, and sit down together.

WORK TOGETHER

FOOD ISN'T FACTUAL: It seems that it should be. You can see it, smell it, touch it, taste it. But it still means very different things to each one of us. What's amazing to me is how different the messages are. I grew up with a dad and grandfather who always grabbed a piece of pie and ate it *first,* declaring that they wanted to eat dessert while they still had room to enjoy it. I've run into a few others like them, but most people have learned that dessert is eaten last and only after their plates have been cleaned up.

Before we can work with our child's temperament, we have to be aware of the messages we have received from parents, relatives, teachers, or friends about the *right* way to eat. Here's what other parents have said:

"In our house eating was very controlled. We had to try one bite of everything, eat very defined amounts, and not leave the table until we were excused."

"My mom had an aunt who always bugged her about how skinny she was. My mom hated it and as a result never said anything to us about food. If we were full and there was one bite left on our plate, it stayed there. There wasn't any pushing."

"Breakfast was our big meal of the day. Everyone had to be seated at the table at seven thirty A.M. It didn't matter what time you'd gone to bed, you were to be at the breakfast table. I am not a breakfast eater and never have been. To this day the sight of pancakes is revolting to me."

"Half of my mom's relatives were very obese and half were not. She was really worried that we would take after the obese side of the family and be discriminated against. She wouldn't let us eat any sugar and never allowed second helpings."

"We never really talked about food. We ate when it was served.

Got ourselves a snack if we were hungry, and that's it. It was never a very big deal."

Look at your food messages. Check to see if they are interfering with a sensitive response to your child's temperamental needs. Do they allow you to accept your responsibility to provide nutritious food and to allow your child to decide whether and how much he will eat? When your expectations and responsibilities are clear, it is easier to work with your child's temperament.

1. If Your Child Is Intense

TEACH HIM GOOD MANNERS: Cooking an entire meal only to have your spirited child sit down, take one look, and scream, "YUK!" is a very frustrating experience. If you have a child who reacts intensely, tell him it is all right to refuse food, but he needs to say, "No, thank you. I don't care for any." Even a young toddler can say, "No, thank you."

I offered this advice in class one day. A parent responded with a very serious frown. "You don't think it will work?" I asked, responding to her expression.

"I just hope it does," she answered. "Last week we had dinner at my in-laws. Graham is very intense. He didn't like the sweet potatoes my mother-in-law put on his plate. He screamed when she plopped them down, but she didn't seem to notice. He scooped them up in his hand and threw them against the wall. I was mortified."

"That's toddlers," I said. "He's certainly making clear his responsibility to choose what he eats. But let's help him stick to throwing balls instead of food. Tell him he can say 'No, thank you' or choose not to eat it, but make sure he knows it isn't all right to throw food."

A few weeks later she reported back. "I was really dreading going to dinner at my in-laws again, especially after what happened last time. But I tried what you suggested. Before we went, I told him he needed to say, 'No, thank you. I don't care for any.' He's very talkative so he could say it, but I didn't know if he understood me.

"Well, my mother-in-law tried putting zucchini on his plate. 'No, thank you,' he said. She paused and looked at him, almost shocked. He said it again, louder this time, 'No, thank you!'

"I thought, 'Oh no, here we go again,' but she stopped, looked at me, and said, 'Well, I guess he really means it,' and passed him by."

Grandma had fulfilled her responsibility by offering zucchini. And while it's Graham's responsibility to choose whether or not he'll eat zucchini, his decision to decline needs to be respectful.

Intense spirited kids can be taught good manners. They react strongly to foods and need to know the correct words to express their wants and needs. This is especially true for the serious and analytical child who sees the flaws. While it is fine for them to notice the lettuce is slightly brown and choose not to eat it, they need to do so in a tactful manner.

2. If Your Child Is Persistent

Satter advises, "Most struggles over feeding grow out of genuine concern for the child and bad advice. Parents are regularly encouraged to overrule information coming from their children and impose certain foods, amounts of food, or feeding schedules. Whenever you impose rigid expectations, feeding will be distorted."

It's important to know that the amount a child needs from each of the food groups is actually very small. A recommended serving of meat, poultry, or fish for a toddler is a mere one to two tablespoons. One entire egg is considered a "serving" for children eight years and older. Before age eight a mere fraction of the egg is considered an adequate amount.

Mary Darling, a former extension specialist in nutrition at the University of Minnesota, says, "Rely on your child's appetite. Start by giving her a quarter of an apple. Make more available if she wants it, but allow her to tell you when she has had enough." Permitting a persistent child who needs to hear yes to take the lead is a very important factor in developing a positive eating relationship.

INVOLVE YOUR CHILD IN FOOD PREPARATION: Did you know even one-year-olds can dip vegetables or fruit for you, or scrub potatoes and carrots? Two- and three-year-olds can tear lettuce, snap beans, pour from a small pitcher, and mix and shake ingredients. Older preschoolers and young elementary kids can spread toppings, roll dough, beat with an eggbeater, peel with a vegetable peeler, and cut with a table knife. The more that spirited kids are involved in preparing their food, the more likely they are to eat it. You can't cut their toast the wrong way if you let them do it. The syrup is on their pancakes right if they pour it from a small pitcher themselves (you control how much syrup is in the pitcher). The peanut butter is the proper consistency on the sandwich if they've spread it themselves.

It's true that in the beginning it takes you more time to teach them how to do it than to do it yourself, but it is time spent teaching rather than fighting. It feels better. In the long run, kids who are proficient in the kitchen are proud of themselves, are more self-sufficient, and enjoy a diverse array of foods.

Involving any child in food preparation is also a great way to take the pressure off the poison hour—that time of day when the kids need attention and you need to get a meal on the table. If they're standing on a stool at the sink washing the potatoes (to death), you know they're not beating up their brother. Baked potatoes taste great whether they've been washed for a few minutes or fifteen. Set a timer if you need to help the persistent child stop and get them in the oven!

AVOID USING FOOD AS A PUNISHMENT OR REWARD: When you provide a variety of good nutritious food in a positive manner, your child will let you know when he is hungry and when he is full. Bribing him to eat or taking food away from him only disrupts his natural message centers. Once he has lost the ability to read his own body's messages, he becomes more vulnerable to eating disorders. Research has shown that kids who are bribed to eat actually eat less and those who have food taken away from them eat more because they're afraid they won't get what they need. The two most important questions for you to ask are "Are you hungry?" and "Are you full?" Let your child decide from there.

Even dessert can be a nutritious part of the meal, especially if it contains fruit, but no matter what it is, offer your child one serving and allow him to choose whether or not to eat it. Avoid making it a treat he must earn or something you take away as a punishment.

3. If Your Child Is Sensitive

SERVE A VARIETY OF FOODS AT ONCE: Spirited kids are selective eaters. They truly have a better sense of taste and smell than the average person. As a result, they also have stronger reactions to the foods they eat. To avoid feeling unappreciated by their strong objections, serve a protein dish, vegetable or fruit, milk, butter and bread all at the same time. If the smell of your hamburger makes them sick, they can quickly redirect their attention to the bread, fresh vegetables, or fruit cobbler you're serving. Understand that their response really is not an evaluation of your culinary skills. They truly are that sensitive to tastes and smells, but it also doesn't mean that they will never choose to eat that food. Feel comfortable continuing to present it. Watching you enjoy it naturally provides a gentle "nudge," and one day they may surprise you.

BE AWARE OF FOOD ALLERGIES: Experiencing allergies and being spirited are not directly correlated, but many spirited children do have food allergies and intolerances. During an interview Laura said, "Brad is very sensitive to some foods. It took us a long time to figure that out. We thought he was just being picky and stubborn. We would force him to eat. Now we recognize that he doesn't tolerate hamburger and spicy foods. He gets constipated and complains about not feeling well."

When you take the responsibility for serving nutritious foods and allow your child to take responsibility for deciding which ones he will eat, you can feel comfortable respecting his judgment. He isn't just being picky.

If your child has "crazy times" after eating, start recording what he eats and how he behaves afterward. Be particularly observant of foods he craves. Often these are the foods to which he is allergic or intolerant.

TALK ABOUT FEELINGS: Sensitive kids need to hear:

> You have a very good sense of taste. You are selective.
> You'll make a great chef someday.
> Sometimes you need to see a food many times before you're
>   ready to try it.
> It's all right to say, "No, thank you."
> It's all right to say, "I'm hungry."
> It's all right to say, "I'm full."

Sensitive kids need the words to express the feelings and sensations they are experiencing. The more effective they are communicating with words, the easier it is to work with them.

4. If Your Child Is Perceptive

What do you do with the child who requires forty-five minutes to complete every meal? The answer depends on why it takes him forty-five minutes. Is he enjoying a leisurely meal or is he distracted? Sometimes it takes kids forty-five minutes to eat because they're jumping up to look at a bird, give the baby a pacifier, or get the ball they left outside. They're not eating. They're grazing, moving around the table, picking up bits and pieces. The grazer needs limits. For example, you might say, "You can choose to stay at the table and eat. If I see you leave the table, I know you are deciding not to eat now. The choice is yours."

Limits alone may not be enough. You also need to help your perceptive child stay focused by being sure to turn off electronics and pick up stray toys and other distracters before you sit down to eat with him. If you have a leisurely eater, expect it, plan for it, and enjoy the time to relax yourself.

If, however, your child is taking longer to eat because he seems to gag more frequently than other children or has difficulty swallowing and chewing, schedule an appointment with an occupational therapist. She can help you to evaluate his swallowing and chewing muscles and provide exercises to strengthen them if needed.

5. If Your Child Is Slow to Adapt

ESTABLISH A ROUTINE: Young children not only want to eat frequently but need to eat frequently. Their bodies are most comfortable taking in nutrition in small amounts every two or three hours. Monitor your snack and mealtimes carefully. When is your child typically hungry? Establish three specific mealtimes and three snack times throughout your day. Make sure the timing fits your child. You might be running into trouble because you would like to eat dinner at six thirty but your child is ready at five thirty. Rather than asking your child to adjust her schedule, you may have to alter yours by moving your meal to the earlier time until she is older and can last longer. Overtired children do not eat well. Instead they spill, fall out of their chairs, and complain. If an earlier mealtime does not work for the rest of your family, serve your child dinner at five thirty and make the six thirty dinner her bedtime snack. Allow enough time after your meal to complete the bedtime routine so that she also gets the sleep she needs.

SLOW-TO-ADAPT KIDS NEED CLEAR TRANSITIONS: They don't easily stop playing and come in to dinner. You have to allow enough time for them to make the switch.

"I bring Milo in a few minutes early," Brianna said. "I have found that if I have him get the last few things on the table, it allows him transition time. Otherwise he is wiggling in his chair, grouchy, and downright contrary because he is going through transition as he sits down at the table. By helping me beforehand, he seems to work it out of his system."

Remember to clearly forewarn your child that it will be time to eat and help her to find a stopping point. By doing so, you help her to "settle" for the meal.

LET HER KNOW WHAT'S ON THE MENU: "One of the biggest blowups I have ever had with my son," Kate told me, "resulted when I told him in advance that we were going to have burritos for dinner. As I started to prepare them, however, I found I didn't have the ingredients I needed so I decided to make hot tuna-cheese sandwiches instead. He was outside playing, and I was enjoying the peace. As a result, I didn't inform him of the change. I gave him the usual ten-minute warning, then called him in to dinner. He washed his hands, sat down at the table, took one look at the food, and burst into tears. I had surprised him. He was counting on burritos, and the surprise of tuna-cheese sandwiches when he was tired and hungry was too much. It put him right over the edge."

Keep your child informed about the menu. When she knows what to expect, she comes prepared to eat. If you have to make changes, as Kate did, be sure to inform her *before* she gets to the table.

The time before dinner is full of transitions. Kids are arriving home from school, and parents are coming home from work. There are clothes to be changed, food to be prepared, and homework to be started. Energy banks tend to be low at this time of the day and tantrums are more frequent. Providing a nutritious, satisfying snack around three o'clock in the afternoon seems to give spirited kids the energy they need to get through the dinner hour without falling apart. If your child is in child care at that time, be certain to inform your child-care provider and ask her to have a snack available for your child. You may notice a marked difference when you pick your child up.

6. If Your Child Is Irregular

"My two-year-old won't eat supper with us," Sarah told me. "At most she'll sit at the table for five minutes, but she won't eat. Two hours later, she wants cereal. My parents say we should punish her and make her sit down or take away all food after lunch so she's starving at supper. I'm not comfortable with either solution, but I don't know what else to do."

One of the most common questions I am asked about spirited kids and mealtime is "What do you do with the child who won't eat the meal but wants to snack later?" People often view a child's refusal to eat as stubbornness, but the issue probably has little to do with persistence as most people seem to think. The real issue is irregular body rhythms—a child whose body does not easily fall into a regular schedule. If your child is hungry at different times every day, it's because of her natural body rhythms. That's why those scheduled snacks are such an important part of her overall diet.

With an irregular child, you have to look at the whole day, not just one meal, before you can decide whether or not you have a problem. Check to see if she is getting the nutritional food she needs over a period of several days. Toddlers typically eat only one good meal a day. That's normal for this age group. Older children may also eat only one good meal a day, but if you watch carefully, you will see that with that meal, and with regular nutritious snacks, they are getting the food their bodies need over a couple of days. There isn't really a problem.

If you are still concerned, review the growth charts. Is your child consistent with her placement on the chart? If at age two she was at the fiftieth percentile mark, is she still there at age four and six? If so, you don't need to worry. If there is a significant change, you should consult your pediatrician.

You can also monitor your child's activity level. If her energy levels are normal for her, you know she's getting what she needs. You don't need to get upset when she won't eat a particular meal. A healthy snack is planned for the near future anyway.

Even if your child isn't hungry at mealtime, however, it is still vital to ask her to come to the table. Mealtime not only allows us to meet our nutritional needs, but is also a social time for family members to share the day's events. It is important for your child to learn these social skills. You can expect your toddler to come to the table and sit with you for five minutes. As she grows older, you can extend the length of time you expect her to sit with you. This routine teaches her the social skills of the family meal—praying, talking, planning, and eating together. Often, sitting at the table will also trigger the hunger signal allowing her to enjoy the meal with you. Even an irregular child will be more likely to fall into your family's routine if it's repeated every day.

YOU DON'T NEED TO BE A short-order cook: If your snacks fill part of your child's nutritional needs, you don't have to hassle her about not eating a meal and then wanting a snack shortly afterward. It doesn't matter because both the meal and the snack include foods that are essential for a well-balanced diet. To avoid feeling like a personal short-order cook, always include at least one item you know your child enjoys and teach her to prepare her own snacks. By doing so, she'll learn how to get her own needs met and to make healthy choices.

7. If Your Child Is Energetic

Toddlers don't sit easily for extended periods of time. Active toddlers sit for even shorter periods of time. In fact, active individuals—child or adult—don't sit for long periods of time in any kind of chair. Watch active adults in meetings. They wiggle their feet, tap their fingers, get up for a cup of coffee, excuse themselves for the restroom, and use numerous other socially acceptable methods to move. The need is very real.

If you know your child needs to move, make sure she has had exercise before she comes to the table. If you are traveling with her, don't expect her to sit quietly in her car seat for three hours and then sit again while you eat in a restaurant. Plan for her success. Try stopping in a park or rest stop where you can picnic and she can run and jump before you sit down to eat. If that isn't possible, let her walk around the restaurant lobby until the food is served rather than waiting at the table. In some way, find an acceptable outlet for her energy.

Staying at the table depends very much on the age of the child and the situation. For safety's sake and social acceptability, adopting a rule that says "When we eat, we sit at the table" is important.

In Europe most children are expected to stay at the table for more extended periods of time than are their American counter-parts. However, they are also entertained at the table. The adults involve them in the conversation. Books are sometimes brought to the table for children to read until they are excused.

If you would like your child to stay with you at the table, plan to involve her in the conversation, ensure that she has a comfortable chair, and bring along some of her favorite table activities. Understand, however, that your child's need to move is very strong. A pressure builds when she is required to sit for an extended period of time. Make your expectations realistic. Even if you entertain her at the table, long and formal dinners may need to be saved for adult-only evenings out.

Daily exercise is a critical element of healthy eating. Children need at least an hour of physical activity every day. Exercise, combined with wholesome food choices and predictable meals and snacks, helps your child develop healthy habits.

8. If Your Child's First Reaction Is to Reject

Kids whose first reaction is an initial rejection or withdrawal are likely to tell you they hate a new food no matter what it is. Don't be caught by that reaction. If you don't want food left on the plate, ask your child before serving if she cares for any. If she says no, respect it and leave her alone. You are free, however, to remark about how much you are enjoying the new food and to serve it again at another meal. A negative first reaction may make you believe that your child doesn't like a food when she really just needs time to get used to it. When you introduce a new food, be sure to plan something in the meal that she will like. That way you can avoid the worry that she isn't eating anything.

Be aware, too, that it is normal for a toddler to place a food in her mouth and then spit it out. She's exploring, discovering the world of textures and tastes. She is not "rejecting" the food. Continue to offer the food as a choice. Toddlers may actually put a food in their mouth and spit it out from five to fifteen times before they ever choose to swallow it.

ENJOY THE REWARDS

The most effective way of teaching appropriate behavior is reinforcing it when you see it. Let your spirited child know you are pleased when he says, "No, thank you." Comment on how well he has used his napkin or his fork. Compliment him on trying a new food or staying in his chair. Enjoy how capable and independent he becomes as he learns to prepare foods himself.

BE REALISTIC: If your child has been successful for five minutes and now wants to leave the table, you can strongly consider letting her go. End the meal in harmony rather than screams.

If you are concerned about your child's eating, consult with a dietician or check out Ellyn Satter's site at http://www.ellynsatter institute.org.

BE KIND TO YOURSELF: Follow Ellyn Satter's advice: provide the food and meals your child needs, then let yourself off the hook. When you aren't worried about controlling how much your child eats, you can enjoy the conversation much more.

MEALTIME
A Summary

Getting spirited kids to the table, keeping them there, and ensuring that they eat some semblance of a nutritional diet is a major source of consternation for parents of spirited kids. By working with your child's temperament, it is possible to make mealtime more tranquil.

Predict:

For many spirited children their sensitivity fosters strong opinions about what they will and will not eat. Intensity makes their reactions forceful. Persistence results in little tigers who want to do it themselves! Perceptiveness leads to "grazing." And slow adaptability makes it tough to get them to the table in the first place. The bonus traits may also affect mealtime. Irregularity leads to erratic hunger pangs. High energy promotes a desire to eat on the run, and a negative first reaction leads to frequent refusals.

Organize the setting:

Provide a good selection of healthy foods, then allow your child to choose whether and how much he or she will eat.

Make snacks nutritious and available on a predictable schedule; then you don't need to battle with your child about what or when he eats.

Work together:

Look at your messages about food and eating. Check to see if they are interfering with a sensitive response to your child's temperamental needs.

Let your child know that it is acceptable to refuse food, but
   he must do so respectfully and tactfully.

Involve your child in food preparation.

Let your child know what's on the menu and inform him of
   any changes *before the meal*.

Look at several days, not just at one meal, before you decide
   whether or not your child has an eating problem.

Even if your child's first reaction to a new food is negative,
   try serving it again.

Enjoy the Rewards:

Be realistic. Know when to end the meal so you have
   harmony rather than screaming.

Enjoy the ritual of tasty family meals.

18

Getting Dressed

Can you love me as I am, or will socks keep us apart?
—Pastor Dave

There was a church bulletin lying on my desk. The bold type read "From the Assistant Pastor." Maybe one of my staff was trying to tell me something, I thought. I picked it up and started reading.

"It was 'one of those mornings,'" the article began. "'Put on your socks, Ben,' had been my command a few minutes earlier. You see, in our household, putting on Ben's socks is a ritual, an action never done with little thought. Socks must be carefully checked and rechecked for seams, for loose annoying threads or for anything that has the potential of bringing discomfort. The moment of truth comes when the socks are put on. Will they feel just right or should they be adjusted . . . or perhaps be removed entirely and switched to the other foot!"

I started to chuckle. I've never met Assistant Pastor Dave, but we have something in common: children who find getting dressed a major venture. I read on.

"As I said, sock placement is a ritual, and this morning things were not going well at all. I was angry. I didn't want to be angry, but I was. 'How can socks be so difficult to put on?' I asked. His response was a shrug of uncertainty. 'Get your socks on right now!' I yelled. I thought I would be challenged and confronted by my strong-willed youngster, but I was wrong.

"'I need you to help me, Daddy,' were his simple words to me. Ben's need presented me with a question of enormous significance. Can you love without condition? Can you love me as I am, or will socks keep us apart?"

I stopped reading, struck by the impact of Pastor Dave's words. "Can you love me as I am, or will socks keep us apart?" Socks—cotton socks, dress socks, old socks, new socks—whatever shape or form they take, we begin and end most of our days putting on and pulling off socks. It may seem insignificant to most people, but in the family of a spirited child, putting on socks can be a divisive event, parents pitted against wiry little bodies dashing across the room to escape strings that scratch, elastic that's too tight, and fabrics that hurt their skin.

Getting dressed is a major challenge not because the kids want to be stubborn, uncooperative, and free spirits but because of their temperament.

PREDICT

"Check your child's temperament picture," I said to the group. "What temperamental traits make dressing troublesome?"

"Definitely sensitivity," Rob responded. "Anna will only wear pants because she doesn't like the feel of dresses."

"That's funny," Katie remarked, "because I would say sensitivity, too, but Sarah will only wear dresses because pants are too binding."

"Energy is the issue at our house. Jonathon gets one sock on and then he's gone," Jess added.

I continued writing as the list grew. Kids who wanted to wear sweaters in July because of slow adaptability. Intense kids who threw fits because they got stuck pulling a shirt over their head or couldn't get one buttoned.

Check your child's temperament picture. Do textures bother her because she is sensitive? If changing styles or type of clothing is difficult, is it because of adaptability? Is it hard for him to focus on directions because he is perceptive? Is she easily frustrated because of intensity? Whatever your child's temperamental picture, you can predict how she will react to getting dressed. Then you can begin to plan for success. Nobody needs to start *every single day* with a fight.

ORGANIZE THE SETTING

Our goal is to get kids to dress independently, appropriately, and in a reasonable amount of time. That means they need a setting that allows them to stay on task, listen to direction, and to have clothing available that is easy to work with and fits the weather and occasion.

Create a Space to Dress

Think about the things in your setting that make it difficult for your children to get dressed successfully. What vies for their attention?

Katie immediately said the television, and she's right. Television disrupts communication with spirited kids because it sends out its own "listen to me" messages and frequently leads to overstimulation. Consider making it a rule that there isn't any television in the morning—it truly helps the routine go more smoothly.

Detractors can be anything. You will have to figure out what hinders a smooth morning at your house, but the parents in my classes tell me the chief culprits in their homes include the following:

WINDOWS: "Mica dashes to the window to watch the cars. He gets so excited, he makes me excited. Then we're both watching. If I really need to get him dressed, I've got to keep the shades down until we're finished."

OPEN DOORS: "Jasper runs away, because he loves to run. The only place I can get him dressed is in the bathroom with the door shut. To him, an open door is an invitation to run away."

TOYS AND OTHER "THINGS": "It's a joke in our house. The only place Keelin can get dressed is in a barren wasteland. Every toy and object has to be put away or she starts fiddling with it."

TOO MANY CHOICES: The reality is that spirited kids have their favorite outfits, the ones that feel, fit, and look just right. More choices simply complicate the process. Go through your child's closet with her and remove the clutter. Leave only her favorites. Reduce the number of accessories. Every decision takes time and energy.

Look carefully at your setting. Anything that sabotages your child's efforts to stay on task needs to be dealt with or done away with. Help your child cooperate simply by changing the setting.

Once you've gotten rid of the things that prevent success, look for those things that help. Here are a few I've learned:

a. *Appropriate clothes.* If you want your child to dress appropriately, you have to have the right clothes available. If you don't want your spirited child wearing shorts anymore, get them out of his room.

b. *Good organization.* Arrange your child's drawers so there is a "dress-up" drawer, a "school" drawer, and a "play" drawer. Your child can help you decide what goes in each. Choices are then limited to the appropriate drawer.

c. *An indoor/outdoor thermometer.* Use a thermometer as a guide for clothing that fits the weather. Place a thermometer that tells you both the inside and outside temperature in your child's room. Make sure it's big enough to glue a picture of shorts at 70 degrees, a swimming suit at 80 degrees, a sweatshirt at 60 degrees, and a warm jacket at 35 degrees. With these guidelines, even a three-year-old can let the thermometer tell her what kind of clothes to wear today. She can't argue with a thermometer as she can with Mom and Dad. Take the steam out of the battle by letting the thermometer do the work.

d. *A mirror.* Help your child to stay focused and happy by providing a mirror for him to watch his progress.

e. *Easy clasps.* Purchase clothing that slides on easily, has big buttons, Velcro fasteners, or easy-pull zippers in the front. Avoid clothes that are difficult to get on and off.

You can create a setting that encourages your child to dress independently, appropriately, and in a timely fashion. Take a look at your child's setting and make the changes necessary to help your child be successful. If your child is three or older, be sure to include her in the process.

WORK TOGETHER

Differences in expectations are often the cause of conflict when it comes to getting dressed. Although we want our kids to dress independently, we still want them to meet our standards. Our standards and theirs may not match. Spirited children tend to develop their own distinct style at a very young age.

"Jayden is one of those kids that wants to wear shorts in January and his winter jacket in June," Chelsea said. "For a long time I really fought with him over it, but finally I just decided to let him find out for himself, within reason, of course. Now I let him step outside with the shorts on, or I let him wear the jacket. Within minutes he is asking to change."

"I wanted a little girl I could dress up," Emily told me. "When I got one that wasn't interested at all in dresses, I realized it was me that had to deal with the issue of what I wanted my child to look like and what I was willing to let go of."

As we work together to get dressed, we need to look at our own expectations. Are they realistic for this child? Do they fit this situation? We can choose how to adapt the script to each individual.

1. If Your Child Is Intense

TEACH HER TO USE WORDS: Spirited kids seem to fall into two camps when it comes to dressing themselves. One group has a mind-set of "I do everything myself"; the other, "I can't do anything without help." The can't-do kids know that getting dressed can be frustrating. As a result, they tend to seek your help. It helps them to keep their cool, so our task is to get them motivated to try on their own. The can-do kids can get frustrated and intense!

Tara is a do-it-herself kid. She can be exasperating to her parents. "It always happens when I'm late for work," her dad told me. "Inevitably the baby is in his high chair crying to get out. My seven-year-old needs breakfast before he goes to school, and Tara is insisting that she will dress herself. It would be fine if she'd pick something she could get on herself, but, of course, on those days she wants to wear the knit dress with the attached T-shirt. The one with two neck holes and four arm holes that is impossible for her to get on by herself. I wait, banished to the sidelines as she grunts and groans. She gets her arm through one arm hole, but the dress twists around so the other half is behind her. If I attempt to help her, she screeches and slaps at my hand. She works and works until finally in exasperation she pulls it off over her head, throws it down on the floor, and kicks it across the room."

Tara is actually doing what we want her to do. She is attempting to dress herself. She is very motivated and independent. The problem arises when her coordination doesn't match her drive. She needs the words to express the frustration she is experiencing, appropriate outlets for that frustration, and help breaking the task down into parts that can be accomplished more successfully.

If your child is like Tara, talk with her about intensity. Give her the words for frustration and anger. Let her know she can ask for help. Then help her break the process down into small steps that are easier to accomplish. If you're not sure how to do this, keep reading until you reach the section on perceptiveness and dressing.

USE HUMOR: Humor helps reduce frustration, diffuse intensity, and win cooperation. After participating in a class, Kristin wrote to me, "Today started with Wyatt refusing to let me wipe his buns; it wasn't even eight A.M. yet and I could just imagine what the rest of the day would be like if this was how it was starting. Normally I would have demanded that he let me do it and we both would have started screaming. Our lives had seemed like one big battle since the day he was born. This time, however, I decided I wasn't going to fight with him. I was going to figure out how to work with him. We had talked about using humor to avoid a blowup, so instead of demanding, I started sniffing the air. 'Whew, stinky buns!' I exclaimed. I pretended to look behind the shower curtain for those 'stinky buns' and then under the sink. He started laughing and looked under the soap dish himself. Finally we found them on his backside, finished the job, and happily walked out of the bathroom. Before your class I would have been furious. Humor is helping both of us appreciate his spirit."

Getting dressed doesn't have to be a serious event. If you and your child frequently disagree or find yourselves getting upset, play with your intensity. Laugh about your strong reactions. Use your child's sense of humor to make light of a difficult situation. Underwear tried on as a hat or a sock on a hand instead of a foot eases the tension. Shaking your head with a smile on your face reminds both you and your child that you've gone through this before and you will survive.

2. If Your Child Is Persistent

Shopping is a key ingredient to dressing without fussing. When it comes to clothing, we want as many *yeses* as possible with persistent spirited kids. Persistent kids like to choose what they will wear and often have a strong sense of personal style. They know what they like, and they don't like to take no for an answer. That means it is very important that you and your child agree about what clothing is available to wear.

Purchase clothing that is easy to get on, matches any other piece in the dresser drawer, and *feels* good. You can avoid fights over mismatched plaids, flowers, and checks by not buying them or buying only patterned pants and plain T-shirts.

If your spirited child is an infant or toddler, this is easy to do. You can just consider his need for soft, nonbinding clothes and pick them out yourself. There are even websites that specialize in soft clothing. "Another option is used clothing that has been washed many times. It is often softer than new, and cheaper as well."

Once your child is verbal, he will clearly state his opinion about what he will and will not wear. Then it's time for what I call "consensus clothes."

Consensus clothes allow spirited individuals to wiggle their necks freely and stretch their arms. They are clothes that can rub against a body without any irritation. But you can't stop there. If you did, you would have a closet full of baggy sweat pants, oversize cotton T-shirts, loose-fitting sundresses, and well-examined (for lint, seams, and strings) socks. Consensus clothes include clothing that also allows the parents of the spirited individuals to hold their heads high in pride, smile at people passing by, and freely admit that the child standing next to them is theirs.

Consensus clothes help to reduce the strife of getting dressed every morning. The trade-off may be five hours of shopping for a month of relatively painless mornings. Because shopping with spirited kids isn't all that exciting, you can decide which is more valuable to you. Personally I choose consensus clothes because I can mentally prepare myself better than hitting it cold turkey every morning. The key elements to shopping for consensus clothes are the following:

a. *I will listen to you.* Let your child know you are about to take on an arduous task. *Arduous* always throws them off, so you start with a definition instead of an argument. Inform him that you are going shopping. When the uproar has settled (most of them hate shopping), ask him to listen carefully and tell him, "I *will not* make you buy anything you hate. I *will* expect you to be flexible and try on things I suggest." By agreeing to work together, you can both be satisfied that an outfit doesn't fit, looks horrendous, scratches like crazy, or is just what you both want.

b. *Expect to make several shopping trips.* Trying to get an outfit for tomorrow's event is asking for big trouble. Many spirited kids have a negative first reaction. That means the first time they try something on, they will probably hate it. Leave it at the store, pray it doesn't sell quickly, and then talk about it on the way home. Look for things that are similar to old favorites or things to which they are already accustomed. You might say, "That blue outfit really looked nice on you. It reminded me of your favorite yellow outfit. Remember how you didn't like that one at first either? Now you love it and are sad that it is getting too small for you. Think about it and maybe we'll go back and look at it again." Then *be quiet!*

c. *Take a break.* Consensus shopping takes tremendous patience, strong self-control, and a tough skin to avoid letting the piercing gaze of salesclerks penetrate your skin. Never shop on an empty stomach. Shop for an hour, then stop for a snack. The kids won't mind it, even though you're the one who really needs it.

d. *Know when to quit.* At my house, it was actually my spunky daughter who far surpassed her spirited brother in

her strong opinions about clothing and style. We were out
on our fourth attempt to find an outfit for her to wear to a
wedding. We'd been in seven stores and were now entering
our eighth. We had tried on at least fifteen outfits, most of
them of my choosing. There was a dress that looked darling. She hated it—wrong color. A pants outfit with a T-shirt
overblouse was all wrong because the material underneath
was stiff and scratchy. She didn't like the way it felt! A black
pants outfit with a short jacket met with the same reaction.
I tried to tell her to pick one and take it home to show Dad.
It didn't work—she started to cry and reminded me I had
promised her I wouldn't buy anything she hated.

I was losing it, but I hadn't started screaming yet. The
clerk gave me "that look" and asked, "How do you deal with
this?"

I smiled sweetly as I said, "We shop a lot." And when the
clerk wasn't looking, we snuck out of the dressing room and
left the store. It wasn't nice, but it felt good.

I wanted to get angry. I certainly was frustrated that we
couldn't find anything that was acceptable to my daughter,
and yet I realized it was very important to her. She wasn't
saying no to see how far she could push me. She was saying
no because to her the outfits we had tried truly didn't feel
good or she didn't feel attractive in them. Still, two and a
half hours into the fourth shopping trip my tolerance was
wearing thin.

"You're getting frustrated, Mom," she said.

"Yes, I am," I admitted. "Shall we stop at one more store?"
I interjected, determined to get this job done!

She looked at me carefully. "I think we'd better go home,"

she said. "By the look on your face I think your temper needs a break!"

She was right. My temper did need a break. We went home, no one screaming, still friends, and fortunately with six more days until the wedding.

e. *When you find it, buy it.* It wasn't until our sixth shopping trip that we finally found our consensus outfit. This was a record-breaking venture. Usually two or three times out was all we needed. I was lucky—the outfit was even on sale. There are times I spent more money on her clothes than I would like, but I knew that if we finally found the right thing, she would wear it every day—if I let her. In the end we would get our money's worth. If we were shopping for play clothes, I looked for the other colors and bought multiples. So what if the style was the same? It felt good to her, looked all right to me.

If the mere thought of trying on clothing in a public dressing room with your child makes you shudder, bring items home to try. But no matter how you approach it, it is much better for your child to wear the beautiful dress or sharp sweater by choice than to feel coerced. Consensus clothes build a working relationship that has the chance of surviving a spirited adolescence. The long-term value is great. The short-term dividend is peace in the morning.

WHEN THEY CHANGE THEIR MINDS: During the toddler and preschool years especially, you may go through all the steps of shopping for consensus clothes only to find your child has changed his mind. *Never* allow your spirited child to wear anything immediately. Keep the tags on and let him try the clothes on again at home before you take a scissor to the tags. Then, and only then, do the tags come off. If you've done all of these things and he still refuses to wear it, you have definitely earned the right to one full-fledged Tarzan scream of frustration.

After you've got that out of your system, sit down with him and together closely examine the outfit. Find out what is wrong with it. Does the collar come up too high? Is the elastic too tight at the waist? Are the sleeves too short or binding? Take note of these for next time. Be sure that you listen carefully to your child, and do not ignore his complaints. Tuning in will limit the number of outfits that sit in the drawer or closet unworn.

Because spirited kids are so persistent, if an outfit is deemed unsuitable, you may even consider giving it away to someone who can use it. When it sits in the drawer or closet unworn, you may be tempted to cajole them into wearing it. Frequently these efforts end up in frustration and fights. Even in families where the clothing budget is tight, parents have used this solution. Is it wasteful? Carried to the extreme, yes. Respectfully done, however, it recognizes that all of us sometimes make mistakes. We can learn from them and make a better choice next time.

SOMETIMES THERE ARE SITUATIONS WHEN WE must demand that our child wear something that is important to us. It is appropriate to do so, especially at times when our child may not want to wear adequate clothing for the weather or doesn't understand the social norms for a particular situation. As you make your demands, however, be careful that you don't back yourself into a corner as Crystal did.

Crystal had just completed a class called "Children, the Challenge." In the class she learned about natural and logical consequences. The child suffers the consequences of his own decisions. She decided to use this method on her son, who at the time was three. They were scheduled to be at a picnic for his nursery school in thirty minutes. Cory was not getting dressed. Putting natural consequences into effect, she said, "Cory, if you're not dressed when it's time to go, you will go in your pajamas."

What Crystal hadn't learned is that three-year-olds don't understand the social norms of parties. He didn't get dressed and so she felt compelled to take him in his pajamas. He had a ball. It was Crystal who was embarrassed. Make sure your ultimatums don't backfire on you.

3. If Your Child Is Sensitive

BE AWARE OF TEXTURES AND FIT: Libby threw open her closet door, proclaiming, "I have *nothing* to wear!" Her eyes scanned the baskets and hangers within as she perused each item. "That one is too prickly," she announced. "That's the scraggly one. And where are my click-click shoes?"

Socks were also an issue for her. She liked short socks but wanted them pulled up. Unfortunately, even that adjustment didn't feel right. Tights drooped, leaving her with saggy knees and a crotch that hung between her legs. And she detested having them pulled up. Today she wanted the sparkly shirt that Grandma had purchased as a birthday gift in July. It had been tucked away in the attic for at least four months. Her mother was incredulous that she remembered it.

Sensitive kids really can feel the lint, threads, and bumps in their clothing. They notice how clothing whispers, how light reflects off it, and the pressure of it against their skin.

In order to work with them, believe them and select natural fabrics like cotton, which feels good and lies quietly. Avoid synthetics that might ball and irritate sensitive skin.

Be creative as you work with your children. Leggings and tights can keep legs warm for the child who hates pants. Beaded moccasins can replace stiff patent leather shoes. Cotton sweaters look as nice as wool. Boxer shorts are now available for both boys and girls. A hood may work just as well as a tight-fitting hat. Look for an imaginative solution. It's there!

As you purchase clothing, be sure to look inside as well as outside of each piece. It's the inside that touches sensitive skin. It needs to be soft and pleasant. Be certain that tags can be removed without leaving a scratchy edge. Appliqués may be cute on the outside but are frequently stiff and irritating on the inside.

TALK ABOUT FEELINGS: Spirited kids need to understand why getting dressed is so difficult for them. It's important to tell them:

> You react to changes in temperature.
>
> You are sensitive. Your shoes never feel quite right at first, but wear them for a few minutes and see if they feel better.
>
> You are very perceptive. That makes it difficult for you to get dressed because you think of other things to do.
>
> You are full of energy. It's hard for you to stand still long enough to put your clothes on or to have your diaper changed.
>
> You are very persistent. You like to get dressed yourself. It's all right to ask for a little help when you need it.
>
> I think it is the tag that is bothering you. We can cut it out and the shirt will feel more comfortable.

The more extensive your child's vocabulary, the better she can explain to you what she is feeling and what she needs from you. Good communication prevents misunderstandings.

BELIEVE THEM WHEN THEY TELL YOU THEY'RE HOT: Spirited kids are intense and energetic. The blood surges through their veins, making them hot. You might feel negligent letting your child wear a short-sleeved T-shirt when you have on a wool sweater, but it may be all she truly needs. Trust that she will let you know if she's cold. Encourage her to carry the sweater in her backpack so that she has it if she needs it.

KNOW WHEN TO TAKE IT OFF: If you get your child into that special outfit, know when to get her out of it. It is much better to put the frilly dress on your daughter, take a quick picture, and get her out of it while she is still happy. If a special outfit is required for a holiday dinner, don't forget to take the comfy clothes along. Coping with clothing that constantly irritates exhausts your spirited child. When she's exhausted, she stops coping and the meltdowns start.

TRY A LITTLE LOTION OR MASSAGE: Taking a few minutes to rub on lotion or firmly massage sensitive hands and feet can make putting on pants, socks, or mittens easier to bear.

4. If Your Child Is Perceptive

"Ethan is seven years old and still begging me to dress him every morning," his mother complained. "He lies on his bed or slides off it like slow-moving lava until he's on the floor—a lifeless object, incapable of lifting a finger. Fortunately, his three-year-old brother dresses himself, so I can help Ethan if I want to, but quite frankly I've had it. I'd rather just yell at him."

When it comes to getting dressed, Ethan is a can't-do kid. Fortunately, there are ways to motivate him to want to get dressed.

USE YOUR IMAGINATION: Spirited kids have wonderful imaginations. You can use this to motivate them to dress. Ask them what they would like to be this morning, perhaps an astronaut, or a firefighter. Once they've chosen their character, pretend the clothes you are putting on them are their costumes. As you put on their socks, make them astronaut socks. Slide on a sweater that is an oxygen pack. Pull a shirt over their head and call it a space suit. Have fun with it. Becoming an astronaut is much more motivating than putting on jeans. It's also easier for your child to keep his cool when his mind is focused on something interesting and fun.

COMPROMISE: You can also motivate the can't-do kid by encouraging him to take off clothing. Taking off clothing is easier than putting it on. Once he's become proficient taking items off, you can turn your attention to putting them on, by agreeing to put on one sock for him, then prompting your child to put on the other. You put on the T-shirt; he puts on the sweater. As you do it, talk with him about the upcoming day. The distraction can help him move through the task without getting frustrated. Gradually you will want to pull out of this process doing less and less until your child is dressing on his own. You may still have to sit in the room while he dresses, but at least he is getting the clothes on.

VISUAL INSTRUCTIONS CAN HELP: As you direct your child, be sure your instructions are clear and concise. A visual plan may help. There is nothing more frustrating for a child to realize after ten minutes of struggling to get on his boots that his snow pants are still sitting on the bench next to him. Children do not automatically know what to put on first. Create a visual plan that lays out the steps: Snow pants, boots, jacket, hat, and finally mittens. Or, underwear, socks, pants, shirt. By allowing your child to *see* the steps involved, you keep him on task and avoid exasperating missteps.

5. If Your Child Is Slow to Adapt

Dressing is full of transitions. It requires that a child stop doing what he was doing, possibly move to another room, and then switch clothing. It is ripe for conflict for a slow-to-adapt child.

ALLOW TIME: You may wish you could dress your child in ten minutes, but the fact is it may take thirty. Laboring to get the right "feel" and to make the transition from one outfit to another takes a great deal of time and effort for everyone involved. Plan the time you need into your schedule so you don't feel rushed.

SET UP A ROUTINE: It is important to set up a consistent pattern that you follow each morning. Your routine might include a seven A.M. wake-up, and ten minutes to snuggle with Mom or Dad. Don't expect a slow-to-adapt child to wake up, immediately jump out of bed, and start on a task. He can't do it. Allow another twenty minutes to get dressed. If possible, have him dress, toilet, and brush hair before leaving the bedroom area. Coming back later is another transition. Allow forty-five minutes to have breakfast, brush teeth, get backpacks, coats, etc., ready to go at eight fifteen.

CHOOSE AHEAD: Spirited kids like to have time to get used to ideas. Select the next day's outfit the night before. If it is a transitional time of the year, be sure to pick out a warm outfit and a cool one. Let the thermometer make the choice in the morning.

"I've got four kids," Nicole remarked, "and I can tell you, choosing what they will wear the night before is the only way I can get them all out in the morning. We lay out everything—even their mittens and boots. Seeing the items lying there seems to help all of them be prepared and more cooperative—even the ones that aren't spirited."

PREPARE FOR CHANGE IN SEASONS: I remember greeting a group of parents with, "Happy first day of spring." I was met with a huff.

"Happy, my eye," a parent threw back at me. "The last week has been a torture, trying to change clothes from one season to the next."

Spirited kids don't like any kind of change—including changes in clothing demanded by different seasons. Used to long winter pants, they'll pull on the hems of shorts trying to make them longer. They'll scream and throw fits over bulky snowsuits and down jackets. You can ease them into the change by getting the new clothes ready a few weeks early. Pull out a suitcase and pack the new season items in it, then let them play dress up with them. By the time they're ready to wear them for real, they will have adapted.

6. If Your Child Is Energetic

LET HER DO AS MUCH AS POSSIBLE: Even a five-month-old baby can pull off a sock if you loosen it over her heel and then let her grab the end and pull. The more involved in zipping, buttoning, pulling on, or pulling off your child is, the less energy she'll have to roll or run away. As soon as your energetic child can stand, dress her standing up in front of a mirror. You'll be respecting her need to move, but the mirror will grab her attention.

ENJOY THE REWARDS

Once you've gotten your child dressed, cheer. Cheer for yourself, your own patience and ingenuity, and for your child and her continued growth. It does get better. After a recent workshop, a woman came up to me and said, "My daughter is now twelve. When she was a preschooler, getting her dressed was a three-hour venture. She couldn't stand lint in her socks. I would find myself sitting there at seven in the morning pulling out minute balls of lint from her socks, knowing that if I didn't, she would scream for the next hour or tear them off her feet. Today she puts on her socks without a fuss. Her dad asked her if she remembers throwing fits about lint in her socks. She said, 'Of course, I do, and it still drives me crazy. I just tolerate it now.'"

Repetition brings success with spirited kids. The more they do something, the more they become comfortable. The old battles fade away, replaced by those of the next stage of development. Instead of socks, it's hair that won't lie right or makeup that smears—but at least they have their successes to fall back on and to remind them that this too they shall resolve.

LET OTHER PEOPLE HELP: Our spirited classes were a great success *except* for the very end. Every session ended in tears as parents tried to get coats on tired kids who were coping with a transition. It felt awful. Our solution was to make getting on coats the last classroom activity for the kids. The teachers, rather than the parents, helped each child get ready to go. It was a miracle cure. The kids thought it was great fun, and all the parents had to do was throw on their own coats and walk out the door. The only stumbling block was making sure parents were ready to go, too, so kids didn't get overheated. Spirited kids save their biggest battles for their parents. They're most comfortable with you. So whenever you can, let someone else help out. The kids won't mind and it's a break for you.

GETTING DRESSED, EATING DINNER, GOING TO bed at night, and other typical tough times don't need to be a daily battle. You can plan for success. You can prevent problems or at least the frequency of problems by respecting each other's temperaments and adapting your responses accordingly. Dare to be different. *Don't let socks keep you apart.*

GETTING DRESSED
A Summary

It may seem insignificant to most people, but in the family of a spirited child getting dressed can be a divisive event—parents pitted against wiry little bodies dashing across the room to escape the tags that scratch, elastic that's too tight, and fabrics that hurt their skin. Getting dressed is a major challenge because of their temperament.

Predict:
Check your child's temperamental picture. Try your best to figure out what temperamental traits make dressing

troublesome for your child. Sensitivity is often a major issue. Adaptability and intensity may be factors too.

Organize the setting:

Create a space for dressing that helps your child focus on the task at hand.

Avoid power struggles by allowing an indoor/outdoor thermometer to help your child decide what is appropriate to wear for the day.

Purchase clothing that is easy for your child to put on and take off by himself.

Provide a mirror if it will help your child stay focused on dressing.

Work together:

Teach your child the words to describe the frustration she experiences when she is getting dressed, so she can verbalize it rather than scream it.

Purchase clothing that respects your child's budding sense of style.

Believe your child when she tells you she is hot.

Allow time for your child to dress without feeling rushed.

Prepare ahead for a change in season.

Enjoy the Rewards:

Remember, repetition brings success. Over time, dressing will become less of an issue.

Let other people help. If your child goes to child care, let the teacher help her with her coat before you arrive.

PART FOUR
Socializing with Spirit

19

Getting Along with Other Kids

Mother, do you think you'll ever be able to socialize her?
—Megan, the sibling of a spirited child

The moms and their babies had been lounging on the floor in the early-childhood room. The bright rainbow-colored parachute stretched out underneath them. They'd rolled balls, dangled rattles, cooed and gurgled at their reflections in the mirrors, and made faces at each other. The teacher started to sing, "Make a circle. Make a circle, everyone."

A sixth grader standing next to me at the observation window asked, "What is she doing that for? Babies don't know what a circle is."

"That's right," I responded. "They don't. We have to teach them about circles and how to act when a group sits in a circle. Right now we are just exposing them to the idea, but in a few years we'll expect them to know what coming to the circle means."

Social skills and protocol are learned. They are the life skills that we all need for working cooperatively in society. Without giving up dignity or identity, spirited children have to learn how to adapt and accommodate to the group. They have to learn how to manage spirit on their own, without us troubleshooting for them.

The journey your child takes as she moves out from you to interact with others in the neighborhood, at school, and on the team may be an easy one. For many spirited kids, an understanding and acceptance of their style is all they need to be successful. Others, however, may stumble. They might not be welcome in the neighborhood because they are punching and tackling the other kids. They may burst into tears if someone at the bus stop teases them, or they may pull back from other children and adults, refusing to interact or even say hello. Watching your child struggle as he tries to figure out how to get along with others can be a painful experience.

"I just don't know what to do." Ashley sighed. "It has gotten to the point that when I see a group of kids, I start to cringe. Silas will barge right into a group and end up destroying the game. He's only four, so I know he isn't doing it on purpose, but it always ends up with him in tears and the other kids furious. I can feel the icy glares of the parents, silently demanding that I control my 'brat,' but I'm at a loss. I don't know what to do."

Kim sighed. "I almost wish Mya would tackle another child. She's been extremely reserved since she was a baby. When other children say hi to her or come over to play, she looks away and refuses to talk to them."

RECOGNIZING BOUNDARIES

Although many children seem to pick up social skills without guidance, spirited kids who are drenched in their perceptions or fired by their intensity may miss social cues. These are the simple body actions that inform them that they have crossed one or more social boundaries—the guidelines that tell them their voices are

. too loud, their bodies too close, or their intensity is penetrating. Still other spirited children may find themselves overwhelmed by the stimulation of a group and pull away.

If your child is struggling, you will have to help him manage his strong emotional reactions, develop the skills to move smoothly into a group, and work with others to solve problems. As he gains confidence, it is likely you'll see evidence of the future leader he can become.

Create Opportunities to Practice

One of the most important things you can do as your child's social skills coach is to set up opportunities to practice. If your child is one who "pulls back," this may seem counterintuitive to what "fits" for her. "I avoided going out with Jasper," Samantha shared in group one day. "He was perfectly happy staying in his pajamas all day, playing at home with me or on his own. When we did go out, even to the library or the grocery store, he hated it and wanted to go home. That's what he seemed to enjoy the most."

But social skills are learned, and that means your child needs opportunities to practice. If you are caring full-time for your child, include in your schedule a time to "go out" every day. It's easier for your child if some of those activities are repeated each week so that he becomes comfortable with the people and setting. When selecting a preschool program, choose the three-day rather than the two-day option so that he has more time to make friends.

Initially select small group activities, where stimulation levels are low and your child is not put on the spot to perform. Being the center of attention can be overwhelming to him. That skill will come later, once he's had lots of practice and tucked many successes under his belt.

"That's so true!" Amanda exclaimed. "Libby hated a tumbling. class because each child had to perform individually, but she loved her music class. There were only six kids and they all sang together. Initially she didn't want to participate. The teacher was so accepting. She invited Libby to just watch until she was ready, and whenever she sang the hello song, she'd always ask Libby if she wanted her name sung. When Libby shook her head no, the teacher would say, 'Okay, maybe next week.' It took several weeks, but shortly Libby was letting them include her in the hello song and singing with the rest of them."

Social skills are critical for a spirited child to fully utilize his strengths. If your child is an infant or a young toddler, sit on the floor with him in front of you rather than on your lap when you are in group situations. Or if you can, lie on your side on the floor, with your child sitting in front of you. That way you are literally on the sideline, offering a comforting backup but leaving the playing field wide open in front of your child so that it's easy for him to move out toward the other children and the toys. Avoid wrapping your body around him to protect him or holding him while you're standing. The journey to the floor and friends is that much more threatening to your child if it begins by being set down.

If your child is experiencing difficulty with peers, try inviting slightly younger, socially adept children to your home. Research has shown that practice with younger children can be a very effective way to learn social skills, skills that will ultimately carry over to interactions with older children. You'll want these sessions to be successful, so keep them short. One hour may be enough.

Watch carefully to see what happens. That will help you identify the *fuel source* behind your child's struggles. Frequently it will be a temperament trait that is influencing what is happening, but it's also necessary to understand the stages of social development.

DETERMINE YOUR CHILD'S SKILL LEVEL

Five-year-old Jacob loves to play with Mathew. Jacob is the boss and Mathew follows. But whenever Ryan joins the group and refuses to follow Jacob's direction, trouble erupts. Jacob gets upset, often pushing Ryan out of the group.

Social skills, like all skills, have developmental stages that build on top of each other. In order to understand the true fuel source behind Jacob's reaction and to identify what skills he needs to strengthen, you have to know the stages. With assistance from my colleague Lynn Jessen, I've simplified them into four key steps.

- Stage one: It's mine! Commonly seen in the toddler years when children are learning about possession of objects. They do not share. That will come later.
- Stage two: Children can interact side by side with similar materials. Each child has his own blocks and builds separate structures.
- Stage three: Children are playing side by side but are now able to take turns. You will see one put a block on the stack and then the other child add another block to the same stack.
- Stage four: Children develop special friendships and can either lead or follow in cooperative play. At this stage you will see children working together to build a castle, sharing ideas, negotiating, and problem solving.

Even though Jacob is five and you might expect him to play cooperatively, it's apparent he's not quite there. To coach him, you will have to step in where he is developmentally. Work first on ownership by suggesting that each of the children could have their own possessions, such as a pile of blocks. The next step is to encourage taking turns working on one structure. After demonstrating success at this level, you can nudge them toward more cooperative play.

Stay tuned in, making suggestions or offering a helping hand as needed. Catch your child being successful and reinforce it by saying something like:

> You both played with your trucks.
> Great job taking turns.
> Good listening.
> You used words to tell Amy you wanted a turn.
> You worked together to make . . .

Remember, practice makes better, and success builds on success.

LEARNING TO ENTER A GROUP

I stood at the observation window with a group of parents. "Watch carefully as your child joins another child," I told them. "Tell me what you see."

"Liam is arguing with Ben over a chunk of Play-Doh. He just grabbed it away from him," said Kari, her words sharp with frustration.

"Mica is standing back and watching the kids in the housekeeping area. He isn't joining in," Sara remarked, her voice dropping in disappointment, then rising as she exclaimed, "Now he is. He waited for an empty chair and then sat down. Now he's chatting with Laura and Braden."

Why was Mica successful in joining a group and Liam wasn't?

It could be that Liam is still at the social development stage of learning to take turns, or it could be related to his temperament.

Research shows that kids who move into a group without drawing immediate attention to themselves, ask relevant questions, and avoid disagreeing with other group members are more socially successful than kids who don't.

This is important information for serious and analytical kids who are prone to make evaluative comments the minute they enter a situation. You may have to teach him to *stop*, make eye contact, say hello, and *listen*. By listening, he can size up the situation and ask relevant questions, or find something with which he can agree. When he is tuned in to what is going on, he can enter successfully. Once he is part of the group, he can make his suggestions for change.

The Child Who "Pulls Back"

For the cautious child who holds back, the issue is often one of inaction rather than action. This child may make an initial attempt to approach and even to hover but never actually to enter the group. Research demonstrates that half of first attempts to enter a group are met with rejection. When your child's initial attempt fails, he needs you to encourage him to try again.

That's why, when he freezes, turning to you to bury his head in your lap, you should avoid the temptation to protect him from this disconcerting experience. That action communicates to your child, "There's something to fear; Mom and Dad are protecting me." While it's important to offer a reassuring hug, avoid pulling your child into your lap and smothering him with kisses and hugs. Instead, comfort him for a moment, stop talking, and then, when you sense a slight relaxation of his body, gently encourage him to move forward and explore. He needs to feel safe in order to do so. So you might say something to comfort him like, "That's a very interesting toy. It reminds me of one you have at home. Look at Elsa's smile; she seems very nice. Maybe you could show her that toy."

When your child begins to move toward others, note that he may turn back to look at you. He's checking your face to discover how he should be reacting. Offer a smile and a nod, encouraging him to continue. While your role is to nurture, it is essential that you tenderly nudge him onto the playing court where he can practice his skills. Your winning smile of confidence eases the path.

BE AWARE OF SPACE

Once your child is working within a group, the boundaries that determine personal space become important. Individuals need a certain amount of space to feel comfortable and work effectively. The extroverted, and especially the high-energy extroverted spirited child, is notorious for invading the space of others because he is so anxious to share his ideas.

In the classroom one day I observed Nora and Damon playing with a train. Each had a locomotive with six cars attached, and they were whirling their trains around and around the track. Nora was so anxious to catch up with Damon and show him her train that she rear-ended his cars and derailed them. Damon burst into tears.

"Nora, look where your locomotive is," the teacher said. "See how it's touching Damon's train. He is telling you that he doesn't like it. You need to keep your train a few inches behind Damon's so you both can use the track." She then showed Nora where her train needed to be. Nora paused, waited for Damon to straighten his train on the track, and then rolled again. She did her best to stay three inches back, jerking to a stop but stopping.

Nora wanted to play with Damon. She didn't intend to upset him, but the thrill of the motion and the desire to share her excitement had blinded her to the limits. She needed help getting the picture—an awareness of the invisible line—but once she had it, she was successful.

Whether it is telling your child to look where her feet are so that she can see when she is standing too close, or where her hands are so that they aren't in someone else's face or touching someone when they don't want to be touched, you are helping your child to learn about the space needs of others. This awareness is important to keep her from invading someone else's space and potentially offending them.

If, despite your coaching, your child continues to bump into others or tackle or wrestle them down, make an appointment with an occupational therapist for sensory work. The sensations the body receives from this physical contact actually calm the body. An occupational therapist can teach your child more appropriate strategies to get that same input.

Intense spirited kids can also cross social boundaries with their voices. Mia was the loudest kid in class. She snarled, snorted, squealed, giggled, and stormed like no other. The other kids cupped their hands over their ears when they saw her coming.

"Mia, I love your enthusiasm," I heard her teacher explain, "but sometimes it is overwhelming to others. Look at the other children. They are covering their ears. See how they back away from you. Notice how they flinch when you shout. Your voice is hurting their ears. I know you don't mean to hurt their ears. Listen to your voice, and try to speak softly." The teacher's words helped Mia to understand the consequences of her behavior.

Over several weeks I watched as the teacher worked with Mia, catching her not when she was loud but when her voice was appropriate. "What a nice, comfortable voice, Mia," she would remark. "That's the voice your friends like to hear." Frequently a child doesn't know what an appropriate voice sounds or feels like. Catching her doing it correctly and modeling that voice tone for her is the best way to teach her.

It is not unusual to find spirited kids in leadership roles and as popular group members. It just takes a keen eye and a little help from you.

RESOLVING CONFLICTS WITH WORDS INSTEAD OF FISTS

Stephen Porges, Ph.D., from the University of Chicago writes, "Social engagement requires a perception of safety." Excitement and apprehension can send your child, especially your intense child, to the red zone of tense energy. Remember, in the red zone your child's heart is beating faster; it's harder to make eye contact or to even cue in on the human voice. It's more likely that he'll move into that state of fight, flight, or freeze. He stops thinking and shifts into a survival reaction. Intense children have to learn to manage these intense reactions in order to keep thinking and performing appropriately in social situations.

During class one morning, Caleb, Greg, and Ben were pretending to camp. A picnic of plastic hot dogs and grapes was spread out on the table. Caleb picked up a hot dog. Without warning, Ben snatched it out of his hand, bellowing, "*Mine!* You can't have it. It's *mine!*" Caleb lunged for the hot dog. Ben slugged him. The blow glanced off Caleb's cheekbone.

And herein lies the challenge. When your child becomes upset and angry, it can be very tempting to react in anger as well. But what your angry child needs more than anything is your help to calm down. When you recognize that his outburst isn't intentional and isn't an immutable reaction, it's easier to see your role as his coach. Being a coach does not imply that we allow our intense spirited children to be aggressive. We can demand that they use their intensity appropriately—even when things don't go quite as expected. Fortunately for Ben, his teacher was a very skilled coach.

As I watched Caleb and Ben, the classroom teacher moved in front of Ben. Bending down to his level, she commanded, "Stop. I will not let you hurt Caleb. The rule is no hitting. No matter how angry you are, you may not hit."

Ben looked almost relieved. Caleb definitely appreciated the support. Spirited kids need to know that we, the adults in their lives, will take charge when there is a possibility of injury or harm. We will enforce the rule. We will not allow one child to hurt another. Stopping potentially dangerous behavior doesn't mean placing blame. It clarifies the rules and sets the stage for more positive problem-solving techniques.

After checking that Caleb was unhurt, and recognizing that Ben was flooded, the teacher used the same strategies we discussed in chapter 8, "Meltdowns." Choosing to listen and understand first, she said to Ben, "I think you had something important to tell Caleb. What did you want to tell him?"

Ben continued to swing at Caleb, who was now standing, leaning against the teacher. The teacher stroked Caleb's back and Ben's arm, attempting to calm both of them and to restrain Ben from hitting again. "I can see you are very angry right now."

"Ben, listen to your body," she stated firmly, then continued more softly. "You are very tense. Look at your hands—see how they are fisted? Do you feel your eyes squinting? You are very tight. Come and sit over here."

She propelled him gently to a calming basket, talking softly to him. "When your hands are still and your eyes can look at me, we will go back and talk to Caleb," she said. She stayed with him, not saying anything, letting her closeness and soft body language tell him she was there to support him and that she cared. Caleb came, too, but after a few comforting strokes, he moved back to the "camp."

Spirited kids have to be taught that it is acceptable to pull out of a situation when they are frustrated or upset. When a young child is overwhelmed by his intensity, as Ben was, he needs help figuring out what happened and what went wrong. By calming him rather than becoming angry with him, you help him to get his brain back in gear, allowing him to think of a better, more acceptable response. This supportive practice strengthens his skills and helps him to switch from his first reaction to a more effective learned one.

In the video *On Their Own with Our Help*, infant specialist Magda Gerber advises that when two children are in conflict, you need to address the aggressor more than the victim. The aggressor is more frightened. He doesn't realize what has happened. He doesn't know what to do about it unless he has been taught.

Ben's body slumped against the teacher's until he gradually climbed onto her lap. Knowing the importance of going back for the redo—the teachable moment—she said, "Let's go talk to Caleb." Ben nodded and allowed her to lead him back to the "campsite."

"Tell Caleb what you want," she said. "Tell him with words that you were angry." Ben tightened, and the teacher gently placed a hand on his.

"I don't want to share," he said. "I had it first."

"Caleb, what would you like to say?" the teacher asked, turning to him.

Caleb responded, "It was my turn. You have had all the hot dogs and now I want a turn."

When kids fight, especially intense, sensitive kids, we've got to talk about the feelings of everyone involved. Spirited kids have to learn how to express their own feelings and also how to *listen* to those of others. Empathy has to be learned. By talking about feelings, we also allow kids to express their emotions and diffuse their intensity. This is a time for sharing, not an opportunity to determine blame.

Seems simple, doesn't it? Of course, it doesn't usually work as smoothly as it did in this classroom.

"My kids would just turn around and scream, 'I hate you,'" Andy remarked when I shared this story with the group.

"Yeah, Beatrice wouldn't have anything decent to say," Maggie added. "Last night she told her brother that she would like to rip his face off and run it through the blender."

If the physical attack turns to verbal threats, your child is not ready to talk yet. His words tell you that he needs to continue his time-out. You might tell him, "I can see you are still too upset to work this out." Then insist that he return to a quiet spot. But later, when he is ready, bring him back to resolve the issue. Too often, spirited kids are removed from the conflict and never brought back. As a result, they don't learn how to express their feelings appropriately or to solve the problem with words instead of fists.

In chapter 9, I talked about being problem solvers and looking for *yes*. Resolving conflict in a positive, healthy way means coming to a resolution that all can accept. Once the kids have talked about their feelings, it's time to explore their interests. "What happened with Ben and Caleb?" the group asked, wanting to know the end of the story.

I continued. The teacher didn't solve it for them. Instead, she clarified the issue and asked questions to get them both thinking. "It seems like you both wanted that hot dog," she said. "How could you work this out?"

As I watched, the two four-year-olds faced each other. I waited, wondering what their response would be, knowing it was essential to avoid jumping in and taking over. They both squinted and hopped on one foot. It was Ben who said, "I'm full. You can have the hot dogs. I'm going to take a nap." He crawled into the sleeping bag, a loud snort escaping as he snored in his "sleep."

The group sat silently contemplating the ending to this tale, as though questioning whether it really could happen this way, before Tiffany offered, "It does work. It's hard to believe, but it does."

Yesterday my kids had the day off from school. They are each so different. It's difficult to find something everyone is willing to do together. Tasha is a strong introvert. Megan is an extreme extrovert. I thought I would take them both to the zoo, but they immediately started complaining. They didn't want to go to the zoo. I didn't care, so I said, "What would you like to do?" Tasha wanted to stay home. Megan wanted to invite three friends over and go roller-skating. Neither one of them is old enough to be left alone, so we had to come up with something that everyone could agree on. We obviously had a problem!

"Tasha, you want to stay home, and Megan, you want to go roller-skating," I said. "Is that really what you want?"

Tasha nodded her head yes. Megan started to complain that Tasha never wants to do anything that she wants to do.

"Do you really want to skate?" I asked Megan, trying to distract her.

"No, but I want to be with my friends," she insisted. That was a little easier.

"All right, you want to be with friends and Tasha wants to be at home. What could we do?"

We made a list of things to do: putting up the badminton net and playing a game, baking, watching a movie, and hosting a video game competition. They each moaned and groaned during the process, but I insisted that they not evaluate until we had a long list. Then we went back through all of the ideas.

We decided that Tasha and I would bake, and Megan would invite three friends over for badminton. They had a great time playing and by the time they were finished, Tasha and I had a snack prepared and ready for them. It wasn't what I had expected, but it didn't cost anything and everyone had a good time.

Looking for yes teaches kids to respect different points of view. It allows persistent kids to unlock and work cooperatively. It reduces frustration because everyone knows they will be heard. With young children, especially intense spirited children who have to work so hard to manage their strong emotions, you have to practice solving problems with them before you can leave them to their own devices. Otherwise, it's like leaving them at the pool and saying, "I'm sure you can figure out how to swim."

When you first begin helping children find yes with their peers,

they may have trouble coming up with ideas. You can offer suggestions, but soon, with practice, they'll be able to do it themselves.
By four or five years of age, kids start to look for *yes* on their own.
They'll run into the house to grab a timer so each person can
have a five-minute turn on the swing. They'll make up a rhyme
that allows each child a turn at the jump rope. If one activity isn't
working, they'll think of another. They'll recognize that different interests drive the choices, and they'll look for ways to make
everyone happy.

Understanding how to find *yes*—to work cooperatively with
others to solve problems—is a critical social skill. It can be used
to stop the battles between persistent kids and their parents. It
works in the classroom, and it can work at home with siblings and
friends too.

Learning to Handle Teasing

Siblings tease, children tease, lovers tease. Learning to handle
teasing is an important social skill but a potentially touchy lesson
for spirited kids. Expect some good-natured teasing to go on, but
teach your child to pay attention to the facial expressions, words,
and body language of others, which indicate the limit. Just like
other social boundaries, the limit for fun and appropriate teasing
may have to be taught. Make sure your child understands that
statements that shame, ridicule, or hurt others are not allowed.
Teasing cannot be an excuse for verbal abuse. Kids don't know
what *verbal abuse* means. You have to teach them. When one
child starts to call another "Stick Legs," "Stupid," or any other
deriding name, you have to say, "Stop. That's verbal abuse. It is not
allowed in our family."

When spirited kids are on the receiving end of teasing, their intensity can make them a susceptible target. If they are embarrassed or angry, their reactions may overwhelm them.

During an interview, I asked eight-year-old Sokim about the last time someone teased her.

"I was on my scooter," she told me. "I had on headphones so that I could listen to music. I just wanted to be alone. Lindsey kept bugging me. She was saying, 'Your butt sticks out,' and Allison was calling me names. I wanted to kick and swear at them. I wanted to beat them up. I knew I was going to cry because they hurt me. They really made me mad. I didn't do anything. They didn't have any right to say what they did."

"What did you do?" I asked. "Did you beat them up?"

"No," Sokim replied, shaking her head. "I knew I wasn't supposed to hit them, even if I felt like it. I needed my mom to tell them to leave me alone, but she didn't hear them, so I sucked it up. I wouldn't let them see it upset me. I stood up real straight, like my dad had told me to do, and stared right at them. Then I went into the house. If I can get away a few minutes, I can stop how mad I am. I watched some funny videos. It helped me cool down."

Sokim had learned to cope with being teased. Even though she reacted very strongly to the antagonizing words of the other children, she had learned to keep her cool. She stood tall and then went into the house and stepped away from the abuse.

It isn't always possible to "face down" or step away from the teasers, but the more options a child knows to stop the flood of emotion created by teasing, the more successful she will be. Talk with your child about teasing. What is acceptable for her to do? Teach her to call for an adult's help. If no one is available, can she walk away? Can she tell the aggressor to stop? Can she talk with someone else? Can she use a little humor or sometimes even agree with her tormentor? That's what Jason did.

I was standing at the entry of our local high school when I saw sixteen-year-old Jason. He had locked his keys in his pickup truck. Now he was waiting at the door for his mom to bring another set. That's when Joe, the six-foot-three football player, sauntered up and started giving him a bad time. "Lose your keys? Have to call your momma?" Jason smiled, nodding in agreement. "Yeah, pretty stupid," he said, and added, "but not as bad as locking myself out of my car at Homecoming." Joe blushed, laughing as he nodded in agreement and stepped away. Something told me Joe's Homecoming date had had to wait with him while his "momma" brought the keys! Jason's touch of humor combined with a bit of "teasing back" did the trick.

Sometimes the teasing is more hurtful, and a direct verbal confrontation of the abuser is called for. Your child may need a little help with this. Six-year-old Tommy was not the only boy in his class being tormented by Katie. For some unknown reason Katie had targeted the boys, often running up to them and kicking them in the shins without any provocation. Bridger, a kindhearted and gentle child, was uncertain how to cope. Fortunately, he had a teacher who knew how. She taught her entire class to not only say *stop* but also to sign *stop*. Whenever Katie approached ready to kick, Bridger, or any other child who was being targeted, would turn, bring the side of their right hand down on the open palm of their left and clearly demand STOP!

Katie jerked to a halt, and when she did, the teacher immediately moved in to help. Wrapping her arms around Katie, she could be heard saying, "I will not allow you to hurt someone. See Bridger's face. Do you think he's happy? No, he looks sad. I know you didn't mean to hurt him. Your body was moving so fast. Did you want to play with him? How else could you tell him that?" Within days, Katie was no longer kicking, and Bridger, the kindhearted child, stood tall, striding just a bit more confidently across his classroom.

Encourage your child to talk with you so you know what she is experiencing. Be sure she has identified her options. Know, too, that when the teasing moves across the line to bullying, it is time for the adults to step in.

Learning to Share

Sharing is one of the most challenging social skills for all children to learn. The limits are so unclear. Moms and Dads don't share their cars with the neighbors, and yet kids are supposed to. Mom takes a sip of Dad's glass, but a toddler isn't supposed to snitch a drink from someone else's bottle. We share some things but not everything. It is all very confusing.

The younger the child, the more difficult it is to share. Toddlers are just learning what ownership means. They don't want to share. They are actually going through the developmental stage in which they are learning what's *mine*.

"Well, that's good to know," Steve said. "At Christmas we gave our eighteen-month-old son an engineer's dream, a child-size locomotive for him to ride. The whistle tooted, the bell rang, and if you pushed the red button, 'smoke' escaped from the chimney. I loved it and so did he. In fact, he loved it so much that he was dragging his cousin off of it and bellowing every time she came near."

To protect your toddler's reputation, save the locomotive until the cousins go home. When other kids are invited over, pull out several cars, a whole pile of building blocks, or any other toys that come in multiples. Avoid toys that require toddlers to take turns. Toddlers aren't developmentally ready to be very gracious. In fact, you may find that for a few months, sharing may be so difficult for your toddler that the only place he can play successfully with another child is in a neutral location—a local park, playground, or other setting where no one owns the toys.

Older kids can be expected to share some, but sensitive spirited kids, especially introverts, are very protective of their possessions. Teach your child to put away the things she does not want to share before other children come to play. Help her select items she is comfortable letting others use. Talk about her feelings. Respect them, but let her know that sharing and doing nice things for others is an important part of friendship.

When you see her being successful, compliment her. You might say to her:

> Mica was thrilled that you let him ride your bike. I think you really made him feel good.
> You did a great job sharing your new ball with Teagan. She seemed to enjoy playing with you.
> I know it was hard for you to let Amy have a turn, but you did a good job of sharing with her.

Reinforce those social skills! Help her to recognize those she has and encourage her to use them more.

SURVIVING TRANSITIONS

Social interactions include many transitions. When someone enters or leaves a game, it is a transition. Winning a game or losing a game is an ending. A change in the rules or in an activity demands a quick response. Putting away toys, going outside, greeting a friend, or saying good-bye all require an adjustment. For a child who is slow to adapt, coping with these transitions can be very challenging.

"Maybe that's what happened to Kai," Lyssa remarked. "He and Cody were playing catch in our front yard. Luke called, asking to play with Kai. I was busy and didn't feel like walking outside to give Kai the phone, so I just told Luke, 'Come on over; he's outside playing ball. I'm sure you can join the game.'

"Luke rode over on his bike and, because I had given permission to do so, immediately joined the game. I realize now, this was all a surprise to Kai. Within minutes I heard the bickering. 'You can't play. He's not out. It's my turn.' When I walked outside, Kai was in a rage. The peaceful ball field was now a battleground."

"Your hunch is probably correct," I responded. "Kai is a slow-to-adapt kid. I suspect he was surprised and couldn't cope. He probably didn't know what hit him. All he knew was that a rush of anger stung him, and he reacted with angry words."

If you can, forewarn your child about upcoming changes in social situations, but if you can't, teach him to recognize them himself. When he understands and can state that he is upset because someone unexpectedly joined his game or that he is experiencing discomfort because a change has occurred, he is better able to cope. He can step back, take a deep breath, or do whatever he needs to do in order to calm himself. He'll release his frustration appropriately. The outbursts will stop and the number of his successes in social situations will increase.

Losing a game is an especially painful transition for the spirited child because it is an undesirable transition that he didn't plan for or expect. Slow adaptability combines with an intense frustration for a potential blowup. Spirited kids need help learning to win or lose in style. Sit down with your child and explain to him how a good winner acts. Let him know that you expect him to shake hands, set the ball aside, and be respectful of the losing team's feelings. Talk, too, about what it feels like to lose. Teach him that it is not all right to throw a ball down on the court. It is not acceptable to refuse to shake hands. It is not appropriate to whine and complain about the referees or the performance of his teammates. Kids don't necessarily know the appropriate protocol—you have to teach them. If you aren't sure how to help your child cope with the transitions involved in social situations, see chapter 13 for more ideas.

UNDERSTANDING THE SOCIAL NEEDS OF INTROVERTS AND EXTROVERTS

Oftentimes when I talk with parents who are worried about their child's social skills, I realize the real issue is recognizing the differences between introverts and extroverts. It is important to remember that popularity or social skills cannot be measured by the number of friends your child does or does not have. In chapter 5, I explained how introverts and extroverts interact with others. Introverts are frequently not given full credit for their social skills because they are more selective with their friendships. If you are an extroverted parent, you may worry that your introverted child doesn't have friends because he is not eager to invite other children home to play. Remember that introverts form deep, longlasting relationships with a few good friends. Their social skills may be excellent, but they are more particular and take longer to form their relationships. If your child is playing successfully with at least one other child, you probably don't need to worry. He has social skills. He is just being selective in how he uses them. Remember, introverts enjoy and need time alone. Being alone and being lonely are not the same thing to an introvert.

CELEBRATING SUCCESS

It does take energy and a keen eye and ear to help your spirited child develop his social skills, but over time you will be rewarded as you see him skillfully resolve a problem, get elected student council representative, or negotiate a group decision. Spirited kids can get along with others. By learning to use their intensity, persistence, and perceptiveness well, they often grow up to be outstanding leaders and politicians.

In *Fortune* magazine, Walter Guzzardi wrote, "At least one of [John] Deere's contemporaries tinkered with adding steel to plows, but only Deere had the wit to persist with the idea, to take the product to the farmer, to preach its virtues and to price it right."

I'll bet my bottom dollar—he was spirited!

20

Holiday and Vacation Hot Spots

When she was little, she would scream so shrilly
in a store that people would part the line to let me go first.
Today that shrill voice is so amazing. She was the
featured soloist at the holiday concert.
—Teri, mother of Emily, age sixteen

I never expected to spend my son's first Christmas hiding in my mother-in-law's bathroom, but that's where I found myself. I was doing my best to soothe my infant son's wails while his cheeks stretched taut, tinged purple under the stream of tears. I didn't remember any of my older sisters and their babies hiding in the bathroom. Yet as I sat on the throne nearly drowning in my own pity, I realized that I had spent most of his first holidays right there—restraining myself from flushing both of us down the tube. It had started with his Grandma's birthday and continued right through Halloween, Thanksgiving, and now Christmas.

The day never began that way. He'd flash his big blues at anyone and gurgle and goo to their hellos. Perched on my lap, he was Mr. Charm, a politician working the crowd. Then it would happen. I could feel his body stiffen against mine. The cycling of his legs and arms became jerky, like a washing machine off-balance. His hands fisted, knuckles whitened. The smile slipped from his face as he erupted into fire-engine wails. The only way I could calm him was to take him outside or to sit in the bathroom (the one quiet room in the house) with the lights out, softly talking to him and stroking his face. Sometimes I cried too.

Holidays, birthday parties, family gatherings, vacations, and special celebrations can prove to be a virtual minefield for spirited kids and their parents. They are filled with hot spots—the people, places, and things that rub against the grain of spirited children's temperaments and drive them wild.

Close your eyes and think about your child's last birthday party. Now try Halloween, Thanksgiving, and vacation. What hot spots did you hit?

"Santa Claus," Mike remarked. "She is scared to death of him."

"Shopping," Kelsey added, and the others joined in.

"My mother's living room. It's full of glass."

"Presents—they weren't hers."

"Bedtime—she couldn't sleep and then she was exhausted."

The list grew. Each hot spot was unique, and yet there were commonalities—temperamental traits. Surprise triggers lurked at the dinner table, in crowds, and at the theater because of sensitivity; in the presents and at naptime because of slow adaptability. High energy levels made sitting quietly in a place of worship, at Grandma's house, or in the car a major effort. A hotel, a strange pillow, and numerous other seemingly insignificant situations brought discord simply because they were new and different.

The special challenge of this minefield of holiday and vacation hot spots is for your child to learn to negotiate it with friends, relatives, and hundreds of strangers. To be successful, he needs your extra support and instruction.

ESTABLISH REALISTIC EXPECTATIONS

Kim's steps scraped across the threshold, her gait restricted by two-year-old Ellie, plastered to her right thigh. Their eyes scanned the ground in front of them instead of the faces around them gathered for the "Holiday Hot Spots" class. Good cheer was not in evidence. I pulled them aside.

"Looks like it's been a tough week," I began, attempting to voice my concern yet allowing her to take the lead.

Her voice was quiet, tired, as she spoke. "The issue is really more mine than the kids. I'm exhausted with the holidays. I get up, go to work, come home, and then I need to shop, bake, and decorate. I know Ellie is spirited. I'm aware that she is more excited, more sensitive than the other kids. I understand that she needs me, but sometimes I just don't have it in me."

During holidays and vacations spirited children need us more than ever to help them cope. It takes energy to provide that support. Unfortunately, we are often drained by baking, shopping, entertaining, cleaning, driving, or other activities. When our kids need us the most, we're not available. Sometimes in order to bring joy to holidays and vacations, we have to let go.

Traditions are supposed to be fun—an opportunity to come together as a family and celebrate. We collect them as we go along, gathering some from the family we grew up in, some from our spouse's family, and some from friends. The result can be an *overload* of traditions—too many *shoulds* that lose their joy. That's what happened to Kim. Her list grew every year. She had not allowed herself to factor in the energy drain of caring for a young child, especially a spirited one. As a result, she and Ellie zinged through the holidays like two pinballs bouncing from one score to the next.

When you plan your celebrations or vacations, make your plans, then cut them in half. Don't sabotage yourself, thinking that you can do it all or that if only you were more capable, you would be able to handle this. You have a spirited child. You are working harder. You are exploring more feelings, teaching more skills. You are preparing a child who is *more* for life.

Permission in hand, Kim went home to slash her *shoulds*. She told me later it began with sugar cookies. "Every year we *must* make sugar cookies," she said. "It's a family tradition."

> I was rolling them out. The kids were bawling, my husband was yelling at them to shut up, and the dog was peeing on the floor at the door. This was supposed to be fun? I don't even like sugar cookies. I threw the dough in the garbage, sat down, and started a list: "What's fun" and "What isn't." Then I began reeling off the things we do: "Go to Aunt Vera's."
>
> The kids responded by chanting, "No, no, no. We won't go."
>
> I agreed, but for the moment had the sense to keep my mouth shut. "Making sugar cookies," I continued.
>
> "I like the frosting," my husband said, "but making the dough and rolling them out is too much trouble."
>
> I concurred. We kept going through all the traditions we have collected. It was quite a list. But now I have this list. The things that are fun! This year we're staying home and having Aunt Vera come to our house. We're not making sugar cookies, but we did buy some at the bakery and let the kids frost them.

When you are honest with yourself and accept the reality of what it means to be the parent of a spirited child, you can grant yourself permission to go home rather than to one more event and to say no to lunch at one grandparent's house and dinner at the other. Everything doesn't have to happen this year or during this vacation. As your child grows and becomes more skilled, you will be able to expand your journey. This year Grandpa and Grandma need to come to you, but maybe a year from now you and your child will both be ready for that trip. Enjoy the stages and grow with them—gradually. You don't need to work at having fun. By setting realistic expectations for yourself, you will have the stamina and forethought to help your child learn to negotiate the hot spots smoothly.

CHECK YOUR CHILD'S EXPECTATIONS

"I dreaded carving the jack-o'-lantern this year," Todd said. "Ashley always gets so upset when it doesn't turn out the way she expected. This year I decided to be a little smarter. I suggested that she get a piece of paper and draw different jack-o'-lantern faces on it until she found just the one that she liked. She worked about twenty minutes until she had the right one. Then she took an erasable marker and drew the face right on the pumpkin. When she was done, we started cutting.

"First I cut out the eyes, following the lines she had drawn—no problem. Then I started on the nose. She had drawn a round nose with two dots in it for nostrils. I cut it out leaving the dots like an *i*—again no complaints. I couldn't believe my luck. I moved on to the mouth and cut just as she had drawn it. She loved the results! There wasn't even one outburst."

Spirited kids never forget their favorite traditions. Their excitement builds for days until they can hardly stand it. Their imaginations run wild creating an image of what the holiday or vacation should look and be like. To prevent a major blowup or letdown, talk with them about what they remember from last year's celebration or vacation. What did they enjoy? What are they looking forward to again this year? You may not be able to meet all their expectations—that's fine—but at least you have discovered them at home, in private, and not in a room filled with other people.

Talking ahead will also help you prevent the tears of disappointment when you cut the jack-o'-lantern the "wrong" way or forget the game you played last year. It will also give your child time to figure out how she could take responsibility for these things herself. Of course, there will still be disappointments and surprises, but the fewer the better.

SHARE INFORMATION WITH RELATIVES AND STRANGERS

"Eva is the first grandchild. It really is wonderful all of the attention that is showered on her, but the relatives grab her the minute we walk in the door. She reacts by hiding behind us, clinging to my leg, or hitting them if they keep pushing. She absolutely detests being kissed. She'll wipe it off, sneer, and say, 'Oh, yuk!' It hurts my dad. I'm embarrassed; my husband gets angry. What a mess!"

Helping relatives and strangers understand and work with your spirited child is crucial to her success. They need to know she wipes off their kisses because she is a sensitive introvert, not because she doesn't like affection. She refuses to take off her coat when she arrives and doesn't run to Grandpa as her cousins do because she is slow to adapt.

Most people want to build a relationship with your child, but they may not be sure how to go about it. All they have are the techniques they have learned in the past and what they observe and learn from you and your child. Share with them what you have discovered. Talk about the techniques that work and don't work and explain why. If they question your newfangled ideas about parenting techniques, remind them that like everything else, new information and research are always coming out. Learning new skills is helpful.

Celebrations and vacations require individuals to adapt to one another. Spirited kids need to learn the skills to be successful in these situations. Other people need to treat the spirited child respectfully and allow him to practice.

"But what if they don't?" Melissa asked. "At Thanksgiving we met my parents at a hotel. My dad took Justin in the pool. Justin doesn't swim, but he loves the water. Dad put him in an inner tube and started pulling him through the water. It scared Justin, and he yelled 'Stop!' but Dad ignored him and kept whirling him around the pool. I finally had to jump in and 'save' Justin."

Sometimes, as the parent of a spirited child, you have to directly step in and help your child. You might have to tell your father to stop—which isn't always very easy. Use it as an opportunity to teach. You might say, "Dad, Justin is asking you to stop. Please listen to him. He is just learning to swim and needs a chance to practice. He'll feel more comfortable and have more fun if you work within the shallow end." Or, "Dad if you let him watch first, he'll join you in a few minutes."

"But what if you tell the other person and he won't listen?" groaned Brianna.

"Don't go there very much," drawled Cody.

If the other people are not listening to your suggestions and your child is not being successful, you may need to make some choices. You can choose to visit less frequently or shorten the length of your visits. You can invite people to your home, where you have more control of the situation.

As children mature and become more capable of managing their temperaments, they will be able to handle difficult situations. Limiting your visits when your child is a toddler doesn't mean you will always have to do so. But it is better to keep the interactions short and successful rather than long and dreadful. Help your child be successful—a little bit at a time.

PREPARE FOR ENTRY

Teaching your child how to greet exuberant relatives and friends can enhance relationships. If your child gets off to a good start, the whole event is likely to go more smoothly. Greeting people can be tough for a spirited child, especially if he is an introvert, slow to adapt, and experiences a negative first reaction.

When greeting others, your child needs your support. Don't let her tears or reluctance embarrass you. With your words and with your actions, send her the message that you are there to help her. You understand. You know she can be successful.

If your child is an infant or toddler, plan to hold her on your lap. If possible, sit with her on the floor when meeting or greeting people for the first time. When you are on the floor with her, she can freely move out from you to the others without having to go through the experience of being put down. When you're on the floor, it is much more comfortable for a young child to move out to others and run back to you to check in.

If your child is older, teach him to say hello, shake hands, or give a high-five and then find a comfortable place from which to observe until he is ready to participate. The big overstuffed chair in the living room may be a perfect place, or the stool at the kitchen counter might work. Any place is fine that allows him to pull out of the action a little bit but not appear antisocial.

Talk to him about his need to check things out before entering a new situation. Teach him to let others know that he learns best by watching and will be very happy to play with them after an initial warm-up. Even professional teams get a warm-up before they play the game and show us their stuff. Remind him of successes from the past, like the first time he met his teacher. Let him know that he is more experienced and skillful at greeting people than he might think.

If you know there will be a crush of people, arrive early.

"That really works for us," Amanda remarked immediately when I offered this suggestion in class. "It takes Christopher a day to warm up. If we're only visiting for a weekend, it's half over before he's ready to roll. We now do our best to arrive earlier than anyone else—if possible, an entire day early. That gives us time to go through the issues of a new table, a new bed, a new house, and all that stuff before the crowd hits."

Allowing your child time to become comfortable with unfamiliar surroundings before having to cope with new people reduces the energy drain on him. It helps him to be successful.

Entry time can be shortened by showing your child photographs or making video calls. Kids from toddlers on up can benefit by a preview of Uncle Jay's portrait or a look at Grandpa and Grandma's house. Find resources on the Internet depicting the new places to which you will be going. Go online for virtual tours. Talk about the things you will see and do and the people you will meet.

WATCH OUT FOR CROWDS

Holidays and vacations are often filled with crowds: people in lines, packed in stores, in the parking lots, and at Grandma's house. In a crowd, spirited kids are blasted with a barrage of sensations. Like human sponges, they absorb the tension of the adults around them. The odors of turkey and mashed potatoes mix with perfumes and sweat. Twinkling and flashing lights; blaring music; tinkling bells; and singing, swearing, and chattering voices are all absorbed by spirited children. Within minutes they can become overwhelmed by the sensations flooding their bodies. Some simply crumple, whimpering at your feet; others let loose, screeching and howling or running wildly.

"We all know you can't spend your life avoiding crowds," I said to the group. "So how can you help your child cope?"

"Actually we have learned to avoid some crowds," Mike offered. "We found he can be successful if there aren't crowds day after day. When we went to Florida, we planned one day at Disney, the next lounging at the pool. One day at Epcot, the next at the beach. The beach was crowded, but because of the open space, it wasn't overwhelming. As long as we gave him those breaks, he did fine—and so did I."

"I just called my aunt and said, 'Listen, the boys are going to go nuts if they are cooped up all day. You've got to clean up your basement so they can play,'" Nicole stated.

The others listened to her, mouths hanging open in amazement. "You called your aunt and told her to clean her basement? Didn't she get angry?" Erica questioned incredulously.

"My aunt is a good lady. She just forgets what it is like to have little kids, so I reminded her. I told her she didn't have to do it, but if she didn't, we were coming late and leaving early. It worked. She

cleaned it up, and we were able to send them down to the basement to run around, and just get away from all of the other people.
Everyone had a great time. She even invited us back next year."

Erica shook her head in amazement. "I haven't got Nicole's
guts, but I do have a backpack ready to go with us next week for
Thanksgiving dinner at my sister's. In it I have packed four of the
kids' favorite books, one bag of Play-Doh, and one of games. If the
kids start to get wild, I'm ready."

"During the holidays I never take my kids shopping," Jessica
offered.

"How do you avoid it?" Megan questioned.

"I wait until someone can watch them. Sometimes I get a sitter,
trade off with the neighbor or whatever, but I don't take them.
The displays are more abundant, closer together, and just beg to be
grabbed. The stimulation overwhelms me, and I have no patience
with them. They are much better off at home without me."

"I guess we're brave," Rob remarked. "We do take ours shopping.
I hate to shop, though, so we only go for about an hour. They seem
to handle that amount of time all right."

Every situation and child calls for a different approach, but the
next time you and your spirited child will be exposed to crowds,
think about what you can do to help him be successful. It may
mean not going, as it did for Jessica, or limiting your exposure like
Rob and Mike. It could be creating an introvert or time-out space,
as Nicole did. Or, like Erica, you can bring along soothing/calming
activities. Whatever you decide to do is fine; just think about it
ahead of time and take the actions necessary to help your child be
successful. If your child is older, involve him in the plans.

Introverted spirited children especially need quiet breaks from
the crowd. Talking with people, listening to them, and answering
their questions is draining to the introvert. When you know that

you will be spending an extended period of time with a group, you need activities that allow your child to escape from the crowd without appearing unsociable. No matter how skilled he has become, he will still need his downtime. If you are an introvert, you will too.

If you or your child is an extrovert, understand that you are enjoying the group more than the introverts in your family. Respect their limits. Stay tuned in to stimulation levels. When you are having a good time, it is easy to miss the cues that stimulation limits are being hit.

BEWARE OF GIFTS

How can gifts be a hidden trigger for spirited kids? Every emotion for the spirited child is intense, whether it is happiness or disappointment. Gifts either excite us or dash our dreams. Gifts also include an element of surprise. Slow-to-transition kids hate surprises. Serious and analytical spirited kids get into trouble because they are not effusive with their praise. This can be disappointing for gift givers, who have spent hours shopping, searching for just the right gift only to have it opened by a straight-faced kid who has to be reminded to say thank you. Are spirited kids ungrateful brats? Are they spoiled? No, but they do need help learning to handle gift giving gracefully.

Set your child up for success by buying gifts that encourage the kind of behavior you want. A scooter or bike received during a Minnesota winter begs to be ridden through the living room. If you don't want your spirited child to be tearing through the house, don't give him a scooter or bike when it is 10 degrees below zero. Wait for spring or summer. Make sure you like any books or music you purchase. Persistent kids will demand to hear their favorites over and over again. If you can't stand them, you are liable to suffer needlessly. And beware of electronic and battery-operated toys, which add noise and high stimulation levels to an already very stimulating environment.

Many spirited kids like toys that allow them to use their imaginations and to experiment. Items such as little toy people, blocks, Legos, play houses/villages, tool kits, music and audio stories, and dress-up clothes are classics that can be used in many different ways.

Spirited kids also enjoy active toys like scooters, tricycles, trampolines, bicycles, and jungle gyms. Make sure you have a place to use them and to store them. Physical toys need to be monitored closely to prevent rev-up. When actions start to get wild, it is time for soothing/calming activities.

A camera can be a perfect gift. Put one into the hands of a high-energy child and suddenly it's socially acceptable for him to be roaming around the room or up on the stairs looking down on the group, snapping shots rather than sitting at the table. A camera also gives the highly perceptive child a "focus" and a role as the recorder of the event. Just be sure that, if the camera is on a mobile device, the older child knows he can't share the photographs without the subjects' permission.

It's not uncommon for spirited kids to get into trouble with gifts because they want to open them *now!* All kids get excited about gifts, but intense kids can hardly contain themselves. You may want to consider opening a few gifts early to diffuse the excitement. Perhaps gifts could be opened first and other activities could follow. Whatever you decide, let your child know what to expect. Help him to find a way to diffuse his excitement.

Remember that although a key element of gift giving is surprise, a surprise is a transition, and slow-to-adapt kids don't like transitions. You can still help your child enjoy gifts by helping her manage the surprise. Give her hints about what is beneath the wrapping paper. Tidbits of information can help her prepare herself and work through her feelings.

Eight-year-old Asher had desperately wanted a microphone for her birthday. She loved to sing. To keep her from knowing that she was getting one, her mother told her that microphones were too expensive so she shouldn't expect one.

Unbeknownst to her mother, Asher was devastated, wallowing for days in her disappointment. Gradually, though, she worked through it and by her birthday was prepared to receive something else. Her mother beamed at her as she handed Asher the box containing the microphone. She was pleased with herself that this time she had something Asher really wanted.

Asher opened the box, took one look, burst into tears, and fled from the room. Her mother gasped first in surprise and then in anger. She was annoyed and disappointed that no matter what she did, it never seemed to please Asher.

What she didn't understand was that her daughter wasn't ungrateful. Asher was overwhelmed. Forced to transition much too quickly, she was unable to recover and fled to hide her intense feelings. If you know you will not be able to give your child an anticipated gift, be honest with her. If there just might be a special package, don't lie. Hint that it might be there. Don't force her to deal with her intense disappointment or surprise in front of others.

Of course, there are times you don't know what's in the box. You can't avoid all the surprises, but you can help your child by playing "what if." "What if you feel like crying?" you might ask. "What would you do? Where could you go? Could you run into the bathroom, sit on my lap, or go to your bedroom? If thrills are racing through your body, can you whoop and holler? Can you run around the kitchen, or do you need to head out the door? What happens if your brother gets a gift you think is better than yours? What if only Sadie has presents? How will you feel?" "What if" helps your child deal with the possibilities and prepare for disappointment. When she is prepared, she is much more likely to behave well.

Finally, when it comes to gifts, analytical spirited kids need to learn about manners. They have a keen eye for quality, style, and quantity. This comes in handy when you're shopping for a major appliance but can be a bit embarrassing at a birthday party. Without thinking, analytical kids make comments like "Oh, yuck! Look at that trim," "What an ugly shirt," and "I already have that book," the kind of comments that can pull you, scarlet-faced, right under the table. If you want your child to be respectful and tactful, teach her the exact words you want her to say, such as "Aunt Sue, what an interesting sweater!" or "Grandma, this is one of my favorite books!" Don't let your analytical child loose without some guidelines and practice.

As your child learns to handle gift giving gracefully, look for the things she has done well. Remark about her enthusiasm, her success in waiting for a turn, or the nice thank-you hug she gave Grandpa. Highlight her gifts within.

BE READY FOR CHANGES IN CLOTHING

Holidays and celebrations often call for stiff, scratchy, dressy clothes that aren't worn every day. For spirited kids who adapt slowly and are sensitive to textures, dressing up can cause a huge battle. But it doesn't have to be that way.

Don't let the day of the event be the first time your child sees his new outfit. Remember, spirited kids need time to get used to things. Leave your child's clothes out several days in advance of the event, allowing him to look at them, try them on and wear them, and even smell them. If he wants to wear them, set a timer so there isn't a fight over when he has to take it off if he decides he loves the outfit and doesn't want to save it for the event. Practice helps to ensure that when the special occasion comes, the outfit won't feel brand new anymore. Once he has worked through his first negative reaction, you can expect a more cooperative child.

If it is a costume he'll be wearing, use the words *dress-up clothes* with him. All preschoolers are learning the difference between what is real and what is not. Spirited preschoolers with their rich imaginations may be uncomfortable with costumes because they might not be quite certain whether they will become the character if they are dressed as one. Even if they've figured out that they aren't really the character, they may still act like him. Select costumes that encourage the kind of behavior you want!

As you select dressy clothes, consider your child's style. Spirited kids are creative thinkers. Their ideas of style and yours may be quite different. You can allow yourself to say, "My child is her own person. I can teach her basic standards, and then I can step back and allow her to have her own style without feeling embarrassed." A nice thing about spirited kids is that they prepare us early for adolescence. While others fight with their teenagers over clothes, we will have already resolved those issues years ago.

Stepping back and allowing your child her own style isn't always easy. At least it wasn't for Tiffany and her daughter Libby—a modern young woman, even at age five.

"From the time she could talk, Libby let it be known that she *hated* dresses," Tiffany told me. "I literally had to wrestle her into one, and then she would pout. I couldn't stand the disagreements, so I began backing off, only insisting on a dress for very special occasions. We were going to be celebrating my parents' anniversary at a very posh restaurant. Libby was five and had picked out a dressy pants outfit that she wanted to wear. I really mulled this one over. Do I let her wear the pants? I worried. Will it embarrass my parents if she walks into the event dressed like that?

"Finally I decided that it was a nice outfit. I would let her wear it because she felt so much more attractive in it than in a dress.

"I was still a nervous wreck on the day of the event. That's when my mother walked out of her bedroom dressed—in pants!

" 'Do I dare wear this?' she asked, turning to me. 'It's so much more comfortable than a dress.'

"Libby burst into applause. 'Grandma, are you spirited too,' she squealed, grabbing her around the waist and hugging.

"I laughed. Appreciating spirit seems to be benefiting more than just Libby."

HELP THEM SLEEP

Dealing with bedtime can be one of the most frustrating hot spots on vacation or during holidays—at least it has been for Emily.

"It takes Damon hours to unwind at a hotel or at someone else's house. It's always been that way. Of course, my sister has the kid you just lay down in bed and he goes to sleep, no matter where he is. She's out chatting with everyone, and I'm stuck in the back bedroom with a wailing kid. It doesn't seem fair. Worst of all, it makes me feel so ineffectual, but I can't make him sleep. The only thing I can do is to help him unwind. The older he gets, the shorter it's been, but it has been a long, embarrassing haul."

Getting enough sleep is always important but especially during the holidays and on vacation. When your child is well rested, he has the energy to cope, but spirited kids often have trouble sleeping in new and different situations.

Show him where he will be sleeping before bedtime so it's not a surprise. Plan to give him more support at bedtime than you do at home. The younger the child, the more challenging it will be because you can't explain to him what is bothering him. Expect it to take him longer to wind down and fall asleep. You may need to sit with him or rock him to help him calm.

Be sure to bring along your props—his own pillow or blanket, sound machine, and any other items that help him feel more comfortable and cue him that this is sleep time. Rigorously protect his nap and bedtime. Avoid skipping naps or changing bedtimes from one day to the next.

As your child grows, talk with him about the need for wind-down time in new situations. Encourage him to read to himself, to breathe deeply, and to relax each muscle before retiring. Let him know he is all right. He is just excited.

IF YOU TRAVEL—CLARIFY EXPECTATIONS

Traveling adds another whole dimension to holidays and vacations. Long hours spent in a cramped automobile or airplane can leave you with a migraine before you ever arrive at your destination. That's why you have to plan for the journey.

I've always admired my friend Vickie for her energy and skill as a parent. But the day she called me and told me she had put five kids—two spirited, three spunky—ages two and a half to thirteen in a car and driven eleven hundred miles, I began to doubt her grasp on reality. In telling me about the trip, she even used the term *vacation* to describe this trek.

How did she survive? She planned for success. It wasn't chance. It wasn't luck. She was *prepared*. She set up a clear expectation for good behavior. Driving down the highway screaming at kids in the backseat is not a relaxing journey—better to establish clear expectations that encourage good behavior and allow you to focus on the road.

"I used the timer on my phone and brought along a bunch of poker chips," Vickie told me. "I told the kids that for every fifteen minutes in the car that they did not fight, played quietly, and stayed in their seat belts, they would earn a poker chip."

At this point I doubted the intelligence of her children, but she wasn't done yet.

"When they had four chips, they could turn them in for a dollar." Now there was something I could identify with.

"Even the two-year-old loved it," she exclaimed. "I'd set the timer for fifteen minutes. When it went off, anyone who had met the expectations got a poker chip. I experimented a little going twenty to thirty minutes between chips, but that didn't work.

It had to be every fifteen minutes. All I had to do when voices started rising was to say 'Are you earning your chip?' and things quieted down fast."

"How much did this cost you?" I asked.

"Twenty-one dollars apiece," Vickie said. "And that was their spending money for the trip. It was great, no nagging for this or that. I'd just tell them it was their money, and they could spend it however they wanted. It really helped them understand the value of a dollar. The eight-year-old would ask me how much is this or that—he came home with fifteen dollars because he wanted to save for something special.

A transparent expectation set a tone of cooperation. The children knew what they could choose to do and what would happen if they did it. The incentive for good behavior was in place.

Clear expectations alone are not enough though. A timer, poker chips, and dollar bills aren't all you need to buy hours of peace in the car. Vickie did admit there had been more. She had stopped every two hours to let everyone out of restraints and give them a chance to run around. They had eaten picnic lunches in parks and at rest stops where the kids could run, climb, and play with the balls she had brought along. Each child had a plastic bucket of paper, markers, books, and simple games. They sang songs and played trivia games, asking questions about familiar nursery rhymes and stories the older kids knew. Due to the high stimulation levels, playing video games and watching movies in the car was limited. The nights were spent at hotels with a pool.

To ensure that you do not arrive at the resort or Grandma's house frazzled, plan for the journey. Bring along activities, expect to sing and tell stories, and know when it's time to pull off the road and take a break. Many times the greatest joy of a celebration or vacation is the journey there.

Time-zone changes are also an issue when traveling. If the time difference is an hour and you plan to stay for only a weekend, consider staying on your "home time" rather than throwing off the schedule. If the time shift is greater than one hour or you'll be staying longer, maintain your routine, but shift it to the new time zone. Get outside for exposure to morning light which will help re-set the body clock to the new time zone.

Upon returning home, expect that it can take up to three weeks for your children and you to recover from significant time-zone changes. During that time reduce the demands, expect to offer more support at bedtime and to have frequent middle-of-the-night awakenings and early-morning rising times. Meltdowns may increase during this time too. Everyone will recover, but it does take time.

Create a Travel Hub

Last year you rented a quaint little cottage and for two weeks basked in the sun. Your spirited child swam in the lake, dug in the sand, and after the first night slept soundly. It was a wonderful vacation.

This year you decided to add more excitement. You toured the East Coast by car, a new hotel, a different city each night. It was a disaster. Your child was a wreck and so were you.

What happened? A child who is slow to adapt and one who experiences a negative first reaction can't cope when the changes and new experiences come too fast. To help your child be successful, consider establishing a travel hub—one hotel, one relative's home, or one campground that you stay at for two or three days before moving on to another hub. By establishing hubs, you allow your child time to adapt to new places. He has a chance to check things out and feel secure. He'll sleep better and have more energy to cope.

You can also extend your hub by buying groceries and bottled water. Sensitive kids react to new foods and changes in the water. The more familiar the setting and the food, the easier it will be for them to adapt.

The younger the child, the more important the hub is to him. Over time and with many successes under her belt, the older child will become more flexible and the hub less important. Success builds on success. Soon that slow-to-adapt two-year-old will be the seasoned nine-year-old ready for a trip across the country.

Make Time for Exercise

Sam is a great swimmer, so when his mom took him to a conference, they made a plan. After taking a flight and then driving two hours to reach their destination, their first activity would be a swim in the pool. It was just what both of them needed to relax after their strenuous journey. Afterward, they snacked on familiar, healthy foods and then headed to the evening reception. Six-year-old Sam was the hit of the night, a perfect gentleman, thanks to the swim that filled his body with soothing, calming hormones and a few healthy snacks that kept him from starving. Exercise calms our body, making it easier to cope with new situations, handle crowds, and wait patiently. Every day, include it in your family's plans. Everyone will benefit.

Plan for the Letdown

Spirited kids tend to fly high during celebrations and vacations and crash afterward. They truly can go to extremes. Be prepared. Don't push yourself so hard that you don't have the energy to help your child transition back to a normal routine. Older kids can make their own plans. Eleven-year-old Hazel told her mother, "I love how I feel at Christmas, but I hate how I feel afterward. I'm saving this present to open when I feel rotten." And she did.

Holidays, celebrations, and vacations do require more planning when you are the parent of a spirited child. At times it can feel like a great deal of work. But when you've done your job well, these events with a spirited child are full of special delights. They are enriched by their enthusiasm, zeal, and exuberance.

21

Success in School

I didn't want him to be "discussed." I wanted him to be treasured.
—Katie, mother of two

Why isn't it easy to send kids off to school? You'd think we'd be happy—appreciative of the break. And perhaps you are. It is a relief, a milestone. Still, you may find your eyes filling, your vision blurred as your son or daughter mounts the school-bus steps for the first time—alone—or releases your hand and enters that preschool classroom—leaving you behind. She's on her own to face the world. You gulp, hoping that she will be treasured by those she encounters rather than discussed as an oddity or a troublemaker. But you don't know and you stand there praying that she will be successful, that she will enjoy school, make friends, and bring a smile rather than a frown to her teacher's face.

Spirited kids can prosper in school. You can find them participating in the concert band, in the starring roles of the school plays, as members of the winning teams, and in the enhanced learning programs. They can be successful in a Montessori school, in a local public school, in a parochial school, or in a private school. The type or location of the school doesn't really matter. What does matter is that there exists a warm, positive climate, a regard for children's perspectives, differentiated learning, and pro-active behavior management. In a school where this occurs, spirit blooms.

Spirited kids make up only 15 to 20 percent of the population, so it can be a challenge to find the right schools for them. They need a classroom that has a rich smorgasbord of teaching techniques and an individualized structure, or they will always feel pressured to adapt to a learning style that isn't their own. Kids who are constantly forced to conform never feel completely comfortable. They become exhausted and frustrated and may end up acting out or giving up. Sometimes the meltdowns occur at school, but more often they happen at home where it is safe to let loose. Fortunately, spirited kids don't need perfect classrooms that fit their temperament 100 percent of the time—just a majority of the time. When children can work within their preferred style most of the time, it isn't a major issue to occasionally work out of their preferred style. So how do you help your spirited child thrive in school? There are three key factors: (1) find a quality classroom, (2) work with the school, and (3) take steps at home to support your child.

IDENTIFYING A QUALITY CLASSROOM

One day during a workshop I said to the group, "If you live in a metropolitan area, you probably have an assortment of schools your child may attend. If there is only one school available, it likely has several classrooms at each grade level from which you may choose. And even if there is little to no choice, it's still important to recognize whether or not your child is in a quality classroom."

A loud groan rose in the room as I shared this message. I turned to Nicole, a young single mom. "What am I supposed to look for?" she asked. "I don't have a master's degree in education. I don't know a good curriculum when I see one. I'm not even sure I know a good teacher."

"It's easy," I responded, "because you know your child. You don't need a master's degree to select a good school. All you have to do is go into a classroom to observe, pick out a child who reminds you of your own, and see how she fares. You'll want to look at three key elements: emotional support, instructional support, and classroom management. I'll give you a checklist to show you what I mean."

Emotional Support

- ✔ **Joy:** Teachers, children, staff members, and parents visiting the classroom seem happy.
- ✔ **Calm:** Your "gut" relaxes the minute you step in the door. There are no sudden clinches or flips of your stomach, tightening of the neck muscles, shoulders suddenly shooting up to hang from your earlobes, or eyes widening. Instead you find yourself relaxing, and drawn to enter. You *want* to be part of this classroom. There is no inner warning system shouting, "Flee while you can!"
- ✔ **Cherished:** Images of the children's home lives, cultures, and interests splash across the walls adding color and a clear message: all are welcome

here. Children are called by name. Questions
about the new puppy, baby, or Grandma's illness
quickly attest to the fact that the adults know these
children.

✔ **Respected:** Real conversations occur. Children's
opinions and ideas are valued. When a child answers a teacher's question with a "left-field" response, it's not met with a scornful declaration,
"We are not talking about that right now!" Instead
there is recognition and respectful redirection:
"Oh, you had a different idea, and I want to talk
with you about that later."

Instructional Support

✔ **Knowledgeable:** You will hear children animatedly
call "Teacher, Teacher," eager to share their discov-
eries. Their eyes are sparkling. They are excited
to tell you what they are learning, know why they
are learning it, and in what ways it is important to
them.

✔ **Vibrant:** Materials are stimulating, activities diverse, and instruction is presented visually, verbally, and physically. Movement is integrated
throughout the day. Models and demonstrations
are abundant. Creativity is encouraged. Children
work in small groups or individually. No matter
whether your child is an introvert or an extrovert,
there is something for him.

Classroom Environment

✔ **Safe:** Expectations are clear, simple, consistent, and visible. An approaching adult is perceived as a helping hand, not as a threat. Children know what appropriate behavior is and have been proactively taught effective strategies to resolve conflicts. You are not surprised when you hear one child demand to another, "You have to share!" But rather than war breaking out, the other child responds: "Well, that's one idea. Why don't we trade instead?"

✔ **Organized:** There is a classroom routine that is clearly conveyed.

✔ **Warm:** Reassuring hugs, gentle touch, and listening ears are used as the antidote for tears and even angry shouts. There is no shaming or shouting.

✔ **Comfortable:** The classroom environment supports health and well-being. Children aren't wrinkling their noses, squinting their eyes, or demonstrating other signs of discomfort or irritation. They seem physically comfortable. When you stop to breathe deeply and absorb the smells of the room, or focus on the lighting and temperature, you feel comfortable too.

If you find a classroom that looks, feels, and sounds like this, there is no doubt you have found a great one.

"I'm checking out a school this week," Nicole replied. "I'll try it."

The next week I was anxious to hear about Nicole's experience and so were the others in the group.

"It was fantastic," she blurted out before we had even had a chance to sit down.

I observed two classrooms in the same school. What a difference! In both rooms I could find a child who reminded me of my son Marc. One even looked like him, and they both liked to bounce around the room like Marc does. In one classroom the teacher seemed very comfortable with the kids moving around the room to different tables and learning centers. They were all deeply engaged in the materials, conversing—yet they were all very focused. The teacher was up and down, moving with them, joking, laughing. She really seemed to like all of them. I heard her ask the little boy I was watching how his new baby brother was, and then she asked another if his dad was still in Japan. Her sincerity and interest were readily evident.

Nick, the little boy I watched, skipped across the room to show her a line of the letter A he'd written. "Look!" he exclaimed, "I made apples!" Realizing he'd only comprehended a segment of an earlier lesson, she never missed a beat. "Wow, that's great! You made the letter A." Drawing out the A sound, she continued, "Aaaaaple, begins with an A." Then she offered, "Let's check our letter chart and see if your A matches the one on it." Nick seriously perused the chart, searching for a matching letter. When he finally found it, he leaped with joy, triumphantly pointing out the match. She gave him a high five and he went off to write more examples of the letter A.

When there was a break, I asked her about Nick. She

smiled and said, "He's my best errand runner, and he's got a great sense of humor."

During group time the children drew close to her, except for two. One was on the outskirts of the group lying on the floor, not disrupting in any way. Another was playing with a gadget, looking up every few seconds as the teacher turned the pages of her book. It was apparent he was listening, and in no way disturbing the group. There was no reprimand.

But then he crossed the line. He added a "motor" to the gadget, his voice rising. All heads turned toward him. The teacher motioned him to join her. Wrapped an arm around him, drew him to her, and whispered in his ear offering him a choice to join the group, or take a break. He chose to set down his gadget and sit next to her chair. She went on. No shouts, threats, shaming, or berating occurred. The lines were clear; respectfully and confidently enforced.

In the second classroom, I picked out Alex, another boy that reminded me of Marc. In this classroom the kids were in their chairs much longer. Alex was absolutely squirming and biting his pencil. The teacher told them that if they did not write their letters like the examples, they would be sent back to kindergarten. I think she was joking, but I could tell from the look on Alex's face he thought she was serious.

Like Nicole, you can identify a classroom that fits your child. You can feel and see it by simply observing a child like yours functioning in that room. Let your ear confirm the warm conversations that verify this teacher's sensitivity. Enjoy the melody of lively discussions among children. Tune in to what the educators call scaffolding, the words that gently nudge a child to the next level of understanding or a more complex way of thinking. Believe what you see, the smiles, the body language of joy, and the proud displays of hard work and growth. And when a child does need to be redirected, heed your gut. Does it knot in shame, or is there a mere twinge when you realize a simple mistake has been made, but the expectation and the support is there to ensure that next time the child will be able to make a better choice?

Don't let reputation or hearsay blur your vision or block your intuition. A great classroom for one child might be a disaster for another because their temperaments are different. That's why you can't rely on your neighbor's suggestion, especially if your child's personality is nothing like the kid's next door. You've got to get into the classroom and find the one that fits your child.

If this is a child-care program, observe to see if the children sleep. Children's ability to sleep at naptime is a marker of the emotional atmosphere. They must feel emotionally safe to sleep.

And if you have an extrovert, take note of whether teachers complain when children raise their hands too much and ask too many questions or if these children are viewed as quick thinkers who are confident in their knowledge.

If your child is slow to adapt, watch for the transitions. Do you see an agenda for the day on the board so that everyone knows what to expect? Is there a predictable routine? Do you hear a forewarning before a transition occurs? How many transitions are there, and is the child like yours moving through them comfortably, or is he stumbling?

If your child is intense, pay close attention to the emotional climate. Check to see how teachers respond to emotions and what activities are available to diffuse the intensity. A child in the red zone experiences neural static that disrupts learning. Megan Gunnar at the University of Minnesota states, "How children feel is as important as how they think."

If your child is perceptive, listen for the directions. Are they clear and presented both verbally and visually?

If your child is energetic, is movement integrated into the classroom? Researchers have noted that a little bit of movement improves attention span. Five years ago Ward Elementary began the Read and Ride program. Staff equipped a classroom with enough exercise bikes to accommodate an entire class of students. Throughout the day teachers could bring the children to use them. The kids who spent the most time in the program achieved an 83 percent proficiency in reading. Those who spent the least time in the program had failing scores—only 41 percent proficiency. Movement matters.

A highly sensitive child needs to know where she'll be eating lunch. If there isn't a cafeteria and the children are eating at their desks, this child may struggle to survive the afternoon immersed in the smells of bananas and tuna fish sandwiches.

And don't forget your introvert, who needs some place in the room where he can take a break, enjoy a few moments of quiet, and get some space! Whatever traits are important for your child, check to see how they are managed in this particular classroom.

"What do you do after you have found the right classroom?" Nicole asked. "I know I want Marc in Mrs. Jensen's class, the first one I saw, but the school policy says that parents can't pick their child's teacher."

"Schools create policies like that," I explained, "so that fifty parents don't request Mrs. Jensen and then get angry that they don't all get her. It is a protective device."

In reality, school principals and teachers want to work with you.

They want your child to be successful. It is perfectly all right and very advisable for you to write a letter to the principal describing the qualities of your child and the type of teacher you think he would be most successful with. For example, Nicole might write a letter like the following:

> *Dear Principal,*
>
>   *My son Marc will be entering your school in September. I would like you to know a little bit about him. He is very energetic and athletic. He loves to play soccer and basketball. He seems to learn best with a teacher who is comfortable with activity in her room and offers many opportunities for movement. He is also very sensitive and responds best to someone with a soft voice. Loud voices frighten him.*
>
>   *Recently I visited your school. Mrs. Jensen seemed to have many of the qualities that would match well with Marc. I hope you will consider this when determining Marc's classroom placement. If it is not possible for him to be in Mrs. Jensen's classroom, I would appreciate it if you would place him in a classroom with someone of similar style.*
>
>   *Thank you. If you have questions for me, you can reach me via phone or e-mail at . . .*

To the best of their ability, the *majority* of principals will honor your request. They want you and your child to be happy. They really will respect your input. Write your letter in the spring, while the principal still has flexibility placing children. The later in the summer your letter arrives, the more difficult it is to place your child in a specific classroom. Keep your letter concise and to the point. Let the principal know the *one* most important thing for your child. But do include an opening for the principal to make a different choice. Trust that she knows her staff. Perhaps after reading your letter or meeting your child, she may realize that the best match for your child would be with a different teacher. And she may also know a few things about Mrs. Jensen that you didn't see during your visit. Work as a team, believing that both of you are striving to create the best "fit" for your child.

By taking the time to find a quality classroom that fits your child *before* he starts, you will have alleviated many potential problems. You will have found a setting that you believe will nurture your child. You'll trust it and so will your child. Trust puts us in the green zone of calm energy, ready to learn.

WORK WITH THE SCHOOL

Years of research consistently show that children whose parents are involved in their school and education are more successful than children whose parents are not involved. Take advantage of every opportunity you have to participate at your child's school. Obviously this may be limited by other demands, but to the best of your ability attend conferences, open houses, and performances. Volunteer to work in the classroom or to assist with a field trip. The more involved you are in your child's school, the more likely you are to develop good lines of communication. A few hours spent at a school picnic or other casual event talking with your child's principal or meeting the other kids in his class and their parents may help you to prevent problems from occurring. If issues do surface, those friendly school picnic conversations may carry over and allow you to solve problems much more quickly and cordially.

SHARE INFORMATION

"Should I warn the teacher?" Ben joked. "Seriously, what should I tell Cassidy's teacher? Should I keep quiet and let her find out by herself, or do I tell her what he's like at home? I don't want to bias her, but I want to help if I can."

You don't need to warn your child's teacher, but you do want to inform her. On the first day of school the teacher meets her class, a group of kids assigned to her. She has to learn quickly what is special and unique about each individual. You can help her by sharing information. As you do, remember our discussion about labels in chapter 2. Use words that highlight your child's strengths and minimize her weaknesses.

"Hey, I did the right thing then," Katie piped in. "The school where Ethan goes has a morning where parents come with their kids. When I talked to his teacher that day, I simply mentioned what he was like. I told her that starting school might be difficult for him. I asked her to let me know if she wanted me to work with him on anything. I also found out that 'a clown' would be taking class pictures the next week. I let her know that he was afraid of clowns and might need a little extra support. The next week I called her just to check in on how things were going. She said I was right, he didn't like the clown, and because she knew it, they had made a plan ahead of time that he would stand right next to her. He did it and was so proud of himself."

"I let Libby's teacher know that she is a very strong introvert," Lindsey added. "I think she was relieved when I told her Libby often works best if she is able to sit slightly back from the rest of the group. She likes to practice in her mind before participating. Sometimes it may seem like she's not listening, but she's taking in everything!"

By describing your child's typical reactions and sharing effective techniques for working with him, you give your child's teacher the information she needs to be effective. Everyone gets off to a good start as the teacher realizes you support her and are willing to help her educate your child.

WHEN THERE IS A PROBLEM

"I'm so tired." Tara sighed softly. "I'm so tired of Kara's teacher complaining about her. What do you do when you have tried everything we have talked about and it's not working? Kara has now been out of school more than she's been in it. She was sick and at first we thought she had a flu, but I know it's more than that. We think she's afraid of her teacher. She's never had a man before, and this one tends to bellow. He's not yelling at her, but she's so sensitive that just the thought of someone possibly getting angry makes her apprehensive. We've talked with the teacher and sent him e-mails, but it feels like he thinks I'm just making excuses for her. I swear whenever I'm talking, he's thinking up replies rather than listening to me. We brought the principal in, but all he would say was 'She's going to run into difficult people in life, and she needs to learn to deal with it.' There's a kernel of truth to that, you know, but my little girl is hurting—bad. Can I expect an entire institution to change for one kid?"

Tara's pain was real. We all felt it. Her drooping body spoke of a parent's pain, the deep gut-wrenching twist that strangles your belly and makes you gulp for air when you fear that you can't protect your child, when you don't know what to do to help her.

"Sometimes," I assured her, "despite your very best efforts, your child will face challenges at school. To find a solution, you are going to have to advocate for her. You are going to have to ask the questions and seek the answers and support you need to help your child be successful. It isn't easy to be an advocate. It takes a great deal of time, energy, and emotional stamina. At times you may feel powerless, but you aren't. There are definitely things you can do to improve the situation."

I turned to the group and said, "Think about it. What can you do to advocate for your child?"

"Don't assume one negative experience will carry to another," Cal responded. "Last year I just couldn't work with the principal at my son's school. I tried, but I couldn't do it. I started getting upset with the entire system, but then someone told me to talk to the principal's boss. I did. The guy was great. He gave me written information, talked with me about the issue, and then sat down with the principal and me and helped us resolve the problem. To this day, I'm grateful to that man."

It hurts when our kids experience problems in school. It hurts a lot. It can be embarrassing, and it can also remind us of our own school experiences where we felt powerless or in pain. These emotions can create barriers that put everyone on the defensive. Teachers know when you're angry, but teachers are people too. They have stress at home and maybe at school too. And they have twenty-five or more kids to educate each day. If we aren't thoughtful in our approach to them, our demands may feel overwhelming and they will back away from us. At the same time you shouldn't have to take a course in assertiveness to be able to talk to your child's teacher. Now more than ever you need to use your good communication skills to work with the school personnel and other resources.

Schedule a meeting with your child's teacher. A face-to-face conversation is a much more effective way to resolve problems than via e-mail. When you want someone to listen to you, start by finding a point she has made that you can agree with even if that requires turning a negative into a positive. For example, if Kara's teacher has said she's too emotional, Tara might say, "We find her to be very sensitive and caring at home too." By finding a point to agree on, you have set a cooperative tone. Minds will be open for listening.

Listen carefully as your child's teacher talks, and to the best of your ability, set aside your own interests while you try to understand hers. If she makes a statement you don't comprehend, ask for an explanation. Be aware of your tone of voice. Use a tone that lets the teacher know you are trying to understand, not interrogating her. For example, if a teacher tells you your child isn't getting her work done, ask, "Could you please give me a recent example?" Dig deeper to find out when the problem is occurring. Is it happening on certain days, in every class, or only when she is finishing math worksheets? If it is a behavioral issue, what preceded the problem? And don't forget to ask the teacher what she thinks your child may have been feeling in that situation. Doing so helps you identify your child's emotions that may be fueling the behavior. If the teacher remarks that your child is simply being stubborn, or lazy, remember that these are "shut-down" behaviors we discussed in chapter 7 that indicate something is causing your child stress.

If you can't figure out what the underlying feelings and needs are, review the temperament traits to help you identify where the problem may lie. Is your child crying at the beginning of the school day because it is a transition? Is your child fighting in line because he is an introvert who needs more space? Is he being distracted because he is perceptive and his chair is next to the aquarium? Is she slow completing her work because she is highly perceptive, reviewing all of the details before she can find a starting point? Discover the real issue and you can find your common interests. Include your child in the investigative work by asking him what he's thinking when he does his work or what he's experiencing. His answer may surprise you.

As you talk with the teacher, don't assume that she is familiar with temperament. The temperament research is often very briefly included in university curriculums; as a result, you may have information she doesn't. Share this book with her. Let her know that this information has been helpful to you. She may not even have thought of linking behavior problems to a misunderstanding of temperament.

Allowing the teacher to be heard first calms her, opening her to listening to you. Restate your understanding of what is important to her to be certain you have it right. These problem-solving steps are the same ones we discussed in chapter 9.

Once you have clarified what is important to the teacher, think about and explain what is important to you. Focus on your *interest* not your *position*. For example, Tara might say, "I want Kara to feel comfortable in the classroom," not "I want Kara out of your classroom!" By focusing on interests, you avoid blaming. This takes down the defense barriers and lets you move to creative solutions.

That solution may already be occurring in the classroom. If you have been in the classroom to participate or to observe, point out what the teacher is doing that works for your child. For example, if your child has been getting into trouble for not sitting quietly you might say, "I noticed when you let Dylan lie on the floor, he could really concentrate." The best solutions are those things that the teacher is already doing—she just needs to do more of them. The second best are things she is already doing but that would be more effective if they were presented in a different order. For example, you might say, "I noticed that when you did calisthenics in the middle of group time, Dylan sat still afterward. Would it be possible to start group time with calisthenics?"

If things aren't going well in the classroom, look for successes from the past. You might say: "Last year Dylan was able to complete his work when Mrs. Romero used learning centers. Would it be possible for you to use this technique also?" Or, "Would you mind talking with Mrs. Romero? She might have ideas that could be helpful." Another possible source of solutions is ideas that work at home, but make sure these will work in a group setting.

Remember as you offer solutions that teachers have temperaments too. They may experience a negative first reaction, be slow to adapt, or lock in easily. Don't force a solution. Offer your ideas, and then agree to talk again later after you have both had time to process.

Be aware of your own temperament as well. If you are intense, realize that your intensity may burn through your calm demeanor. Take along a friend or spouse who can talk and listen too, so you can pull out of the conversation and take deep breaths if needed. If you are an introvert and need time to process information, ask for another meeting.

Using other resources may also be helpful. Ask the principal or school psychologist to meet with you and the teacher. If you have a child-care provider, grandparent, or someone else who knows your child well, they might also be helpful.

When your child experiences a problem, expect to find a solution. The majority of teachers are very committed to their profession. They want your child to be successful in their classroom. Be flexible and creative as you work with them, and remember, spirited kids don't need perfect classrooms that fit their temperament 100 percent of the time—just a majority of the time.

It was three weeks before I saw Tara again. She strode confidently into the center. "We went back to the school ready to advocate," she said, "not to blame." She emphasized the words, expressing her discomfort with them yet realizing they had been helpful to her. "I tried to figure out how to explain my concerns," she said. "I was sitting at swimming lessons when I realized we don't start the kids out in the deep end. We start them out in the shallows, where they can be successful. I went back to the principal and agreed with him. I said, 'You're right, she is going to meet people she doesn't get along with.' He liked that, then I said, 'But, you know, when we teach kids to swim, we don't put them in over their heads, and I think the same thing is true when we teach kids how to get along with other people. I think Kara is in over her head and drowning.' He listened! He called the teacher in and we all sat down. Together we decided to move Kara, not because he was a bad teacher, but because it wasn't working for Kara. It felt all right to everyone, and the results were immediate. Kara hasn't missed a day in the last ten."

Spirited kids can be successful in school. By working together, parents, teachers, and kids who understand spirit and know how to manage it well can make school a positive and fun experience—a place where individual styles are appreciated and spirit blooms.

SUPPORT SCHOOL SUCCESS AT HOME

BEFORE THE SCHOOL YEAR BEGINS: Even if you can't choose which classroom your child is in or what school she will attend, you can still plan to support her success at home. Talk with your child about school. What is she excited about? What is she worried about?

"With Mica, our oldest, I found out quite by accident that he was scared to death to ride the school bus," Crystal responded. "I never thought of that as a problem, but it really was for him. Fortunately, our neighbor drove the bus, so she took Mica with her one day and let him get inside one."

If your child is going to ride a school bus, make sure that the first time she ever looks inside one isn't the day she is expected to get on it and ride by herself. Find out where the bus garage is and go look at a school bus. The folks who work in transportation departments for a school district take their jobs very seriously. They are proud of what they do and will usually be more than happy to let you take a look at a bus.

You can also check with your local park or community education departments, or other programs to see if they are planning any field trips that include a ride on a school bus. Register for it and let your child's first bus ride be with you, the person she trusts the most.

If your child will be walking to school, practice with her, traversing the route before the first day of school.

Find out what the drop-off policy is. Many schools insist that children be dropped in the school drive and escorted into the school by teachers. If this is the case you will want to role play drop-off. Select a quiet weekend morning. Enlist another adult who will pretend to be the teacher greeting your child. Drive up to the drop-off point, open the door, and allow your child to step out. The other adult will greet her as the teacher would and walk her to the school door. Practice always makes things better.

"Sarah was really worried about who her teacher would be," Brent added, as our discussion continued. "She also wanted to know what her room looked like and where the bathroom was located."

Many schools post classroom assignments before school begins, but if your school doesn't, call about a week before the starting day and find out who your child's teacher will be and her classroom number. You can also ask when the teachers will be setting up their classrooms. Then go to the school with your child, visit her classroom, check out the bathrooms, the drinking fountains, the lunchroom, playground, media center, and gymnasium, and meet the teacher and the principal. This relaxed, comfortable visit can alleviate a great deal of stress for the child who is slow to adapt or experiences a cautious first reaction.

Whether it is riding buses, finding out who the other kids are in the classroom, picking out clothes, or meeting the teacher, do what your child needs to do in order to feel comfortable on the first day of school. Reducing her stress increases the likelihood that she will get off to a good start. You may even want to consider reducing all outside commitments for the entire month of September. This allows your slow-to-adapt child to focus her energy on feeling comfortable in her new classroom.

SEND YOUR CHILD TO SCHOOL IN THE GREEN ZONE: "I let Braden sleep in," Cody told the group. "He'd gotten to bed late. I thought it would make things go more smoothly this morning, but then we were short on time and rushing. I had his clothes ready, but he still had unfinished homework—he hates homework. Quite frankly, he hates school! I ended up dragging him to the bus stop."

Increase the odds for your child's success in school by ensuring that he's physically ready. The psychologist Gahan Fallone of Mercy Clinic Behavioral Health–Lark in Springfield, Missouri, states, "If parents want their children to thrive academically, getting them to sleep on time is as important as getting them to school on time." While this is true for *all* children, it's especially important for spirited children.

Family meals are also critical. Research consistently demonstrates that the family meal is a better indicator of academic achievement than participation in sports or the arts. Presumably the additional time with you calms your spirited children, increases the likelihood that they will be eating nutritional foods, and enhances their vocabulary as you converse during the meals. So create a family schedule that includes a regular bedtime and predictable mealtimes and then stick to it!

Finally, be emotionally and physical available in the morning. It's challenging to do because there are so many demands on your time, but a few minutes spent completely focusing on your child makes a difference. Brenda found this to be true. "Ricky was throwing a fit every morning about going to school, but once he got there, he was fine," Brenda told the group. "I realized I'd seen this behavior before when he started nursery school, but that was only three days a week, half days, and the meltdowns weren't as explosive. It was his teacher who suggested that he needed warm-up time and maybe we just had to support him as he transitions into first grade. I started spending more time helping him to get ready in the mornings. That extra support seemed to be all that he needed. The meltdowns stopped after about four weeks."

REENTRY: Often, spirited children hold it together at school but fall apart the moment they reunite with you. Even when school is a good fit for your child, coping with the stimulation, interacting with peers, following rules, and staying focused is hard work. By the time you see them it's likely they are exhausted and, because you are an emotional haven to them, they fall apart. You can predict that this transition will be tough and plan for success.

Talk with your child. Help him understand that after school he's drained and that's okay, but it is not acceptable to hit, kick, scream, or be rude. Instead you can make a plan together to ease the transition. Ask him what he needs to feel better after school. Does he want a snack? Does he want someone to talk to or play with, or would he prefer alone time? Does he want to be active or quiet? Would he like noise or no noise? Does he need space? Does he need choices? Would he prefer to be in an activity after school or to go home? Is it better for him to get his homework finished immediately or does he need a break? Use the temperament chart to think about each trait and what might bring him back to the green zone.

Then together create a visual plan of what will happen after school. The extroverts may want to include snack, talk time, active play, a timer app to alert them to when it's almost time to stop, homework, and dinner in their plan. The introverts may include snack, quiet alone time, play, homework, dinner. There is no right or wrong plan. Just create one that fits you and your child, gives him predictability, and brings his body back to the green zone.

HOMEWORK: "But how do you get them to do their homework?" Katie asked. "Imogene starts this high-pitched whining and says, 'It's so hard. I can't do it. I need help.' Do I ignore it? Do I tell her to stop? I'm so tired of clashing."

Completing homework requires being calm. When your child is whining, rolling on the floor, running away, refusing to do it, or complaining that she can't get started, she's letting you know she's in the red zone and unable to think clearly.

That's why a reentry plan is so helpful. It brings your child back to the green zone before she begins homework and takes the surprise out of when it is to be completed. You can teach your child to stop and check. Are her arms, legs, and voice quiet? Is her breathing slow and deep? These are signs she is in the green zone. If she is not, she can take deep breaths, drink cold water, or do a visualization of a beautiful place.

Figuring out the right environment is also important. Experiment with your child to discover what fits her best. Does she work more efficiently if she sits at the kitchen table near you or in a quiet spot? Does background music help her focus or does it distract? Does she prefer an exercise ball to a chair or sitting to standing?

Once your child is calm and settled in a suitable work environment, assist her in breaking tasks into small steps. Time her while she reads one page or completes one worksheet line. If she has ten pages to read and each one takes her three minutes to complete, the assignment will require approximately thirty minutes. Would she prefer to read in three ten-minute segments with breaks in between or complete the entire assignment at one time? She can choose and plan accordingly. Together decide what the breaks will be, like getting a glass of water, walking around the table, or listening to a song. Will they be longer breaks such as ten minutes of reading after school, and ten more the next morning with the final ten completed the next day?

If there are multiple tasks, encourage her to begin with an easy one. A quick success will help her keep going. And if it is a long writing task, teach her to stop in the middle of a sentence so it's easy to pick up and go again.

Homework does not need to be a daily skirmish. By taking the time to set your child up for success, you help her understand what she needs in order to work most efficiently and gain skills in project management. Soon she'll be completing homework with little to no assistance from you.

DIG DEEPER: Temperament is a key factor in school success and an important one to explore. It is not, however, at the core of every problem. If your child's struggles at school persist, it may be due to a mismatch of temperament, but it could also be the result of learning differences, poor health, or many other factors.

In class Ben told us, "Courtney experienced severe stomach problems. We thought it was stress, but the school made changes for us and the pain persisted. It ended up that she had a kidney problem that required surgery."

If, despite all efforts, your child continues to struggle, schedule a complete physical and psychological examination. Get the information you need before deciding how to proceed.

Check too on your own stress. "We ended up going for family counseling," Rob offered. "Elizabeth was letting loose at school, but the real issue was that my wife and I were experiencing problems in our relationship. Elizabeth picked up our stress and acted out at school. It really had nothing to do with what was going on in the classroom."

Remember, spirited kids are the emotional barometer of your family. If you are experiencing major stresses within your family relationships, you may have to address them before the problems at school can be resolved.

Involve your child's school counselor. He or she can work with your child to help him cope with a divorce, death, or other traumatic situations. Some schools even have support groups for kids who are hurting because of these issues.

Spirited children can be successful in school. It you haven't found it this year, try again and keep working on the school situation. Don't wait. You can find solutions. I've seen it. You can believe it.

PART FIVE
Enjoying Spirit

Epilogue

The Rose in My Garden

And every time I held a rose
It seems I only felt the thorns . . .
—Billy Joel

I wish that I could say that after reading this book, you will live happily ever after, no pain, no hassle, in perfect harmony with your spirited child. I have been truthful with you throughout this book. I have shared with you only real emotions and tried techniques. I won't lie to you now. I can't promise that there will be no hassles. There will be. Change takes time. Building a relationship is a process that occurs over years, and every stage of development brings new challenges that force you to stretch, learn, and grow in different ways. Remember, our motto is *progress, not perfection*.

There will still be days when you think you are wasting your time waiting for your slow-to-adapt child to adjust. When you huff and puff and pull at the reins ready to move on, feeling tethered by your child. On those days reread this book. Use it as a friend, a guide from those who have been there before you. As you review the material, you will find ideas that didn't seem to apply when your child was four but are extremely effective now that he is eight. Grab them and use them.

On the good days, pat yourself on the back, recognizing and appreciating what you are already doing well. Sometimes improving your relationship with your spirited child is merely a matter of doing more of what you already do well.

Do not fear intensity. Don't let it scare you. Intensity is passion, zest, and vitality. It's true that there will be days when it will wear you out. Then kiss your child good-bye, go for a walk, and take a break.

As you learn about your spirited child, learn about yourself. Become more aware of how stimulation, transitions, and new situations affect you. Be more cognizant of your energy level, your own need for routine, your joy in change.

Love your spirited child for who she is. Let her make you laugh. Let her share with you how she sees, hears, and experiences the things around her. Allow her to enrich your life. Because she is more, she will make you more.

Spirited kids are like the roses in my garden. They need more attention. Throw a little water on the other flowers and they grow. Not the rose—it needs special treatment. It has to be pruned and guided in its growth.

Other flowers can be plucked, pulled, and mauled by a preschooler and still last for weeks on your dining room table. If you treat a rose roughly, it will wilt in your hands or stab you, make you bleed.

But there is not another flower like the rose in my garden. Its rich perfume fragrance titillates my senses. Its satin-soft petals tickle my fingers. Its blooms are so vibrant they stir my soul. Spirited kids are like roses—they need special care. And sometimes you have to get past the thorns to truly enjoy their beauty.

Index

About the Author

Mary Sheedy Kurcinka, Ed.D., is an internationally recognized lecturer and parent educator. Born on a third-generation dairy farm in Minnesota, Mary now lives with her husband in Bozeman, Montana. She is the proud mother of one son and one daughter—now adults with whom she loves to spend time. A former director of one of Minnesota's largest Early Childhood Family Education programs, Mary is the founder of the Spirited Child and Kids, Parents, and Power Struggles workshops and is the director of ParentChildHelp. She is the bestselling author of *Raising Your Spirited Child; Raising Your Spirited Child Workbook; Kids, Parents, and Power Struggles;* and *Sleepless in America.*